Better Homes and Gardens®

ANNUAL
Recipes
2005

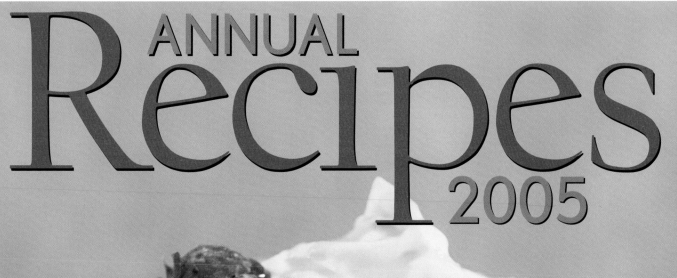

French-Toasted Angel Food Cake
page 105

Meredith® Books
Des Moines, Iowa

Bittersweet Bark with Cinnamon Candies
page 24

THE YEAR OF 2005 WILL ALWAYS BE A STELLAR ONE FOR THE *BETTER HOMES AND GARDENS®* FAMILY BECAUSE IT MARKS THE LATEST INCARNATION OF OUR LEGENDARY TEST KITCHEN. An icon in the industry and in North American culture, the Better Homes and Gardens® Test Kitchen has improved how we cook at home for a remarkable 77 years. Our facilities have grown and changed over the years, of course, but we've always remained true to the Test Kitchen's mission of bringing you the tastiest, no-fail recipes on the planet. With the unveiling of the latest and newly improved Better Homes and Gardens® Test Kitchen, we are better poised than ever to deliver on this promise. In addition, our Test Kitchen expresses the best ideas in today's home design: It combines the style that homeowners want with the ease of function and care they deserve. Ideally, the kitchen is not only for cooking, it's also for dining, entertaining, and relaxing. Our new facilities reflect this kitchen-centric thinking.

If you need more reasons to spend time in your kitchen, we have them right here. The great recipes, tips, and ideas you'll find in *Better Homes and Gardens® Annual Recipes 2005* will keep you inspired for many cooking days to come. In one volume, you have every recipe that appeared in *Better Homes and Gardens®* magazine in 2005, plus additional information about choosing the best ingredients, entertaining, wine tasting, healthy dining, saving time and money, and simply eating and living well.

The food editors of *Better Homes and Gardens®* magazine keep an eye out for trends but never lose sight of the fresh, simple, and delicious foods that fit into your busy lifestyle. Cook seasonal or special occasion dishes, or try our "Quick, Quicker, Quickest" weeknight recipes for everyone's favorite bird—chicken (see *page 90*). Start a "Moms' Cooking Club" (see *page 40*); we show you how laughing and sharing with friends while cooking makes preparation time fly by.

You can be sure every time you step into your kitchen with this book, the home economists in the Better Homes and Gardens® Test Kitchen have done their homework in theirs. Every recipe we publish has been tested, tasted, and retested to make sure it's perfect—not only that it's as simple as possible, but also that it looks great and tastes delicious. You can count on every recipe, every time you make it.

Karol

KAROL DEWULF NICKELL, EDITOR IN CHIEF
Better Homes and Gardens® magazine

Better Homes and Gardens® Annual Recipes 2005
Editor: Jessica Saari
Contributing Recipe Editor: Janet Figg
Contributing Writers: Ellen Boeke, Lisa Kingsley
Associate Design Director: Som Inthalangsy
Copy Chief: Terri Fredrickson
Publishing Operations Manager: Karen Schirm
Senior Editor, Asset and Information Manager: Phillip Morgan
Edit and Design Production Coordinator: Mary Lee Gavin
Book Production Managers: Pam Kvitne, Marjorie J. Schenkelberg,
    Rick von Holdt, Mark Weaver
Contributing Copy Editor: Amanda Knief
Contributing Proofreaders: Gretchen Kauffman, Susan J. Kling, Jody Speer
Indexer: Elizabeth Parson
Editorial Assistant: Cheryl Eckert
Test Kitchen Director: Lynn Blanchard
Test Kitchen Product Supervisor: Maryellyn Krantz

Meredith® Books
Executive Director, Editorial: Gregory H. Kayko
Executive Director, Design: Matt Strelecki
Managing Editor: Amy Tincher-Durik
Senior Editor/Group Manager: Jan Miller
Senior Associate Design Director: Ken Carlson

Publisher and Editor in Chief: James D. Blume
Editorial Director: Linda Raglan Cunningham
Executive Director, New Business Development: Todd M. Davis
Executive Director, Sales: Ken Zagor
Director, Operations: George A. Susral
Director, Production: Douglas M. Johnston
Director, Marketing: Amy Nichols
Business Director: Jim Leonard

Vice President and General Manager: Douglas J. Guendel

Better Homes and Gardens® Magazine
Editor in Chief: Karol DeWulf Nickell
Executive Editor: John Riha
Creative Director: Bradford W.S. Hong
Managing Editor: Lamont D. Olson
Art Director: Michael D. Belknap
Deputy Editor, Food and Entertaining: Nancy Wall Hopkins
Editor: Jeanne Ambrose
Associate Editors: Richard Swearinger, Stephen J. Exel
Editorial Assistants: Karen Pollock, Anna Anderson

Meredith Publishing Group
President: Jack Griffin
Executive Vice President: Bob Mate
Vice President, Corporate Solutions: Michael Brownstein
Vice President, Creative Services: Ellen de Lathouder
Vice President, Manufacturing: Bruce Heston
Vice President, Finance and Administration: Karla Jeffries
Vice President, Consumer Marketing: David Ball
Consumer Product Associate Marketing Director: Steve Swanson
Consumer Product Marketing Manager: Wendy Merical
Business Manager: Darren Tollefson
Consumer Marketing Director of Operations: Chuck Howell

Meredith Corporation
Chairman and Chief Executive Officer: William T. Kerr
President and Chief Operating Officer: Stephen M. Lacy

In Memoriam: E. T. Meredith III (1933-2003)

ISSN: 1083-4451. ISBN: 0-696-22404-6.

Test Kitchen

Our seal assures you that every recipe in *Better Homes and Gardens® Annual Recipes 2005* has been tested in the Better Homes and Gardens® Test Kitchen. This means that each recipe is practical and reliable, and meets our high standards of taste appeal. We guarantee your satisfaction with this book for as long as you own it.

All of us at Meredith® Books are dedicated to providing you with information and ideas to enhance your home. We welcome your comments and suggestions. Write to us at: Meredith Books Editorial Department, 1716 Locust St., Des Moines, IA 50309-3023. Title is available by mail. To order editions from past years, call 800/627-5490.

Pictured on the front cover: German Chocolate Cupcakes (page 12).

Pictured on the back cover (clockwise from top left): Great Grilled Burger (page 165); Dressed-Up Deli Chicken (page 101); PB&J Ice Cream Sandwiches (page 14); Tres Leches Cake (page 82); Flank Steak Vinaigrette Salad (page 68); and Chicken Chowder (page 46).

Pork with Raisin Sauce
page 262

Double Thumbprint Cookies
page 27

Meal planning takes on a whole new meaning with *Better Homes and Gardens® Annual Recipes 2005*: It's so easy! We know you're always pressed for time, but that doesn't mean you want to forego fresh, delicious, home-cooked food enjoyed at your own table. We've organized this book in a month-by-month format so you can find just the recipe you need for any occasion, situation, or taste—whether it's a romantic Valentine's menu (see *page 22*) or 10-minute popcorn chicken and homemade slaw for busy weeknights (see *page 101*). If, during the year, a recipe in *Better Homes and Gardens®* magazine caught your eye but escaped your schedule, it's right here—along with more than 400 other great recipes, stories, tips, and ideas for menu planning and entertaining with ease and flair. (Check out how to host a wine-tasting party, *page 85*.) As a bonus, you'll also find:

Healthy Recipes and Nutrition Information: A "Healthy" icon found next to the recipe nutrition facts means that it meets certain calorie, fat, sodium, and cholesterol guidelines. For example, a main dish will be about 400 calories and contain no more than 12 grams of fat per serving to earn the healthy badge of honor. See page 334 for more information about our nutrition guidelines.

Fast Recipes and Preparation Times: All of the recipes in the book have preparation times that will aid in your meal-prep schedule, but those marked "Fast!" can be on the table in 30 minutes or less.

Kid-Friendly Recipes: Go beyond mac 'n' cheese and hot dogs with these fun recipes containing ingredients kids will love. Of course, even the recipes that don't have a kid-friendly icon might pass the taste test at your house—so go ahead and give them all a try!

Prizewinning Recipes: You'll find the top $400 and $200 blue-ribbon winners from the magazine's monthly Prize Tested Recipes® contest starting on page 252. On the opposite page of each monthly contest, you'll also find several bonus Honor Roll winners. These recipes didn't make it into the magazine but were too good to leave out of the *Better Homes and Gardens® Annual Recipes 2005* book.

Menu Ideas: Planning a party and looking for ideas of what recipes to serve together? Starting on page 302, you'll find a selection of menus that incorporate the Prize Tested Recipes® and Honor Rolls. This section helps you match tastes for mistake-proof dinner parties every time!

Ingredient Substitution Guide: In a pinch and out of baking powder? See the easy-to-read Emergency Substitutions chart on page 335 that will help you substitute an ingredient you might not have with one you do have.

2005 CONTENTS

Overnight Oats with Fruit
page 158

Hot Dogs and Texas Tomato Chutney
page 139

Triple Green Bean Salad
page 111

BBQ Chicken Burgers and Waffle Fries
page 95

Out-and-About Cheesecake
page 180

Beef and Sweet Pepper Pasta
page 42

Three-Herb Deviled Eggs
page 65

Mandarins and Ice Cream Cake
page 15

JANUARY

German Chocolate Cupcakes
page 12

MELTY, SCRUMPTIOUS, AND OOZING WITH FLAVOR,
THESE ICE CREAM DESSERTS WILL SWEEP THE WINTER
BLUES RIGHT OUT THE DOOR.

Warm Up with Ice Cream

PB&J Ice Cream Sandwiches
page 14

Toasted S'More Snowballs
page 17

Gingerbread Tumble
page 11

Warm up with *Ice Cream*

Gingerbread Tumble

TOPPED, LAYERED, AND SANDWICHED WITH MOUNDS OF
LUSCIOUS ICE CREAM, THESE DECADENT CONFECTIONS CAN
BE SIMPLIFIED BY PURCHASING BAKERY GOODIES OR
PERSONALIZED BY CREATING HOMEMADE CAKES AND COOKIES.

Toss a crowd-pleasing centerpiece in one big bowl, set out six spoons, and let everyone dig in. For Gingerbread Tumble, spice up vanilla ice cream with freshly grated ginger, then watch it turn into a melty heap over warm gingerbread and cinnamon-kissed pears. The surprise shortcut: The gingerbread is made with a mix.

Gingerbread Tumble

PREP: 30 MINUTES **FREEZE:** 4 HOURS

- 1 quart vanilla ice cream, softened
- 2 to 3 tsp. grated fresh ginger or 1/2 to 1 tsp. ground ginger
- 1 14- or 14 1/2-oz. pkg. gingerbread mix or 9×9-inch purchased gingerbread
- 2 cups sugar
- 3/4 cup butter
- 1 tsp. ground cinnamon
- 9 small pears, peeled, cored, and halved, or three 16-oz. cans pear halves, drained

1. In a bowl combine softened ice cream with ginger. Cover and freeze 4 hours or overnight.

2. Prepare gingerbread mix according to package directions using the 9×9×2-inch pan option. Cool. Cut into 2-inch chunks.

3. In a 12-inch skillet cook and stir sugar, butter, and cinnamon over medium-high heat 3 minutes. Carefully add pears; stir to coat. Cook and stir 8 to 10 minutes more for fresh pears or 3 minutes for canned.

4. To assemble, place gingerbread in a 3-quart shallow bowl or casserole. Top with scoops of ice cream and pears. Drizzle with half of the sauce in skillet. Pass remaining sauce. Makes 10 to 12 servings.

EACH SERVING: 748 cal., 36 g total fat (16 g sat. fat), 114 mg chol., 418 mg sodium, 106 g carbo., 5 g fiber, 5 g pro. Daily Values: 18% vit. A, 11% vit. C, 13% calcium, 14% iron.

When paired with something warm from the oven, ice cream in winter is a delicious incentive for everyone to gather around a board game or to share a quiet afternoon hunkered down with good books. To give everyone more time for reading, playing, and snuggling, our recipes all start with ice cream from the carton and give you the choice of buying or baking the accompanying cookies, cakes, and crusts.

The heart of each idea on these pages is delicious contrast. Hot meets cold: Rivers of hot caramel sauce turn the towering mound on top of the German Chocolate Cupcakes into a nutty, creamy avalanche that's part sauce, part frozen wonder. Spicy faces off with sweet: Two kinds of ginger highlight the creaminess of the vanilla ice cream in the Gingerbread Tumble. Crunchy yields to soft: Crisp, freshly baked cookies hug icy scoops in the PB&J Ice Cream Sandwiches.

These treats also can be adapted for kids or grown-ups, for parties, or for quiet family-only nights. For instance, make a child-friendly version of the Anise Coffee and Ice Cream by pouring in hot chocolate instead of coffee. Turn German Chocolate Cupcakes into pretty pink packages by substituting strawberry cupcakes for the chocolate variety and topping with cherry ice cream and white chocolate shavings. Beneath the Toasted S'More Snowballs, replace chocolate with rocky road ice cream.

However you put your stamp on them, these goodies go together in less than an hour, can be made ahead of time, and have their good looks built in—there's no fussing with garnishes or hard-to-get ingredients.

This is the time of year when kids are home from college, grandparents fly in for a week, and friends visit from near and far. When your home brims with conversation and laughter, serve these catalysts of fun and joy. These are the desserts that entice guests to linger and, when it is finally time to head home, leave them with a tale about how a cold slab of frozen milk became the warm heart of winter.

Greet the new year with German Chocolate Cupcakes created from rounds of chocolate ice cream, purchased or homemade cupcakes, and a crunchy nut-and-caramel topper.

German Chocolate Cupcakes

For a super shortcut, start with purchased cupcakes and use a scoop of ice cream for the Chocolate-Pecan Ice Cream "Frosting."

PREP: 25 MINUTES **BAKE:** 25 MINUTES **FREEZE:** 4 HOURS

Cut into slabs of ice cream with a round cookie cutter for cupcake "frosting."

  1 recipe Chocolate-Pecan Ice Cream "Frosting"
  1 cup all-purpose flour
$1/2$ tsp. baking soda
$1/4$ tsp. salt
  2 oz. sweet baking chocolate
$1/4$ cup water
$1/2$ cup butter, softened
$1/2$ cup sugar
  2 eggs
$1/2$ tsp. vanilla
$1/2$ cup buttermilk
     Prepared caramel ice cream topping
$2/3$ cup Toasted Coconut Topping (see recipe, *right*)

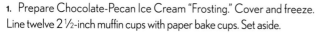

1. Prepare Chocolate-Pecan Ice Cream "Frosting." Cover and freeze. Line twelve 2½-inch muffin cups with paper bake cups. Set aside.

2. Preheat oven to 350°F. In a small bowl stir together flour, baking soda, and salt; set aside. In a saucepan combine chocolate and water. Cook and stir over low heat until melted; cool 10 minutes.

3. In a large bowl beat butter with an electric mixer on medium to high speed for 30 seconds. Beat in sugar until fluffy. Add eggs and vanilla; beat on low speed until combined, then beat on medium speed 1 minute. Beat in chocolate mixture. Add flour mixture and buttermilk alternately to beaten mixture, beating on low speed after each addition just until combined. Spoon into cups, filling about two-thirds full.

4. Bake 25 minutes or until a wooden toothpick inserted near centers comes out clean. Let stand 10 minutes; remove from pans. Cool.

5. Just before serving, heat caramel ice cream topping until warm. Remove papers from cupcakes; place cupcakes on plates or in shallow bowls. Top each cupcake with one round of "Frosting." Top with Toasted Coconut Topping and drizzle with warm caramel ice cream topping. Makes 12 servings.

CHOCOLATE-PECAN ICE CREAM "FROSTING": Line a cookie sheet with waxed paper; set aside. Slice ½ gallon chocolate ice cream into slabs about 2 inches thick. Use a cookie cutter to cut rounds from ice cream slab (see photo, *above*). Place ice cream rounds on prepared cookie sheet. Press ¾ to 1 cup toasted pecan pieces or halves into surface of ice cream. Serve on cupcakes immediately. Or cover and freeze ice cream "frosting" for 4 to 24 hours.

EASY CHOCOLATE-PECAN ICE CREAM "FROSTING": Follow instructions above for Chocolate-Pecan Ice Cream "Frosting," except for "Frosting" use an ice cream scoop to remove 12 generous scoops from ½ gallon of chocolate ice cream. Place scoops on prepared cookie sheet. Continue as directed above. (See photo, *front cover.*)

TOASTED COCONUT TOPPING: With a vegetable peeler, shave strips from a peeled, halved coconut. Place in a shallow baking pan. Toast in a 350°F oven for 10 minutes or until edges are lightly browned, stirring occasionally. If using purchased raw chip coconut, toast 2 to 3 minutes.

EACH SERVING: 411 cal., 25 g total fat (12 g sat. fat), 80 mg chol., 261 mg sodium, 43 g carbo., 2 g fiber, 6 g pro. Daily Values: 11% vit. A, 1% vit. C, 10% calcium, 8% iron.

German Chocolate Cupcakes

WHAT BETTER WAY TO FIGHT OFF THE JANUARY CHILL THAN BY HOSTING A LIGHT AND CHEERY POST-HOLIDAY PARTY? THESE SNAZZY DESSERTS CAN BE THE STARS OF THE GATHERING OR MERELY AN AFTER-DINNER TREAT WITH COFFEE.

Bake a bedtime snack solution: Create these two-bite PB&J Ice Cream Sandwiches from a roll of slice-and-bake peanut butter cookie dough, vanilla bean ice cream, and a jar of jam. Assemble, wrap individually, then fill a whole freezer shelf.

PB&J Ice Cream Sandwiches

SQUARE COOKIES

Make PB&J Ice Cream Sandwiches (recipe, *right*) with 6 Graduated Square Cutters ranging from 1³/₈ to 2⁵/₈ inches. Sets of cutters are dishwasher-safe and nest in a metal storage tin. Specify AAJ804872 for squares ($14.95). Shipping, handling, and sales tax will be added to your order total. Call 800/881-4066 or visit www. bhgcatalog.com.

Kid Friendly PB&J Ice Cream Sandwiches

PREP: 40 MINUTES **BAKE:** 8 MINUTES **FREEZE:** 4 HOURS

- ¼ cup all-purpose flour
- 1 18-oz. roll refrigerated peanut butter cookie dough
- 6 Tbsp. preserves, such as raspberry, cherry, or strawberry
- 1 pint vanilla bean ice cream

1. Preheat oven to 350°F. Knead flour into cookie dough. On a lightly floured surface, roll dough into a 13½×9-inch rectangle. Cut into 1½-inch squares. Transfer to ungreased cookie sheets. Bake for 8 to 10 minutes or until edges are firm. Cool on cookie sheets for 1 minute. Transfer to a wire rack. Cool completely.

2. Place 1 teaspoon jam on flat side of 1 cookie. Top with a scoop of ice cream (about 1½ tablespoons) and another cookie. Repeat with remaining cookies, jam, and ice cream (there will be extra cookies). Wrap and freeze 4 to 48 hours. Makes 16 sandwiches and 22 extra cookies.

EACH ICE CREAM SANDWICH: 175 cal., 9 g total fat (3 g sat. fat), 23 mg chol., 104 mg sodium, 22 g carbo., 0 g fiber, 3 g pro. Daily Values: 3% vit. A, 1% vit. C, 5% calcium, 3% iron.

Mandarins and Ice Cream Cake

PREP: 1 HOUR **FREEZE:** 5 HOURS **STAND:** 10 MINUTES

- ⅓ cup butter, melted
- 1½ cups crushed purchased spiced biscotti (about 6 oz.)
- 1 pint vanilla ice cream
- 1 8-oz. carton mascarpone cheese
- 1 pint orange sorbet, softened
- ½ cup orange marmalade
- 1 11-oz. can mandarin orange sections, drained, or
    6 to 8 clementines, peeled and cut into segments

1. Line a 2-quart square baking dish with foil, extending foil over edges of dish. In a bowl stir together butter and crushed biscotti. Spread in prepared baking dish. Press firmly to form an even crust. Freeze.

2. In a chilled bowl stir ice cream to soften. In another bowl stir mascarpone cheese to soften. Slowly add the softened ice cream to the mascarpone, stirring well (mixture may be slightly lumpy). Spoon into crust-lined dish and spread evenly. Freeze 1 hour or until firm. Spoon sorbet on top of ice cream mixture and spread with the back of a spoon. Cover; freeze 4 hours or until firm.

3. Let frozen mixture stand at room temperature for 10 minutes. Lift from pan using foil. In a small saucepan cook and stir marmalade just until heated through. Stir in orange sections.

4. To serve, cut ice cream mixture into 9 squares. Top each square with some of the citrus mixture. Makes 9 servings.

EACH SERVING: 420 cal., 27 g total fat (15 g sat. fat), 87 mg chol., 152 mg sodium, 43 g carbo., 2 g fiber, 9 g pro. Daily Values: 19% vit. A, 40% vit. C, 6% calcium, 3% iron.

Mandarins and Ice Cream Cake

Dazzle your book club with this frozen orange-and-mascarpone creation called Mandarins and Ice Cream Cake. Pile on a chunky, hot topping of marmalade and mandarin oranges for a flavor that will remind you of a Creamsicle®.

DIP UP THESE DELIGHTS

Create a **FROSTY SWIZZLE STICK** by poking a cinnamon stick into an ice cream ball. Great in hot chocolate or coffee.

Chop a frozen chocolate-coated ice cream bar and pile the chunks onto a **FRESH-FROM-THE-OVEN GOOEY PUDDING CAKE** or **CHERRY PIE.**

Scatter spoons of mascarpone cheese, dried apricots, and dried pears over scoops of vanilla ice cream for **AN EASY, ELEGANT DESSERT.**

Start the day with ice cream. A flavorful scoop melting over hot oatmeal is **A SPECIAL-OCCASION SUBSTITUTE FOR MILK.**

Scoop ice cream into a tall glass and top with **ORANGE SODA.**

Anise Coffee and Ice Cream

Pour a perfect end to dinner with this unique dessert: Anise Coffee and Ice Cream. Brew coffee, slice up ice cream, and you're done.

Anise Coffee and Ice Cream
Instead of coffee, make hot chocolate for the kids.

 START TO FINISH: 20 MINUTES

- ⅓ cup ground dark roast coffee
- 2 tsp. anise seeds, crushed
- 2¼ cups cold water
- 1 pint vanilla ice cream

1. Prepare coffee in a drip coffeemaker according to manufacturer's directions using amounts of coffee, anise seeds, and water listed above.
2. Meanwhile, carefully remove ice cream from package and cut into 8 large chunks. Place ice cream into cups. Pour about ¼ cup of coffee around ice cream. Serve immediately. Makes 8 servings.

EACH SERVING: 96 cal., 7 g total fat (4 g sat. fat), 34 mg chol., 23 mg sodium, 9 g carbo., 0 g fiber, 1 g pro. Daily Values: 5% vit. A, 5% calcium, 2% iron.

Chocolate Stout Shake
 PREP: 25 MINUTES

- ¼ cup chocolate stout beer or stout beer
- ½ cup prepared chocolate fudge ice cream topping
- ½ gallon vanilla bean ice cream
- 1 cup milk
- 8 purchased chocolate-and-nut-covered pretzel rods (optional)

1. In a saucepan heat beer and chocolate topping until warm.
2. Meanwhile, in a blender combine ice cream and milk, half at a time. Cover and blend until combined. Divide ice cream mixture among 8 glasses. Drizzle with beer mixture and, if desired, serve with chocolate-covered pretzel rods. Makes 8 servings.

EACH SERVING: 436 cal., 25 g total fat (16 g sat. fat), 139 mg chol., 122 mg sodium, 46 g carbo., 0 g fiber, 7 g pro. Daily Values: 20% vit. A, 22% calcium, 6% iron.

Chocolate Stout Shake

Melt dad's heart with a sturdy combination of chocolate-flavor stout, hot fudge, and ice cream. Serve this fast Chocolate Stout Shake with a pretzel rod to tide him over until dinner.

Put a smile on everyone's face with Toasted S'More Snowballs, a chocolaty-marshmallow cross between baked Alaska and that old campfire favorite. Assemble this three-ingredient recipe beforehand and pop it in the freezer. Three minutes in the oven will add a toasty golden crunch to the topping.

Kid Friendly Toasted S'More Snowballs

PREP: 25 MINUTES **FREEZE:** 1 HOUR **BAKE:** 3 MINUTES

- 12 graham cracker squares
- 12 small scoops chocolate fudge or rocky road ice cream (about 1½ cups)
- 1 7.2-oz. pkg. fluffy white frosting mix

1. Line a baking sheet with waxed paper. Arrange cracker squares on waxed paper. Use a small scoop to place a mound of ice cream on each cracker square. Cover and place in freezer.

2. Prepare frosting mix according to package directions. Place frosting in a large pastry bag fitted with a large round tip (¼ inch). Pipe frosting over each frozen ice cream mound to cover (see photo, *right*). Or use a spoon to spread frosting over each mound, spreading to cover. Freeze at least 1 hour (cover loosely after frosting is firm).

3. Preheat oven to 500°F. Transfer squares to a greased baking sheet. Bake, uncovered, for 3 to 4 minutes or until frosting is golden brown. Serve immediately. Makes 12 servings.

EACH SERVING: 120 cal., 2 g total fat (1 g sat. fat), 6 mg chol., 91 mg sodium, 25 g carbo., 0 g fiber, 1 g pro. Daily Values: 1% vit. A, 1% calcium, 2% iron.

Pipe frosting over the ice cream, making sure you cover the scoops completely to prevent them from melting during baking.

Say Cheese

If you're looking for new pairings for cheese, this matchmaker has them. At Montage Resort & Spa Loft Restaurant in Laguna Beach, California, fromage maître d' Starr Cornwall delights in helping people understand the 20 varieties of cheeses from the Loft's Cheese Gallery. "Cheeses range from fresh and tangy to stinky and nutty, sharp, and even fruity," Cornwall says . "When you serve cheese at home, you want to have a mixture of varieties from mild to pungent so a wide range of taste buds is covered." She recommends a trio of soft-ripened cheese, blue cheese, and goat cheese, paired these ways.

Buttery soft-ripened cheese is divine with fresh berries and a glass of Champagne or Pinot Noir. Try Mt. Tam Triple Cream cheese from Point Reyes, named after Mt. Tamalpais in California.

Ripe blue cheeses are delightful partners to fresh dates, walnuts, or dried fruits. Serve with full-bodied red wines such as Zinfandel or Shiraz, or cider. One of Cornwall's favorites is St. Agur blue cheese.

Creamy, mild goat's milk cheese is a mouthwatering match to decadent pieces of honeycomb, apples or pears, and a buttery Chardonnay or crisp Sauvignon Blanc. Humboldt Fog, a goat's milk cheese made by Cypress Groves in California, has a bloomy rind and a line of ash through the center that helps the cheese develop in complexity as it ages.

Starr Cornwall

Soft-ripened

Blue

Goat's milk

Where to get it: Montage Resort & Spa Loft Restaurant, Laguna Beach, California, 949/715-6000. Cheeses: Cowgirl Creamery, 866/433-7834 or www.cowgirlcreamery.com; Cheese Store of Beverly Hills, 800/547-1515 or www.cheesestorebh.com.

Deliciously savory when served plain with their food and wine complements, these cheeses also perform wonderfully when transformed into luscious appetizers.

Artichoke and Goat Cheese Bundles
PREP: 40 MINUTES **BAKE:** 14 MINUTES

- 2 Tbsp. butter
- 1/3 cup chopped shallots or sliced green onions
- 1 Tbsp. snipped fresh thyme or 1/2 teaspoon dried thyme, crushed
- 1 clove garlic, minced
- 1 9-ounce pkg. frozen artichoke hearts, drained and chopped
- 2 Tbsp. dry white wine or chicken broth
- 8 oz. soft goat cheese (chèvre)
- 1/8 tsp. salt
- 18 sheets frozen phyllo dough (9×14-inch rectangles), thawed
- 6 Tbsp. butter, melted

1. Preheat oven to 375°F. For filling, in a large skillet melt the 2 tablespoons of butter over medium heat. Add shallots, thyme, and garlic; cook and stir about 3 minutes or until shallots are tender. Add artichoke hearts and wine to the mixture in skillet. Simmer, uncovered, about 3 minutes or until liquid evaporates. Remove from heat. Stir in goat cheese and salt. Cool slightly.

2. Place one sheet of phyllo dough on a cutting board or other flat surface. Lightly brush to edges of dough with some of the melted butter. Place another sheet of phyllo on top; brush with butter. Repeat with a third sheet of phyllo. (Keep remaining phyllo sheets covered with plastic wrap until needed.)

3. Trim stacked phyllo sheets into a 12×8-inch rectangle; cut into six 4-inch squares. Place about 2 teaspoons of the filling in the center of each square. Bring the four corners of each square together; pinch and twist slightly to make a bundle. Place on an ungreased baking sheet. Repeat with remaining phyllo dough, butter, and filling. Brush with any remaining butter.

4. Bake for 14 to 15 minutes or until golden brown. Cool slightly on a wire rack; serve warm. Makes 36 appetizers.

EACH SERVING: 52 cal., 4 g total fat (1 g sat. fat), 3 mg chol., 78 mg sodium, 2 g carbo., 1 g fiber, 2 g pro. Daily Values: 3% vit. A, 1% vit. C, 1% calcium, 1% iron.

Blue Cheese-Walnut Rolls
PREP: 20 MINUTES **BAKE:** 15 MINUTES

- 1/2 of a 15-oz. pkg. folded refrigerated unbaked piecrust (1 crust)
- 2/3 cup toasted, finely chopped walnuts
- 1/3 cup crumbled blue cheese
- 1 Tbsp. finely snipped fresh parsley
- 1/4 tsp. ground black pepper
- 1 Tbsp. milk
- 2 tsp. grated Parmesan cheese
  Finely snipped fresh parsley

1. Preheat oven to 425°F. Grease a baking sheet; set aside. Let piecrust stand at room temperature as directed on the package.

2. Combine walnuts, blue cheese, 1 tablespoon of the parsley, and pepper. Set aside.

3. On a lightly floured surface, unfold piecrust according to package directions. Spread filling evenly over the crust. Cut pastry circle into 12 wedges. Starting at the wide ends, loosely roll up wedges. Place rolls, tips down, on prepared baking sheet.

4. Brush rolls lightly with milk. Sprinkle with Parmesan cheese and remaining parsley. Bake for 15 minutes or until golden brown. Serve warm. Makes 12 rolls.

EACH ROLL: 139 cal., 10 g total fat (1 g sat. fat), 8 mg chol., 130 mg sodium, 9 g carbo., 3 g fiber, 3 g pro. Daily Values: 1% vit. C, 2% calcium, 1% iron.

FEBRUARY

Melted Ice Cream Mousse
page 29

Double Thumbprint Cookies
page 27

WITH OR WITHOUT THE HELP OF CUPID'S ARROWS,
THIS DELIGHTFUL MENU IS SURE TO INSPIRE AN
OUTPOURING OF GASTRONOMIC LOVE.

Cupid's Guide to Valentine's Dinner

Plus

Warm Cannellini Salad with Prosciutto Chips
page 24

Raspberry Meringues
page 33

be my valentine

Poached Halibut and Peppers
page 28

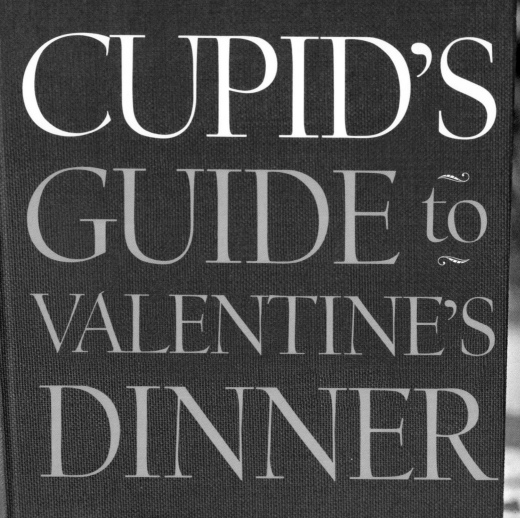

CUPID'S GUIDE to VALENTINE'S DINNER

A Colorful Menu

Sparkling Pomegranate Spritzers
Parmesan Breadsticks
Warm Cannellini Salad with Prosciutto Chips
Poached Halibut and Peppers
Roasted Thyme Tomatoes
Bittersweet Bark with Cinnamon Candies
Melted Ice Cream Mousse
Double Thumbprint Cookies

Sparkling Pomegranate Spritzers

Prosecco is a sparkling wine from Italy. Other dry (nonsweet) sparkling wines work well too. Look for bottles labeled "brut" or "extra dry." Those will be the least-sweet options.

 START TO FINISH: 5 MINUTES

- 2 Tbsp. 100% pomegranate juice* or cranberry juice, chilled
- Splash orange liqueur, such as Cointreau or Grand Marnier (about 1/2 tsp.)
- Prosecco or sparkling wine, chilled

1. For each spritzer, in a small tumbler or flute combine pomegranate juice and Cointreau. Fill glass with Prosecco or sparkling wine. Makes 1 serving.

*NOTE: Some pomegranate juices are filtered to be clear and some are left in their natural state; either will work in this recipe.

EACH SERVING: 106 cal., 0 g total fat, 0 mg chol., 7 mg sodium, 6 g carbo., 0 g fiber, 0 g pro. Daily Values: 6% vit. C, 1% calcium, 3% iron.

Sparkling Pomegranate Spritzers

BY ELIZABETH SCHATZ PHOTOGRAPHS BY TINA RUPP PRODUCED BY JESSICA THOMAS FOOD STYLING BY ANNE DISRUDE PROP STYLING BY CHRISTINA WRESSELL

V

alentine's Day is the perfect time to stir up something special for those you cherish, especially with this I-adore-you dinner menu from entertaining guru Jennifer Rubell. "It's romantic and fun to celebrate a love-filled holiday with your family or friends," Rubell says.

Jennifer Rubell

HEART-WARMING FLAVORS

The menu you serve on Valentine's Day should be a special feast, including favorite flavors with a few surprising twists. Make the most simple appetizers look and taste decadent: add a newly discovered aromatic cheese, such as a blue or Stilton, to a cheese plate; or brush toast points with a lemon, basil, or truffle butter. Kick up the heat with a spicy broth for the seafood main course. Leave out the hot peppers for little diners. A mild fish such as halibut or cod pleases every palate and goes well with the white bean and prosciutto salad. Don't forget the chocolate. What is Valentine's Day without it? Make favorite chocolate confections rich and decadent: incorporate unique spices and flavors, such as cinnamon, citrus, mint, and rosemary; or make a chocolate dessert from your childhood and share a happy memory with your own children.

Warm Cannellini Salad with Prosciutto Chips

You can substitute cooked bacon pieces for the prosciutto.
PREP: 15 MINUTES **BAKE:** 25 MINUTES

- 4 to 6 slices prosciutto (3 to 4 oz.)
- 3 Tbsp. olive oil
- 3 cloves garlic, minced
- 2 Tbsp. lemon juice
- 2 tsp. snipped fresh sage
- 1/4 tsp. sea salt or a dash of salt
- 4 cups fresh arugula or mixed greens
- 1 19-oz. can cannellini beans (white kidney beans), rinsed and drained

1. Preheat oven to 375°F. Arrange prosciutto in a single layer on a large baking sheet. Bake for 25 minutes; do not move prosciutto during baking. Set aside.
2. For dressing, in a small saucepan heat oil over medium heat. Cook garlic in hot oil until it begins to brown. Remove from heat. Stir in lemon juice, sage, and salt; set aside.
3. Arrange arugula, beans, and prosciutto on individual plates. Drizzle with warm dressing. Serve immediately. Serves 4 to 6.
EACH SERVING: 268 cal., 12 g total fat (2 g sat. fat), 6 mg chol., 761 mg sodium, 38 g carbo., 13 g fiber, 18 g pro. Daily Values: 10% vit. A, 12% vit. C, 10% calcium, 18% iron.

Warm Cannellini Salad with Prosciutto Chips

> This chocolate bark can go straight from the freezer to the table, and guests can serve themselves by breaking off their own pieces. Any leftover bits can be sent home in gift bags.

Bittersweet Bark with Cinnamon Candies

Feel free to substitute crushed toffee for the cinnamon candies.
Fast! **PREP:** 10 MINUTES **COOK:** 8 MINUTES **FREEZE:** 10 MINUTES

- 8 oz. bittersweet chocolate, broken into chunks
- 1/3 cup red cinnamon candies

1. Place parchment paper on platter; set aside. In small heavy saucepan melt chocolate over medium-low heat; stir often.
2. When melted (about 8 minutes), remove from heat. Working quickly, stir in about 1/3 of the cinnamon candies. Immediately turn chocolate out onto parchment paper. With the back of a spoon spread out chocolate mixture until candies are in a single layer. Sprinkle remaining candies on top and place in freezer for 10 to 15 minutes or until hard. Leave bark in freezer until ready to break off pieces to serve. Makes 4 servings.
EACH SERVING: 336 cal., 20 g total fat (12 g sat. fat), 0 mg chol., 4 mg sodium, 48 g carbo., 4 g fiber, 4 g pro. Daily Values: 2% calcium, 11% iron.

WHETHER YOU'RE WOOING YOUR PARTNER OVER A CANDLELIT DINNER OR CATERING TO A GROUP OF FUN-LOVING FRIENDS, THIS IRRESISTIBLE CHOCOLATE CONFECTION IS THE PERFECT WAY TO WRAP UP THE EVENING.

Bittersweet Bark with Cinnamon Candies

Start the evening with a stress-free appetizer that guests can dip to their hearts' content. Set out a bowlful of fast-to-make Parmesan Breadsticks with a trio of tasty sauces—a quick blender dip and two ready-to-serve store-bought favorites.

Parmesan Breadsticks

Parmesan Breadsticks

Leftover breadsticks taste great with a soup or salad.

 PREP: 15 MINUTES **BAKE:** 10 MINUTES PER BATCH

> 1 12-oz. loaf baguette-style French bread (16 to 24 inches long)
>   Nonstick cooking spray
> ½ cup olive oil
> ¾ cup grated or finely shredded Parmesan cheese
> 1 recipe Red Pepper Sauce or purchased marinara sauce
>   Flavored oils, such as lemon, basil, or garlic (optional)

1. Preheat oven to 375°F. Cut loaf crosswise in half, then cut in half lengthwise. Then cut each half lengthwise into long ¼- to ½-inch-wide strips. (Cut bread so there is crust on each strip.)

2. Line a 15×10×1-inch baking pan with foil; lightly coat with cooking spray. Arrange half of the breadsticks in a single layer; drizzle with half of the oil. Using a spatula or tongs, carefully turn breadsticks to coat with oil. Sprinkle with half of the Parmesan.

3. Bake for 10 to 12 minutes or until browned and crisp. Repeat with remaining breadsticks, oil, and cheese. Transfer to a platter. If desired, serve with Red Pepper Sauce and/or flavored oils.

4. To store leftover breadsticks, place in a covered container and store at room temperature for 2 days or in the freezer up to 1 month. Makes 12 to 15 servings.

RED PEPPER SAUCE: In a large skillet cook 4 red sweet peppers, coarsely chopped, and 2 shallots, chopped, in ¼ cup olive oil over medium heat about 10 minutes until tender, stirring occasionally. Remove skillet from heat. Add ½ cup dry white wine; 4 cloves garlic, minced; 2 tablespoons snipped fresh flat-leaf parsley; ½ teaspoon salt; and ¼ teaspoon ground black pepper. Stir to combine. Return to heat. Bring mixture to boiling; reduce heat. Cover and simmer 10 to 15 minutes until peppers are very tender. Cool slightly. Transfer to a food processor. Add 2 tablespoons snipped fresh flat-leaf parsley and 2 tablespoons olive oil; cover and process until almost smooth. Makes about 1½ cups.

EACH SERVING: 179 cal., 11 g total fat (2 g sat. fat), 4 mg chol., 249 mg sodium, 15 g carbo., 1 g fiber, 4 g pro. Daily Values: 8% calcium, 5% iron.

Double Thumbprint Cookies

Let your children or friends add their thumbprints to these precious cookies and bake them while you serve coffee. The guests can then fill their own cookies with their favorite flavor of jam.

Kid Friendly Double Thumbprint Cookies

Pile these pretty hearts on a plate and let guests fill them with assorted jams and preserves.

PREP: 45 MINUTES **BAKE:** 7 MINUTES PER BATCH

- ½ cup butter, softened
- ¼ cup granulated sugar
- ¼ cup packed brown sugar
- 1 tsp. baking powder
- ½ tsp. salt
- 1 egg
- 1 Tbsp. milk
- 1 tsp. vanilla
- 2 cups all-purpose flour
- ¼ to ⅓ cup cherry jam or preserves, or seedless raspberry preserves

1. Preheat oven to 375°F. In a large bowl beat butter with an electric mixer on medium to high speed for 30 seconds. Add granulated sugar, brown sugar, baking powder, and salt. Beat until mixture is combined, scraping sides of bowl occasionally. Beat in egg, milk, and vanilla until combined. Beat in as much of the flour as you can with the mixer. Stir in any remaining flour.

2. Shape dough into ¾-inch balls. For each cookie, place 2 dough balls side-by-side with one side touching (see photos, *right*) on an ungreased or parchment paper-lined cookie sheet. Press a thumb into each ball to form an indentation in each. Press in center of each with thumb and taper bottom of cookie with fingers to form a heart shape. Repeat with remaining dough balls, leaving about 2 inches between cookies.

3. Bake for 7 to 9 minutes or until edges are lightly browned. Remove from oven; transfer to a wire rack. While warm, fill each indentation with jam (snip any large pieces of fruit). Cool completely. Makes about 30 cookies.

TO STORE: Place filled cookies in a single layer in covered storage containers and store at room temperature up to 3 days or freeze up to 3 months.

EACH COOKIE: 81 cal., 3 g total fat (2 g sat. fat), 16 mg chol., 74 mg sodium, 11 g carbo., 0 g fiber, 1 g pro. Daily Values: 2% vit. A, 1% calcium, 2% iron.

Poached Halibut and Peppers

Poached Halibut and Peppers

For extra panache, pour the remaining broth into a pitcher and pass it so guests can pour the juices over their fish.

PREP: 20 MINUTES **COOK:** 11 MINUTES

- 1½ cups dry white wine such as Sauvignon Blanc or Pinot Grigio, or chicken broth
- 1 cup water
- 1 medium yellow sweet pepper, chopped (¾ cup)
- 3 Tbsp. drained capers
- 4 cloves garlic, minced
- ¼ to ½ tsp. crushed red pepper
- 4 halibut steaks (1½ to 1¾ lb.), or
- 4 cod or other whitefish fillets
  Salt and freshly ground black pepper
- 2 Tbsp. basil oil or olive oil
  Coarsely chopped fresh parsley

1. For poaching liquid, in a large skillet combine wine, water, sweet pepper, capers, garlic, and crushed red pepper. Bring to boiling; reduce heat. Simmer, uncovered, for 7 minutes, stirring occasionally.
2. Place fish in a single layer in the poaching liquid in the skillet. Season with salt and black pepper. Spoon liquid over fish. Return to simmer. Cook, covered, 4 to 6 minutes per ½-inch thickness of fish until fish flakes easily when tested with a fork. Remove fish to serving platter. Spoon or pour cooking liquid into a small serving pitcher. Drizzle cooked fish with oil. Sprinkle with fresh parsley. To serve, place fish in individual serving bowls; pass remaining broth. Makes 4 servings.

 EACH SERVING: 338 cal., 11 g total fat (1 g sat. fat), 54 mg chol., 437 mg sodium, 8 g carbo., 1 g fiber, 37 g pro. Daily Values: 11% vit. A, 289% vit. C, 11% calcium, 13% iron.

Roasted Thyme Tomatoes

Serve these rosy tomatoes alongside scrambled eggs or quiche for brunch.

PREP: 20 MINUTES **ROAST:** 45 MINUTES

- 8 plum tomatoes (1½ lb.)
- 4 tsp. olive oil
- 5 sprigs fresh thyme, stems removed (1 Tbsp. dried thyme leaves)
- ¼ tsp. salt
- ¼ tsp. ground black pepper
  Coarse brown sugar (optional)
  Fresh thyme sprigs (optional)

1. Preheat oven to 375°F. Halve tomatoes lengthwise. Scoop out seeds and center membrane. Place tomatoes in a shallow roasting pan, cut sides up; drizzle with oil. Combine thyme, salt, and pepper; sprinkle mixture over tomatoes.
2. Roast, uncovered, for 45 minutes. Remove from oven. If desired, sprinkle with sugar and top with thyme. Serve warm. Serves 4 to 6.

 EACH SERVING: 71 cal., 5 g total fat (1 g sat. fat), 0 mg chol., 154 mg sodium, 7 g carbo., 2 g fiber, 2 g pro. Daily Values: 29% vit. A, 38% vit. C, 2% calcium, 4% iron.

Melted Ice Cream Mousse

A no-fail, extra chocolaty version of the dessert favorite.

PREP: 20 MINUTES **CHILL:** 2 HOURS

  1 pint chocolate ice cream
  1 cup whipping cream
  1/3 cup unsweetened cocoa powder

1. Place ice cream in a medium saucepan. Heat over low heat until melted. Transfer to an extra large mixing bowl; cover and chill about 1 hour or until cold.

2. Add whipping cream to melted ice cream. Beat with an electric mixer on high speed for 5 to 6 minutes or until soft peaks begin to form. Sift cocoa powder into the chocolate mixture. Beat on low speed for 1 minute or until combined, scraping sides of bowl twice.

3. Pour into serving bowl. Cover and chill for 1 to 6 hours until ready to serve. Makes 6 to 8 servings.

EACH SERVING: 253 cal., 20 g total fat (12 g sat. fat), 70 mg chol., 49 mg sodium, 16 g carbo., 1 g fiber, 4 g pro. Daily Values: 15% vit. A, 1% vit. C, 13% calcium, 6% iron.

RICH AND CREAMY, SMOOTH AND DECADENT—NO MATTER HOW YOU CHOOSE TO DESCRIBE THIS WHIPPED DESSERT, YOUR MOUTH WILL MERELY DEFINE IT AS *PERFECTION*.

Melted Ice Cream Mousse

CURRIED POTATO SALAD
Add a dash of curry to red-potato salad. Top toast with salad and radish sprouts.

TURKEY SANDWICH Top toast with deli turkey, mashed potatoes, and dried cherries soaked in warmed balsamic vinegar and sherry.

PEANUT BUTTER RASPBERRY
Spread toast with crunchy peanut butter. Add raspberries, crème fraîche, and crumbled bacon.

CILANTRO SALAD Toss cilantro and torn arugula with Italian dressing. Spread toast with goat cheese and top with salad.

ANTIPASTO Toss purchased antipasto mix with shredded smoked whitefish and fresh oregano or basil. Top toast with mixture.

WHITE CHEDDAR CHUTNEY
Spread toast with butter. Layer with white cheddar cheese. Top with purchased pear or apple chutney.

BY **STEPHEN EXEL** PHOTOGRAPHS BY **GREG SCHEIDEMANN, [N] HAUS FOTO** FOOD STYLING BY **SUSAN BROWN DRAUDT**

TOAST OF THE TOWN

Remember the toast point? Somehow, this classic accompaniment to

dips and spreads, sliced meats, and smoked salmon got lost in a shuffle of artisan breads and bruschetta. Toast points—toasted bread cut into quarters—get a new attitude when topped with a creative combo of ingredients straight from the grocery store aisles.

TAIL OF THE SEA

Find an excuse to celebrate, then make an impression with this succulent lobster salad.

It's hard to imagine that lobster was once so abundant that it was often used as bait by fishermen in the 19th century. Nowadays lobster may be a luxury, but the tasty payoff is well worth the splurge. The king of seafood has a mild, sweet flavor that makes it outstanding on its own. But when combined with a touch of citrus and thyme—as it is in this salad—lobster takes on a refreshingly lively flavor.

When shopping for frozen lobster, be sure it is sealed tightly in a moistureproof package. Plan on thawing the lobster on a plate in the refrigerator for up to 24 hours before you will be using it.

If you can't find deep-red blood oranges, substitute any other fresh oranges that are available in your market. Grapefruit is a tasty alternative too.

BY **SHELLI MCCONNELL** PHOTOGRAPHS BY **SCOTT LITTLE**

Lobster and Citrus Salad
PREP: 30 MINUTES **COOK:** 8 MINUTES

- 4 8-oz. frozen lobster tails, thawed in the refrigerator
- 3 blood oranges or regular oranges
  Blood orange juice or orange juice
- 8 cups mesclun greens or other salad greens
- 2 shallots, finely chopped
- 3 Tbsp. salad oil
- 2 Tbsp. grapefruit juice or orange juice
- 2 tsp. snipped fresh thyme or ¼ tsp. dried thyme, crushed
  Freshly ground pepper (optional)

1. In a 3-quart saucepan bring 6 cups *water* and 1 teaspoon *salt* to boiling. Add lobster. Simmer, uncovered, for 8 to 12 minutes or until shells turn bright red and meat is tender. Drain; let stand until cool enough to handle.

2. Meanwhile, peel and section oranges over bowl to catch juices. Add enough additional juice to make ⅓ cup; set aside. In a large bowl toss together the salad greens and orange sections. Divide the salad mixture among 4 dinner plates.

3. For dressing, in a medium skillet cook shallots in hot oil until tender. Carefully add the ⅓ cup orange juice, the 2 tablespoons grapefruit juice, and the thyme. Bring to boiling; keep warm.

4. To remove lobster meat from shell, insert a fork and push the tail meat out in one piece. Remove and discard the black vein that runs the length of the tail meat. Slice the tail meat, making ½-inch medallions. Arrange lobster medallions on top of greens. Spoon dressing over salads. If desired, sprinkle with black pepper. Serve immediately. Makes 4 main-dish servings.

EACH SERVING: 253 cal., 11 g total fat (2 g sat. fat), 81 mg chol., 442 mg sodium, 13 g carbo., 2 g fiber, 25 g pro. Daily Values: 14% vit. A, 68% vit. C, 9% calcium, 8% iron.

Lobster and Citrus Salad

GRAB THE PICKLED BEETS

Roasted Beets, Fennel, and Parsnips

Those shiny purple-red disks

that add a sweet vinegar snap to your lunchtime fare are a salad bar classic. At home, a jar of whole or sliced pickled beets goes a long way to create winter side dishes to serve with roasted meats and chicken.

- Fill a cored apple with chopped pickled beets; bake.
- Puree beets with chicken broth; then heat to make a soup.
- Mix pickled beets with pears and sage; puree for a spread.
- Warm chopped beets and strawberry preserves for a quick and delicious sauce.
- Roast whole pickled beets with onions and almonds.

Roasted Beets, Fennel, and Parsnips with Warm Caraway Vinaigrette (recipe, *right*) is an easy side dish to serve alongside a company roast or burgers. When roasting pickled beets, keep the beets separate in the pan so the juices don't stain other vegetables. Roasted pickled beets don't need peeling, so there's not a lot of mess.

BY **STEPHEN EXEL** PHOTOGRAPHS BY **GREG SCHEIDEMANN, [N] HAUS FOTO**
FOOD STYLING BY **BROOKE LEONARD**

Roasted Beets, Fennel, and Parsnips
PREP: 20 MINUTES **ROAST:** 40 MINUTES

- 2 16-oz. jars whole pickled beets, drained
- 3 medium parsnips, peeled and cut into 1-inch pieces
- 1 medium fennel bulb, cut into thin wedges
- 2 Tbsp. olive oil
- 1 tsp. caraway seeds, crushed
- ¼ tsp. salt
- ¼ tsp. freshly ground black pepper
- 1 recipe Warm Caraway Vinaigrette
  Sea salt (optional)

1. Preheat oven to 400°F. Place beets in one side of a shallow roasting pan. Place parsnips and fennel in opposite side of pan. Drizzle with oil. Sprinkle with caraway seeds, ¼ teaspoon salt, and pepper. Stir to coat, keeping beets separate from other vegetables. Roast in preheated oven 40 to 45 minutes or until vegetables are lightly browned and tender, stirring once or twice.

2. Prepare Warm Caraway Vinaigrette. In a serving bowl toss roasted vegetables with vinaigrette. If desired, sprinkle with salt. Serve immediately. Makes 6 side-dish servings.

WARM CARAWAY VINAIGRETTE: In a saucepan combine 2 tablespoons white wine vinegar; 1 tablespoon olive oil; ½ teaspoon sugar; ¼ teaspoon crushed caraway seeds; 1 small clove garlic, minced; and a dash of freshly ground black pepper. Bring to just boiling.

EACH SERVING: 201 cal., 7 g total fat (1 g sat. fat), 0 mg chol., 509 mg sodium, 34 g carbo., 7 g dietary fiber, 2 g pro. Daily Values: 22% vit. C, 4% calcium, 6% iron.

HAVE A HEART

Even kids know the way to another's

heart is with a playfully sweet nibble and a *message d'amour*. That's why a hard meringue is perfect for helping little ones send valentines—especially when they come with a message of love printed in red ink. Have the kids pen their missives by taking a cue from the words printed on tiny valentine-heart candies, finding inspiration from favorite love songs, or just writing whatever comes from the heart.

Then, help them whip up a batch of crunchy heart-shape meringues. You take care of the basic recipe; they'll have a blast piping out the pink sweets. A few tips for successful meringues:
■ Work with squeaky-clean bowl and beaters. The tiniest bit of residual oil, butter, or cream can deflate your meringue.
■ Draw heart outlines with a pencil on parchment paper to use as a guide when shaping meringues.
■ Snip the corner of a plastic food storage bag and fit it with a pastry tip as an alternative to a pastry bag.
■ Store meringues in an airtight container up to 2 weeks.

BY **JUDITH FERTIG** PHOTOGRAPHS BY **JOYCE OUDKERK POOL**

FOOD STYLING BY **POUKÉ**

Kid Friendly Raspberry Meringues

PREP: 30 MINUTES **STAND:** 30 MINUTES **DRY:** 1 HOUR

    2 egg whites
    1 Tbsp. seedless red raspberry jam (at room temperature)
    6 drops red food coloring
   1/3 cup superfine sugar or
       granulated sugar
   1/3 cup sifted powdered sugar
   1/8 tsp. cream of tartar
       Valentine messages written on parchment paper strips

1. Let egg whites stand, covered, in a stainless-steel or glass mixing bowl at room temperature for 30 minutes. Meanwhile, cover 2 baking sheets with baking parchment paper.
2. Preheat oven to 300°F. In a small mixing bowl stir together raspberry jam and red food coloring. Set aside.
3. In a small bowl combine superfine sugar and powdered sugar; set aside. Uncover eggs and add cream of tartar. Beat with an electric mixer on medium speed until soft peaks form (tips curl). Add sugar mixture, 1 tablespoon at a time, beating for 5 to 7 minutes on medium speed or until stiff glossy peaks form (tips stand straight) and sugar is dissolved.
4. Use a spatula to gently fold 1/2 cup of the meringue mixture into the jam; then gently fold jam mixture into remaining meringue.
5. Using a pastry bag or plastic food storage bag fitted with a large round or star tip (Wilton 2 D), pipe meringue into 2-inch hearts on the parchment.
6. Place baking sheets in preheated oven. Turn off oven. Let meringues dry in oven, with door closed, for 1 hour or until dry and crisp. Remove from oven. Let cool on parchment. Gently remove meringues. Tuck a message into each meringue. Makes about 20 meringue cookies.

LEMON MERINGUES: Prepare as above, except omit raspberry jam and red food coloring. Use a spatula to gently fold 1½ teaspoons finely shredded lemon peel into meringue after it has reached stiff-peak stage. Proceed with Step 5, above.

EACH MERINGUE: 23 cal., 0 g total fat , 0 mg chol., 6 mg sodium, 6 g carbo., 0 g fiber.

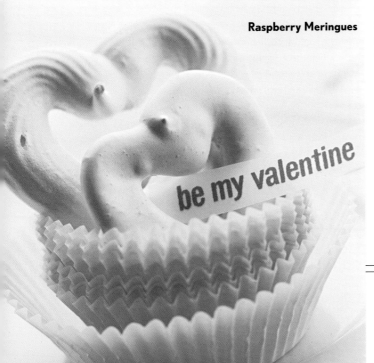

Raspberry Meringues

be my valentine

SAVING MEMORIES

We sent a digital camera along as TV anchor Julie Chen recorded her family's cooking secrets. We got pictures; she got a journal full of tradition and a new appreciation for Mom.

Julie Chen is on a mission to preserve her family's holiday recipes and traditions that her mother has upheld for decades.

"I don't think of my parents as old," says Julie, co-anchor of CBS's *The Early Show*, "but I have to start thinking about which memories and stories and traditions I want to record."

So with notebook in hand, she spent a day in the kitchen with her mother, Wan-Ling Chen, recording every dash and dollop as her mom prepared a Chinese New Year dinner for friends and family.

The holiday is time traditionally set aside for people to get together for a major feast and to focus on family and the hopes for luck and prosperity in the upcoming 12 months.

The meal itself is a leisurely two hours. At the center of the table sits the Chinese Hot Pot, a kind of Asian fondue in which a pot of boiling water is used to cook meats, fish, and vegetables one at a time. As the food cooks, it turns the water into broth that's served at the end with noodles as a soup.

Keeping a journal of the holiday was eye-opening for Julie. "You don't realize how much work it is until you write it all out. It made me appreciate all the hard work my mom went through every year for us as a family to celebrate Chinese New Year."

With recipes now in hand, Julie is ready to host her own celebrations, incorporating ideas both from traditional Chinese culture and from her own life.

Chinese Hot Pot
START TO FINISH: 75 MINUTES

- 1 recipe Dipping Sauce
- 8 oz. fresh or frozen peeled, deveined shrimp
- 8 oz. fresh or frozen sole, cut into 2-inch pieces
- 8 oz. boneless beef top loin steak
- 3 cups shredded napa cabbage
- 1 cup sliced fresh shiitake mushrooms
- 1 cup fresh bean sprouts, trimmed
- 2 medium carrots, thinly bias-sliced
- 1 8-oz. can sliced bamboo shoots, drained
- 1 tsp. salt
- 2 Tbsp. sliced green onions
- 1 1-inch piece fresh ginger, peeled and thinly sliced
- 4 oz. rice stick noodles

1. Prepare Dipping Sauce. Thaw shrimp and sole, if frozen. Thinly slice beef into bite-size strips. Arrange beef and seafood on a platter; set aside.

2. Arrange vegetables (except onions) on a separate platter; set aside.

3. In a large saucepan bring 8 cups *water* and the salt to boiling. Pour into a firepot, electric wok, or electric skillet on the dining table. Light burner under pot or turn on wok or skillet to medium heat.

4. To serve, give each person a soup bowl, a smaller bowl to hold Dipping Sauce, and a small wire strainer, chopsticks, or a slotted spoon. Dip beef, seafood, and vegetables into simmering water for 1 to 2 minutes until done, then dip into Dipping Sauce and eat. (Beef should no longer be pink; fish should flake easily; shrimp should turn opaque; and vegetables should be crisp-tender.)

5. When all beef, fish, seafood, and vegetables are cooked, add green onions, ginger, and noodles to broth. Cook 3 minutes or until noodles are tender. Remove and discard ginger pieces. Pour broth and noodles over any remaining beef, seafood, and vegetables in soup bowls. Stir Dipping Sauce into each bowl to taste. Makes 6 to 8 servings.

DIPPING SAUCE: In a small bowl stir together ½ cup reduced-sodium soy sauce; ¼ cup snipped fresh cilantro; ¼ cup sliced green onions; 1 tablespoon toasted sesame oil; 1 small fresh jalapeño pepper, seeded and finely chopped (see note, *page 143*); 2 teaspoons sugar; 2 teaspoons rice vinegar; 2 teaspoons grated fresh ginger; and 2 cloves garlic, minced. Allow to stand, covered, 1 hour before serving. Makes about ¾ cup.

EACH SERVING: 270 cal., 5 g total fat (1 g sat. fat), 93 mg chol., 1,293 mg sodium, 29 g carbo., 3 g dietary fiber, 26 g protein. Daily Values: 59% vit. A, 31% Vit. C, 11% calcium, 18% iron.

BY RICHARD SWEARINGEN PHOTOGRAPHS BY GREG SCHEIDEMANN, [N] HAUS FOTO FOOD STYLING BY JILL LUST

Chinese Hot Pot

"MY MOM IS LIKE A PROFESSIONAL CHEF WHO ADDS A LITTLE THIS, A LITTLE THAT, AND WHEN I ASK FOR MEASUREMENTS SHE ESTIMATES," SAYS JULIE *OPPOSITE*, WITH HER MOTHER, WAN-LING CHEN.

In good taste

FOOD AND ENTERTAINING

Pairs to Share

Create quick little nibbles by pairing biscuits or mixed nuts and dried fruit with other goodies for an instant celebration, suggests Anne Callahan, co-owner with husband Mark, of Uniquely Together. Their gourmet food company specializes in delicious munchies meant to be matched with other foods quickly and simply. "Pairing food and flavors is fun, exciting, and creative," Anne says. For example, the popular company's biscuits can be crushed and used for breading chicken and fish; sweeter ones can go into piecrusts or over ice cream. Nut mixes jazz up salads or can be stirred into cream cheese or salsa. **WINE NUTS AND CHAMPAGNE BISCUITS:** Uniquely Together; 800/613-7276; www.uniquelytogether.com.

▪ Wine nuts and Stilton pita pizza Dried grapes, almonds, and crunchy-coated Japanese peanuts are among the treats you'll find in Uniquely Together's Wine Nut Mix. Scatter it across a pita pizza topped with pungent blue cheese and a sprinkle of fresh lemon peel. Bake in the oven just until the cheese melts.

▪ Champagne biscuits and lemon curd These slightly crumbly biscuits studded with black currants have a buttery flavor that is especially yummy when you dip them in a smooth, tart lemon curd and end with a nibble of dried fruit.

Wine nuts and Stilton pita pizza

Champagne biscuits and lemon curd

Sweet Treat

ChikaLicious Dessert Bar is a wonderful place to plant yourself for some sweet indulgences. The intimate dessert bar has Manhattanites looking at dinner's finale with new eyes. The menu is strictly desserts with a wine list that offers appropriate matches. Among chef/owner Chika Tillman's offerings is a tiny, perfect Warm Chocolate Tart with Pink Peppercorn Ice Cream and Red Wine Sauce. ChikaLicious Dessert Bar, 203 E. 10th St. (at 2nd Ave.), New York, New York; 212/995-9511.

Adding interesting ingredients to purchased ice cream is the quick and easy way to make a "homemade" dessert for the family. To get you started, here are some more fun recipes straight from the Better Homes and Gardens® Test Kitchen.

Sweet Herb Ice Cream
PREP: 10 MINUTES **FREEZE:** 4 HOURS

2 cups vanilla ice cream
2 Tbsp. coarse sugar
4 tsp. snipped fresh lemon thyme, cinnamon basil, pineapple sage, or lemon verbena
Fresh herb sprigs (optional)

1. In a chilled medium bowl stir ice cream just to soften, using a wooden spoon to press ice cream against side of bowl. Quickly stir in sugar and thyme. Cover and freeze for 4 hours or until firm. Store, tightly covered, in the freezer for up to 1 week. If desired, garnish with fresh herb sprigs. Makes 4 servings.
EACH SERVING: 104 cal., 5 g total fat (3 g sat. fat), 19 mg chol., 35 mg sodium, 15 g carbo., 0 g fiber, 2 g pro. Daily Values: 4% vit. A, 2% vit. C, 6% calcium, 1% iron.

Balsamic Berries over Ice Cream
PREP: 20 MINUTES **STAND:** 1 HOUR

2 cups sliced strawberries
¼ cup sugar
1 Tbsp. balsamic vinegar
Butter
¼ cup pine nuts
Dash ground cloves
2 cups vanilla ice cream

1. In medium bowl combine strawberries, 2 tablespoons of the sugar, and the balsamic vinegar. Cover; let stand 1 to 2 hours.
2. Meanwhile, line a cookie sheet with foil. Butter the foil; set aside. In a small skillet combine the remaining sugar, the pine nuts, and cloves. Cook over medium heat, shaking skillet occasionally, until sugar begins to melt. Do not stir. Reduce heat to low and cook, stirring constantly with a wooden spoon until sugar is melted and pine nuts are golden brown. Remove from heat. Immediately pour pine nut mixture onto prepared cookie sheet. Cool completely. Break into pieces.
3. To serve, scoop ice cream into dishes. Top with berries and sprinkle with pine nut mixture. Makes 4 servings.
EACH SERVING: 319 cal., 18 g total fat (9 g sat. fat), 71 mg chol., 54 mg sodium, 37 g carbo., 2 g fiber. Daily Values: 10% vit. A, 71% vit. C, 10% calcium, 8% iron.

TRY THIS

Recreate ChikaLicious' peppery, exotic Valentine's treat by softening 1 quart of vanilla ice cream and stirring in 1 tablespoon of pink peppercorns, slightly crushed. Place in a chilled, freezer-safe container; cover and refreeze. Serve with a chocolate tart, cake, or brownie. Drizzle with red wine or raspberry or chocolate sauce.

MARCH

SPRING IS IN THE AIR! ENJOY THE RETURN OF WARM WEATHER BY GETTING OUT OF THE KITCHEN QUICKER WITH A LESSON FROM MOMS' COOKING CLUB.

Chicken Chowder
page 46

Moms' Cooking Club

Chicken Mac and Cheese
page 45

Herbed Beef and Barley Soup
page 44

Enchiladas with Fresh Mango Salsa
page 51

Moms' cooking club

WITH A LITTLE PLANNING AND LOT OF FRIENDSHIP, MOMS' COOKING CLUBS ACROSS THE COUNTRY HAVE TURNED MEAL PREPARATION FROM A DAILY NUISANCE INTO A SOCIABLE GATHERING.

BY **RICHARD SWEARINGER** RECIPES BY **JENNIFER KALINOWSKI** PHOTOGRAPHS BY **JAMES CARRIER, SUSIE CUSHNER, GREG SCHEIDEMANN** FOOD STYLING BY **KAREN SHINTO** PROP STYLING BY **CAROL HACKER**

Meatball Sandwich with Spicy Mayo

PREP: 15 MINUTES PLUS MEATBALLS **BROIL:** 1 MINUTE

- 1 recipe Mealmaker Meatballs (see recipe, *page 44*)
- 3/4 cup light mayonnaise or salad dressing
- 2 to 3 Tbsp. snipped fresh cilantro
- 1 to 1 1/2 tsp. chili powder
- 6 ciabatta or other hearty buns, split
- 4 oz. Monterey Jack cheese with jalapeño peppers or Monterey Jack cheese, shredded (1 cup)
- 1 small carrot, shredded (about 1/3 cup)
- 1/2 of a small peeled jicama, shredded (about 1/3 cup)
- 1 to 2 jalapeño chile peppers, seeded and thinly sliced (see note, *page 143*)

1. Prepare and bake Mealmaker Meatballs. In a small bowl stir together mayonnaise, cilantro, and chili powder; set aside. Set oven to broil and arrange oven rack 4 inches from heat.

2. Place ciabatta, split sides up, on a large baking sheet. Divide and sprinkle cheese on bun bottoms. Broil about 1 minute or until buns are toasted and cheese is melted. Spread cut sides of bun tops with mayonnaise mixture. Place hot meatballs on bun bottoms. Top each with carrot, jicama, and jalapeño slices. Makes 6 servings.

COOKING CLUB DIRECTIONS: Prepare and bake meatballs. Cool slightly. Divide and transfer to plastic storage or freezer containers for each member. Cover and refrigerate up to 2 days or freeze up to 1 month. If refrigerating meatballs, place mayonnaise mixture, cheese, carrot, jicama, and jalapeño peppers in separate storage containers. If freezing meatballs, prepare mayonnaise mixture, cheese, carrot, jicama, and jalapeño peppers at serving time.

REHEATING AND SERVING: Thaw frozen meatballs in the refrigerator. Place meatballs on the rack of a broiler pan. Broil 4 inches from the heat about 5 minutes or until heated through, turning once. Assemble as above.

EACH SERVING INCLUDING MEATBALLS: 537 cal., 24 g total fat (9 g sat. fat), 106 mg chol., 1,010 mg sodium, 53 g carbo., 3 g fiber, 28 g pro. Daily Values: 23% vit. A, 6% vit. C, 23% calcium, 26% iron.

Meatball Sandwich with Spicy Mayo

Embrace your workweek with the peace of mind that comes from a fridge full of home-made dinners ready to serve.

We'll show you how to start your own Moms' Cooking Club and create delicious ready-made meals to tote home and tuck into the refrigerator or freezer. Our plan gives you simple-to-prepare, family-tested recipes that you'll make again and again. We'll show you how to get started, tell you what tools you'll need, and even provide the grocery list.

Cooking groups form for lots of reasons. Many are made up of busy moms looking to jazz up the routine of feeding the family and create dinners more efficiently. Neighbors, people with children the same age, and those who share your taste in food are all great candidates for membership in a cooking club.

We suggest setting a standing date for your group to meet, then e-mail or deliver copies of each recipe to all members and figure out what equipment to bring. You'll need at least two or three of several basic cooking tools on hand, including vegetable peelers, kitchen knives, cutting boards, and measuring spoons. Extra Dutch ovens and 12-inch frying pans are helpful too, as are pot holders and trivets. Also have plenty of plastic wrap and plastic bags for storing chopped vegetables and other ingredients before they're cooked.

It's best to shop the day before the actual cooking day. One strategy is for each club member to buy her own groceries, with the host of the day providing milk, eggs, and spices. Other groups may prefer to have one person shop and then to reimburse the shopper.

You'll make the most of your time when everyone pitches in and does most of the chopping, cutting, and measuring first. Consider dividing up the frying, boiling, baking, and other tasks based on who likes to do which jobs.

Once you bring the dishes home, adjusting them to your family's taste is easy. For example, try giving the soups a flurry of fresh herbs before serving or add parsley and vegetables to a macaroni and cheese dish.

The real reward of these ideas, and the Moms' Cooking Club, is that they combine the joy of group effort—women helping women—with the sense of fulfillment from having a refrigerator filled with delicious meals, ready to reheat and set on your family's dinner table.

Multiply the amount of ingredients in each recipe by the number of members in your group to determine the amount of groceries to buy.

For instance, if there are three members in your group, and you decide to make the recipes based on meatballs, you'll need 9 pounds of ground beef. For three chicken recipes and four members, you'll buy 16 pounds of chicken breasts.

Take advantage of the ready-to-photocopy grocery lists we've provided. Each includes all the ingredients you'll need to make one set (beef, chicken, or meatless) of recipes. To the left of each ingredient is a blank space for you to jot down the amount of each you'll need to buy for your group.

Finally, each member should have a sturdy box or cooler on hand to transport the finished food home.

BEEF GROCERY LIST

MEAT COUNTER

_____ slices bacon or peppered bacon
_____ lbs. lean ground beef

PRODUCE

_____ butternut or acorn squash
_____ carrots
_____ fennel bulbs
_____ bunches fresh cilantro
_____ garlic bulbs (figure about 12 cloves to a bulb)
_____ jalapeño chile peppers
_____ jicama
_____ onions
_____ parsnips

BAKING/SPICES/CANNED GOODS

_____ chili powder
_____ dried Italian seasoning
_____ dried oregano or dried thyme
_____ cayenne pepper
_____ 26-oz. jars spicy red pepper pasta sauce
_____ light mayonnaise or salad dressing
_____ oz. dried pappardelle pasta or fettuccine
_____ oz. quick-cooking barley
_____ 14-oz. cans reduced-sodium chicken broth
_____ quarts apple juice
_____ olive oil or cooking oil

DAIRY

_____ eggs
_____ oz. Italian fontina or mozzarella cheese
_____ oz. Monterey Jack cheese with jalapeño peppers
_____ oz. shredded Parmesan

BAKERY

_____ loaves French or Italian bread (for crumbs)
_____ ciabatta or other hearty buns

Beef and Sweet Pepper Pasta

START TO FINISH: 40 MINUTES

1 recipe Mealmaker Meatballs (see recipe, *page 44*)
8 oz. dried pappardelle pasta or fettuccine
1 medium fennel bulb, trimmed and cut into thin bite-size strips
1 medium onion, quartered and thinly sliced
2 medium carrots, thinly bias-sliced
2 cloves garlic, minced
1 Tbsp. olive oil or cooking oil
1 26-oz. jar spicy red pepper pasta sauce or mushroom and ripe olive pasta sauce
  Salt and ground black pepper
4 oz. Italian fontina or mozzarella cheese, shredded (1 cup)
2 oz. Parmesan cheese, finely shredded (½ cup)

1. Prepare and bake Mealmaker Meatballs. In a large pot or kettle cook pasta according to package directions until just tender; drain.

2. Meanwhile, in a 10-inch skillet cook fennel, onion, carrots, and garlic in hot oil over medium heat for 7 minutes or until vegetables are tender. Return pasta to cooking pot. Add vegetable mixture, meatballs, and sauce to pasta; toss to coat. Heat through. Season to taste with salt and pepper. Top with shredded cheeses. Makes 6 servings.

COOKING CLUB DIRECTIONS: Prepare as above, except do not heat vegetables and pasta through. Divide pasta-meatball mixture and transfer to 4-quart storage containers or 1-gallon resealable plastic bags for each member of the club. Divide cheese in resealable plastic bags. Refrigerate pasta mixture and cheese up to 2 days. To freeze, transfer to 4-quart freezer containers or 1-gallon resealable plastic freezer bags. Freeze up to 1 month.

TEST KITCHEN TIP: You can cook a double batch of the vegetables by using a 12-inch skillet; the vegetables will cook in 15 minutes.

REHEATING AND SERVING: Thaw pasta mixture and cheese, if frozen, in refrigerator for 1 to 2 days or until completely thawed. Transfer refrigerated or thawed pasta mixture to a 3-quart microwave-safe casserole; add ¼ cup water. Microwave, covered, on 100% power (high) for 15 to 20 minutes or until heated through, gently stirring every 5 minutes. Serve as above.

EACH SERVING INCLUDING MEATBALLS: 515 cal., 22 g total fat (9 g sat. fat), 112 mg chol., 935 mg sodium, 47 g carbo., 5 g fiber, 31 g pro. Daily Values: 57% vit. A, 17% vit. C, 33% calcium, 20% iron.

WHEN THE FAMILY CALLS FOR SPAGHETTI AND MEATBALLS, GIVE THEM A VERSION WORTHY OF APPLAUSE!

Beef and Sweet Pepper Pasta

Herbed Beef and Barley Soup

Herbed Beef and Barley Soup

START TO FINISH: 1 HOUR

> 1 recipe Mealmaker Meatballs (see recipe, *left*)
> 4 slices bacon or peppered bacon
> 1 medium onion, chopped (1/2 cup)
> 2 cloves garlic, minced
> 1 1- to 1 1/2-lb. butternut or acorn squash, peeled and cut into 3/4-inch pieces (about 4 cups)
> 2 medium carrots, cut into 3/4-inch pieces
> 2 medium parsnips, cut into 3/4-inch pieces
> 4 14-oz. cans reduced-sodium chicken broth
> 1 cup apple juice or water
> 1 tsp. dried Italian seasoning or dried thyme, crushed
> 1 cup quick-cooking barley
> Salt and ground black pepper

1. Prepare and bake Mealmaker Meatballs. In a 4-quart Dutch oven cook bacon until crisp. Remove bacon, reserving 1 tablespoon drippings in pan. Drain bacon on paper towels; set aside.

2. Cook onion and garlic in reserved drippings over medium heat until tender. Add squash, carrots, and parsnips; cook for 5 minutes more, stirring occasionally. Add broth, apple juice, and Italian seasoning. Bring to boiling; stir in barley. Simmer, covered, for 10 to 15 minutes or until barley and vegetables are tender. Add meatballs; heat through. Season to taste with salt and ground black pepper.

3. To serve, ladle into bowls. Crumble cooked bacon and sprinkle over individual servings. Makes 6 to 8 servings (12 cups total soup).

COOKING CLUB DIRECTIONS: This soup is not recommended for freezing. Prepare as above, except divide cooked bacon among small resealable plastic bags for each member. Quick-chill soup by placing Dutch oven in a sink filled with ice water for 10 minutes, stirring frequently. Transfer soup to 4-quart storage containers for each member. Cover and refrigerate soup and bacon up to 3 days.

TEST KITCHEN TIP: To make a double batch, use an 8-quart Dutch oven.

REHEATING AND SERVING: To serve, transfer soup to a 4-quart Dutch oven. Bring soup to boiling, stirring frequently. Serve as above.

EACH SERVING INCLUDING MEATBALLS: 402 cal., 13 g total fat (5 g sat. fat), 89 mg chol., 1,117 mg sodium, 47 g carbo., 7 g fiber, 23 g pro. Daily Values: 60% vit. A, 25% vit. C, 7% calcium, 18% iron.

Kid Friendly Mealmaker Meatballs

PREP: 25 MINUTES **BAKE:** 15 MINUTES

> 1 egg, beaten
> 1/2 cup soft French or Italian bread crumbs*
> 1/4 cup finely chopped onion
> 2 cloves garlic, minced
> 1 tsp. dried oregano or dried thyme, crushed
> 1/2 tsp. salt
> 1/8 tsp. cayenne pepper or 1/4 tsp. ground black pepper
> 1 lb. lean ground beef

1. Preheat oven to 400°F. Line a 15×10×1-inch baking pan with foil; set aside. In a large bowl combine egg, bread crumbs, onion, garlic, oregano, salt, and pepper. Add beef; mix well. Shape into 24 meatballs (about 1 tablespoon mixture per meatball). Arrange meatballs in prepared pan. Bake 15 minutes or until juices run clear. Drain off fat. Makes 24 meatballs.

*NOTE: Use a blender or food processor to make soft bread crumbs. About 1 1/2 ounces of bread makes 1 cup of crumbs.

TEST KITCHEN TIP: The job is quick when one person makes the meatballs while others perform other tasks. Set aside a spot at the kitchen table for the meatball maker to sit.

EACH MEATBALL: 41 cal., 2 g total fat (1 g sat. fat), 21 mg chol., 71 mg sodium, 1 g carbo., 0 g fiber, 4 g pro. Daily Values: 1% calcium, 3% iron.

Chicken Mac and Cheese

PREP: 40 MINUTES **BAKE:** 20 MINUTES **STAND:** 10 MINUTES

- 1 lb. skinless, boneless chicken breast halves
- 1 to 2 tsp. dried Italian seasoning, crushed
  Salt and ground black pepper
- 1 Tbsp. olive oil
- 8 oz. dried mostaccioli, ziti, or penne pasta
- 1 medium onion, chopped (½ cup)
- 2 cloves garlic, minced
- 3 Tbsp. butter
- 3 Tbsp. all-purpose flour
- 2 Tbsp. tomato paste
- 3 cups milk
- 8 oz. smoked cheddar or Swiss cheese, shredded (2 cups)
  Salt and ground black pepper
- 2 cups soft sourdough or French bread crumbs
- 2 oz. finely shredded Parmesan cheese (½ cup)
- 3 Tbsp. butter, melted

1. Preheat oven to 350°F. Cut chicken into bite-size pieces. In a 10-inch skillet cook chicken, Italian seasoning, salt, and pepper in hot oil over medium heat until chicken is no longer pink (170°F). Remove chicken from skillet; set aside.

2. In a large pot or kettle cook pasta according to package directions until just tender. Drain; return pasta to pot.

3. Meanwhile, in the same skillet in which chicken was cooked cook onion and garlic in 3 tablespoons hot butter over medium heat until tender. Stir in flour until well combined. Stir in tomato paste. Add milk. Cook and stir until mixture is thickened and bubbly; reduce heat. Add cheddar cheese. Stir until cheese is almost melted. Remove from heat. Season to taste with salt and ground black pepper. Add sauce and chicken to cooked pasta in pot; stir to coat. Spoon mixture into a 2-quart square or rectangular baking dish.

4. In a small bowl stir together bread crumbs, Parmesan cheese, and 3 tablespoons melted butter. Sprinkle crumb mixture over pasta mixture. Bake, uncovered, for 20 to 25 minutes or until crumb mixture is golden and edges are bubbly. Let stand 10 minutes before serving. Makes 6 servings.

COOKING CLUB DIRECTIONS: Prepare casserole as above for each member, except divide the crumb mixture into small resealable plastic bags or resealable plastic freezer bags. Do not bake. Cover pans with foil to refrigerate or wrap with moistureproof and vaporproof wrap to freeze. Refrigerate up to 24 hours or freeze casserole and bread crumb mixture up to 1 month.

Chicken Mac and Cheese

TEST KITCHEN TIP: Use a blender or food processor to make soft bread crumbs. About 1½ ounces of bread makes 1 cup of crumbs.

REHEATING AND SERVING: Thaw casserole and bread crumb mixture, if frozen, in refrigerator overnight. Bake refrigerated or thawed casserole, covered with foil, in a 350°F oven for 20 minutes. Uncover and top with bread crumb mixture. Bake, uncovered, for 35 to 40 minutes more or until crumb mixture is golden and edges are bubbly. Let stand 10 minutes before serving.

EACH SERVING: 675 cal., 34 g total fat (18 g sat. fat), 132 mg chol., 771 mg sodium, 49 g carbo., 1 g fiber, 42 g pro. Daily Values: 21% vit. A, 4% vit. C, 55% calcium, 16% iron.

CHICKEN GROCERY LIST

MEAT COUNTER
_____lbs. skinless, boneless chicken breast halves

PRODUCE
_____bunches fresh cilantro (optional)
_____garlic bulbs (figure about 12 cloves to a bulb)
_____onions
_____jalapeño chile peppers
_____oz. fresh ginger (or ground ginger)
_____medium green, yellow, or red sweet peppers
_____6-oz. pkg. baby spinach
_____zucchini and/or yellow summer squash

BAKING/SPICES/CANNED
_____ground cumin   _____ground coriander
_____sesame seeds   _____crushed red pepper
_____Italian seasoning
_____olive oil   _____salad oil
_____soy sauce   _____rice vinegar
_____all-purpose flour
_____hoisin sauce
_____14-oz. cans reduced-sodium chicken broth
_____12-oz. cans tomato paste
_____oz. dried mostaccioli, ziti, or penne pasta
_____6-oz. pkg. rice sticks (rice noodles)

DAIRY
_____lbs. butter   _____quarts milk
_____8-oz. cartons dairy sour cream
_____oz. smoked cheddar, Gruyère, or Swiss cheese
_____oz. shredded Parmesan or Romano cheese
_____oz. Monterey Jack cheese, asadero cheese, or
white cheddar cheese (optional)

FREEZER CASE
_____10-oz. pkg. frozen baby lima beans or frozen
shelled sweet soybeans (edamame)

BAKERY
_____loaves sourdough or French bread (for crumbs)

Chicken Chowder
PREP: 40 MINUTES **COOK:** 15 MINUTES

1 lb. skinless, boneless chicken breast halves
1 Tbsp. olive oil or cooking oil
1 medium onion, chopped ($\frac{1}{2}$ cup)
1 medium green, yellow, or red sweet pepper, coarsely chopped
3 cloves garlic, minced
2 to 3 jalapeño chile peppers, seeded and finely chopped (see note, _page 143_)
2 small zucchini and/or yellow summer squash, coarsely chopped
2 14-oz. cans reduced-sodium chicken broth
1 10-oz. pkg. frozen baby lima beans or one 12-oz. pkg. frozen sweet soybeans (edamame)
2 tsp. ground cumin
2 tsp. ground coriander
$\frac{1}{4}$ tsp. each salt and ground black pepper
1 8-oz. carton dairy sour cream
2 Tbsp. all-purpose flour
Salt and ground black pepper
Snipped fresh cilantro (optional)
Shredded Monterey Jack or asadero cheese (optional)

1. Cut chicken into cubes. In a 4-quart Dutch oven heat oil over medium heat. Add chicken, onion, sweet pepper, garlic, and jalapeño pepper; cook and stir until chicken is browned and vegetables are tender. Add zucchini; cook 2 minutes more. Add broth, lima beans, cumin, coriander, the $\frac{1}{4}$ teaspoon salt, and the $\frac{1}{4}$ teaspoon ground black pepper. Bring to boiling; reduce heat. Simmer, uncovered, for 5 minutes. In a small bowl stir together the sour cream and flour.

2. Whisk sour cream mixture into soup. Cook and stir until thickened and bubbly; cook and stir for 1 minute more. To serve, ladle into bowls. Season to taste with additional salt and ground black pepper. If desired, sprinkle with cilantro and cheese. Makes 6 servings (8 cups total chowder).

COOKING CLUB DIRECTIONS: Prepare as above through Step 1. Divide flour-sour cream mixture into small storage or freezer containers for each member. Divide soup and transfer to 3-quart storage containers or 3-quart freezer containers for each member. Cover and refrigerate up to 3 days or freeze up to 1 month.

TEST KITCHEN TIP: You can use a 12-quart pot to make a double batch. Cook chicken a pound at a time (if you try to cook more, the chicken won't brown).

REHEATING AND SERVING: Thaw chowder and sour cream mixture, if frozen, in refrigerator 24 hours. Transfer thawed or refrigerated chowder to a 4-quart Dutch oven. Bring to boiling, stirring frequently. Stir sour cream mixture and add. Cook and stir until thickened and bubbly; cook and stir 1 minute more. Serve as above.

EACH SERVING: 291 cal., 12 g total fat (6 g sat. fat), 62 mg chol., 730 mg sodium, 21 g carbo., 5 g fiber, 25 g pro. Daily Values: 11% vit. A, 44% vit. C, 9% calcium, 13% iron.

WITH THE RICH HUES OF RED, GREEN, AND YELLOW, THIS CHOWDER IS AS PLEASING TO THE EYE AS IT IS TO THE PALATE.

Chicken Chowder

Asian Chicken Salad

Asian Chicken Salad

This recipe can be served either as a cold or warm salad. To heat, microwave chicken breasts and noodles until heated through.

START TO FINISH: 1 HOUR **CHILL:** 1 HOUR

> 6 medium skinless, boneless chicken breast halves (2 to 2½ lb.)
> Salt and ground black pepper
> 2 Tbsp. hoisin sauce (from the Asian section of the supermarket)
> 1 6-oz. pkg. rice stick noodles
> 1 recipe Asian Dressing
> 1 6-oz. pkg. baby spinach
> 1 Tbsp. toasted sesame seeds
> Slivered green onions (optional)

1. Preheat oven to 375° F. Arrange chicken breast halves in a 3-quart rectangular baking dish or a 13×9×2-inch baking pan. Sprinkle with salt and pepper. Brush tops of chicken breasts with hoisin sauce. Bake, uncovered, for 35 to 40 minutes or until chicken is no longer pink (170°F). Cool slightly; cover and chill at least 1 hour or until ready to serve (up to 2 days).

2. Meanwhile, cook rice stick noodles according to package directions. Drain; rinse with cold water. Drain well. Snip cooked rice stick noodles in a few places; transfer to a resealable plastic bag. Close bag. Chill until ready to serve. Prepare and chill Asian Dressing.

3. To serve, arrange spinach on 6 serving plates. Top spinach with cooked rice stick noodles. Place chilled chicken breasts on rice sticks. Drizzle with Asian Dressing. Sprinkle with sesame seeds and, if desired, green onions. Makes 6 servings.

ASIAN DRESSING: In a screw-top jar combine ¾ cup rice vinegar, ⅓ cup salad oil, 3 tablespoons hoisin sauce, 2 tablespoons soy sauce, 1½ teaspoons grated fresh ginger or ¼ teaspoon ground ginger, and ¼ teaspoon crushed red pepper. Cover and shake well; chill until ready to serve (up to 1 week).

COOKING CLUB DIRECTIONS: Divide cooked chicken, cooked rice stick noodles, spinach, and sesame seeds into resealable plastic bags for each member. Divide Asian Dressing into plastic storage containers. Refrigerate up to 1 day.

TEST KITCHEN TIPS: You can bake two batches of chicken breasts at once. If you don't have two 3-quart dishes, chicken can be baked in several different size pans. Line the pans with foil to help cleanup. Make all the dressing at once and divide into individual containers.

SERVING: Assemble as above in Step 3.

EACH SERVING: 434 cal., 16 g total fat (3 g sat. fat), 88 mg chol., 733 mg sodium, 30 g carbo., 1 g fiber, 38 g pro. Daily Values: 56% vit. A, 14% vit. C, 7% calcium, 13% iron.

Vegetable Soup with Corn Bread Croutons
PREP: 40 MINUTES **BAKE:** 12 MINUTES **COOK:** 15 MINUTES

- 1 recipe Corn Bread Croutons
- 1 28-oz. can whole Italian-style tomatoes
- 2 medium leeks, sliced, or 1 medium onion, chopped (½ cup)
- 1 Tbsp. olive oil or cooking oil
- 1 8-oz. pkg. fresh mushrooms, quartered
- 1 large yellow or red sweet pepper, coarsely chopped
- 4 cloves garlic, minced
- 3 cups water
- 1 15- to 19-oz. can cannellini beans (white kidney beans), rinsed and drained
- 1 tsp. coarse sea salt or ½ tsp. salt
- ¼ tsp. freshly ground black pepper
- 8 oz. spinach leaves (about 4 cups)

1. Prepare Corn Bread Croutons; set aside to cool.
2. Remove tomatoes from can, reserving liquid. Coarsely chop tomatoes. In a 4-quart Dutch oven cook leeks in hot oil over medium heat until tender, stirring occasionally. Add mushrooms, sweet pepper, and garlic; cook 5 minutes more, stirring occasionally. Add water, tomatoes and reserved liquid, cannellini beans, salt, and black pepper. Bring to boiling; reduce heat. Simmer, uncovered, for 5 minutes; stir in spinach. Serve with Corn Bread Croutons. Makes 6 to 8 servings (about 10 cups total soup).

CORN BREAD CROUTONS: Preheat oven to 350°F. Grease 2 large baking sheets; set aside. In a medium bowl lightly beat 1 egg. Add one 8½-ounce package corn muffin mix, ⅔ cup finely shredded Romano or Parmesan cheese, and 2 tablespoons milk. Drop into small mounds by scant teaspoonfuls onto prepared baking sheet(s). Lightly sprinkle with freshly ground black pepper and, if desired, coarse sea salt. Bake for 12 to 14 minutes or until golden. Remove from baking sheet; let cool completely on a wire rack. Store Corn Bread Croutons in an airtight container at room temperature up to 1 day or in the refrigerator up to 3 days (let stand 30 minutes at room temperature before serving). Makes about 28.

COOKING CLUB DIRECTIONS: Divide cooked mushrooms, sweet pepper, and garlic among 3-quart storage containers or freezer containers for each member. Into the same containers divide water, undrained tomatoes, beans, salt, and black pepper. Divide Corn Bread Croutons among members; place in resealable plastic bags or freezer bags. If refrigerating, divide spinach in plastic bags. If freezing, spinach should be purchased at preparation time. Cover and refrigerate up to 3 days or freeze up to 3 months.

Vegetable Soup with Corn Bread Croutons

TEST KITCHEN TIP: This recipe can be made in double batches in a 6-quart Dutch oven or kettle.

REHEATING AND SERVING: Thaw frozen Corn Bread Croutons and soup for 48 hours in refrigerator, if frozen. Transfer thawed or refrigerated soup to a 4-quart Dutch oven. Bring soup just to boiling. Reduce heat and simmer, uncovered, for 5 minutes. Stir in spinach.

EACH SERVING: 345 cal., 11 g total fat (2 g sat. fat), 42 mg chol., 933 mg sodium, 52 g carbo., 6 g fiber, 15 g pro. Daily Values: 53% vit. A, 159% vit. C, 21% calcium, 26% iron.

Pesto Lasagna Pie

Pesto Lasagna Pie

This recipe can also be made in a 13×9×2-inch baking pan.

PREP: 50 MINUTES **BAKE:** 60 MINUTES **STAND:** 20 MINUTES

- 12 dried regular or whole wheat lasagna noodles
- 1 recipe Lemon-Parsley Pesto or 1 cup purchased pesto
- 1 egg, slightly beaten
- 1 15-oz. container ricotta cheese
- 1 8-oz. pkg. shredded Italian blend cheese or mozzarella cheese (2 cups)
- 1/4 tsp. salt
- 1/4 tsp. ground black pepper
  Nonstick cooking spray
- 2 cups chopped fresh spinach
- 1/2 of an 8-oz. pkg. fresh mushrooms, thinly sliced
- 1 28-oz. can whole Italian-style tomatoes
  Fresh flat-leaf parsley leaves (optional)

1. Preheat oven to 375°F. In a 4-quart or larger pot cook noodles according to package directions until just tender. Drain noodles; rinse with cold water. Drain well; set aside.

2. Prepare Lemon-Parsley Pesto; set aside. In a medium bowl stir together egg, ricotta cheese, 1 cup of the shredded Italian blend cheese, the salt, and pepper; set aside.

3. To assemble lasagna, lightly coat the inside of a 9-inch springform pan or 13×9×2-inch baking pan with nonstick cooking spray. Arrange 4 of the cooked noodles in the bottom of the pan, trimming and overlapping as necessary to cover bottom of pan with 1 layer of noodles. Top with spinach. Spoon half of the ricotta cheese mixture over spinach, spreading evenly. Spoon one-third of the pesto over ricotta layer, spreading evenly. Top with another layer of noodles, trimming to fit. Top with mushrooms. Spread remaining ricotta cheese mixture over mushrooms. Spread half of the remaining pesto over ricotta layer. Top with another layer of noodles and remaining pesto. Drain tomatoes. Slice, quarter, or halve tomatoes and place on top of layers.

4. Place springform pan in a foil-lined shallow baking pan. Bake, covered, for 45 minutes. Uncover and sprinkle with remaining Italian blend cheese. Bake, uncovered, for 15 minutes more or until cheese is melted and lasagna is heated through. Cover and let stand for 20 minutes before serving. Carefully remove sides of pan. If desired, top with parsley leaves. To serve, cut lasagna into wedges. (For 13×9×2-inch pan, bake, covered with foil, in a 375°F oven for 40 minutes; uncover and sprinkle with remaining cheese. Bake, uncovered, 5 minutes more or until cheese is melted and lasagna is heated through.) Makes 8 to 10 servings.

LEMON-PARSLEY PESTO: In a food processor combine 4 cups fresh spinach leaves (about 8 ounces); 1/2 cup fresh flat-leaf parsley; 1/3 cup grated Parmesan or Romano cheese; 1/3 cup toasted pine nuts or walnuts; 2 cloves garlic, quartered; 2 tablespoons olive oil; 2 teaspoons finely shredded lemon peel; 2 tablespoons lemon juice; and 1/4 teaspoon salt. Cover and process until nearly smooth. (If desired, use a blender and add 2 to 4 tablespoons water with the spinach leaves.) Makes about 1 cup.

MEATLESS GROCERY LIST

PRODUCE

____leeks ____lemons (for juice and peel)
____garlic bulbs ____oz. fresh mushrooms
____onions ____mangoes
____yellow or red sweet peppers
____jalapeño or serrano chile peppers
____pkg. spinach
____bunches cilantro
____fresh flat-leaf parsley (optional)
____16-oz. pkg. firm or extra-firm tub-style tofu or 15-oz. cans black or pinto beans

BAKING/SPICES/CANNED

____ground cumin ____olive oil
____oz. pine nuts or walnuts ____all-purpose flour
____coarse sea salt
____nonstick cooking spray
____oz. regular or whole wheat lasagna noodles
____8½-oz. packages corn muffin mix
____28-oz. cans whole Italian-style tomatoes
____15- to 19-oz. cans cannellini beans
____purchased mole sauce

DAIRY

____milk ____eggs
____finely shredded Romano or Parmesan cheese
____oz. asadero cheese, Monterey Jack, or sharp cheddar cheese
____15-oz. container ricotta cheese
____8-oz. pkg. shredded Italian blend cheese
____oz. dairy sour cream
____dozen 6- to 7-inch flour or corn tortillas

COOKING CLUB DIRECTIONS: Prepare lasagnas as directed for each member, except do not add tomatoes and do not bake. Cover each pan with plastic wrap (if freezing, also wrap in aluminum foil). Package remaining cheese in a resealable plastic bag or a resealable freezer bag for each member. Refrigerate up to 24 hours or freeze up to 3 months.

TEST KITCHEN TIP: It's possible to make up to a quadruple batch of ricotta mixture at one time.

REHEATING AND SERVING: Thaw lasagna and cheese, if frozen, in the refrigerator 48 hours before baking. Place thawed or refrigerated lasagna on a foil-lined baking sheet. Remove plastic wrap; top lasagna with tomatoes. Preheat oven to 375°F. In springform pan bake, covered with foil, for 60 minutes; uncover and sprinkle with remaining cheese. Bake, uncovered, 15 minutes more or until heated through. (For a 13×9×2-inch pan, bake, covered with foil, for 40 minutes; uncover and sprinkle with remaining cheese. Bake, uncovered, 5 minutes more or until cheese is melted and lasagna is heated through.) Cover and let stand for 20 minutes before serving. If desired, sprinkle with parsley. Carefully remove sides of pan, if necessary. To serve, cut lasagna into wedges.

EACH SERVING: 418 cal., 23 g total fat (10 g sat. fat), 76 mg chol., 577 mg sodium, 32 g carbo., 2 g fiber, 23 g pro. Daily Values: 57% vit. A, 38% vit. C, 37% calcium, 22% iron.

Enchiladas with Fresh Mango Salsa

If you're planning to freeze this dish, do not make the Mango Salsa until serving time.

PREP: 40 MINUTES **BAKE:** 30 MINUTES

    Nonstick cooking spray
 1 dozen 6- to 7-inch flour or corn tortillas
 1 medium onion, chopped (½ cup)
 2 cloves garlic, minced
 1 medium jalapeño or serrano chile pepper, seeded
    and finely chopped (see note, page 143)
 1 Tbsp. olive oil or cooking oil
 ⅓ cup dairy sour cream
 ¼ cup purchased mole sauce (available in the Hispanic
    food section of supermarkets or at Hispanic
    specialty markets)
 2 Tbsp. water
 1 16-oz. pkg. firm or extra-firm tub-style tofu (fresh
    bean curd), drained and cut into ½-inch cubes,
    or two 15-oz. cans black beans or pinto beans,
    rinsed and drained
 8 oz. asadero cheese, Monterey Jack cheese, or sharp
    cheddar cheese, shredded (2 cups)
 1 cup dairy sour cream
 2 Tbsp. all-purpose flour
 1 tsp. ground cumin
 ¼ tsp. salt
 ¾ cup milk
 1 recipe Mango Salsa or 1½ cups
    purchased salsa

1. Preheat oven to 350°F. Coat one 13×9×2-inch (3-quart) rectangular baking dish or two 11×7×1½-inch (2-quart) rectangular baking dishes with nonstick cooking spray; set aside. Stack

the tortillas, wrap tightly in foil, and bake for 10 minutes or until warm. Or microwave half of the tortillas at a time between 2 pieces of waxed paper on 100% power (high) for 30 seconds.

2. Meanwhile, for filling, in a large skillet cook onion, garlic, and jalapeño pepper in hot oil until tender; remove from heat. Stir together the ⅓ cup sour cream, the mole sauce, and water; add to skillet along with tofu and half of the cheese. Spoon ⅓ cup of the tofu mixture onto one edge of each tortilla; roll up. Place, seam sides down, in prepared baking dish or dishes.

3. For sauce, in a medium bowl combine the 1 cup sour cream, flour, cumin, and salt; whisk in milk. Pour evenly over filled tortillas.

4. Bake, covered, for 25 minutes until heated through. Top with remaining cheese. Bake, uncovered, for 5 minutes more or until cheese melts. Serve enchiladas topped with Mango Salsa. Makes 6 servings.

MANGO SALSA: In a small bowl combine 1 large mango, seeded, peeled, and chopped (1½ cups); 2 jalapeño or serrano chile peppers, seeded and finely chopped (3 tablespoons) (see note, page 143); 2 tablespoons snipped fresh cilantro; and 1 tablespoon lemon or lime juice. Divide and place in a storage container and refrigerate up to 2 days.

COOKING CLUB DIRECTIONS: Prepare as above for each member of the club, except do not bake. Cover baking dishes with foil. Divide cheese among resealable plastic bags. Prepare salsa as a above for each member of the club. (Mango Salsa cannot be frozen. If freezing enchiladas, prepare salsa just before serving.) Divide among resealable plastic bags.

TEST KITCHEN TIP: Make multiple batches of sauce and filling at the same time. It's also quicker to shred all cheese at the same time. You can make a quadruple recipe of the Mango Salsa in a single bowl as well.

REHEATING AND SERVING: Refrigerate up to 72 hours or freeze up to 1 month. Chill or freeze remaining cheese separately in resealable plastic bags or freezer bags. If frozen, thaw enchiladas and cheese in the refrigerator overnight before reheating. To serve, bake, covered, in a 350°F oven for 40 minutes. Top with remaining cheese. Bake, uncovered, for 5 minutes more or until cheese is melted. Serve with Mango Salsa.

EACH SERVING: 824 cal., 35 g total fat (15 g sat. fat), 57 mg chol., 1,243 mg sodium, 98 g carbo., 7 g fiber, 31 g pro. Daily Values: 23% vit. A, 30% vit. C, 35% calcium, 34% iron.

Enchiladas with Fresh Mango Salsa

Quick Eggs Benedict

FIX A FAST BREAKFAST

Somehow, time catches up with us,

even on supposedly lazy weekends. Still, Saturday and Sunday morning meals can be a treat without spending much time in the kitchen.

Quick Eggs Benedict is a rendition of a familiar favorite. Instead of making the traditional hollandaise sauce, save time by substituting a stir-together sauce of sour cream, mustard, lemon juice, and milk. A big dollop on top of a speedy poached egg still gives you that burst of lemony flavor with a tasty twist. Stick to the traditional Canadian bacon if you wish, or try layering on thin slices of smoked salmon for a new taste sensation. You may even find some extra time to spend with the Sunday paper.

BY **STEPHEN EXEL** PHOTOGRAPHS BY **GREG SCHEIDEMANN** FOOD STYLING BY **BROOKE LEONARD**

Tweak the traditional for speedy versions of morning meals. Quick Eggs Benedict does the trick in just 20 minutes.

Quick Eggs Benedict

 Fast! **START TO FINISH:** 20 MINUTES

- ¼ cup dairy sour cream or crème fraîche
- 1 tsp. lemon juice
- ¾ to 1 tsp. dry mustard
- 3 to 4 tsp. milk
- 4 eggs
- 4 ½-inch-thick slices crusty French bread or lightly toasted French bread
- ¼ lb. thinly sliced smoked salmon or 4 slices Canadian bacon
  Diced red sweet pepper (optional)
  Salt and ground black pepper

1. In a bowl combine sour cream, lemon juice, and dry mustard. Add milk to desired consistency. Set aside.

2. Lightly grease 4 cups of an egg poaching pan.* Place the poacher cups over pan of boiling water (water should not touch bottoms of cups); reduce heat to simmering. Break an egg into a measuring cup. Carefully slide egg into poacher cup. Repeat with remaining eggs. Cover; cook 6 to 8 minutes or until the whites are completely set and yolks begin to thicken but are not hard. Run a knife around edges to loosen eggs. Invert poacher cups to remove eggs.

3. Top each bread slice with smoked salmon. Top with poached egg. Top with mustard-sour cream mixture and, if desired, red sweet pepper. Season with salt and pepper. Makes 4 servings.

*NOTE: If you don't have an egg poaching pan, lightly grease a 2-quart saucepan with cooking oil or shortening. Fill the pan halfway with water; bring to boiling. Reduce heat to simmering. Break one egg into a measuring cup. Carefully slide egg into water, holding the lip of the cup as close to the water as possible. Repeat with remaining eggs, spacing eggs equally. Simmer, uncovered, 3 to 5 minutes or until whites are completely set and yolks begin to thicken but are not hard. Remove eggs with a slotted spoon.

EACH SERVING: 206 cal., 10 g total fat (4 g sat. fat), 225 mg chol., 481 mg sodium, 14 g carbo., 1 g fiber, 14 g pro. Daily Values: 9% vit. A, 1% vit. C, 7% calcium, 9% iron.

INSTANT INDIA

Indian food, all the rage these days,

is yours to enjoy at home with one secret ingredient: a jar of mild or hot Indian curry paste. It's available in many large supermarkets and ethnic food stores, and ideal for use as a rub or as the base for a sauce.

Indian curry paste is really a family of products, with nearly a dozen styles available. Each represents a seasoning combination and hotness level unique to a different region of India.

Curry paste seasonings typically include pepper, cumin, coriander, turmeric, cloves, tamarind, and chilies. The aromatic spices are first blended and ground, then preserved in oil to maintain freshness.

Indian cooking sauces, in jars or cans, are an easy alternative to the curry pastes. These are less concentrated in flavor, but simple to use: Just heat cooked meat, poultry, fish, or vegetables with the sauce.

The beauty of these sauces is that you don't have to invest in lots of different spices and unfamiliar ingredients or spend hours over a hot stove to enjoy a taste of India at home. A simple "stir-in and simmer" brings Bombay right to the doorstep.

BY **NANCY BYAL** PHOTOGRAPHS BY **COLLEEN DUFFLEY** FOOD STYLIST **BROOKE LEONARD**

Busy People's Indian Chicken
PREP: 35 MINUTES **COOK:** 20 MINUTES

- 4 medium skinless, boneless chicken breast halves (about 1 pound)
- ¼ cup purchased Indian curry paste
  Nonstick cooking spray
- 1 medium onion, coarsely chopped
- ½ cup chicken broth
- 1 recipe Cumin Rice
  Steamed sugar snap peas (optional)

1. With a knife, score chicken on both sides by making shallow diagonal cuts across the surface. Brush chicken liberally with curry paste; let stand at room temperature 30 minutes.
2. Coat a skillet with cooking spray; add onion. Cook onion over medium heat until just tender and beginning to brown, stirring

occasionally. Remove onion from skillet; set aside. Add chicken to skillet; cook over medium heat for 8 to 10 minutes or until chicken is tender and no longer pink, turning once. (Reduce heat as necessary to prevent burning.)

3. Remove chicken from skillet. Slowly add broth to skillet, scraping up crusty bits. Return chicken and onion to skillet. Simmer, uncovered, for 3 to 5 minutes or until liquid thickens slightly. Transfer chicken to serving platter; drizzle with onion mixture. Serve with Cumin Rice and, if desired, sugar snap peas. Makes 4 servings.

CUMIN RICE: In saucepan toast 2 teaspoons cumin seeds over medium heat for 1 minute; cool. Add 2 cups water and ¼ teaspoon salt to seeds in saucepan; bring to boiling. Add 1 cup uncooked basmati or long grain rice. Return to boiling; reduce heat. Cover; simmer about 15 minutes. Makes 3 cups.

EACH SERVING: 377 cal., 11 g total fat (1 g sat. fat), 66 mg chol., 905 mg sodium, 38 g carbo., 3 g fiber, and 31 g pro. Daily Values: 4% vit. C, 7% calcium, and 19% iron.

Busy People's Indian Chicken

In good taste
FOOD AND ENTERTAINING

Be-Deviled

In the South, deviled eggs are a staple side dish of a big Sunday lunch of fried or roasted chicken with all the trimmings. Plates with shallow wells designed for holding these morsels can still be found in antiques shops and culinary stores. The most amusing ones have a handle in the middle resembling a chicken surveying the scene like a good mother hen overseeing her young. Introduced during the Depression, deviled eggs were a way of stretching eggs past their prime into a complement to lunch or dinner. After World War II, deviled eggs began to appear at cocktail parties as a prelude to a buffet supper. Egg plates were convenient for passing because the little wells kept each egg in place. By the mid-1980s egg plates seemed old-fashioned, but now they're back on the table due to a renewed interest in vintage-style dining ware. Because deviled eggs have always been considered an hors d'oeuvre, egg plates have remained a novelty item in the tabletop world, never a part of a pattern or set. If eggs aren't on the menu, fill the wells with small colored candies or use them to display decorated Easter eggs.
—Stephen Harrison

EGG PLATES: 11-inch deviled egg plates, $12 each, BIA Cordon Bleu; 800/242-2210.

OH, MY LITTLE DUMPLING

Gnocchi, small Italian potato dumplings, can be an alternative to pasta, rice, or "just-the-usual" potato side dish. Combine them with meatballs, spinach, and your favorite red sauce, or serve them drizzled with olive oil and smothered in shaved Parmesan. Eliminate one or two steps when making homemade gnocchi with Ecco La Pasta Gnocchi Flour, an add-water flour mix. In 10 minutes you'll have fresh gnocchi. **ECCO LA PASTA GNOCCHI FLOUR:** 8-oz. pkg. for $4; 877/257-7216; www.eccolapasta.com.

PHOTOGRAPHS BY **KIM CORNELISON** FOOD STYLING BY **JANET PITTMAN**

SMOOTH ROLLING

Tender, flaky pastry is easy to make with a few simple rules.

- Measure ingredients accurately.
- Cut in shortening or butter until the mixture resembles coarse crumbs. Don't overwork.
- Add water gradually; toss gently.
- To roll out dough with no sticking, flour the work surface and rolling pin. A silicone-covered rolling pin creates its own nonstick surface, so there's no need to flour it.
- Roll pastry to an even thickness.

SILICONE ROLLING PIN: **SIL-PIN**, $50, Fiesta Products; 732/396-9759.

Spring Slant On Potpies

With March coming in like a lion, potpies are a great dinner choice for this transitional month.

Put a seasonal spin on your favorite potpie recipe. At PotPie cafe in Kansas City, Missouri, owners John Williams and Sarah Ponak fill March's menu offering with a springy combination of lamb, white beans, tomato, and rosemary. John also suggests trying fava beans, spring onions, and morel mushrooms. **POTPIE,** 904 Westport Rd., Kansas City, Missouri; 816/561-2702.

HIT THE BUNNY TRAIL

Top Easter cupcakes, pies, and ice cream or frozen treats with marshmallow bunnies dressed for the occasion. Frost a marshmallow with purchased frosting; then roll it in flaked coconut. Attach two miniature marshmallows for feet and decorate with candies for the eyes, nose, and whiskers. For ears? Use kitchen shears to cut a strip from the top edge of a large marshmallow. Attach the ears with a bit of frosting.

APRIL

CELEBRATE THE MOVE INTO A NEW HOUSE BY THROWING A LIGHT-HEARTED BASH WITH FRIENDS AND NEIGHBORS. AS LONG AS YOU FIND THE BOX WITH THE DISHES, THE REST OF THE UNPACKING CAN WAIT!

Flank Steak Vinaigrette Salad
page 68

1-2-3 Cheesecake
page 77

Three-Herb Deviled Eggs
page 65

Housewarming Potluck

Housewarming Potluck

WITH THE CULTURAL SIGNIFICANCE OF GOOD LUCK AND WARM WISHES, THIS FOOD SPREAD IS THE PERFECT BUFFET TO SERVE AT A CASUAL HOUSEWARMING PARTY. GOOD FOOD AND GOOD FRIENDS QUICKLY TURN "HOUSE" INTO "HOME."

Almond Sandwich Cookies

Kid Friendly

You'll love how quickly these lacy cookies come together—not only are they perfect as a take-along to a housewarming, but they also make a delightful addition to a bridal shower or luncheon. When baking, be sure to place the dough for each cookie at least 3 inches apart on the baking sheet; the cookies will spread when baked.

PREP: 30 MINUTES **BAKE:** 10 MINUTES PER BATCH

- 1 cup rolled oats
- 1 cup sugar
- 2 Tbsp. all-purpose flour
- 1 tsp. ground cardamom
- 1/4 tsp. salt
- 1/4 tsp. baking powder
- 1 egg, slightly beaten
- 1/2 cup butter, melted
- 1 tsp. vanilla
- 1 cup slivered almonds
- 1 recipe Vanilla Cream

1. Preheat oven to 325°F. Line a cookie sheet with parchment paper or line cookie sheet with foil and lightly coat with nonstick cooking spray; set aside.

2. In a large mixing bowl combine oats, sugar, flour, cardamom, salt, and baking powder. In a medium bowl whisk together egg, butter, and vanilla until well combined. Add egg mixture to the flour mixture; stir until well combined. Add the almonds and stir until distributed.

3. Drop level teaspoons of dough 3 inches apart on prepared cookie sheet. Bake for 10 to 12 minutes or until edges are brown. Let cookies cool completely; then peel from parchment paper or foil. Repeat with remaining dough.

4. For each sandwich cookie, spread bottom side of a cookie with a rounded teaspoon of Vanilla Cream. Place a cookie, top side up, on top of filling. Makes 30 to 36 filled cookies.

VANILLA CREAM: In a large mixing bowl beat together 1/3 cup butter, softened, with 1 cup powdered sugar until smooth. Beat in 1 teaspoon vanilla. Gradually beat in an additional 3/4 cup powdered sugar until mixture is smooth.

EACH SANDWICH: 139 cal., 8 g total fat (3 g sat. fat), 21 mg chol., 62 mg sodium, 16 g carbo., 1 g fiber, 2 g pro. Daily Values: 3% vit. A, 2% calcium, 2% iron.

Almond Sandwich Cookies

M oving into a new home is a great time for a celebration. What better way to mark this milestone than a housewarming potluck? Hosting a potluck for friends who have recently moved sets just the right note of warmth for settling into a new home. The smiling faces of friends and family are all the decor that's needed.

Anything goes when setting up for a gathering at the initial stage of moving in. Put aside worries about the house not being "done." Use boxes as tables and plug in the lamps.

The loan of a few essentials will help the homeowners' empty kitchen become functional. Start with a 12-inch skillet; a practical all-purpose knife; a coffeemaker; a can opener; stacks of paper plates, napkins, and cups; plastic knives, forks, and spoons; and. if possible, a microwave oven.

Ask friends to bring foods that reflect housewarming traditions in their own families along with foods that represent familiar or new cultural traditions. In many cultures certain foods symbolize good fortune, prosperity, and welcome. In Germany, pork is a symbol of good luck, and the English and colonial Americans used pineapples as a sign of hospitality; therefore, a Pineapple and Rosemary Glazed Ham is a genial anchor to a potluck spread.

Black-eyed peas, prepared for good luck in the Southern United States, are the main ingredient in Black-Eyed Pea and Spring Green Salad.

Sesame, considered a good-fortune food in Japan, dresses up seasonal vegetables in Sesame Vegetable Salad. Eggs, universally symbolic of new beginnings, become spring-fresh with dill, parsley, and chive in Three-Herb Deviled Eggs.

Many cultures use salt and bread to christen a new home. Create a version of this tradition with Pretzel Bread Houses complemented with easy stir-together mustards. In Scandinavia, almonds represent wishes of good fortune; bake Almond Sandwich Cookies as a sweet alternative to the salty Pretzel Bread Houses. For a refreshing beverage, serve effervescent Strawberry and Sage Shrub, which incorporates the American Indian tradition of using sage to cleanse a new home.

In the same way that an old-fashioned barn raising and the suburban Welcome Wagon helped a household get established, today's housewarming lays the foundation for a home where family and friends will gather for years to come.

BY STEPHEN EXEL PHOTOGRAPHS BY JAMES CARRIER FOOD STYLING BY WILLIAM SMITH PROP STYLING BY KAREN JOHNSON AND SUSAN STRELECKI

Sesame Vegetable Salad

Sesame Vegetable Salad

Eliminate the chicken for a vegetarian version of this salad.

PREP: 50 MINUTES **COOK:** 8 MINUTES **CHILL:** 1 HOUR

- 1 lb. chicken breast tenderloins, halved crosswise
  Salt and ground black pepper
- 1 Tbsp. olive oil or cooking oil
- 1 lb. fresh asparagus, trimmed
- 1 lb. fresh sugar snap or snow pea pods, trimmed
- 6 cups watercress, tough stems removed
- 2 medium yellow sweet peppers, seeded and cut into thin strips
- 1 cup grape tomatoes
- 1 recipe Garlic Ginger Soy Dressing
- 1 Tbsp. sesame seeds, toasted

1. Sprinkle chicken lightly with salt and black pepper. In a large skillet cook chicken in hot oil over medium-high heat for 6 to 8 minutes or until no longer pink, turning to brown evenly. Remove chicken from skillet. Cool slightly; place in an airtight container. Chill at least 1 hour and up to 2 days until ready to serve.

2. In a large saucepan cook asparagus spears and pea pods, covered, in a small amount of boiling salted water for 2 to 4 minutes or until crisp-tender. Drain; rinse with cold water. Drain well. Use immediately or place in an airtight container and chill up to 2 days.

3. To serve, in very large bowl gently toss together chilled chicken, asparagus spears, pea pods, watercress, sweet peppers, and tomatoes. Add Garlic Ginger Soy Dressing; toss well. Sprinkle with sesame seeds. Makes 12 servings.

GARLIC GINGER SOY DRESSING: In screw-top jar combine ½ cup rice vinegar; ⅓ cup olive oil; 1 clove garlic, minced; 2 teaspoons *each* honey and soy sauce; 1 teaspoon sesame seeds, toasted; ¾ teaspoon ground ginger; ¼ teaspoon salt; and ⅛ teaspoon ground black pepper. Cover; shake well. Serve immediately or refrigerate up to 1 week; shake well before serving.

EACH SERVING: 158 cal., 8 g total fat (1 g sat. fat), 22 mg chol., 159 mg sodium, 9 g carbo., 2 g fiber, 11 g pro. Daily Values: 23% vit. A, 125% vit. C, 6% calcium, 9% iron.

Pineapple and Rosemary Glazed Ham

If you use canned pineapple for the glaze, use the canned juices for the ½ cup pineapple juice.

PREP: 30 MINUTES **BAKE:** 2½ HOURS **COOK:** 20 MINUTES

Pineapple and Rosemary Glazed Ham

1 8- to 10-lb. cooked bone-in ham, rump half or one
   4- to 6-pound cooked boneless ham
1¼ cups packed dark brown sugar, divided use
3 Tbsp. Dijon-style mustard
2 Tbsp. snipped fresh rosemary or 2 tsp. dried
   rosemary, crushed
½ cup pineapple juice
¼ cup Dijon-style mustard
1 medium (4 lb.) pineapple, peeled, cored, and
   coarsely chopped (4½ cups), or three 20-oz. cans
   pineapple tidbits, drained (set aside ½ cup juice)
1 recipe Grilled Pineapple Slices (optional)

1. Preheat oven to 325°F. Place ham in a shallow roasting pan. Score ham by making diagonal cuts, ¼ inch deep, in a diamond pattern. Insert an oven-going meat thermometer into center of ham, not touching the bone, if present. Bake for 1¾ hours if using bone-in ham or 1 hour if using boneless ham.

2. Meanwhile, in a bowl combine 3 tablespoons of the brown sugar, the 3 tablespoons mustard, and rosemary. Brush mixture over ham. Bake for 15 minutes more. Meanwhile, for glaze, in a 2-quart saucepan combine the remaining brown sugar, the pineapple juice, and ¼ cup mustard. Bring to boiling over medium heat, stirring frequently. Remove ½ cup glaze to brush over ham. Set aside.

3. Bake ham 30 minutes more or until thermometer registers 140°F, generously brushing with the ½ cup glaze several times during baking.

4. Meanwhile, add pineapple to the remaining glaze in saucepan. Bring to boiling; reduce heat. Simmer, uncovered, for 20 minutes. Transfer ham to serving platter; slice ham. Serve with pineapple sauce and, if desired, Grilled Pineapple Slices. Makes 16 to 24 servings.

GRILLED PINEAPPLE SLICES: Cut two peeled, cored pineapples in ½-inch slices. Lightly brush both sides with cooking oil. Lightly sprinkle with snipped fresh rosemary. Heat indoor grill or grill pan. Grill slices just until they start to brown, turning once. Serve alongside ham.

EACH SERVING: 305 cal., 8 g total fat (3 g sat. fat), 74 mg chol., 1,898 mg sodium, 24 g carbo., 1 g fiber, 33 g pro. Daily Values: 12% vit. C, 4% calcium, 10% iron.

Black-Eyed Pea and Spring Green Salad

Black-Eyed Pea and Spring Green Salad

French breakfast radishes have an elongated shape and sweeter taste than their rounder counterparts. For extra crispness, soak radishes in ice water for 1 to 2 hours before using.
PREP: 25 MINUTES **COOK:** 40 MINUTES

- 1 16-oz. pkg. frozen black-eyed peas
- 8 green onions, washed and trimmed
- 8 cups mixed spring salad greens
- 2 cups French breakfast radishes or small radishes, washed, trimmed, and cut in large pieces
   Coarse salt
- 1 recipe Caramelized Sweet Onion Vinaigrette

1. In a large saucepan cook black-eyed peas, covered, in lightly salted boiling water for 40 minutes or until tender. Drain; rinse with cold water until beans feel cold. Drain well.

2. Place whole green onions on a platter and arrange salad greens on top. Top with radishes. Spoon peas over radishes. Sprinkle all with coarse salt. Serve with Caramelized Sweet Onion Vinaigrette. Makes 8 side-dish servings.

CARAMELIZED SWEET ONION VINAIGRETTE: In a medium to large covered skillet cook 1 large sweet onion, chopped (1 cup), in 1 tablespoon cooking oil over medium-low heat for 13 to 15 minutes or until onions are tender, stirring occasionally. Uncover; cook and stir over medium-high heat for 3 to 5 minutes more or until onions are golden. Remove from heat; set aside to cool. In a small bowl whisk together 1/2 cup salad oil, 1/2 cup cider vinegar, 1 tablespoon honey, 1/4 teaspoon salt, and 1/8 teaspoon ground black pepper. Stir in onion mixture. Cover and chill up to 1 week. Makes about 1 1/2 cups.

EACH SERVING: 246 cal., 16 g total fat (2 g sat. fat), 0 mg chol., 172 mg sodium, 23 g carbo., 4 g fiber, 6 g pro. Daily Values: 7% vit. A, 19% vit. C, 5% calcium, 11% iron.

Strawberry and Sage Shrub

PREP: 40 MINUTES **STAND:** 1 HOUR

- 3 16-oz. pkg. frozen unsweetened whole strawberries or three 12-oz. pkg. frozen unsweetened red raspberries or combination of both
- 1 cup sugar
- 3/4 cup honey
- 1/2 cup water
- 1 Tbsp. finely shredded lemon peel
- 1/2 cup lemon juice
- 2 tsp. whole pink peppercorns (optional)
- 1/2 cup fresh sage leaves or 2 tablespoons dried sage, crushed
- 4 to 6 cups ice cubes
- 2 750-ml bottles Champagne or two 1-liter bottles club soda, chilled
  Fresh sage leaves (optional)
  Fresh strawberries or raspberries (optional)

1. In 4-quart Dutch oven combine frozen strawberries, sugar, honey, water, lemon peel, lemon juice, and, if desired, peppercorns. Cook, uncovered, over medium heat until mixture comes to boiling, stirring frequently. Remove from heat. Stir in sage. Let mixture stand, uncovered, for 1 hour.

2. For syrup, press strawberry mixture through a fine-mesh sieve; discard solids (you should have 4 to 5 cups sieved syrup). Syrup may be covered and refrigerated up to 3 days.

3. To serve, combine the syrup and ice cubes. Slowly add Champagne. If desired, garnish with additional fresh sage leaves and fresh berries. Makes 14 to 16 servings.

EACH SERVING: 220 cal., 0 g total fat, 0 mg chol., 3 mg sodium, 41 g carbo., 2 g fiber, 1 g pro. Daily Values: 2% vit. C, 4% iron.

Strawberry and Sage Shrub

Pretzel Bread Houses

Kid Friendly — Pretzel Bread Houses

Store these salty treats, wrapped in plastic wrap and tightly covered, at room temperature up to 3 days.

PREP: 1 HOUR **BAKE:** 12 MINUTES PER BATCH

    4 to 4½ cups all-purpose flour
    1 pkg. active dry yeast
    1 Tbsp. fennel seeds or coriander seeds, crushed
    1 Tbsp. sugar
    1 tsp. salt
 1½ cups warm water (120°F to 130°F)
    2 Tbsp. cooking oil
    1 egg white
    1 Tbsp. water
      Coarse sea salt
      Herbed Dijon Mustard, Ball Park Mustard, and/or
      Horseradish Honey Mustard

1. In a mixing bowl stir together 1¾ cups of the flour, the yeast, fennel seeds, sugar, and the 1 teaspoon salt. Add the 1½ cups warm water and the oil. Beat with an electric mixer on low to medium speed for 30 seconds, scraping sides of bowl. Beat on high speed for 3 minutes. Using a wooden spoon, stir in as much of the remaining flour as you can.

2. Turn dough out onto a lightly floured surface. Knead in enough of the remaining flour to make a moderately stiff dough that is smooth and elastic (6 to 8 minutes total). Shape dough into a ball. Divide in half. Cover; let stand for 10 minutes. Preheat oven to 425°F. Lightly grease baking sheets; set aside.

3. Roll each dough half to a 13-inch square on a lightly floured surface. Using a 3½×3¼-inch house-shape cookie cutter or desired cutter, cut 12 shapes from each square.* Arrange cutouts on prepared baking sheets about 2 inches apart. In a small bowl combine egg white and the 1 tablespoon water. Brush each cutout with egg white mixture and sprinkle with coarse salt. Bake about 12 minutes or until golden brown. Remove and cool on wire racks. Serve with Herbed Dijon, Ball Park, and/or Horseradish Honey Mustards. Makes 24 pretzels.

HERBED DIJON MUSTARD: In a small bowl stir together one 8-ounce jar Dijon-style mustard (¾ cup), 3 tablespoons packed brown sugar, 2 tablespoons dry white wine, and 1 tablespoon snipped fresh marjoram. Makes about 1 cup.

BALL PARK MUSTARD: In a small bowl stir together one 8-ounce jar yellow mustard (¾ cup) and ¼ cup packed brown sugar. Stir in ⅓ cup chopped peanuts just before serving. Makes about 1 cup.

HORSERADISH HONEY MUSTARD: In a small bowl stir together one 8-ounce jar honey mustard (¾ cup) and ¼ cup horseradish sauce. Makes about 1 cup.

*NOTE: Gather dough scraps and gently pull dough to shape into a ball. Cover and let rest for 10 to 15 minutes. Roll out dough to ¼-inch thickness and cut out additional houses or shapes as directed, *left*. Or divide ball into 8 pieces. Roll each piece into a 12-inch-long rope. Shape each rope into a pretzel by crossing one rope end over the other about 4 inches from each end, forming a circle. Twist once. Bring ends up and over the top of the circle. Press ends just under the top of circle to seal. Brush, sprinkle, and bake as directed, *left*.

EACH PRETZEL: 84 cal., 1 g total fat (0 g sat. fat), 0 mg chol., 117 mg sodium, 15 g carbo., 1 g fiber, 2 g pro. Daily Values: 1% calcium, 5% iron.

Three-Herb Deviled Eggs

This recipe results in one whole egg per serving. If you prefer servings of half-eggs, simply cut the cooked eggs in half lengthwise.

Fast! **START TO FINISH:** 30 MINUTES

> 1 recipe Hard-Cooked Eggs
> ¼ cup mayonnaise or salad dressing
> ¼ cup dairy sour cream
> 2 to 3 tsp. Dijon-style mustard
> 2 Tbsp. snipped fresh parsley
> 2 Tbsp. snipped fresh dill or 1½ tsp. dried dillweed
> 2 Tbsp. snipped fresh chives or 1½ tsp. dried chives
> Sea salt or salt
> Freshly ground black pepper
> Paprika or cayenne pepper (optional)

Three-Herb Deviled Eggs

1. Prepare Hard-Cooked Eggs. Cut off tops of eggs about one-third from the top; gently scoop out yolks with a small spoon. Cut a small thin slice off the rounded bottoms so eggs will sit flat. (Set aside tops for another use.)

2. Place yolks in a bowl; mash with a fork. Add mayonnaise, sour cream, and mustard; mix well. Stir in parsley, dill, and chives. Season to taste with salt and black pepper. Gently stuff egg yolk mixture into egg bottoms. If desired, sprinkle tops with paprika. Makes 12 servings.

HARD-COOKED EGGS: Place 12 eggs in a single layer in a large Dutch oven. Add enough cold water to just cover eggs. Bring to rapid boiling over high heat. Remove from heat; cover and let stand for 15 minutes. Drain. Run cold water over eggs or place them in ice water until cool enough to handle; drain. To peel eggs, gently tap each egg on the countertop. Roll the egg between the palms of your hands. Peel off eggshell, starting at the large end.

TEST KITCHEN TIP: Hard-cooked eggs made with eggs that have been refrigerated 1 week to 10 days after purchase are easier to peel.

EACH SERVING: 121 cal., 10 g total fat (3 g sat. fat), 217 mg chol., 130 mg sodium, 1 g carbo., 0 g fiber, 7 g pro. Daily Values: 8% vit. A, 2% vit. C, 3% calcium, 4% iron.

BUDGET COOKS, REJOICE. HERE'S A PIECE OF MEAT YOU CAN REALLY SINK YOUR TEETH INTO!

Grilled Marinated Flank Steak

SAVORY, TENDER FLANK STEAK

BY **STEPHEN EXEL** PHOTOGRAPHS BY **GREG SCHEIDEMANN, [N] HAUS FOTO** FOOD STYLING BY **CHARLES WORTHINGTON**

Marinated and grilled to perfection,

this cut of beef plays the starring role for a casual dinner party or a weeknight family supper. Dinner featuring this economical cut of steak, thinly sliced and served alongside three flavorful toppers, comes together quickly. Serve with tortillas and shredded lettuce for tasty options that allow everyone time for lively conversation. The added attraction is grilling enough steak to set aside for a meal later in the week.

The three chop-and-stir toppers (see Zesty Toppers, *page 68*), Quick Steak Sauce, Artichoke-Bean Spread, and Sweet Pepper Salsa, are quick to prepare; two are made ahead and refrigerated. Sweet Pepper Salsa accompanies both recipes, Grilled Marinated Flank Steak and Flank Steak Vinaigrette Salad (see recipe, *page 68*). Quick Steak Sauce goes classic with a piquant blend of raisins, soy sauce, molasses, and brown sugar. The Artichoke-Bean Spread goes Mediterranean with lemon peel and green onion; the salsa has a cool-hot attraction from jicama and serrano pepper.

Reserve some flank steak to serve later in the week in a seasonal salad that's satisfying enough for dinner (see recipe, *page 68*).

Grilled Marinated Flank Steak

PREP: 30 MINUTES **MARINATE:** 30 MINUTES **GRILL:** 17 MINUTES

- 1 1½-lb. beef flank steak
- ⅓ cup red wine vinegar
- 2 large cloves garlic, minced
- 2 Tbsp. Dijon-style mustard
- 2 Tbsp. snipped fresh cilantro
- ¼ tsp. crushed red pepper
- 4 10-inch flour tortillas
  Shredded lettuce
- 1 recipe *each* Sweet Pepper Salsa,
  Artichoke-Bean Spread, and Quick Steak Sauce,
  (see recipes, *page 68*)

1. Trim fat from steak. Score steak on both sides by making shallow diagonal cuts at 1-inch intervals in a diamond pattern. Place steak in a resealable bag set in a shallow dish; set aside. In a small bowl stir together vinegar, garlic, mustard, cilantro, and red pepper until well combined. Pour over steak in bag. Seal bag. Marinate in refrigerator for 30 minutes. Drain steak, discarding marinade.

2. Place steak on rack of uncovered grill directly over medium coals. Grill for 17 to 21 minutes or until an instant-read thermometer inserted in center registers 145°F for medium-rare doneness or 160°F for medium doneness. (Or preheat gas grill. Reduce heat to medium. Place meat on rack over heat. Cover and grill as above.) To serve, thinly slice steak against the grain. Wrap and refrigerate half of the steak up to 3 days for use in the Flank Steak Vinaigrette Salad (see recipe, *page 68*).

3. Serve remaining steak in flour tortillas with lettuce, Sweet Pepper Salsa, Artichoke-Bean Spread, and Quick Steak Sauce. Makes 4 servings.

EACH SERVING: 271 cal., 9 g total fat (3 g sat. fat), 34 mg chol., 270 mg sodium, 23 g carbo., 1 g fiber, 22 g pro. Daily Values: 3% vit. A, 2% vit. C, 6% calcium, 16% iron.

ZESTY TOPPERS

SWEET PEPPER SALSA

In a bowl toss together 2 medium green sweet peppers, finely chopped; 1 fresh serrano pepper, seeded and chopped (see note, *page 143*); 1/2 cup peeled, finely chopped jicama; 1/4 cup finely chopped red onion; 2 Tbsp. snipped fresh cilantro; 1 Tbsp. red wine vinegar; and 1/4 tsp. salt. Cover and chill. Makes about 2 1/2 cups. (Reserve 1 cup for the salad, *right.*)

QUICK STEAK SAUCE

In a blender combine 1/4 cup red wine vinegar, 1/4 cup chopped onion, 1/4 cup raisins, 2 Tbsp. tomato paste, 1 Tbsp. molasses, 1 Tbsp. packed brown sugar, 1 Tbsp. soy sauce, and 1/4 tsp. black pepper. Cover and blend until smooth. Refrigerate, covered, up to 1 week. Makes 3/4 cup.

ARTICHOKE-BEAN SPREAD

Drain one 6-oz. jar marinated artichoke hearts, reserving marinade. Coarsely chop artichokes; set aside. In food processor combine the marinade from artichoke hearts; one 15-oz. can garbanzo beans, rinsed and drained; 2 Tbsp. thinly sliced green onion; and 1 Tbsp. finely shredded lemon peel. Cover and process until smooth. Stir in artichokes. Season to taste with salt and black pepper. Refrigerate, covered, up to 3 days. Makes about 2 cups.

Flank Steak Vinaigrette Salad

 START TO FINISH: 30 MINUTES

- 1 recipe Mustard-Cider Vinaigrette
- 1 cup Sweet Pepper Salsa (see recipe, *left*)
- 3/4 lb. tiny new potatoes, scrubbed and quartered
- 1/2 lb. sugar snap peas, trimmed
- 6 cups purchased torn mixed salad greens, such as mesclun
- 8 oz. cooked beef flank steak, thinly sliced and chilled; or reserved Grilled Marinated Flank Steak (see recipe, *page 67*)

1. Prepare Mustard-Cider Vinaigrette. Stir into Sweet Pepper Salsa. Cover and chill.
2. In a saucepan cook potatoes in a small amount of lightly salted boiling water for 10 minutes. Add peas; cook 1 minute more. Drain. Rinse in cold water. Drain again; set aside.
3. In very large bowl combine salad greens and potato mixture; toss. Place flank steak slices or reserved sliced Grilled Marinated Flank Steak in medium bowl. Toss with 1/2 cup vinaigrette mixture. Add remaining vinaigrette to lettuce mixture; toss to coat. To serve, place tossed salad on serving platter. Top with flank steak. Makes 4 main-dish servings.

MUSTARD-CIDER VINAIGRETTE: In a screw-top jar combine 1/3 cup olive oil, 1/3 cup cider vinegar, 1 to 2 teaspoons sugar, 1 tablespoon snipped fresh cilantro, 1 teaspoon country-style mustard, 1/4 teaspoon salt, and 1/8 teaspoon ground black pepper. Cover and shake. Serve immediately, or cover and store in refrigerator up to 1 week. Shake before serving.

EACH SERVING: 417 cal., 24 g total fat (5 g sat. fat), 34 mg chol., 332 mg sodium, 26 g carbo., 5 g fiber, 23 g pro. Daily Values: 12% vit. A, 87% vit. C, 6% calcium, 23% iron.

Flank Steak Vinaigrette Salad

BUSY DAYS CALL FOR TIGHT TIME MANAGEMENT, BUT EVEN THEN A GOOD TIME CAN BE HAD. CHECK OUT THESE SPEEDY PARTY RULES FOR A LESSON IN FAST AND FUN FAMILY GATHERINGS.

FAST FUN: HOST A 1-HOUR PARTY

BY **STEPHEN EXEL** PHOTOGRAPHS BY **GREG SCHEIDEMANN, [N] HAUS FOTO** FOOD STYLING BY **SUSAN BROWN DRAUDT**

Spring has its set of child-

centered social obligations—recitals, plays, sports events. A fun one-hour party beforehand can start those events off on a high note. Kids love the festivity, and you can enjoy a casual drink and snack with the parents. Host up to 25 friends for a guaranteed good time.

This kind of get-together is easy and won't break the bank. Keep the food stress-free. Serve just a few nibbles that don't require plates or forks, such as an easy party mix and a couple of tempting dips. Two-Way Maple Peanut Mix is designed to be served two ways: To half, you add a dash of crushed red pepper and dried cranberries for adult tastes; then, for the kid-friendly version, chunks of milk-chocolate candy bar are tossed in. Serve filling hummus-style Roasted Red Pepper and White Bean Spreads on Cumin-Spiced Flatbreads. The spreads quickly whirl together in the blender. Everything can be made the night or afternoon before the party.

Offer a signature drink to ease the beverage duties. You can make Pomegranate Fizzes with or without wine (have bottled water on hand as an alternative). The bubbly drinks have a full, rich berry flavor and a deep red color to match. Pour out some fizzes in advance to take care of the initial rush—plastic or inexpensive tumblers from the discount store will do nicely. To give the party a little pizzazz, mix the drinks with a CO_2 siphon of carbonated water.

You'll be able to set up in just a couple of hours. Start the party at six. At seven, everyone's out the door. At 7:10, the serving dishes are in the dishwasher (ask a friend to stay and help), and at 7:30, you're in your seat waiting for the curtain to rise.

Total cost to entertain 25 people? For the ingredients in these recipes and the paperware, about $70.

Roasted Red Pepper and White Bean Spreads
PREP: 25 MINUTES **CHILL:** 2 HOURS

 ½ cup olive oil
 1 12-oz. jar roasted red sweet peppers, well drained
 4 cloves garlic, minced
 1 Tbsp. coriander seeds
 3 15- to 19-oz. cans cannellini beans, rinsed and drained
 1½ tsp. sea salt or 1 tsp. salt
 1 tsp. ground white pepper
 1 recipe Cumin-Spiced Flatbreads

1. In a skillet heat ¼ cup of the oil over medium heat. Add roasted peppers, garlic, and coriander seeds. Cook and stir for 2 minutes. Transfer mixture to a food processor. Cover; process until mixture is smooth. Transfer to bowl; set aside.

2. Place beans, salt, and white pepper in a food processor. Add the remaining ¼ cup oil; process until mixture is smooth. (Or mash mixture with a potato masher until almost smooth.) Cover both mixtures; chill 2 to 24 hours. Serve bean mixture and red pepper mixture with Cumin-Spiced Flat Breads. Makes 20 appetizer servings.

CUMIN-SPICED FLATBREADS: Split 12 pita bread rounds; cut into wedges. Place in a single layer on baking sheets. Brush with ½ cup olive oil. Sprinkle with 2 teaspoons ground cumin and 1 teaspoon sea salt. Bake in a 350° F oven for 12 to 15 minutes until crisp and golden brown.

EACH SERVING: 237 cal., 11 g total fat (2 g sat. fat), 0 mg chol., 493 mg sodium, 30 g carbo., 4 g fiber, 7 g pro. Daily Values: 51% vit. C, 5% calcium, 11% iron.

Pomegranate Fizzes

PREP: 20 MINUTES **CHILL:** 2 TO 4 HOURS

- ¼ cup mint leaves
- 4 cups pomegranate juice or cranberry juice
- ¼ cup sugar
  Ice
- 2 32-oz. bottles club soda or three 750-ml bottles dry white wine

1. Place mint leaves in a pitcher. Use a wooden spoon to bruise leaves. Add pomegranate juice and sugar; stir to dissolve. Cover and chill 2 to 4 hours. Remove mint leaves with a slotted spoon; discard.* For each serving, fill a glass with ice. Pour 3 to 4 tablespoons pomegranate mixture over ice. Top with club soda (about ¼ cup per serving). Makes 20 servings.
*NOTE: Syrup may be stored for 48 hours after mint has been removed.
EACH SERVING: 40 cal., 0 g total fat, 0 g chol., 21 mg sodium, 10 g carbo., Daily Values: 10% vit. C, 1% calcium, 2% iron.

Pomegranate Fizzes

Kid Friendly Two-Way Maple Peanut Mix

PREP: 25 MINUTES **BAKE:** 20 MINUTES **COOL:** 1 HOUR

- 1 cup maple syrup
- 2 Tbsp. butter, melted
- 8 cups cocktail peanuts
- 1 to 1½ tsp. crushed red pepper
- 3 cups pretzel sticks
- 1 cup dried cranberries
- 1 6-oz. bar milk chocolate, broken into bite-size pieces

1. Preheat oven to 350°F. Line two 15×10×1-inch baking pans with foil. Grease foil, set pans aside. In a bowl stir together syrup and butter; stir in peanuts. Place half of the mixture (4 cups) in a single layer in one baking pan. Stir crushed red pepper into remaining mixture in bowl; place in a single layer on second baking pan. Bake, uncovered, for 20 minutes, stirring twice. Stir 1½ cups of the pretzels and the cranberries into the mix with the crushed red pepper. Stir the remaining pretzels into the other mixture. Coat 2 large sheets of heavy foil with nonstick cooking spray. Spoon mixture onto the foil. Cool completely, about 1 hour. Break mixture into clusters.
2. Transfer the red pepper mixture into one serving bowl. Add chocolate to other mixture; transfer to a second serving bowl. Serve or store, tightly covered, up to 5 days. Makes 32 (½-cup) servings.
EACH SERVING: 301 cal., 21 g total fat (5 g sat. fat), 3 mg chol., 191 mg sodium, 21 g carbo., 4 g fiber, 10 g pro. Daily Values: 1% vit. A, 4% calcium, 5% iron.

Two-Way Maple Peanut Mix

HEALTH BY THE GLASS

Juicing gets more vegetables

into your family's diet—the delicious way. You'll love how easy it is to whip up a batch of Mother Nature's finest.

A recent study by the Baylor College of Medicine in Houston showed children approaching middle school have a marked decrease in vegetable consumption. Adults aren't faring much better.

If your family is on the lookout for easy, palatable ways to squeeze more produce into your busy lifestyle, consider a juice extractor, which can juice vegetables as well as the more traditional fruit.

"One of the great benefits of juicing is that it's full of enzymes that are important for the body. They're needed for many chemical reactions that go on, like digestion and absorption," says Pat Vasconcellos, a registered dietitian and spokesperson for the American Dietetic Association. "If you cook vegetables, those enzymes are destroyed."

For busy parents, the quick preparation and cleanup also make juicing a welcome way to provide nutrition. Whipping up a big pitcherful in the morning provides a refreshing shot of vitamins and starts everyone's day on the right foot.

GETTING STARTED

If your family is new to juicing, start with a base juice of carrots and apples: ½ of a large cored apple (or an entire small cored apple) and about 5 washed carrots per person.

Even if you go no further in your juicing adventures, this healthful drink will serve you well because it's packed with essential nutrients such as beta-carotenes. If you choose to step up to bolder flavors, add in small handfuls of additional vegetables at first until your family's palate adjusts. As with the apple-carrot blend, don't hesitate to add fruit if you need to sweeten any of your juices. "You'll still have a cup of juice packed with veggies," Vasconcellos says. "There's nothing wrong with adding an apple."

Here are some more recipe ideas to get you and your family juiced.

BY **KATHLEEN M. REILLY** PHOTOGRAPHS BY **GREG SCHEIDEMANN, [N] HAUS FOTO**

KID-PLEASERS

 Carrot-Apple-Beet Juice

A straightforward favorite, this juice is sweet and tasty. The beet turns the juice a cool purple color that kids love.

Fast! **START TO FINISH:** 10 MINUTES

- 1 small apple, cored
- 4 carrots
- ½ medium young beet, cut into wedges (1 cup)

1. Scrub the produce well. Juice the apple first; then alternate juicing the carrots and the beet. Serve chilled or over ice. Makes 1 serving.

Kid Friendly Super Green Juice

It's hard to get kids to eat spinach and celery, but they won't even notice them in this vivid green drink.

PREP: 15 MINUTES **CHILL:** 30 MINUTES

- 1 small handful fresh parsley (about ¼ cup)
- 1 cup pineapple chunks
- 6 cups spinach leaves
- 1 stalk celery
- 1 medium orange or tangerine, peeled and seeded

1. Wash veggies. Bunch up parsley and push it through the feed tube with pineapple, spinach, celery, and orange. Cover and chill 30 to 60 minutes or until well chilled. Stir and pour into an ice-filled serving glass. Makes 1 serving.

 Veggie Smoothie

A vegetable smoothie? It's true. This is a fun way to get growing bodies the nutrition they need.

Fast! **START TO FINISH:** 15 MINUTES

- 2 cups lightly packed spinach
- 1 large green apple, cored
- 1 large banana, peeled, cut into chunks, placed in a food-safe bag, and frozen
- ½ cup milk
- 1 Tbsp. peanut butter

1. Wash spinach and apple. Juice spinach and apple. Pour into a blender. Add frozen banana, milk, and peanut butter. Cover and blend. Serve immediately. Makes 2 servings.

Ginger Ale

Adventurous kids will crave this alternative to soda. And so will adults. The combination of parsnips and pears gives it an intriguing and zingy taste.

 START TO FINISH: 15 MINUTES

- 2 medium parsnips
- 2 medium pears, cored
- 1-inch-thick slice of fresh ginger
- 16 oz. carbonated water, chilled

1. Juice the parsnips, pears, and ginger. Divide among 4 serving glasses. Add carbonated water. Stir right before serving. Makes 4 to 6 servings.

GROWN-UP TASTES

Good Morning Juice

Drink this juice first thing in the morning; it'll give you the energy to start your day right.

 START TO FINISH: 15 MINUTES

- 5 carrots (about 13 oz.)
- 1 large cucumber (about 12 oz.)
- ¼ cup mint leaves or ginger mint leaves
- 1-inch slice of ginger
- Dash of salt

1. Scrub produce, slice into pieces, and feed into juicer. Season with salt. Cover and chill, if desired. Stir before serving. Serve over ice. Makes 2 servings.

Super Tomato Juice

This doesn't have the high sodium of the canned drink, and it's as flavorful as anything you can get at the store.

 START TO FINISH: 15 MINUTES

- 2 medium carrots
- 4 medium vine-ripened tomatoes, quartered
- 1 large red or yellow sweet pepper, stemmed, seeded, and cut up
- ½ medium cucumber, peeled (about 6 oz.)
- ¼ tsp. salt
- Few dashes bottled hot pepper sauce
- Kalamata olives, lime wedges, and cracked black pepper (optional)

1. Juice carrots, tomatoes, sweet pepper, and cucumber. Stir in salt and hot pepper sauce. Chill or serve over ice. Stir well before serving. If desired, skewer kalamata olives and lime wedges on wooden toothpicks; top juice with skewers and, if desired, cracked black pepper. Makes 4 servings.

From top to bottom: Veggie Smoothie, Carrot-Apple-Beet Juice, and Super Green Juice

Sunshine in a Glass

Because it's rich in antioxidants, this juice boosts your skin's ability to protect itself from the damaging effects of the sun.

 START TO FINISH: 10 MINUTES

- 4 carrots (10 oz.)
- 1 medium sweet potato (12 oz.)
- ½ cup packed parsley sprigs
- Dash salt
- Dash black pepper

1. Scrub produce well and cut into small chunks. Feed into juicer. Add salt and pepper. Serve over ice. Makes 1 serving.

MAKE IT FAST... WITH LOVE

The Getz family (*left*) take a spin in their car. They are, clockwise from front right, Marian; her husband, Greg; and sons, Jordan and Ben.

With big, bold strokes of a black

permanent marking pen, Marian Getz copies a recipe onto an 8½×11-inch piece of paper and attaches it, at eye level, to her kitchen cupboard. You can't miss it. The large print makes it nearly impossible to skip an ingredient or a step. And it doesn't get messy sitting on the countertop while flour and butter are flying.

Marian, executive pastry chef at Wolfgang Puck Cafe in Lake Buena Vista, Florida, is a master of step-saving shortcuts and kitchen wisdom. She has to be, she says. She's a time-pressed mom with a two-hour commute to work and a family of four to feed—and two of them are teenage boys. In addition, Marian's home is the neighborhood hangout for her sons' ever-hungry friends.

"I love nurturing and caring and feeding my family," Marian says. "My passion is cooking, but I'm a very busy person. And sometimes I just want to curl up in a chair and read."

To create a little "curl up" time, Marian streamlines her recipes, breaking them down to the bare bones to cut back on the number of ingredients or steps. That's how her 1-2-3 Cheesecake evolved.

"I'm notorious for deconstructing recipes," she says. "I get annoyed by extra steps. I'm willing to make mistakes to find a better way."

The cheesecake, which she calls "the best in the world," started out as a recipe from a magazine. She made it, loved it, but hated the fact that it required many ingredients and time-consuming steps.

"I thought I could get away without making the crust. So I chucked the crust," she said. "Take away the crust and a big chunk of the time and work are gone.

"Then I thought, does it really need lemon zest, vanilla, salt, sour cream? Nope. Just sugar, cream cheese, and eggs. It's even easy to remember: 1 cup of sugar, 2 pounds of cream cheese, and 3 eggs."

For her fall-apart flaky Hurry-Up Biscuits she uses heavy cream in place of the standard shortening or butter. The cream makes the biscuits a simple stir-together, eliminating the step of cutting shortening into the mix.

Marian uses the basic biscuit as a jumping-off point for other creations. She adds grated cheese and/or chives to make a savory dinner biscuit. For breakfast scones she tosses in a little extra sugar, nuts, and chocolate, or maybe dried fruit. Other times she'll drop the biscuits onto bubbling-hot fruit, sprinkle it with coarse sugar, and bake it as a cobbler.

She often doubles the batch of biscuits and freezes a dozen or so balls of dough to use later. (See tips, *opposite*.) The frozen biscuits are especially good when the family craves something homemade on a hectic day.

"Pop the biscuits in the oven along with a sheet pan of raw bacon [375°F for about 20 to 25 minutes]," she advises. "Then you'll have time to do a load of laundry, check your e-mail, iron, feed the animals, take out the garbage, and still smile smugly to yourself while everything cooks."

Marian's culinary adventures began when she was growing up in the Congo as the daughter of missionaries. Books, she says, were an unaffordable luxury in the primitive community where they lived. So Marian snuggled up with her mother's cookbooks, paging her way through *Joy of Cooking* and *Mastering the Art of French Cooking*, often reading by candlelight because they had no electricity.

That's also the time her love of sharing through food developed. She often bakes extras, including big pans of macaroni and cheese, or three cheesecakes at a time, so she has plenty to give away to someone in need. "My best personal tip," Marian says, "is to cook with love."

BY **JEANNE AMBROSE** PHOTOGRAPHS BY **COLLEEN DUFFLEY**

1-2-3 Cheesecake

Just before serving, top this dessert with sliced plums and finely shredded lemon peel. Or drizzle with honey or warm jam.

1-2-3 Cheesecake
PREP: 25 MINUTES **BAKE:** 70 MINUTES
COOL: 1 HOUR **CHILL:** OVERNIGHT

- 1 cup sugar
- 4 8-oz. pkgs. cream cheese, softened
- 3 eggs

1. Preheat oven to 275°F. Line the outside of an 8-inch springform pan with heavy foil. Grease the bottom and sides inside the pan; set aside.

2. In a large mixing bowl beat sugar and cream cheese with a sturdy handheld or a freestanding electric mixer on medium to high speed for 8 to 10 minutes, scraping twice, until mixture is smooth and the sugar is dissolved.

3. Stir in eggs just until combined. Pour the batter into prepared pan. Place in a shallow roasting pan. Place roasting pan on the oven rack. Add 1 inch of very hot water to the roasting pan.

4. Bake for 70 to 75 minutes or until center appears nearly set when shaken.

5. Carefully remove springform pan from water bath and let cool on a wire rack for 15 minutes. Run a thin metal spatula around edge of the cheesecake to loosen from sides of pan. Cool for 45 minutes more. Cover and chill overnight.

6. To serve, remove sides of the pan. Makes 10 servings.

TEST KITCHEN TIP: For added flavor, add 1 tsp. finely shredded lemon peel or 1 tsp. vanilla to cheesecake batter with eggs.

EACH SERVING: 413 cal., 33 g total fat (20 g sat. fat), 163 mg chol., 290 mg sodium, 22 g carbo., 0 g fiber, 9 g pro. Daily Values: 26% vit. A, 8% calcium, 8% iron.

TIPS FROM MARIAN

- Cut cheesecake with dental floss. This way, you can easily cut a perfect 8-inch cheesecake into 12 or even 24 slices, which is impossible to do with a knife. This works for any soft cake.

- One of my favorite tools: the stand mixer. The beauty of a stand mixer, other than it's more powerful than a handheld mixer, is that it's hands-free. You can do something else while you're creaming the butter and sugar.

- To quickly cool puddings, fillings, or ice cream bases, fill a resealable plastic bag with ice cubes, close the top, and float the bag in the mixture. The mixture will cool in no time.

- Use an ice cream scoop to place biscuit batter on a cookie sheet lined with parchment paper. Freeze. Transfer frozen biscuits to a freezer bag. When you're ready for biscuits, pull out as many as you need and bake them.

So-Easy Chocolate Soufflé

So-Easy Chocolate Soufflé

 Fast! **PREP:** 15 MINUTES **BAKE:** 12 MINUTES

Nonstick cooking spray
Sugar
4 oz. semisweet chocolate, chopped
½ cup whipping cream
4 egg whites
2 Tbsp. sugar

1. Preheat oven to 400°F. Coat insides and rims of four 6-ounce ramekins with nonstick cooking spray. Sprinkle with sugar and set on a baking sheet; set aside.
2. In a small microwave-safe bowl combine chocolate and cream. Microwave on 100% power (high) for 1½ to 2 minutes or until smooth, stirring twice. Divide in half. Cover and cool to room temperature.
3. In a medium mixing bowl beat egg whites with an electric mixer on medium speed until foamy. Gradually add the 2 tablespoons sugar, beating until soft peaks form (tips curl).
4. Gently fold half of the cooled chocolate mixture into the beaten egg whites until combined. Spoon mixture into prepared ramekins. Bake for 12 to 15 minutes or until a knife inserted near the centers of soufflés comes out clean. Serve immediately. To serve, use a spoon or knife to split open the centers of the soufflés; pour in remaining chocolate mixture. Makes 4 servings.
EACH SERVING: 294 cal., 20 g total fat (12 g sat. fat), 41 mg chol., 67 mg sodium, 25 g carbo., 2 g fiber, 6 g pro. Daily Values: 9% vit. A, 2% calcium, 8% iron.

Hurry-Up Biscuits

These biscuits taste great by themselves, or use the batter to make a flaky topping for Hurry-Up Biscuit Cobbler

Fast! **PREP:** 15 MINUTES **BAKE:** 15 MINUTES PER BATCH

- 3 cups all-purpose flour
- 4 tsp. sugar
- 4 tsp. baking powder
- 1 tsp. salt
- 2 cups whipping cream

1. Preheat oven to 375°F. Lightly grease 2 cookie sheets or line with parchment paper; set aside. In a large bowl stir together flour, sugar, baking powder, and salt with a fork until well combined.

2. Add cream all at once. Stir gently with fork just until combined.

3. Drop dough into 16 mounds 1 inch apart on prepared cookie sheets using an ice cream scoop (size 16) or 2 large spoons (if necessary, shape into mounds with hands). Bake 15 to 17 minutes or until golden brown. Serve warm. Makes about 16 biscuits.

EACH BISCUIT: 186 cal., 11 g total fat (7 g sat. fat), 41 mg chol., 217 mg sodium, 18 g carbo., 1 g dietary fiber, 3 g pro. Daily Values: 9% vit. A, 4% calcium, 6% iron.

FOR CHEESY BISCUITS: Prepare Hurry-Up Biscuits as above; add 1 cup finely shredded or grated Parmesan cheese to flour mixture in Step 1.

MAKE AHEAD: Dough mounds can be frozen up to 1 month. To freeze, place mounds in a single layer on a baking sheet or tray. Cover and freeze until firm. When firm, place in freezer containers. Cover and freeze up to 1 month. To bake, arrange dough mounds on greased or parchment-paper-lined baking sheets. Bake frozen mounds in a 375°F oven for 18 to 20 minutes or until golden brown.

HURRY-UP BISCUIT COBBLER: Prepare Hurry-Up Biscuits as directed through step 2; set aside. Meanwhile, in a large saucepan combine 1 cup sugar, 2 tablespoons cornstarch, and ¼ cup water. Stir in 6 cups (two 16-ounce packages) fresh or frozen unsweetened pitted tart red cherries. Cook and stir over medium heat until thickened and bubbly. Divide mixture among eight 8- to 12-ounce ovenproof coffee cups or individual casserole dishes. Drop 1 or 2 mounds of batter on top of each cup. (Freeze any remaining batter as directed in Make-Ahead instructions.) Bake in a 375°F oven for 25 to 30 minutes or until topping is golden brown and mixture is bubbly. Makes 8 servings.

EACH SERVING: 524 cal., 23 g total fat (14 g sat. fat), 82 mg chol., 436 mg sodium, 75 g carbo., 3 g fiber, 7 g pro. Daily Values: 37% vit. A, 4% vit. C, 10% calcium, 15% iron.

Hurry-Up Biscuit Cobbler

CURED SALMON

Its silky texture and salty-sweet taste

belie how quickly and simply you can prepare cured salmon—at home, in about 30 minutes. The lion's share of the work is done in the refrigerator, where the salmon chills for 48 hours before serving. For variations on Classic Cured Salmon, try the maple-sage or mustard-ginger cures following the recipe steps.

Cured salmon is a brunch buffet star and a versatile ingredient too. Toss it into fettuccine Alfredo, incorporate it into gazpacho, or layer it on a grilled cheese sandwich. And it's right at home on a Sunday morning bagel smeared with cream cheese.

BY **STEPHEN EXEL** PHOTOGRAPHS BY **GREG SCHEIDEMANN, [N] HAUS FOTO**
FOOD STYLING BY **BROOKE LEONARD**

Classic Cured Salmon
PREP: 30 MINUTES **CHILL:** 48 HOURS

- 1/3 cup coarse kosher salt
- 1/4 cup sugar
- 2 1 1/2-lb. *each* center-cut salmon fillets, skin on
- 2 tsp. shredded lemon peel
- 1 cup coarsely chopped fresh dill, loosely packed (some stems are okay)
- 1 tsp. cracked black peppercorns

1. For cure mixture, in a bowl combine salt and sugar; set aside. Remove salmon from refrigerator. Scrape off any loose scales. Rinse fish; pat dry. Place, skin sides up, on cutting board. Using a very sharp knife, lightly score the skin of each fillet diagonally in a diamond pattern about every 3 inches (do not make deep cuts).

2. With a clean spray bottle filled with water, spray the skin of one fillet to moisten. Sprinkle with 2 tablespoons of cure mixture, sprinkling lightly on the tail or thin end of the fillet and sprinkling more heavily on the thicker end. Lightly spray again with water to help mixture stick.

3. Place fillet, skin side down, in a 2-quart rectangular baking dish. Spray with water. Sprinkle with 2 tablespoons of cure mixture, sprinkling lightly on thin end and more heavily on thick end. Sprinkle with lemon peel, dill, and peppercorns (*Photo 1*).

4. Turn second fillet skin side down. Spray with water. Sprinkle as before with 2 tablespoons cure mixture. Spray again. Turn fillet over; place, skin side up, on first fillet, tail (thin) end over thicker end (*Photo 2*). Sprinkle with remaining cure mixture; spray again.

5. Cover with plastic wrap. Weight with a glass baking dish filled with dried beans or a heavy plate (*Photo 3*). Refrigerate. Using two spatulas or your hands, turn fish every 12 hours, spooning liquid in the dish over fish. After 48 hours, remove fish from dish. Separate fillets. With a paper towel carefully wipe away cure mixture and other ingredients.

6. Transfer fish to a cutting board, skin sides down. Using a very sharp knife, thinly slice the flesh away from the skin at a diagonal, starting at tail end. Salmon should cut easily from skin. Thinly slice flesh (*Photo 4*). Wrap and store any remaining salmon in refrigerator up to 2 days. Makes 2 1/2 pounds (20 servings).

MAPLE-SAGE VARIATION: Substitute 1/4 cup maple syrup or packed brown sugar for granulated sugar. Substitute 1/2 cup snipped fresh sage for the dill. Omit lemon peel.

MUSTARD-GINGER VARIATION: Substitute 1 teaspoon crushed mustard seeds for black peppercorns. Substitute 1/3 cup grated fresh ginger (2 ounces) for the dill. Omit lemon peel.

EACH SERVING: 45 cal., 2 g total fat (0 g sat. fat), 15 mg chol., 783 mg sodium, 1 g carbo., 0 g fiber, 6 g pro. Daily Values: 1% calcium, 1% iron.

Classic Cured Salmon served with its traditional accompaniments: dark pumpernickel, herbed cream cheese, capers, chopped cooked egg, lemon, and pickled red onion.

THE CAKE TO CELEBRATE

Tres leches translates to "three milks," and that's exactly what makes this cake so moist. It's a sweet white cake soaked in a mixture of condensed, evaporated, and whole milk or whipping cream. The layer cake is also topped with whipped cream frosting. You'll find it almost melts in your mouth, a decadent result of simple beginnings. For many, the best part of the cake is the three-milk sauce. So generously is it used that it pools on the serving plate.

Mexico, Nicaragua, and Guatemala all claim the creation of Tres Leches Cake. It has become the ultimate celebration cake in those countries since the late 1800s. Serve it for birthdays, brunches, Sunday dinner dessert, or for any special occasion. Make the cake the day before you want to serve it so the flavors meld in the refrigerator.

To keep the celebration easy, this Tres Leches Cake (it's pronounced tress LEH-chays) starts with a white cake mix. A bit of lime peel stirred into the batter and a layer of fresh strawberries add spring flavor and color to this dessert. Dress up your version with other berries or a drizzle of fruit-flavored liqueur. You can also substitute chunky fruit preserves for the fresh fruit.

BY **STEPHEN EXEL** PHOTOGRAPHS BY **GREG SCHEIDEMANN, [N] HAUS FOTO**
FOOD STYLING BY **CHARLES WORTHINGTON**

Tres Leches Cake

Why cool cakes exactly 10 minutes before turning them out? That length of time allows the cake to firm up yet still be easily removed from the pan.
PREP: 45 MINUTES **BAKE:** 50 MINUTES **CHILL:** 8 HOURS

    1   2-layer-size regular white cake mix
   3/4 cup butter, softened
    6   eggs
   1/2 cup water
    2   Tbsp. finely shredded lime peel
    3   cups fresh strawberries, chopped
    1   recipe Tres Leches Sauce
    1   cup whipping cream
   3/4 cup granulated sugar
    1   tsp. vanilla

1. Preheat oven to 350°F. Grease and flour a 10-inch springform pan; set aside.
2. In a mixing bowl combine cake mix, butter, eggs, and water. Beat on low speed until combined. Beat on medium speed for 2 minutes (batter will be thick). Stir in lime peel. Spread batter in prepared pan. Bake 50 minutes or until a wooden skewer inserted near the center comes out clean.
3. Cool in pan on a wire rack for 10 minutes (cake may sink during cooling). Loosen cake from sides of pan; remove sides. Lift cake from pan bottom using a wide metal spatula. Cool cake completely on a wire rack (the bottom of the cake should be cool to the touch).
4. Line an 11-inch round straight-side Dutch oven or other 11-inch diameter container with plastic wrap, allowing wrap to hang over edges. Using a serrated knife, split cake in half horizontally. Place top half of cake, cut side up, in prepared container. Top with strawberries. Place cake bottom, cut side down, on strawberries. Press down lightly.

Almost any straight-side, flat-bottom vessel, such as a Dutch oven (Photo 1, *right*) or a glass salad bowl, works to soak Tres Leches Cake. To remove the cake, place a serving platter on top of the cake container, hold both together, and quickly invert (Photo 2). Some of the liquid may not have absorbed into the cake; use a platter or plate deep enough to catch any of the excess.

5. Using a long-tined fork or wooden skewer, poke holes in cake layers across the entire surface. Slowly pour 4 cups of the Tres Leches Sauce over cake. Cover cake; chill 8 to 12 hours or overnight. Cover and chill remaining mixture.

6. About 1 hour before serving, slowly pour 1 cup of the remaining Tres Leches Sauce over cake. Cover; chill cake and remaining sauce until serving time.

7. To serve, in a chilled bowl combine whipping cream, sugar, and vanilla. Beat with an electric mixer until stiff peaks form. Remove cake from refrigerator; uncover. Place a serving platter with a lip, upside down, over the container; carefully invert. Remove plastic wrap. Spread whipped cream mixture over top and sides of cake. Some of the Tres Leches Sauce will seep from cake as it stands. Serve immediately with the remaining Tres Leches Sauce on the side. Makes 12 to 16 servings.

TRES LECHES SAUCE: In a saucepan combine two 12-ounce cans evaporated milk, two 14-ounce cans sweetened condensed milk, and 2 cups whole milk or whipping cream. Cook over medium heat just until boiling, stirring frequently. Remove from heat. Transfer to a large bowl. Cover; cool completely. Makes about 7½ cups sauce.

EACH SERVING: 764 cal., 37 g total fat (20 g sat. fat), 208 mg chol., 584 mg sodium, 93 g carbo., 1 g fiber, 16 g pro. Daily Values: 24% vit. A, 56% vit. C, 48% calcium, 9% iron.

The puddinglike texture of Tres Leches Cake is a pleasant change from a standard white cake. Its richness makes it a treat to savor.

Tres Leches Cake

HORSERADISH BITES BACK

In spring, the spiciness of horseradish

is a welcome wake-up for taste buds. This ever-faithful companion to the carved roast beef sandwich has fresh appeal when served au naturel—straight from the root. You'll get the same peppery bite associated with bottled horseradish (which contains vinegar as a preservative), but the flavor will be a little less bitter and less astringent. Consequently, fresh horseradish has a sneaky heat that horseradish lovers crave.

Shop in the produce section for roots that are hard, dry, and free from knots or deep blemishes. To use fresh horseradish, peel away the outer skin to reveal only as much of the creamy white interior as you'll need. Then slice, grate, chop, or grind as you wish. At this point, volatile oils are released and their potent fumes can cause tears, so when you work with fresh horseradish, be sure your kitchen is well ventilated.

A hand grater works when you want a small amount of horseradish, but consider using a food processor or blender for larger amounts or for finely chopping the root. First, coarsely dice the peeled root. Then place it in a food processor or blender and process or blend until finely chopped. Add a splash of water to the mixture if you're looking for a creamier consistency.

Be sure to use freshly grated horseradish promptly. The pungent aroma will fade quickly, and what will remain is that hit of heat. Store the unused root in a cool, dry place or bundle it in plastic wrap and place it in the refrigerator.

BY **STEPHEN EXEL** PHOTOGRAPHS BY **JOYCE OUDKERK POOL**
FOOD STYLING BY **POUKÉ**

GRATE STUFF

TOP A FISH
Combine freshly grated horseradish with sourdough bread crumbs, melted butter, fresh herbs, and lemon juice to crust a fillet of fish.

GREENS WITH KICK
Start with a pile of lightly sauteed greens or spinach leaves. Add a sprinkling of grated horseradish for a spicy boost of flavor.

BURGER TOPPERS
Smother a burger with sauteed onions, then grate a bit of fresh horseradish over all.

Look for horseradish in the produce section of supermarkets. It is usually available year-round.

WINE MAKES GOOD SCENTS

Can you tell when a wine is

"lemony" or has an aroma that's "cherrylike?" A way to test—or heighten—your wine sense is to throw a wine-tasting party that allows guests to compare aromas and flavors in wines to foods. The party is more than fun; it's also an exercise that draws guests into lively conversation while teaching lessons that make drinking wine more enjoyable.

Here's how it's done: Set out glasses, each holding a slice or sample of food that's used to describe wines (see Wine-Food Combinations, *right*). Then pour guests a glass of wine and let them compare the aroma and flavors wafting from their glass to the sample foods.

Start with one or two kinds of wine, a couple of glasses for each person, and four or five extra glasses to hold the sniffables. Buy one bottle of each type of wine for every four people (you'll get about five glasses from a 750-ml bottle).

Focus on aromas first; they're easier to identify. Then move on to flavors, which will be more obvious once you know what you're tasting for.

The wine-tasting exercise makes an abstract idea concrete. For example, when you compare a Chardonnay or a Merlot to a slice of lemon or a few cherries, those qualities in the wine suddenly snap into focus.

Let the party snacks you serve at the gathering take a backseat to the wine. Consider just a few nibbles, such as baguette slices, nuts, and a hunk of Brie or other mild cheese. Put away any scented candles; they interfere with the ability to smell the wine.

The reward is that everyone learns or advances a skill: the ability to name the flavors in the glass. Once you can do that, you'll better appreciate wine and be able to identify the flavors you like. You'll know to buy wines with flavor descriptions that suit your tastes. Labels that read "aromas of peach, pear, and plum" are no longer poetry but useful buying advice.

BY **STEPHEN EXEL** PHOTOGRAPHS BY **JOYCE OUDKERK POOL**
FOOD STYLING BY **POUKÉ**

WINE-FOOD COMBINATIONS

WHEN SERVING CHARDONNAY
- Pear slices
- Pineapple
- Shortbread cookies
- Peach slices (canned or fresh)
- Grapefruit
- Green apple slices
- Buttered popcorn

WHEN SERVING SAUVIGNON BLANC
- Lime peel
- Cantaloupe slices
- Apricots (canned or fresh)
- Peaches (canned or fresh)
- Banana slices
- Pineapple slices
- Pear slices
- Green sweet pepper

WHEN SERVING ZINFANDEL
- Black pepper
- Raspberries
- Strawberry jam
- Walnuts
- Fig bars
- Cocoa powder

WHEN SERVING MERLOT
- Cherries or cherry jam
- Prunes
- Fruitcake
- Toasted hazelnuts
- Cloves
- Licorice
- Coffee
- Cinnamon

You'll find the aroma of raspberries in many red wines, including Merlots, Cabernet Sauvignons, and Shirazes.

In good taste
FOOD AND ENTERTAINING

Cakes in Bloom

Serve a platter of sweet rose-topped treats.
Russell Millner of Russell's Bakery in Austin, Texas, found a simple way to top cupcakes with huge buttercream flowers. Fit a pastry bag with a large petal tip (Wilton size 125 or larger) and pipe directly onto the cupcake. To begin, place the wide end of the tip on the center of the cupcake and, squeezing gently, give the cupcake a full turn to create a cone for the center of the rose. Form the petals by placing the wide end of the tip at the base of the cone and make small arch-shape strokes. Work from the center outward, gradually making each stroke larger. Stagger each stroke so the petals are off-set. Russell's Bakery & Coffee Bar, 3339 Hancock Drive, Austin, Texas; 512/419-7877.

Rice Pudding Deluxe

Visit New York City's Rice to Riches rice pudding bar and you'll find amazing combinations of flavors for this ultra creamy dessert.
According to owner Pete Moceo, sushi rice is best for that creamy texture. "It's fatter, stouter, and puffier," Moceo says. "It has a bolder taste and texture and keeps its shape better." The best source for sushi rice is Asian markets or specialty grocery stores.

BEST NEW SPRING FLAVORS: Moceo suggests using fruit to embellish your favorite rice pudding recipe. For example, mash pineapples, cook them until soft and saucy, and stir the cooled sauce into rice pudding. Fresh berries, such as strawberries or blackberries, are also delicious add-ins. Rice to Riches, 37 Spring St. (between Mott and Mulberry), New York, New York, 10012; 212/274-0008; www.ricetoriches.com.

USING SIMPLE SYRUPS

Infused with flavors such as lavender and Meyer lemon, simple syrups add refreshing taste when stirred into lemonade, iced tea, or iced coffee. Add a dash of the syrup to sparkling wine or a light white wine. To add flavor to desserts, stir simple syrups into frostings; also use them to glaze cakes and other baked goods. Use them to flavor a base for homemade ice cream or sorbet; or drizzle them over purchased ice cream or sorbet. Stirred together with fresh herbs, such as mint or basil, simple syrups can be brushed over trout, whitefish, or salmon before grilling or broiling. In this season of changeable weather, a dash stirred into a cup of hot water is delightful.

SIMPLE SYRUPS: Lavender Infused, $11; Classic, $12; Sonoma Syrup Co.; 707/996-4070; www.sonomasyrup.com.

PHOTOGRAPHS BY KIM CORNELISON
FOOD STYLING BY JANET PITTMAN

Healthy family
NEWS EVERYONE NEEDS TO STAY WELL

Plan with Cans

Trying to squeeze more fruits and vegetables into your family's diet? Don't forget your trusty can opener. "Canned foods are a great convenience," says Liz Weiss, a registered dietitian and author of *The Moms' Guide to Meal Makeovers.* "You can open a few cans and pull together a healthy meal in no time." The boon goes beyond convenience. "With canned food, you're not sacrificing quality," adds Carolyn O'Neil, a registered dietitian and author of *The Dish on Eating Healthy and Being Fabulous!* "You can even get bigger, bolder flavors from some canned foods because they're concentrated." Here are a few creative suggestions from Weiss and O'Neil on using canned produce.

- **ARTICHOKE HEARTS** A great source of fiber, vitamin C, folate, and magnesium. Try canned artichoke hearts in pasta salads or tossed salads.
- **BABY CORN** Rich in fiber and folate, this is a great addition to any stir-fry.
- **BEANS** All kinds are high in protein, fiber, and antioxidants. Add chickpeas to salads. Blend black beans into meat loaf or burgers. Toss red beans into rice dishes.
- **BLACK OLIVES** Loaded with healthy fats. Throw slices on Mexican dishes, pizza, soups.
- **BLUEBERRIES** The antioxidant level in canned blueberries is actually higher than that of fresh. Gently fold wild canned berries into a muffin mix. Or add them to cereal.
- **PEACHES** are brimming with vitamin C. Taste summer year-round by using as an ice cream topping, a smoothie ingredient, or just as a snack.
- **PUMPKIN** Canned pumpkin also has a higher concentration of antioxidants and fiber than fresh. Fold a few spoonfuls into canned tomato soup for some extra flavor.
- **SPINACH** Heat a drained can of spinach with a bit of extra virgin olive oil and some coarse salt for a simple side dish loaded with antioxidants and vitamin C. —DOUG DONALDSON

PHOTOGRAPHS BY **GETTY IMAGES** (CANNED FOOD)

MAY

Chicken and Biscuit Kabobs
page 97

WITH OVER A DOZEN
QUICK AND EASY CHICKEN
CHOICES, YOU'LL HAVE
DINNER VARIETY GALORE!

Quick Quicker Quickest

Chicken in a Phyllo Nest
page 94

French-Toasted Angel Food Cake
page 105

Quick, quicker quickest

Chicken, Goat Cheese, and Greens
page 103

STRAPPED FOR TIME? PICK FROM OUR SPEEDY CHICKEN RECIPES—
SOME TAKE JUST 10 MINUTES—AND YOU'LL HAVE TIME TO SPARE
FOR YOUR FAMILY AND OTHER THINGS THAT REALLY MATTER.

Chicken with Creamy Mushrooms

30 minutes

Sliced mushrooms and butter sizzle together in a skillet, flavoring the pan before the chicken is sautéed.

Chicken with Creamy Mushrooms

Save time by buying sliced mushrooms. Skinless, boneless chicken breasts that have not been marinated also work well in this dish.

START TO FINISH: 30 MINUTES

- 1 lb. sliced fresh mushrooms, such as button or shiitake
- 3 Tbsp. butter
- 6 Italian-marinated skinless, boneless chicken breast halves (about 2 lb.)
- 3 Tbsp. rice vinegar or white wine vinegar
- 1½ cups whipping cream
- 3 Tbsp. capers, drained
- ¼ tsp. freshly ground black pepper
- Steamed fresh vegetables (optional)

1. In a 12-inch skillet cook mushrooms, uncovered, in 1 tablespoon of the hot butter over medium-high heat about 5 minutes or until tender. Remove mushrooms from skillet.

2. Reduce heat to medium. Add the remaining 2 tablespoons of the butter and the chicken breast halves to skillet. Cook, uncovered, for 8 to 12 minutes or until no longer pink (170°F), turning once. Remove chicken from skillet and keep warm.

3. Remove skillet from heat; add vinegar, stirring to loosen browned bits in bottom of skillet. Return skillet to heat. Stir in cream, capers, and pepper. Bring to boiling; boil gently, uncovered, for 2 to 3 minutes or until sauce is slightly thickened. Return mushrooms to skillet; heat through. Cut each chicken piece in half horizontally to make two thin pieces. Top with mushroom sauce. If desired, serve with steamed vegetables. Makes 6 servings.

EACH SERVING: 456 cal., 34 g total fat (19 g sat. fat), 183 mg chol., 967 mg sodium, 7 g carbo., 1 g fiber, 33 g pro. Daily Values: 22% vit. A, 1% vit. C, 5% calcium, 5% iron.

BY JEANNE AMBROSE PHOTOGRAPHS BY COLLEEN DUFFLEY FOOD STYLING BY WILLIAM SMITH

Y

ou've got an hour before the kids are off to rehearsal, or soccer, or cheerleading practice. Dinner? Done.

Any one of these simple supper options can be on the table easily in less than 60 minutes, making a delicious impression on family or guests. Whether it's a casual midweek meal or a Sunday afternoon feast, chicken satisfies any occasion. It's a comfort-food mainstay, pleasing just about everyone's palate. It's gentle on the budget too.

When it comes to chicken, is there a multipurpose cut—a one-cut-fits-all? We think so: boneless breasts, followed closely by boneless thighs. When you have little time, those are the pieces that can be taken swiftly from casual to company-special while providing standout flavor.

For instance, thighs take on a fresh citrus taste when lemon wedges are baked along with the chicken. Breasts, cooked quickly in a skillet, can be sauced, sliced, served on a bun, or topped on a salad.

The quest for fabulous low-stress meals gets a boost from ready-to-eat packaged chicken available from the grocery store. Among the speediest ingredient is refrigerated grilled chicken—complete with grill marks—easily tossed on a salad or over pasta with a little sauce. The chicken strips are flavored with various spice blends, including Italian, Southwestern, and Mexican.

Keep some handy helpers, such as breaded chicken breast strips and nuggets (ready to heat and eat), taco-seasoned shredded chicken, or marinated breasts, stashed in the fridge or freezer. Even no-frills chicken pieces waiting to be sprinkled with your favorite seasoning or splashed with a bottled marinade can be baked or sautéed in a jiffy.

Want to add more wow? Grab some specialty sauce at the grocery store. Chicken provides the perfect foundation for layering flavor.

Of course there's everyone's fast-food favorite: whole roasted chicken, hot from the deli. The basic roasted bird can be the centerpiece for a special day, or it can be sliced or shredded to use a variety of ways.

Although chicken may be the ultimate convenience food, you may substitute pork, beef, turkey, or tofu in most of these recipes. Hints are provided in the recipes.

Start with easy chicken ideas and, before you know it, dinner's ready. After all, the best place to get fast food is at home.

Swiss chard tucked around a chicken breast serves as a snug wrap for an herb-enhanced feta cheese stuffing.

Chard-Wrapped Chicken

To put the meal on the table 10 minutes quicker, bake the chicken as directed and skip the roasted carrots. Instead, serve the carrots steamed or cooked in the microwave oven with a bit of butter and a sprinkling of salt and fresh herbs. Dill is especially delicious.

PREP: 15 MINUTES **BAKE:** 35 MINUTES

- 1 recipe Roasted Carrots and Onions
- ¼ cup olive oil
- 2 Tbsp. snipped fresh dill, oregano, or sage
- 1 clove garlic, minced
- ¼ tsp. ground black pepper
- ½ cup crumbled feta cheese
- 6 medium skinless, boneless chicken breast halves
- 6 Swiss chard leaves, stems trimmed

1. Preheat oven to 375°F. Prepare Roasted Carrots and Onions and place in oven. Meanwhile, in a small bowl combine oil, 1 tablespoon of the snipped herbs, the garlic, and pepper. In another small bowl combine feta cheese and 1 tablespoon of the oil mixture. Mash mixture together with the back of a spoon to form a paste.

2. Top each chicken breast with some of the feta mixture, pressing firmly. Wrap center portion of each chicken breast with a Swiss chard leaf, leaving ends exposed. Place wrapped chicken breasts in a 3-quart rectangular baking dish.

3. After carrots have been in the oven for 10 minutes, add chicken to oven. Bake, uncovered, for 25 to 30 minutes or until chicken is no longer pink (170°F). Sprinkle chicken with remaining 1 tablespoon snipped fresh herbs. Makes 6 servings.

ROASTED CARROTS AND ONIONS: In a 2-quart rectangular baking dish combine one 1-pound package peeled fresh baby carrots; 1 medium onion, cut into thin wedges; 1 tablespoon olive oil; ¼ teaspoon kosher salt or salt; and ⅛ teaspoon ground black pepper. Toss to coat. Bake as directed.

EACH SERVING: 344 cal., 16 g total fat (4 g sat. fat), 99 mg chol., 390 mg sodium, 10 g carbo., 3 g fiber, 38 g pro. Daily Values: 195% vit. A, 12% vit. C, 12% calcium, 10% iron.

Meaty chicken thighs, orzo (rice-shape pasta), lemon, and kalamata olives create a heavenly aroma while baking.

Kalamata-Lemon Chicken

You can get dinner on the table quicker by skipping the browning step and placing the ingredients in a 2-quart rectangular baking dish. The baking time won't change, but your prep time will be nearly nothing. Pour on additional hot broth if you're in the mood for soup.

PREP: 10 MINUTES **BAKE:** 35 MINUTES

- 1 to 1¼ lb. skinless, boneless chicken thighs
- 1 Tbsp. olive oil
- ⅔ cup dried orzo
- ½ cup drained, pitted kalamata olives
- 1 14-oz. can chicken broth
- ½ of a lemon, cut into wedges or chunks
- 1 Tbsp. lemon juice
- 1 tsp. dried Greek seasoning
- ¼ tsp. each salt and freshly ground black pepper
  Hot chicken broth (optional)
  Snipped fresh oregano (optional)

1. Preheat oven to 400°F. In a 4-quart Dutch oven brown chicken in hot oil over medium-high heat for 5 minutes, turning once. Stir in orzo, olives, broth, lemon wedges, lemon juice, Greek seasoning, salt, and pepper. Cover; bake for 35 minutes or until chicken is tender and no longer pink (170°F).

2. Serve in shallow bowls. If desired, add additional broth and top with snipped oregano. Makes 4 servings.

EACH SERVING: 309 cal., 11 g total fat (2 g sat. fat), 91 mg chol., 837 mg sodium, 24 g carbo., 2 g fiber, 27 g pro. Daily Values: 1% vit. A, 14% vit. C, 2% calcium, 12% iron.

Chard-Wrapped Chicken

50 minutes

CHICKEN IS COMFORT FOOD FOR THE SOUL. NOW IT'S ALSO THE ULTIMATE CONVENIENCE FOOD WITH THESE SATISFYING NEW RECIPES.

Kalamata-Lemon Chicken

45 minutes

Chicken in a Phyllo Nest

25. minutes

Precooked grilled chicken and bagged spinach are key fuss-free factors for a meal-in-a-bowl salad tossed with balsamic vinaigrette.

Chicken in a Phyllo Nest

Leftover grilled steak or chunks of cooked salmon are appetizing options for the chicken. Marinated tofu works too.

 START TO FINISH: 25 MINUTES

Nonstick cooking spray
10 sheets frozen phyllo dough (14×9-inch rectangles), thawed
1 cup 2-inch pieces green onions (1 bunch)
2 Tbsp. olive oil
12 oz. refrigerated grilled chicken breast strips (3 cups)
1 6-oz. pkg. fresh baby spinach
3/4 cup cherry tomatoes, halved or quartered (optional)
1 Tbsp. snipped fresh tarragon
1/4 tsp. freshly ground black pepper
1/2 cup bottled balsamic vinaigrette

1. Preheat oven to 425°F. Lightly coat a 15×10×1-inch baking pan with nonstick cooking spray; set aside. Roll stack of phyllo sheets into a cylinder shape. With a sharp knife cut phyllo roll crosswise into 1/4- to 1/2-inch strips (see photo, *below*). Gently separate phyllo into strips and spread evenly in the prepared baking pan. Coat phyllo generously with additional nonstick cooking spray. Bake, uncovered, for 8 to 10 minutes or until phyllo strips are golden brown.
2. Meanwhile, in a 12-inch skillet cook green onions in oil over medium-high heat for 1 minute or until just tender. Add chicken; cook and stir until heated through. Remove skillet from heat. Add spinach; cherry tomatoes, if desired; tarragon; and pepper. Toss to combine.
3. Divide phyllo among 6 bowls. Spoon chicken mixture over phyllo. Drizzle with balsamic vinaigrette. Serve immediately. Makes 6 servings.

EACH SERVING: 197 cal., 10 g total fat (2 g sat. fat), 40 mg chol., 760 mg sodium, 14 g carbo., 1 g fiber, 14 g pro. Daily Values: 57% vit. A, 19% vit. C, 4% calcium, 11% iron.

Use a knife to slice rolled-up phyllo dough into strips before baking.

BBQ Chicken Burgers and Waffle Fries

 Kid Friendly BBQ Chicken Burgers and Waffle Fries

Mini burgers bake in just 12 minutes, so let the waffle fries get a head start in the oven before popping in the burgers. Worried about fat grams? Drop the bacon and cheese from the fries and pass the ketchup instead. Or skip the fries and serve a fruit salad.

Fast! **START TO FINISH:** 30 MINUTES

- 1/3 cup bottled barbecue sauce
- 1/3 cup grape jelly or seedless raspberry jam
- 3 cups frozen waffle-cut or thick-cut french fried potatoes
- 4 slices packaged ready-to-serve cooked bacon, chopped
- 2 Tbsp. fine dry bread crumbs
- 2 Tbsp. finely chopped honey-roasted walnuts or almonds
- 1 Tbsp. bottled barbecue sauce
- 1/2 tsp. poultry seasoning
- 1/4 tsp. salt
- 1/8 tsp. ground black pepper
- 8 oz. uncooked ground chicken or turkey
- 1/2 cup shredded Italian-blend cheeses, Monterey Jack cheese with jalapeño peppers, or Gorgonzola cheese
  Snipped fresh chives
- 8 dinner rolls or cocktail-size hamburger buns, split
  Tomato slices and/or lettuce

1. Preheat oven to 425°F. Combine the 1/3 cup barbecue sauce and the jelly. Mix with a wire whisk until smooth. Set aside.
2. Arrange waffle-cut potatoes in a single layer on an ungreased baking sheet. Sprinkle with chopped bacon. Bake for 8 minutes.
3. Meanwhile, in a bowl combine bread crumbs, nuts, the 1 tablespoon barbecue sauce, poultry seasoning, salt, and pepper. Add ground chicken; mix well. Shape into 8 balls; place 2 inches apart on greased shallow baking pan. Moisten the bottom of a glass and press each ball to about 1/4-inch thickness.
4. Place pan of burgers in oven. Bake fries and burgers for 5 minutes. Stir fries; turn burgers. Continue baking burgers and potatoes for 5 minutes more.
5. Sprinkle cheese over fries. Brush barbecue-jelly mixture on burgers. Bake burgers and potatoes 2 minutes more or until burgers are no longer pink in center and cheese is melted on fries.

6. To serve, sprinkle fries with snipped chives. Place mini burgers in dinner rolls with additional barbecue-jelly mixture spooned over. Top with tomato slices and/or lettuce. Makes 4 servings.

EACH SERVING: 537 cal., 21 g total fat (7 g sat. fat), 20 mg chol., 902 mg sodium, 66 g carbo., 4 g fiber, 22 g pro. Daily Values: 4% vit. A, 15% vit. C, 21% calcium, 20% iron.

Chicken and Biscuit Kabobs

> Nuggets of breaded chicken are skewered with pieces of refrigerated biscuit dough and slices of squash for a fun-to-eat meal on a stick.

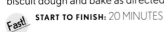

Chicken and Biscuit Kabobs

Cook the frozen chicken in the microwave oven to allow the skewer to be inserted easily. Instead of chicken, you can opt for thick slices of fully cooked smoked sausage. Thread it onto the skewers with the biscuit dough and bake as directed.

START TO FINISH: 20 MINUTES

- ½ of a 13.5-oz. pkg. (12) frozen cooked breaded chicken breast chunks
- 1 4.5-oz. pkg. (6) refrigerated buttermilk or country biscuits
- 1 medium zucchini and/or yellow summer squash, cut into 3×¾-inch strips
- ⅓ cup butter, melted*
- 3 Tbsp. honey*

1. Preheat oven to 400°F. Arrange chicken chunks in a single layer on a microwave-safe plate. Microwave, uncovered, on 100% power (high) for 1 minute (chicken will not be heated through).

2. Use kitchen scissors to snip each biscuit in half. On each of 4 metal or wooden skewers alternately thread chicken pieces, biscuit halves, and squash, leaving about ¼ inch between pieces. Place on ungreased baking sheet. Bake for 10 minutes or until biscuits are golden brown and chicken is heated through.

3. Meanwhile, whisk together melted butter and honey. Drizzle some of the mixture over kabobs. Pass remainder for dipping. Makes 4 servings.

*TIP: Substitute ½ cup honey-butter for the melted butter and honey. Place in a microwave-safe bowl and microwave, uncovered, on 100% power (high) for 35 to 45 seconds or until melted.

EACH SERVING: 376 cal., 22 g total fat (9 g sat. fat), 57 mg chol., 649 mg sodium, 37 g carbo., 1 g fiber, 10 g pro. Daily Values: 11% vit. A, 10% vit. C, 1% calcium, 6% iron.

WHAT'S NEW IN QUICK CHICKEN?

For quicker-than-quick dinner or snack ideas, start with cooked or grilled chicken from the supermarket.

POPCORN CHICKEN

From freezer to table in minutes, these bite-size bits are perfect for snack attacks. Serve with a salad or raw veggies.

GRILLED TO GO

No one will ever know you didn't grill these strips yourself. Look for various flavors, bagged or boxed, available frozen or refrigerated. Just heat and eat in soups, with pasta, or on a bed of salad greens.

15minutes

Mango chutney adds a big hit of spicy-sweet flavor to ready-in-minutes couscous. The speediest ingredient? Precooked flavored chicken.

Couscous Chicken Salad

Couscous Chicken Salad

Swift-cooking couscous is a tiny grain-shape pasta made from semolina flour, a product of durum wheat. Cooked and fluffed, couscous is a good substitute for rice or polenta. Look for couscous in the rice and dried bean section of your grocery store.

 START TO FINISH: 15 MINUTES

- 1 14-oz. can reduced-sodium chicken broth
- 1¼ cups quick-cooking couscous
- ½ cup mango chutney, large pieces cut up
- ¼ cup bottled olive oil and vinegar salad dressing, white wine vinaigrette, or roasted garlic vinaigrette salad dressing
- 1 6-oz. pkg. cooked refrigerated lemon-pepper or Italian-style chicken breast strips, cut into bite-size pieces (about 1½ cups)
- ½ cup golden raisins or raisins
- 1 cup coarsely chopped, seeded cucumber or radishes
   Salt and freshly ground black pepper
- 1 small cucumber, cut into spears

1. In a medium saucepan bring chicken broth to boiling. Stir in couscous. Cover and remove from heat. Let stand for 5 minutes. Fluff couscous lightly with a fork.

2. Meanwhile, in a medium bowl combine mango chutney and dressing. Add chicken, golden raisins, the 1 cup of chopped cucumber, and cooked couscous. Toss to coat.

3. Season to taste with salt and pepper. Serve with cucumber spears. Makes 4 servings.

EACH SERVING: 418 cal., 10 g total fat (1 g sat. fat), 28 mg chol., 873 mg sodium, 62 g carbo., 4 g fiber, 19 g pro. Daily Values: 6% vit. A, 17% vit. C, 4% calcium, 9% iron.

Those beloved kid-pleasing fish-shape crackers inspired this crispy coating for chicken strips. Crushed pretzels would provide a crunchy coating too.

Two-Step Crunchy Chicken Strips

Two-Step Crunchy Chicken Strips

 Kid Friendly Two-Step Crunchy Chicken Strips

As directed, this recipe produces plump pieces of yummy snacking chicken in about 20 minutes. For an even speedier version, start with cooked chicken breast strips from the deli case and proceed as directed.

Fast! **PREP:** 10 MINUTES **BAKE:** 10 MINUTES

Nonstick cooking spray
2½ cups crushed bite-size cheddar fish-shape crackers or pretzels
⅔ cup bottled buttermilk ranch salad dressing or honey Dijon mustard
1 lb. chicken breast tenderloins
Bottled buttermilk ranch salad dressing or honey Dijon mustard (optional)

1. Preheat oven to 425°F. Line a 15×10×1-inch baking pan with foil; lightly coat foil with nonstick cooking spray. Set aside.

2. In a shallow dish place the crushed crackers or pretzels. In another shallow dish place ranch dressing (see photo, *below*). Dip chicken tenderloins into the ranch dressing or mustard, allowing excess to drip off; dip into cracker crumbs to coat. Arrange chicken in prepared pan. Bake for 10 to 15 minutes or until chicken is no longer pink (170°F). If desired, serve with additional ranch dressing or mustard. Makes 4 to 6 servings.

QUICKER VERSION: Use a 10-ounce package of cooked refrigerated chicken breast strips instead of the chicken breast tenderloins. Prepare as above, except bake only 5 to 8 minutes or until heated through.

EACH SERVING: 517 cal., 21 g total fat (2 g sat. fat), 66 mg chol., 1,060 mg sodium, 51 g carbo., 2 g fiber, 33 g pro. Daily Values: 3% calcium, 10% iron.

Dip strips of chicken in buttermilk ranch salad dressing, roll in crushed fish-shape crackers, and bake.

20 minutes

Boiling water is the most time-consuming element of making this super-fast spin on mac and cheese.

Tortellini and Cheese

Any leftover cooked meat is a good substitute for the chicken here. Or skip the chicken altogether because there's plenty of protein in this dish without it.

 START TO FINISH: 20 MINUTES

- 1 9-oz. pkg. refrigerated cheese tortellini
- 1 cup frozen peas, corn, or pea pods
- 1 8-oz. tub cream cheese spread with garden vegetables or chive and onion
- ½ cup milk
- 1 9-oz. pkg. frozen chopped cooked chicken breast

1. In a large saucepan cook tortellini according to package directions. Place frozen vegetable in colander. Drain hot pasta over vegetables to thaw; return pasta-vegetable mixture to pan.

2. Meanwhile, in a small saucepan combine cream cheese and milk; heat and stir until cheese is melted. Heat chicken according to package directions.

3. Stir cheese sauce into cooked pasta-vegetable mixture. Cook and gently stir until heated through. Top with chicken. Makes 4 servings.

EACH SERVING: 505 cal., 26 g total fat (15 g sat. fat), 130 mg chol., 525 mg sodium, 32 g carbo., 2 g fiber, 32 g pro. Daily Values: 33% vit. A, 11% vit. C, 24% calcium, 12% iron.

Tortellini and Cheese

 10 minutes

Popcorn Chicken with Coconut Slaw

Popcorn Chicken with Coconut Slaw

Heap this mixture in a bowl or cup or encase it in a flavored tortilla. Kids will love the tropical twist to this 10-minute meal. Skip toasting the coconut, if you like.

Fast! **START TO FINISH:** 10 MINUTES

1 10- to 12- oz. pkg. frozen cooked, breaded popcorn chicken
½ of a 16- oz. pkg. shredded cabbage with carrot (coleslaw mix) (4 cups)
1 cup mango pieces or quartered strawberries
½ cup raw coconut chips and/or shredded coconut, toasted*
⅓ cup bottled citrus vinaigrette or bottled Italian salad dressing
   Salt and ground black pepper

1. Cook popcorn chicken in the microwave oven according to package directions. Meanwhile, in a bowl combine shredded cabbage with mango pieces and coconut. Add vinaigrette; toss to coat. Add cooked chicken and toss.

2. Divide mixture among 4 goblets or bowls. Season to taste with salt and pepper. Top with additional *coconut*, if desired. Makes 4 servings.

***TOASTING COCONUT:** Preheat oven to 350°F. Place coconut in a shallow baking pan. Bake, uncovered, for 5 to 10 minutes or until toasted, stirring once or twice.

EACH SERVING: 331 cal., 19 g total fat (8 g sat. fat), 17 mg chol., 720 mg sodium, 32 g carbo., 5 g fiber, 9 g pro. Daily Values: 26% vit. A, 66% vit. C, 3% calcium, 6% iron.

Dressed-Up Deli Chicken

A handful or two of herbs and edible flowers dresses up a roasted bird hot from the market rotisserie (*below*). While you're at the store, take advantage of the salad bar and bring home enough greens and veggies to toss together in a big bowl to round out the meal.

 START TO FINISH: 5 MINUTES

1 2- to 2½-lb. purchased roasted chicken*
1 cup fresh edible flowers and/or mixed herbs, such as lavender leaves, thyme, sage, oregano, mint, and/or parsley
⅓ cup balsamic vinaigrette salad dressing or olive oil and vinegar salad dressing

1. Place the chicken on a platter. Sprinkle with ¼ cup of the edible flowers and/or herbs. Slice chicken. Pass remaining herbs; sprinkle with vinaigrette. Makes 4 servings.

***NOTE:** If roasted chicken is chilled, place it on a microwave-safe plate. Loosely cover it with waxed paper. Microwave on high (100% power) for 8 minutes. Prepare recipe as directed above.

EACH SERVING: 416 cal., 25 g total fat (6 g sat. fat), 134 mg chol., 303 mg sodium, 3 g carbo., 1 g fiber, 42 g pro. Daily Values: 16% vit. A, 19% vit. C, 6% calcium, 15% iron.

Dressed-Up Deli Chicken

5 minutes

15 minutes

Let the kids put together their own do-it-yourself tostadas with the help of taco-flavored shredded chicken.

Towering Tostadas

Here's a chance to pile on lots of veggies. For an extra taste of creamy flavor, top each tostada with a dollop of light dairy sour cream, Mexican-style. Look for tubs of shredded chicken in the refrigerated section of a deli. You can also substitute shredded beef or pork.

 START TO FINISH: 15 MINUTES

1¼ cups (½ of an 18-oz. tub) taco sauce with shredded chicken
 4 6-inch tostada shells
¾ cup shredded, peeled jicama; shredded carrot; shredded broccoli slaw mix; or canned black beans, rinsed and drained
⅓ cup shredded Colby and Monterey Jack cheese (about 1 oz.)

1. In a small saucepan cook chicken mixture until heated through. Divide evenly on 4 tostada shells. Top with selected veggies. Sprinkle with cheese. Makes 4 servings.

 EACH SERVING: 174 cal., 8 g total fat (3 g sat. fat), 40 mg chol., 645 mg sodium, 14 g carbo., 2 g fiber, 9 g pro. Daily Values: 7% vit. A, 10% vit. C, 10% calcium, 4% iron.

Towering Tostadas

Chicken, Goat Cheese, and Greens

Company dinner can be a cinch to make when you invite guests over at the last minute. Just pick up a ready-to-eat roasted chicken on your way home from work. More than four for dinner? Serve two chickens.

 PREP: 15 MINUTES **BAKE:** 15 MINUTES

- 1½ lb. Swiss chard, beet greens, and/or mustard greens, trimmed and washed
- 1 2- to 2½-lb. roasted chicken
- 3 Tbsp. olive oil
- 2 Tbsp. lemon juice
- 2 Tbsp. snipped fresh dill, oregano, and/or sage
- ¼ tsp. sea salt, kosher salt, or salt
- ¼ tsp. cracked black pepper
- 1 3- to 4-oz. log goat cheese (chèvre), sliced into rounds or coarsely crumbled

1. Preheat oven to 350°F. Reserve one or two small leaves of chard. Tear remaining chard and place in a 3-quart rectangular baking dish. Remove string from chicken; use the string to tie the chicken legs together. Place chicken on chard in dish. In a small bowl combine oil and lemon juice. Drizzle oil mixture over chicken and chard in dish. Sprinkle 1 tablespoon of the snipped herbs over the chicken and chard. Sprinkle salt and ⅛ teaspoon of the pepper over chard only.

2. Loosely cover baking dish with foil. Bake for 15 to 20 minutes or until torn chard is tender. Meanwhile, sprinkle cheese with remaining 1 tablespoon snipped herbs and the remaining ⅛ teaspoon pepper.

3. Transfer chicken to a serving platter. Place several of the goat cheese rounds on top of chicken. Add reserved chard leaves. Toss cooked chard in dish to evenly coat with cooking liquid. Serve chard and remaining cheese with chicken. Makes 4 servings.

TIP: This recipe doubles easily to serve 8. Double the ingredients and prepare as directed above, except place all the greens and both chickens in a large shallow roasting pan. Bake as directed above.

EACH SERVING: 542 cal., 36 g total fat (10 g sat. fat), 143 mg chol., 620 mg sodium, 7 g carbo., 3 g fiber, 48 g pro. Daily Values: 187% vit. A, 53% vit. C, 13% calcium, 28% iron.

Chicken, Goat Cheese, and Greens

30 minutes

ANGEL FOOD SOARS

Dressed-up angel food cakes (recipes, *opposite*) gain height on pedestals fashioned from dinner plates and overturned mixing bowls. A bit of tacky wax (from crafts stores) affixed to the plate and bowl will keep them together.

1. FRENCH-TOASTED ANGEL FOOD CAKE: Slice one 7- to 8-inch angel food cake into 10 to 12 wedges about 1 to 2 inches thick. In a medium bowl combine 6 eggs, beaten; 1½ cups milk; 3 tablespoons sugar; and 2 teaspoons vanilla. Soak wedges in egg mixture for 1 to 2 minutes per side until completely soaked through. In a skillet or on a griddle melt 1 tablespoon butter over medium heat. Cook 4 wedges for 1 to 3 minutes on each side or until golden brown. Repeat with remaining wedges, adding more butter as needed to the skillet. To serve, stand slices in cake formation. Top with whipped cream or crème fraîche. Drizzle with maple syrup; top with strawberries. Serve immediately. Makes 10 to 12 servings.

EACH SERVING: 275 cal., 12 g total fat (6 g sat. fat), 187 mg chol., 305 mg sodium, 33 g carbo., 1 g fiber, 8 g pro. Daily Values: 11% vit. A, 36% vit. C, 13% calcium, 6% iron.

2. HONEY-ROSEMARY ANGEL FOOD CAKE: In a saucepan heat ½ cup honey until thin enough to brush over cake. Beat together 8 ounces mascarpone cheese and ½ cup whipping cream until light and fluffy. Fold in 1 teaspoon lemon juice and 1 teaspoon snipped fresh rosemary. Slice one 7- to 8-inch angel food cake in half horizontally. Brush tops of layers with the honey. Spread one layer with filling. Top with second layer. Makes 10 to 12 servings.

EACH SERVING: 313 cal., 19 g total fat (11 g sat. fat), 57 mg chol., 235 mg sodium, 36 g carbo., 8 g pro. Daily Values: 4% vit. A, 2% vit. C, 5% calcium, 1% iron.

3. CHOCOLATE-DRIZZLED ANGEL FOOD CAKE: Using a long wooden skewer, generously poke holes all the way through the top of one 7- to 8-inch angel food cake. Drizzle with equal proportions of orange liqueur and orange juice (at least 2 tablespoons each). For the chocolate glaze, in a saucepan melt 6 ounces bittersweet or dark chocolate with ½ cup butter over low heat, stirring frequently. Remove from heat. Whisk in 1½ cups powdered sugar and ¼ cup whipping cream. Spoon evenly over cake. Makes 10 to 12 servings.

EACH SERVING: 396 cal., 23 g total fat (12 g sat. fat), 43 mg chol., 304 mg sodium, 49 g carbo., 2 g fiber, 3 g pro. Daily Values: 10% vit. A, 3% vit. C, 6% calcium, 5% iron.

Smart entertaining can be a devil

of a job. Pulling dessert together can be a lot easier when you dress up an angel food cake fresh from the grocery store. It's a simple shortcut you and your guests will appreciate.

A purchased angel food cake, a few on-hand ingredients, and a little ingenuity will solve the "what's quick and easy to make for dessert?" dilemma. The results for these three fix-ups—French-Toasted, Honey-Rosemary, and Chocolate-Drizzled Angel Food Cake—all have remarkable homemade appeal and taste. The praises from friends and family will make you feel like a saint.

BY **STEPHEN EXEL** PHOTOGRAPHS BY **GREG SCHEIDEMANN, [N] HAUS FOTO**

In good taste
FOOD AND ENTERTAINING

A STACK OF LOVE

Mom: Leave this page open where Dad is bound to see it. Now, Dad: Pay attention! Here's a really simple way to get the kids involved in making breakfast to serve Mom on Mother's Day. Have them stir ingredients such as granola, chocolate chips, orange or lemon zest, chopped nuts, or ground cinnamon or nutmeg into pancake batter. Dad, you can flip the pancakes while the kids decorate a breakfast tray with cards and flowers.

SMOOTH GOING

A busy day of dropping the kids at school, running errands, squeezing in time at the gym, and after-school activities can take a toll on your energy and your time. It can also disrupt healthy eating habits. These three smoothies blend together quickly to get you through a whirlwind day.

Banana Breakfast
For a quick breakfast, blend together half a banana, chopped; ³/₄ cup pineapple chunks; and ½ cup coconut milk.

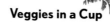

Veggies in a Cup
Serve lunch in a glass. In the microwave oven, steam 3 medium carrots and half a cored, seeded yellow sweet pepper. Blend with 1 cup room-temperature chicken broth and a dash of ginger.

Green Tea Grab-and-Go
For an easy afternoon pick-me-up, blend 1 cup chilled steeped green tea, ½ cup chopped honeydew melon, a sprig of mint, and ice.

PHOTOGRAPHS BY **KIM CORNELISON**

Wine and Spirits

GREAT WINES, MODEST PRICES

When friends are invited and a glass of wine is one of the evening's offerings, the natural impulse is to buy an expensive bottle. Resist the urge.

Plenty of wines are available for $7 to $10 a bottle that will make your friends believe you are a wine expert.

Budget wines taste better than ever for several reasons. Winemakers have been replanting vineyards with grapes that make better wine. (Just as plant breeders strive to offer more robust, more fragrant roses for gardeners, grape researchers work to improve their vines for winemakers.)

At the same time, wine growers are learning how to get more flavor from the grapes they grow by careful timing of watering and pruning. Economics are at work too. When wines cost $7 or $8 a bottle and above, winemakers can afford to use the high-quality grapes that make better wine. These changes, according to one industry expert, mean that today's under-$10 wines would have cost $15 five years ago.

Choosing a good inexpensive wine requires a little experience, some experimentation, and a bit of luck. Here are a few strategies for buying and serving.

▪ Buy two less-expensive wines rather than one expensive bottle. If you can get two different wines on sale for less than $10, buy them and serve both at dinner. Even if you don't like one of the wines, you still have the other bottle. If you like them both, tightly cork and refrigerate any unused portion. It will stay good in the refrigerator up to three days in most cases. (Let red wine stand on the counter about an hour to take off the chill before serving again.) Or save the one you like less for making into sangria.

▪ Buy adventurously; choose a name you've never heard of or a vintage from a country you've never tried. Some of the best low-priced, high-value wines this year come from Australia, Argentina, Chile, Spain, South Africa, and Portugal.

▪ Consider blends in which two or three varieties of grapes are listed on the label, such as Syrah-Merlot or Semillon-Chardonnay. Blending means the winemaker has created more interesting, flavorful wine by melding the best of each grape. For instance, the richness of wine made from Syrah grapes can be blended with the spicy, chocolaty flavors of Merlot grapes. Think of the combination of fruits in a dessert—plain raspberry pie is wonderful, but when you add blueberries, blackberries, and strawberries, there is more complexity and flavor.

—Richard Swearinger

WINES TO CONSIDER

These wines share lower prices, easy drinkability, and all go well with the chicken recipes in this book.

▪ Little Penguin 2004 Shiraz, $8; www.thelittlepenguin.com.
▪ Folonari Valpolicella 2003, $7; www.frederickwildman.com.
▪ Alice White Chardonnay 2004, $7; www.alicewhite.com.
▪ George Duboeuf G.D. Red 2003, $7; www.wjdeutsch.com.
▪ Veramonte 2003 Chardonnay, $8; www.veramonte.com.
▪ J. Lohr Estates Wildflower Valdiguié 2004, $8; www.jlohr.com.

JUNE

Grilled Polenta and Tomato Relish
page 119

MICROWAVE THEM, GRILL THEM, OR DON'T COOK
THEM AT ALL—NO MATTER HOW YOU CHOOSE TO
SERVE THEM, THIS SUMMER'S BOUNTY OF VEGETABLES
WILL LEAVE YOU WANTING MORE.

Summer Fresh and Fast

Rose and Berry Summer Salad
page 117

Hot-off-the-Grill Apricot Pie
page 122

Red and Orange Stuffed Peppers with Honey-Herb Steaks
page 121

SUMMER *fresh* AND *fast*

WHEN GREEN BEANS ARE TENDER AND PEACHES ARE AT THEIR JUICY BEST, IT'S EASY TO CREATE QUICK DINNERS THAT LEAVE YOU PLENTY OF TIME TO CHASE THE FIREFLIES AND SMELL THE ROSES. THE PLAN? STEP AWAY FROM THE STOVE AND LET THE SEASON'S BOUNTY TAKE CENTER STAGE.

Triple Green Bean Salad

BY **RICHARD SWEARINGER** PHOTOGRAPHS BY **ANN STRATTON** FOOD STYLING BY **ANNE DISRUDE**

Triple Green Bean Salad

Smoked salt is available from a number of sources including www.saltcouture.com and www.saltworks.us.

PREP: 10 MINUTES **COOK:** 5 MINUTES **STAND:** 30 MINUTES

- 12 oz. fresh green beans, dry tips trimmed, if required
- 2 Tbsp. water
- ⅓ cup fresh parsley, coarsely chopped
- 4 green onions, sliced (green tops only)
- 2 stalks celery, cut into ½-inch slices
- 2 Tbsp. olive oil
- 2 Tbsp. lime juice
  Smoked sea salt, sea salt, or salt
  Lime wedges (optional)

1. In a 1½- or 2-quart microwave-safe casserole combine green beans and water. Cover and microwave on 100% power (high) for 5 to 7 minutes or just until tender, stirring once after 3 minutes. Drain in a colander. Rinse with cold water; drain again. Transfer to a serving dish. Toss with parsley, green onion tops, celery, oil, and lime juice. Cover and let stand up to 30 minutes.

2. Sprinkle with smoked sea salt just before serving. If desired, squeeze lime wedges over each serving. Makes 4 to 6 servings.

 Healthy

EACH SERVING: 96 cal., 7 g total fat (1 g sat. fat), 0 mg chol., 134 mg sodium, 8 g carbo., 4 g fiber, 2 g pro. Daily Values: 24% vit. A, 36% vit. C, 6% calcium, 8% iron.

Zap in the flavor

Microwave ovens are a summer cook's ally; they don't heat up the kitchen, and the quick cooking leaves time for after-dinner fun.

More important, no other appliance has the ability to time cooking down to the second, making microwave cooking the single best way to coax many fruits and vegetables to the point of perfect tenderness without overcooking them. Peas, squash, eggplant, and most other vegetables sweeten, soften, and develop more complex flavors after only a few minutes in the microwave oven. It's easy to further enhance the flavors by tossing in a handful of herbs or splashing on a little olive oil.

Keep it simple

When fruits and vegetables are so perfect, take advantage of summer's bounty and serve them at their freshest best—no cooking at all. A little slicing or a cool dressing and they're ready to serve. These summer-fresh meals have staying power; they'll satisfy the yen for something hearty and fuel an hour or two of after-dinner work or play. The meats—rotisserie chicken and smoked fish—are ready-cooked from a deli counter. Delis also offer other fortifying foods—cheeses, hearty breads, and dry salamis—that combine with an easy-to-toss medley of chopped vegetables drizzled with dressing.

Go grill crazy

Who wouldn't love to take credit for cooking an entire dinner on the grill? In addition to giving the cook a chance to enjoy the outdoors, grilling adds flavor and texture. Asparagus comes off the grill crispy outside, tender inside; zucchini grilled cut side down takes on smoky sweetness; and pineapple gains richness and sweetness that puts ice cream to shame.

The grill rewards bold choices. Cook two or three vegetables you never dreamed would go together and you'll be delighted by how well they turn out. For instance, beets make a surprisingly hearty side dish when brushed with oil and grilled with red onions and portobello mushrooms.

Carrot-Cucumber Gazpacho uses a carton of carrot juice blended with a couple of whole tomatoes. Then it's your choice of chopped vegetables to add: Try peppery radishes, arugula, corn, and red onions.

Microwave cooking prevents fresh flavor from boiling away in soups and stews such as Shore Chowder. This hearty combination of fish, spinach, tomatoes, and onions has a secret (and easy) ingredient—a healthful dollop of pasta sauce.

Carrot-Cucumber Gazpacho

The color of the soup will be darker or lighter depending on the kind of tomatoes used.

PREP: 25 MINUTES **CHILL:** 1 HOUR

- 2 large (about 1 lb.) tomatoes, quartered and seeded
- 1 1/2 cups carrot juice
- 2 Tbsp. coarsely chopped fresh chives
- 1 medium cucumber, seeded and coarsely chopped (1 1/2 cups)
- 1 1/2 cups fresh corn kernels (3 ears) (optional)
- 1/4 of a jicama, peeled and chopped (1 cup)
- 1/2 cup arugula, shredded
- 1 to 2 Tbsp. prepared horseradish
- 1/2 tsp. salt
- 4 large or 6 small radishes, quartered or cut into chunks
  Shredded arugula (optional)
  Coarsely chopped radishes (optional)
  Fresh corn (optional)
  Lime wedges (optional)

1. In a blender container or food processor bowl combine tomatoes, carrot juice, and chives. Cover and blend or process until smooth. Transfer mixture to a large bowl. Stir in cucumber, corn (if desired), jicama, the 1/2 cup arugula, horseradish, and salt. Cover and refrigerate at least 1 hour or up to 24 hours before serving.

2. Ladle soup into bowls or glasses. Top with the cut-up radishes. If desired, top with additional shredded arugula, radishes, and corn. Pass lime wedges. Makes 5 side-dish servings.

 Healthy **EACH SERVING:** 66 cal., 0 g total fat (0 g sat. fat), 0 mg chol., 270 mg sodium, 15 g carbo., 2 g fiber, 2 g pro. Daily Values: 299% vit. A, 44% vit. C, 4% calcium, 5% iron.

Carrot-Cucumber Gazpacho

Shore Chowder

This recipe will also work well with game fish such as trout.

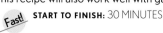 **START TO FINISH:** 30 MINUTES

- 1/4 cup lime mayonnaise or regular mayonnaise with 1/4 teaspoon shredded lime peel stirred in
- 2 cloves garlic, minced
- 1 14-oz. can reduced-sodium chicken broth
- 4 small carrots, peeled and cut into matchstick-size strips, or 1 1/2 cups packaged fresh precut julienned carrots
- 1 1/2 cups purchased puttanesca sauce or 1 recipe Puttanesca Sauce
- 1 cup grape or cherry tomatoes
- 1 lb. fresh or frozen skinless fish fillets, such as cod, sole, or striped bass, thawed and cut into 2-inch pieces
- 2 cups fresh baby spinach
  Sliced baguette-style French bread, toasted if desired

1. In a small bowl combine lime mayonnaise and garlic; set aside.

2. In a 3-quart microwave-safe bowl combine chicken broth and carrots. Microwave, covered, on 100% power (high) for 4 to 5 minutes or until crisp-tender, stirring once halfway through cooking.

3. Uncover carrot mixture. Stir in puttanesca sauce, tomatoes, and fish. Microwave, covered, on 100% power (high) for 3 to 4 minutes or until fish just begins to flake easily, stirring once halfway through cooking. Stir in spinach. Ladle fish and vegetables into serving bowls. Pass mayonnaise mixture with bread slices to serve with chowder. Makes 4 servings.

PUTTANESCA SAUCE: In a large skillet cook 1/2 cup chopped onion and 3 cloves garlic, minced, in 1 tablespoon olive oil over low heat until tender. Add one 14 1/2-ounce can diced tomatoes, undrained; 1/4 cup dry red wine or 1/4 cup chicken broth; 2 tablespoons tomato paste; and 1/8 teaspoon crushed red pepper. Bring to boiling; reduce heat. Simmer, uncovered, for 15 to 20 minutes or until sauce is desired consistency. Stir in 12 pitted kalamata olives; 3 tablespoons snipped fresh parsley; 3 canned anchovy fillets, cut into 1/2-inch pieces; and 1 tablespoon capers, drained and chopped. Heat through.

EACH SERVING: 380 cal., 16 g total fat (2 g sat. fat), 64 mg chol., 1,168 mg sodium, 28 g carbo., 5 g fiber, 26 g pro. Daily Values: 157% vit. A, 38% vit. C, 10% calcium, 17% iron.

SIMMER UP SOME SUPPER WITH THIS SAVORY, VEGGIE-PACKED FISH STEW. THE BEST PART? MOST OF IT IS MADE IN THE MICROWAVE OVEN!

Shore Chowder

Cauliflower Wedges with Lemon Dressing

In this recipe, cauliflower wedges are steamed in the microwave and then drizzled with a lemon dressing. When topped with capers and thin slices of cheese and ham it adds up to a delicious reason to embrace new recommendations to eat seven servings daily of fruits and vegetables.

Cauliflower Wedges with Lemon Dressing

Serrano ham comes from Spain; find it in some specialty markets or at www.tienda.com. Substitute with any other thinly sliced ham.

Fast! **START TO FINISH:** 20 MINUTES

- 2 small heads cauliflower
- 2 to 3 oz. thinly sliced Serrano ham, cooked ham, or prosciutto
- 2 oz. Manchego cheese or Jack cheese, thinly sliced or crumbled
- ¼ cup olive oil or cooking oil
- 2 Tbsp. lemon juice
- 1 clove garlic, minced
- ½ tsp. salt
- ¼ tsp. sugar
- ¼ tsp. dry mustard
- ¼ tsp. freshly ground black pepper
- 2 Tbsp. toasted pine nuts
- 2 Tbsp. capers, drained

1. Remove heavy leaves and tough stems from cauliflower; cut into 4 to 6 wedges each. Place cauliflower in a microwave-safe 3-quart casserole. Add ½ cup *water*. Microwave, covered, on 100% power (high) for 7 to 9 minutes or just until tender. Remove with a slotted spoon to serving plates. Top with ham and cheese.

2. In a screw-top jar combine oil, lemon juice, garlic, salt, sugar, mustard, and pepper. Cover and shake well to combine; drizzle over cauliflower, ham, and cheese. Sprinkle with pine nuts and capers. Makes 4 servings.

EACH SERVING: 207 cal., 18 g total fat (3 g sat. fat), 10 mg chol., 848 mg sodium, 7 g carbo., 4 g fiber, 9 g pro. Daily Values: 3% vit. A, 170% vit. C, 4% calcium, 8% iron.

GOOD TO KNOW

Showing up at farmers' markets and produce aisles is a broccoli-cauliflower relative called Romanesco (roh-mah-NEHS-koh), which—despite its dramatic appearance—has a milder flavor than the usual variety. It's also called Romanesca. To use it in this recipe (*above*), substitute 4 small heads Romanesco for the amount of cauliflower called for in the recipe.

Halve a head of romaine lettuce and pile it high with peaches, mint leaves, and a quarter of a take-out chicken for Southern Chicken Salad. Drizzle all with a creamy mustard dressing. The result? In 20 minutes you can be back at the pool for an after-dinner dip.

Southern Chicken Salad

This recipe is also a great way to use leftover barbecued chicken. The "Southern" part of this dish's name refers to the peaches and chicken, a beloved combination below the Mason-Dixon Line, especially when combined with a creamy mustard dressing.

 START TO FINISH: 20 MINUTES

- ½ cup purchased crème fraîche or dairy sour cream
- ¼ cup white wine vinegar
- 3 to 4 Tbsp. Dijon-style mustard
- 2 cloves garlic, minced
- ½ tsp. salt
- ¼ tsp. ground black pepper
- 2 small heads romaine lettuce
- 4 slices thick-cut bread, toasted, or large slices sourdough bread, toasted
- 2 to 4 Tbsp. purchased honey-butter
- 1 2- to 2½-lb. purchased rotisserie chicken, cut into quarters*
- 4 medium peaches or nectarines, pitted and sliced
- ½ cup lightly packed small fresh mint leaves
- 2 Tbsp. shredded fresh basil or marjoram leaves

Southern Chicken Salad

1. For dressing, in a small bowl whisk together crème fraîche, vinegar, mustard, garlic, salt, and pepper; set aside.

2. Remove a few outer leaves from romaine heads. Reserve removed leaves for another use. Halve romaine heads lengthwise. Spread each toast slice with honey-butter; place one slice on each of 4 serving plates. Top each with a half head of romaine. Arrange chicken and peaches on greens. Sprinkle with mint and basil. Drizzle with dressing. Makes 4 servings.

***NOTE:** Chicken can be warm or chilled in this salad.

EACH SERVING: 677 cal., 36 g total fat (13 g sat. fat), 218 mg chol., 965 mg sodium, 37 g carbo., 3 g fiber, 52 g pro. Daily Values: 25% vit. A, 28% vit. C, 14% calcium, 33% iron.

ADD ELEGANCE TO SUMMER LUNCHES WITH SIMPLE ADDITIONS SUCH AS FRESH-FROM-THE-GARDEN ROSE PETALS.

Rose and Berry Summer Salad

Iced waters—with flavors that come from being steeped with fruit and herbs—are one of the simplest, most refreshing ways to appreciate the best of what summer has to offer. Whether you choose the blueberry-rosemary version or the citrus-melon combination, they'll be a hit during the hot months.

A little finery from the garden—rose petals—adds a lively accent to this guest-worthy Rose and Berry Summer Salad featuring red lettuces. The salad is paired with smoked black cod and a wedge of soft cheese.

Rose and Berry Summer Salad

The brands of sheep's milk cheese found in your grocery store or specialty cheese shop vary around the country, but they are increasingly available. Or refer to www.zingermans.com or www.blacksheepcheese.com.

 START TO FINISH: 25 MINUTES

- 7 oz. soft sheep's milk cheese or Brie cheese
- 6 cups mixed baby greens with baby red lettuce leaves or salad greens such as red romaine, red oak leaf, or other red lettuce leaves
- ¼ cup snipped rose petals or other assorted edible flowers*
- 8 to 12 oz. smoked black cod (sablefish), smoked whitefish, or smoked salmon, bones removed and cut into 6 pieces
- ¼ cup snipped fresh dill
- ¼ cup salad oil
- ¼ cup Champagne vinegar or white wine vinegar
- 1 tsp. sugar
- ½ tsp. ground cardamom
- ½ tsp. coarsely ground black pepper
  Sea salt or salt, and freshly ground black pepper
- 3 cups raspberries or blackberries

1. Cut cheese into thin wedges. In a large bowl toss greens and rose petals.
2. On 6 salad plates arrange cheese, fish, and mixed greens. Sprinkle with dill.
3. For dressing, in a small screw-top jar combine oil, vinegar, sugar, cardamom, and ½ teaspoon coarsely ground pepper. Cover tightly and shake until well combined. Season dressing with sea salt and freshly ground black pepper. Drizzle dressing over fish and greens. Serve with fresh berries. Makes 6 servings.

*NOTE: Use only flowers that have been grown without pesticides or other chemicals. Find them in the produce section of some supermarkets or from mail-order flower and herb farms. Avoid florist-shop flowers, which are sometimes treated with chemicals. Only eat flowers that are known to be edible.

EACH SERVING: 304 cal., 22 g total fat (10 g sat. fat), 47 mg chol., 786 mg sodium, 7 g carbo., 5 g fiber, 18 g pro. Daily Values: 7% vit. A, 25% vit. C, 22% calcium, 5% iron.

Summer-Flavored Waters

PREP: 10 MINUTES EACH CHILL: 2 HOURS

- 2 or 3 slices ripe honeydew melon
- 1 lime, sliced ¼ inch thick
- 4 mint sprigs
- 2 quarts water
  Ice cubes

1. Add melon slices, lime slices, and mint sprigs to a large pitcher. Fill pitcher with the water. Refrigerate for 2 to 4 hours to allow fruit and herbs to transfer flavors to water. To serve, fill glasses with ice. Top with flavored water. Makes 8 (8-ounce) servings each recipe.

 EACH SERVING: 9 cal., 0 g total fat (0 g sat. fat), 0 mg chol., 5 mg sodium, 2 g carbo., 1 g fiber, 0 g pro. Daily Values: 1% vit. A, 3% vit. C, 1% calcium, 0% iron.

HERB-AND-BERRY FLAVORED WATER: Substitute 1 cup fresh blueberries, lightly crushed, and two 4-inch sprigs fresh rosemary, lightly bruised, for the melon, lime, and mint. Fill pitcher with water, refrigerate 2 to 4 hours, and serve as above.

Summer-Flavored Waters

IS THE FAMILY TIRED OF HOMEGROWN TOMATOES BY THE END OF THE SUMMER? KEEP THE JUICY FRUIT FRESH AND INTERESTING WITH THE ADDITION OF CRISPY GRILLED POLENTA.

Grilled Polenta and Tomato Relish

A simple way to add juicy appeal to almost any dish from the grill is to reach for Tomato Relish—vine-ripe tomatoes tossed with tequila dressing. Stack those red and green beauties high along with Grilled Polenta, crusty grilled bread, chicken breasts, or a grilled pork tenderloin.

Grilled Polenta and Tomato Relish

To make this dish without using the stove at all, use purchased polenta.*

PREP: 30 MINUTES **GRILL:** 10 MINUTES **STAND:** 30 MINUTES
CHILL: 3 HOURS

1²/₃	cups water
1	Tbsp. butter
1	Tbsp. packed brown sugar
½	tsp. salt
¾	cup yellow cornmeal
1	cup cold water
½	tsp. salt
3	small red tomatoes, cut into wedges and seeded
3	small green tomatoes, cut into ½-inch slices
1	Tbsp. olive oil
1	Tbsp. tequila or orange juice
1 to 3	tsp. packed brown sugar
1	tsp. chili powder
	Olive oil

1. Line a 9-inch round baking pan with foil, extending foil over edges. Grease foil; set aside. In a medium saucepan bring the 1²/₃ cups water, butter, 1 tablespoon brown sugar, and ½ teaspoon salt to boiling.

2. Meanwhile, in small bowl stir together cornmeal, 1 cup cold water, and ½ teaspoon salt. Slowly add moistened cornmeal mixture to boiling water, stirring constantly. Cook and stir just until mixture returns to boiling. Reduce heat to low. Cook, uncovered, for 10 to 15 minutes or until mixture is very thick, stirring occasionally. Evenly spread the cornmeal mixture in prepared pan. Cool; refrigerate, covered, for 3 to 24 hours.

3. For the Tomato Relish: In a large bowl combine red tomatoes, green tomatoes, the 1 tablespoon olive oil, the tequila, 1 to 3 teaspoons brown sugar, and chili powder. Cover and refrigerate until serving time. Let stand at room temperature 30 minutes before serving.

4. Using foil, lift cornmeal mixture from pan and gently cut into 8 wedges. Generously brush wedges with additional olive oil and grill directly over medium-hot coals for 10 to 15 minutes or until golden, turning as needed to brown evenly. (To prepare indoors: In a 12-inch skillet heat wedges in 1 tablespoon hot olive oil over medium heat for 10 to 15 minutes or until golden, turning occasionally.)

5. To serve, layer 2 grilled polenta wedges with Tomato Relish on each plate. Spoon any of the remaining Tomato Relish mixture over all. Makes 4 side-dish servings.

*NOTE: To use purchased polenta, omit water, butter, the 1 tablespoon of brown sugar, salt, cornmeal, cold water, and salt. Slice a 16-ounce tube refrigerated cooked polenta into ½-inch slices. Grill or cook in skillet as directed in Step 4.

EACH SERVING: 234 cal., 11 g total fat (3 g sat. fat), 8 mg chol., 627 mg sodium, 30 g carbo., 4 g fiber, 4 g pro. Daily Values: 25% vit. A, 38% vit. C, 3% calcium, 6% iron.

Bull's-Eye Burgers

There's one less thing to bring to the table when you shape burgers around fresh onion slices before they go on the grill. In addition to looking delicious, the onion slices keep these Bull's-Eye Burgers moist.

Bull's-Eye Burgers

Start the burgers onion side up to ensure the onion is nestled securely in the beef. Even when the ground beef firms up, turn carefully to keep onions intact.

 PREP: 20 MINUTES **GRILL:** 10 MINUTES

- 1 large sweet onion, such as Vidalia or Maui
- 1 lb. lean ground beef
- 1½ tsp. garlic powder
- ½ tsp. salt
- ¼ tsp. ground black pepper
- 8 red and/or green kale leaves or other desired lettuce, stems removed
- 2 tsp. olive oil
- 4 ¾-inch slices hearty bread or Texas toast, toasted
- 4 slices Swiss cheese (4 oz.) (optional)

1. Peel and cut onion into four ¼-inch-thick slices; reserve remaining onion for another use. Shape beef loosely into four ½-inch-thick patties; sprinkle with garlic powder, salt, and pepper. Press 1 onion slice into the center of each patty and shape meat around onion until top of onion is flush with the surface of the beef patty.

2. FOR A CHARCOAL GRILL: Place patties, onion sides up, on the rack of an uncovered grill directly over medium coals. Grill for 10 to 13 minutes or until meat is done (160°F), carefully turning once halfway through grilling with a spatula. Lightly brush kale leaves with oil and add to grill the last 1 to 1½ minutes of grilling.

FOR A GAS GRILL: Preheat grill. Reduce heat to medium. Place patties, onion sides up, on grill rack over heat. Cover and grill as above. Lightly brush kale leaves with oil and add to grill the last 1 to 1½ minutes of grilling.

3. To serve, place 2 kale leaves on each bread slice. Top with a slice of cheese, if desired, then the beef patty, onion side up. Makes 4 servings.

EACH SERVING: 475 cal., 24 g total fat (10 g sat. fat), 147 mg chol., 648 mg sodium, 31 g carbo., 2 g fiber, 36 g pro. Daily Values: 159% vit. A, 104% vit. C, 35% calcium, 25% iron.

Red and Orange Stuffed Peppers with Honey-Herb Steaks is quick to assemble. Toss cooked rice with dried cherries, squeeze on some lemon juice, and create a memorable side dish from whole sweet peppers. If they're available, use small peppers, one for each person. Finally, dust the steaks with some of the lemon peel, coriander, and pepper mixture.

Red and Orange Stuffed Peppers with Honey-Herb Steaks

Crush coriander or fennel seeds called for in this recipe in a mortar and pestle or with the back of a spoon in the bottom of a small, sturdy bowl.

PREP: 35 MINUTES **GRILL:** 25 MINUTES

- 2 to 4 twelve-inch wooden or metal skewers
- 1 8.8-oz. pouch cooked whole grain brown rice or cooked long grain rice
- 1/3 cup dried tart cherries
- 1/3 cup snipped fresh cilantro
- 4 tsp. finely shredded lemon peel
- 2 Tbsp. lemon juice
- 1 Tbsp. honey
- 1/2 tsp. salt
- 4 small red, yellow, or green sweet peppers (4 oz. each)*
- 1 1/2 tsp. coriander seeds, crushed, or 1 tsp. fennel seeds, crushed
- 3/4 tsp. salt
- 1/2 tsp. freshly ground black pepper
- 2 1- to 1 1/4-lb. beef porterhouse or T-bone steaks, cut 1 inch thick

Red and Orange Stuffed Peppers with Honey-Herb Steaks

1. Soak wooden skewers in water for least 1 hour before grilling. In a medium bowl combine unheated rice (break up any clumps of rice), cherries, cilantro, 2 teaspoons of the lemon peel, the lemon juice, honey, and the 1/2 teaspoon salt; set aside.

2. Cut tops off sweet peppers; reserve tops. Cut a very thin slice from the bottom of each pepper to make a flat surface. Discard bottom slices. Carefully remove seeds and membranes from pepper cavities, keeping peppers intact. Spoon rice mixture into peppers. To help stabilize the pepper, thread peppers, open ends up, onto skewers, poking 2 skewers through each pepper. Replace pepper tops.

3. In a small bowl combine remaining 2 teaspoons lemon peel, the coriander seeds, 3/4 teaspoon salt, and the black pepper. Trim fat from steaks. Sprinkle peel mixture on steaks; rub mixture in with your fingers.

4. **FOR A CHARCOAL GRILL:** Arrange medium-hot coals around outside edges of grill, leaving as large a space as possible in the center for the peppers. Test for medium heat in center of grill. Place peppers, top sides up, on grill rack in center of grill so that they are not over any coals. Cover and grill for 25 to 35 minutes or until peppers are crisp-tender and rice mixture is heated through. During the last half of pepper grilling time, place steaks on grill rack directly over the medium-hot coals around the edge of the grill. Cover and grill to desired doneness, turning once halfway through grilling. Allow 10 to 13 minutes for medium rare (145° F) and 12 to 15 minutes for medium (160° F). Makes 4 servings.

FOR A GAS GRILL: Preheat grill. Reduce heat to medium-hot. Adjust for indirect cooking according to manufacturer's directions. Cover and grill as above.

*__NOTE:__ If you can't find small peppers, use two 8- to 10-ounce sweet peppers and divide the rice mixture into the two peppers. Cut peppers in half to serve.

EACH SERVING: 407 cal., 12 g total fat (4 g sat. fat), 83 mg chol., 811 mg sodium, 38 g carbo., 4 g fiber, 36 g pro. Daily Values: 69% vit. A, 265% vit. C, 3% calcium, 27% iron.

When summer fruit is perfectly ripe, the best way to use it is the simplest. For the apricot pie, a foil pan and a ready-to-use piecrust let you create a dessert that's ready to go on the grill in about 20 minutes. To bake the pie, push the coals to the sides of the grill. Place the pie in the center, close the lid, and bake, using the grill as an oven.

Hot-off-the-Grill Apricot Pie

The chipotle chile powder gives the pie just a hint of heat. The pan size called for is one of the most widely available nationwide, but a half inch either way in the dimensions won't make any difference.
PREP: 20 MINUTES **GRILL:** 40 MINUTES **STAND:** 45 MINUTES

    ½ of a 15-oz. pkg. rolled refrigerated unbaked piecrust (1 crust)
    ¼ cup packed brown sugar
    2 tsp. all-purpose flour
    ⅛ tsp. ground cardamom
    ⅛ tsp. ground chipotle chile pepper or chili powder (optional)
    1 lb. (5 to 6) apricots, halved and pitted, or two 15-oz. cans unpeeled apricot halves in light syrup, drained
    ¾ cup granola with raisins
    2 Tbsp. pistachio nuts or pecan halves
    1 7⅞×5⅜×1⅛-inch disposable foil pan
    Vanilla bean ice cream (optional)

1. Bring piecrust to room temperature according to package directions. Meanwhile, in a medium bowl combine brown sugar, flour, cardamom, and, if desired, ground chipotle pepper. Add apricots. Gently toss until coated; set aside.* In another bowl combine granola and nuts; set aside.

2. Lightly grease disposable pan or lightly coat with nonstick cooking spray; ease crust into pan, allowing edges of crust to hang over edges of pan. Spoon apricot mixture into pastry-lined pan. Sprinkle with granola mixture. Fold crust edges over filling.

3. FOR A CHARCOAL GRILL: Arrange medium-hot coals around outer edges of grill, leaving as large a space as possible in the center. Place pan on grill rack in the center of the grill so it is not over any coals. Cover and grill for 40 minutes or until piecrust is golden brown, fresh fruit is tender, and filling is bubbly.

FOR A GAS GRILL: Preheat grill. Reduce heat to medium. Adjust for indirect cooking according to manufacturer's directions. Place pan on grill rack away from heat. Cover and grill as above.

OVEN METHOD: Preheat oven to 350°F. Place disposable pan on a baking sheet. Bake on the bottom rack of the oven for 50 minutes or until pastry is golden brown, fresh fruit is tender, and filling is bubbly.

4. Remove pan from grill and let stand 45 minutes before serving. Serve warm and, if desired, with vanilla bean ice cream. Makes 6 servings.

*NOTE: If mixture with fresh apricots seems dry, let stand for 10 minutes before transferring to pastry-lined pan.

EACH SERVING: 304 cal., 13 g total fat (5 g sat. fat), 7 mg chol., 141 mg sodium, 44 g carbo., 3 g fiber, 4 g pro. Daily Values: 24% vit. A, 10% vit. C, 4% calcium, 5% iron.

When forming the crust, press gently into the sides and corners but don't trim the top. Its irregular shape adds to the charm of the pie when it's folded in over the filling.

DESSERT FROM THE GRILL TAKES ON NEW MEANING WITH THIS FUN APRICOT PIE. WITH THE EASE OF PURCHASED PIECRUST, ALL YOU HAVE TO DO IS FILL AND GRILL.

Hot-off-the-Grill Apricot Pie

TUSCAN-STYLE
This Italian hybrid cantaloupe is deep orange and has sweeter taste than its American cousin. As the melon ripens, the green exterior grooves turn golden cream color.

SUMMER-RIPE MELONS

Juicy, fragrant, and refreshing melons are ready to enjoy in

salads, chilled soups, and day-camp lunch boxes. Just cut them open to find creamy texture and a panoply of pastel color. Sweet melons—on their own, tumbled over sherbet, or served with sweet and salty appetizers—are the perfect summer treat.

The melon clan includes muskmelons—cantaloupe is the most familiar—and watermelons. See the guide, *opposite*, for muskmelon varieties and qualities.

Test for melon ripeness at the stem end. It should yield a little to gentle pressure; the rest of the melon should be firm. Muskmelons, when ripe, fall away from the stem easily, leaving a rounded hollow at the end. If the stem is attached, avoid it; the melon was harvested too early and time won't help the ripening process. The smell should be fragrant. Store whole melons at room temperature; store cut melons in the refrigerator, tightly covered, for two to three days.

BY **STEPHEN EXEL** PHOTOGRAPH BY **GREG SCHEIDEMANN, [N] HAUS FOTO**

SPRITE This hybrid offspring of honeydew is smaller and super sweet. This one mixes well with citrus fruits.

CRENSHAW Fragrant and spicy-sweet, this melon is one of the most succulent. It ranges from 5 to 9 pounds.

GALIA Aromatic flesh surrounded by a beige rind characterizes this melon. This late-season fruit is very sweet due to its high sugar content.

SHARLYN Use this very perishable melon within two days of purchase. It tastes like honeydew with intense flavor.

ORANGE FLESH HONEYDEW This hybrid honeydew teams well with salty prosciutto and jazzes up a summer fruit salsa.

CASABA With flavor similar to cucumber or squash, this melon adds mellow flavor to salads. It is juicy with little aroma.

LOOKS COUNT

- The fine maze of lines across the surface of melons such as cantaloupe or Galia is called netting. When buying a melon, look for thick, raised netting.
- The crackling across the surface of some melons, such as Sharlyns or Sprites, is not a sign of old age. These are sugar cracks, good indicators of sweetness. The deeper the crackling, the sweeter the melon.
- Weight is important. When shopping, compare the weights of several melons of equal size and then choose the heavyweight. This melon is closer to its picking date; the others have had a chance to dehydrate, losing sweet flavor along with weight.

PHOTOGRAPHS BY COLLEEN DUFFLEY

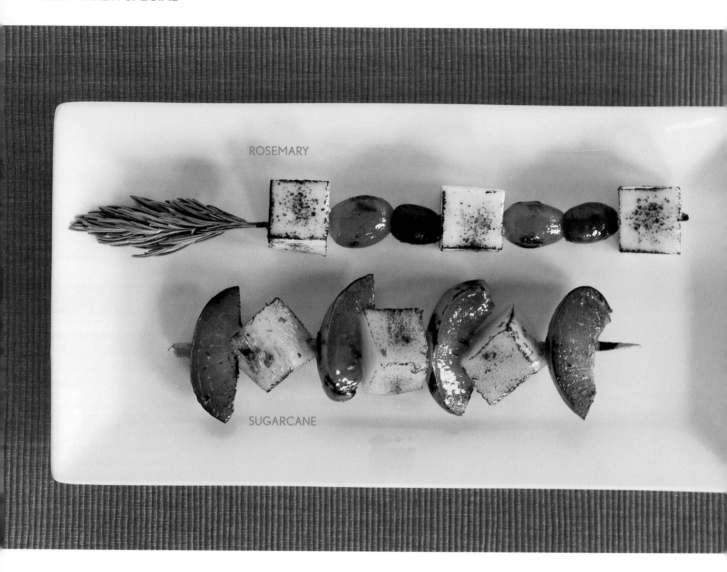

ROSEMARY

SUGARCANE

BRANCH OUT
WITH SKEWERS

Step into your garden, the farmer's market, or grocery store

and pluck a handful of edible skewers for kabobs that yield garden-fresh accents. Sugarcane, lavender, lemongrass, and rosemary each have enormous flavor profiles that penetrate the food they contact. The subtle sweetness of sugarcane or the floral notes of lavender pair well with fruit. Lemongrass adds a citrus tang to seafood, and rosemary's lemony-pine burst permeates cheeses, chicken, and fish. Fresh stems—rather than dried—make sturdier skewers and provide the best flavor.

BY **JUDITH FERTIG** PHOTOGRAPHS BY **GREG SCHEIDEMANN, [N] HAUS FOTO**

LEMONGRASS

LAVENDER

ROSEMARY BRANCHES:
Remove all but 1 inch of rosemary leaves from several 6-inch woody branches. Carefully thread squares of haloumi cheese or queso blanco (cheese may crack slightly), pitted black olives, and cherry tomatoes onto the branches. Cook on a greased grill rack for 1 to 2 minutes on each side or until the cheese becomes golden brown.

SUGARCANE STALKS: Use a paring knife to taper ends of sugarcane stalks to a point. Skewer pineapple chunks and plum slices. Grill on a greased grill rack directly over medium-hot coals for 1 minute on each side. Or skip the grilling and serve fresh fruit, such as banana chunks, cherries, and mango chunks, on the sugarcane skewers.

LEMONGRASS STALKS: Strip the tough outer layers from 6 to 8 lemongrass stalks until they're pencil thin; set aside. In a bowl combine 1/2 cup canned coconut milk, 1 to 2 teaspoons green curry paste, and 1 tablespoon chopped lemongrass. Add 1 pound of fish, cut in 1 1/2-inch cubes. Marinate for 30 minutes. Meanwhile, use a sharp knife to cut a point at one end of each of the lemongrass stalks. Skewer the cubes of fish onto stalks. Grill over medium heat for 2 minutes on each side or until fish flakes easily with a fork.

LAVENDER: Remove and reserve about half of the buds from the lower portion of 6-inch woody lavender branches. Thread halved, pitted apricots onto branches. In a saucepan combine 1/2 cup honey, 1/4 cup butter, and 1/2 teaspoon lavender buds. Cook over medium-high heat until boiling. Reduce heat; cook, uncovered, for 10 minutes. Pour mixture through a sieve to remove lavender buds. Brush sieved mixture onto apricots. Grill on a greased grill rack directly over medium-hot coals for 1 minute on each side.

ADD FLAVOR WITH BRINING

Golden color and distinctive flavor are characteristics of roasted brined chicken.

Put this popular technique of

flavoring a Thanksgiving turkey to work year-round. Brining works equally well for poultry and pork, and grilling or roasting. The cured meat imparts succulent moistness and beautiful golden color.

Begin with the Basic Brine (recipe, *right*)—a solution of water, kosher salt, garlic, and peppercorns—and a whole chicken. Then experiment with other cuts of meat, adding a variety of herbs and spices to the basic recipe to give dinnertime the flavors of Spain, France, or India. Serve complementary side dishes and you'll experience a sophisticated cuisine without leaving home.

Depending on which meat you use, the brining process takes from 1 to 24 hours. Make the timing work to your advantage. While the meat soaks up flavor in the refrigerator, relax and plan the rest of your meal. When it's time to cook, rinse off the brine mixture and cook the meat to golden doneness.

BRINES WITH GLOBAL FLAVORS

Indian-, French-, and Spanish-inspired brine solutions can be made simply by adding flavorful herbs and spices to the Basic Brine (recipe, *right*).

INDIA: To Basic Brine, add two 3-inch sticks cinnamon and 2 tablespoons *each* whole cloves; anise seeds, slightly crushed; and curry powder.

FRANCE: Add one 0.6-oz. jar (½ cup) herbes de Provence, or mix your own blend using at least five of these dried spices: basil, fennel, lavender, marjoram, rosemary, sage, savory, or thyme.

SPAIN: Add 3 tablespoons ground chipotle chile pepper; 3 tablespoons toasted cumin seeds, slightly crushed; and 2 tablespoons coriander seeds, slightly crushed. Caution: Prepare this brine in a well-ventilated area; fumes will be strong.

BY **STEPHEN EXEL** PHOTOGRAPHS BY **GREG SCHEIDEMANN, [N] HAUS FOTO**

Basic Brine

PREP: 15 MINUTES **MARINATE:** 10 HOURS **ROAST:** 1 HOUR
STAND: 10 MINUTES

- 1 gallon water
- 1 cup kosher salt
- 8 medium cloves garlic, peeled and halved
- 2 Tbsp. cracked peppercorns
- 1 3½- to 4-lb. whole chicken

1. In a stockpot bring the water to boiling. Add salt, garlic, and peppercorns. Stir to dissolve salt. Remove from heat; cool. Refrigerate until chilled.

2. Transfer chilled brine to container large enough to hold chicken and brine. Place chicken, breast side down, in container; cover with brine. Cover with plastic wrap. Weight chicken down with a plate to keep it submerged. Marinate in refrigerator for 10 to 12 hours.

3. TO PREPARE CHICKEN FOR ROASTING: Preheat oven to 425°F. Remove chicken from brine; rinse. Place chicken, breast side down, on a rack in a roasting pan; roast for 30 minutes. Turn chicken breast side up. Roast 30 minutes more or until drumsticks move easily in sockets and chicken is no longer pink (180°F). Remove chicken from oven. Cover; let stand 10 minutes before carving.

4. TO PREPARE CHICKEN FOR GRILLING: Prepare grill for indirect grilling. Test for medium heat above the drip pan. Remove chicken from brine; rinse. Place chicken, breast side down, on grill rack over drip pan. Grill, covered, for 30 minutes. Turn chicken breast side up; continue grilling for 45 minutes to 1¼ hours until drumsticks move easily in sockets and chicken is no longer pink (180°F). Makes 4 to 6 servings.

EACH SERVING: 566 cal., 39 g total fat (11 g sat. fat), 201 mg chol., 1,895 mg sodium, 0 g fiber, 50 g pro. Daily Values: 6% vit. A, 6% vit. C, 3% calcium, 12% iron.

In good taste
FOOD AND ENTERTAINING

GET TO THE GRILL

The secret to grilling perfection starts with some basic techniques. Three grill masters offer their advice for perfecting delicious summer grilling.

Elizabeth Karmel, creator of GirlsattheGrill.com and author of *Taming the Flame*, says her favorite tools are two sets of 12-inch locking tongs to turn meats on the grill (forks pierce food, allowing juices to escape). To avoid cross-contamination between raw and cooked foods, Karmel uses one pair marked with red tape to turn uncooked food on the grill and the other, marked with green, to remove cooked food.

Bobby Flay, star of TV show "Boy Meets Grill" and author of *Grilling for Life*, reminds people not to play with their food. "Brush your meat, fish, and vegetables with oil, season with salt and pepper, and place on a hot grill," he says. "Don't touch it for at least two minutes. It needs to form a crust so that it can naturally pull away from the grill. If you begin to turn it before the crust has formed, it will stick."

Steven Raichlen, author of *The Barbecue Bible* and *Raichlen's Indoor Grilling,* suggests letting grilled meats rest on a platter or cutting board a few minutes before serving. This allows the meat to "relax," which makes it more tender and juicy.

MAKING DAD'S FAVORITE PIE

When you need help making Dad's favorite pie, Mom always seems to know best. Monica Schenk, pie maker extraordinaire of Monica's Pies in upstate Naples, New York, says cherry is the favorite her customers snap up as a treat for Dad. Here are her tips for making a perfect cherry pie:

• Always use pastry flour. It has no gluten, so it makes a very tender crust. For a double-crust pie, add 1 teaspoon salt to the pastry for a better-tasting crust.

• For best flavor, use sour or tart cherries and add ½ teaspoon almond extract to the filling mixture.

• Dot the filling with 1 tablespoon of butter before baking for a richer flavor.

• To prevent overbrowning, cover the edge of the pie with foil.

• Bake the pie until the fruit bubbles in the center. To see if the pie is done, spoon out some of the juices through a hole in the top crust. The juice should be clear, not cloudy.

Schenk started her business more than 20 years ago, selling pies on the honor system from a roadside stand. Today Monica's Pies are still all baked by hand, although the business has grown to a four-story pie barn that sells 20,000 pies yearly.

PHOTOGRAPH BY **JEAN LAUGHTON**

THE SECRET'S IN THE SAUCE

Steak sauces have intense flavor well suited to grilled meats. Keep several flavor nuances on hand for experimenting. Virginia Gentleman has a smooth hit of 90-proof small batch bourbon that adds subtle flavor to grilled beef tenderloin steaks. New York restaurant BLT Steak's sauce heats up meaty T-bones with horseradish. Stonewall Kitchen's Mesquite Steak Sauce lends deep smoky taste to grilled chicken or pork chops. Sauces: Virginia Gentleman Bourbon Steak Sauce, $6.95; Ashman Mfg. & Dist.; 800/641-9924; www.thevirginiacompany.com. BLT Steak Sauce, $9; 212-752-7470. Mesquite Steak Sauce, $6; Stonewall Kitchen; 800/207-5267; www.stonewallkitchen.com.

PHOTOGRAPH BY **KIM CORNELISON**

JULY

DO IT YOUR WAY ON INDEPENDENCE DAY! PICK AND CHOOSE FROM THIS SELECTION OF SUMMER FOOD FAVORITES AND CELEBRATE TO YOUR HEART'S CONTENT.

Three-Way Marinade and Sauce
page 136

Four Steps to a Fabulous 4th

Skillet White Beans
page 138

Hot Dogs and Texas Tomato Chutney
page 139

Fourth of July Cherry-Cola Cake
page 144

Firecracker Coconut Dip
page 142

Four steps to a fabulous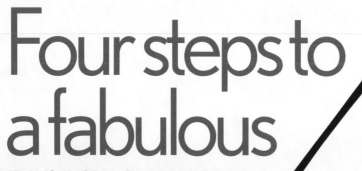

HOLIDAYS JUST WOULDN'T BE AS MUCH FUN WITHOUT A BEVY OF TREATS, SO LET FOOD SET THE MOOD AT YOUR NEXT SUMMER GET-TOGETHER. WHAT'LL IT BE? HOT DOGS AND ICE CREAM, OR RIBS AND COLA CAKE?

Red, White & Blueberry Ice Cream Dessert

Say it with food! For an easy way to show your true colors, layer sorbet and ice cream for patriotic stripes and dot with blueberries.

BY WINIFRED MORANVILLE PHOTOGRAPHS BY TINA RUPP PRODUCED BY DAVID ANGER

Kid Friendly Red, White & Blueberry Ice Cream Dessert

To save time when making the syrup, you can use herbal tea bags that contain hibiscus flowers, such as Red Zinger® brand tea.

PREP: 25 MINUTES **COOK:** 40 MINUTES **COOL:** SEVERAL HOURS
FREEZE: 5 HOURS

2 pints raspberry sorbet, softened
2 pints vanilla ice cream, softened
1 recipe Hibiscus Syrup
   Additional blueberries (optional)

1. Line two 8×4×2-inch loaf pans with foil, extending foil over pan edges; set aside. Spoon 1 pint of raspberry sorbet in each prepared pan; spread evenly. Cover and freeze 1 to 2 hours or until firm. A half hour before spreading second layer, allow vanilla ice cream to soften 30 minutes in refrigerator. Spoon 1 pint softened vanilla ice cream on raspberry sorbet in each pan. Cover; freeze 4 hours or overnight until ice cream is firm. Place serving platter in freezer.

2. To serve, remove ice cream loaves from pans, using foil to lift. Peel back foil and divide each loaf into 8 slices. Place slices on frozen serving platter. Serve with Hibiscus Syrup. If desired, scatter additional blueberries over slices. Makes 16 servings.

HIBISCUS SYRUP: In a large saucepan combine 4 cups water and 3 cups sugar. Bring to boiling, stirring to dissolve sugar. Add 2 cups dried hibiscus flowers or 8 Red Zinger® herbal tea bags. Reduce heat. If using flowers, boil gently for 40 to 50 minutes or until syrup is reduced to 3½ cups. If using tea bags, boil gently for 5 minutes. Remove tea bags with a slotted spoon. Continue boiling gently until tea mixture is reduced to 2½ cups. If using flowers, cool mixture 15 minutes; strain and discard flowers. Cover syrup and cool completely (syrup will thicken as it cools). Whisk 1 teaspoon ground cinnamon into syrup. Add 4 cups blueberries. Makes 4½ cups syrup.

EACH SERVING: 309 cal., 6 g total fat (4 g sat. fat), 34 mg chol., 24 mg sodium, 63 g carbo., 3 g fiber, 2 g pro. Daily Values: 5% vit. A, 8% vit. C, 5% calcium, 1% iron.

1 Choose the food:

Easy now. With sparklers to light, this is no time to fuss in the kitchen. Consider baked beans you don't have to bake. Or tap into a versatile marinade that goes with whatever is your pleasure: ribs, chicken, or pork roast. Too complicated? Hot dogs will do because frankly, franks are just perfect for the Fourth. Choose a recipe or two, then fill in the rest with easy options like potato chips and ice cream.

2 Get the look:

Red, white, and blue carry the day, but this year, let freedom ring. Liberate yourself from banners and bunting. Show off your own style while celebrating America's diversity. Pick up supplies at paper and fabric stores, ethnic markets, and unusual gift shops. A glue stick and scissors are all you'll need to cut and paste your way to crafty eye-candy decorations. For extra fun, let the kids get involved in the decorating. Not only will they be proud to have their work on display, but the colorful projects are sure to keep little hands and minds busy during hot summer days.

3 Add the fun:

It's the frills that signal to guests they're in for a great time. To pull it together in a memorable way, poke around town for some ready-to-hang touches. A trip to ethnic markets and out-of-the way gift shops for unique table decor and party favors will kick the good times up a notch and make for a merry family outing in itself. While you're out, look for unexpected treasure troves at art supply stores and charity shops. Of course, you could let fruit-filled summer recipes play out the red, white, and blue theme. Feel free to spin any idea your own way. Can't find piñatas? Try whirligigs or pinwheels from a garden supply or party supply store. If you love the patriotic gist of the Double-Berry Cooler but forgot to plan ahead, remember—the fruits show off just as colorfully if you serve them as toppings for a simple ice cream sundae. Make it fun. Make it yours.

4 Give a gift:

It's our nation's birthday, and everyone deserves a little something. Remember the thrill of the quirky dime-store find? Tap into that spirit with old-fashioned candies and little treasures, catching them wherever you can. While you're out shopping for everything else, head down uncharted aisles, scope out bottom shelves, and dig deep into bargain bins. If it's red, white, or blue—and inexpensive—go ahead and pick it up. Bring your treasures home and then wrap 'em, stack 'em, or just tuck in a ribbon or two.

Here are more choices than meet the eye. The marinade plays three ways: Mexican, Asian, or charged with orange and sage. Use it on ribs, *opposite*; chicken; or pork roast.

Three-Way Marinade and Sauce

This triple-purpose sauce works wonders on almost any cut of meat.

PREP: 30 MINUTES **MARINATE:** 8 HOURS **GRILL:** 1½ HOURS FOR RIBS AND ROAST; 1¼ HOURS FOR CHICKENS

- 1 8-oz. can tomato sauce
- ½ cup frozen apple juice concentrate, thawed
- ½ cup cider vinegar
- 1 clove garlic, minced
- ½ tsp. dry mustard
- ½ tsp. paprika
- ½ tsp. ground cumin
- ½ to 1 tsp. bottled hot pepper sauce
- 1 recipe Mexican Mole, Sesame-Hoisin, or Orange-Sage Sauce
- 6 to 8 lb. pork loin back ribs or meaty spareribs; one 3- to 3½-lb. boneless pork top loin roast; or two 3½- to 4-lb. whole broiler-fryer chickens

1. In a medium bowl combine tomato sauce, apple juice concentrate, vinegar, garlic, mustard, paprika, cumin, and hot pepper sauce. Stir in one of the flavor variations. Reserve ½ cup of the mixture in a covered container; refrigerate.

2. Place roast, ribs, or chicken in a resealable plastic bag(s) set in a shallow dish; pour in remaining mixture. Cover and refrigerate for 8 hours or overnight, turning bag(s) occasionally. Drain; discard marinade.

3. **FOR RIBS ON A CHARCOAL GRILL:** Arrange medium-hot coals around a drip pan. Test for medium heat above pan. Place ribs in rib racks* on grill rack over drip pan. Cover; grill for 1½ to 1¾ hours or until ribs are tender.

FOR RIBS ON A GAS GRILL: Preheat grill. Reduce heat to medium. Adjust for indirect cooking. Grill as above, except place ribs in a disposable foil roasting pan.

4. **FOR PORK ROAST ON A CHARCOAL GRILL:** Arrange medium-hot coals around a drip pan. Test for medium-low heat above the pan. Place roast on grill rack over drip pan. Cover and grill for 1½ to 2¼ hours or until meat thermometer inserted into roast registers 150°F. Remove roast from grill; cover with foil; let stand 15 minutes. During standing, temperature will rise about 10 degrees.

FOR PORK ROAST ON A GAS GRILL: Preheat grill. Reduce heat to medium-low. Adjust for indirect cooking. Place roast on a rack in a roasting pan; place on grill rack and grill until meat thermometer inserted into roast registers 150°F. Remove roast from grill; cover with foil and let stand for 15 minutes. During standing, temperature will rise about 10 degrees.

5. **FOR CHICKENS ON A CHARCOAL GRILL:** Skewer neck skins of chickens to backs; tie legs to tail. Twist wing tips under backs. For a charcoal grill, arrange medium-hot coals around a drip pan. Test for medium heat above the pan. Place chickens on grill rack over drip pan. Cover and grill for 1¼ to 1¾ hours or until drumsticks move easily in their sockets and chicken is no longer pink (180°F).

FOR CHICKENS ON A GAS GRILL: Preheat grill. Reduce heat to medium. Adjust for indirect cooking. Place chickens over drip pan. Cover and grill as above.

6. Heat ½ cup of reserved sauce and serve with pork or chicken. Makes 8 servings.

MEXICAN MOLE SAUCE: Whisk ⅓ cup purchased mole sauce into marinade.

SESAME-HOISIN SAUCE: Stir ¼ cup hoisin sauce, 2 tablespoons toasted sesame seeds, and 1 tablespoon toasted sesame oil into marinade.

ORANGE-SAGE SAUCE: Whisk 1½ teaspoons ground sage and 1 teaspoon finely shredded orange peel into marinade.

*****NOTE:** Use two grills for the ribs if you don't have a rib rack.

EACH SERVING (RIBS WITH MOLE VARIATION): 361 cal., 16 g total fat (6 g sat. fat), 101 mg chol., 110 mg sodium, 4 g carbo., 0 g fiber, 47 g pro. Daily Values: 1% vit. A, 2% vit. C, 2% calcium, 11% iron.

JALAPEÑO FIRECRACKERS

Wearing plastic gloves to protect hands, use a paring knife to cut through 4 to 6 red jalapeño or other small red chile peppers from just below the stems through the tip end, leaving pepper intact. Rotate and cut again two or three more times to form a brush. To create curls, place in a bowl of ice water; cover and refrigerate overnight. Drain. Rinse out seeds.

THIS MARINADE DOES TRIPLE DUTY BY MAKING A
SENSATIONAL SOAK FOR RIBS, PORK, AND CHICKEN—
NOT TO MENTION ITS THREE DIFFERENT POSSIBILITIES AS A
SERVE-ALONG SAUCE. ONE RECIPE REALLY CAN DO IT ALL!

Three-Way Marinade and Sauce

Skillet White Beans

Old-world character, new-world ease. A touch of balsamic vinegar and a drape of crème fraîche add Italian and French angles to our simplified take on this all-American dish.

Skillet White Beans

Baked beans are a summer staple, but this streamlined version has the same deep, rich flavor without heating up the kitchen.
PREP: 25 MINUTES **COOK:** 25 MINUTES

- 1 large sweet onion, halved lengthwise and thinly sliced (2 cups)
- 3 Tbsp. butter
- 1/3 cup white balsamic vinegar or lemon juice
- 2 Tbsp. packed brown sugar
- 2 Tbsp. snipped fresh sage
- 2 Tbsp. tomato paste
- 1 tsp. salt
- 1/2 tsp. freshly ground black pepper
- 2 15 1/2- or 16-oz. cans navy beans, rinsed and drained
- 2 15 1/2- or 16-oz. cans butter beans, rinsed and drained
- 1 15- to 16-oz. can garbanzo beans (chickpeas), rinsed and drained
  Crème frâiche or dairy sour cream (optional)
  Chopped tomatoes (optional)
  Yellow cherry tomatoes, halved (optional)

1. In a 12-inch skillet cook onion in hot butter over medium heat about 15 minutes or until very tender and browned, turning heat down if onions start to overbrown. Stir in balsamic vinegar, brown sugar, sage, tomato paste, salt, and pepper. Add all beans; stir to coat.

2. Cover and cook over medium heat for 10 to 15 minutes or until heated through, stirring occasionally. Transfer to a serving bowl. If desired, top with crème frâiche and tomatoes. Makes 12 to 14 servings.
EACH SERVING: 225 cal., 4 g total fat (2 g sat. fat), 8 mg chol., 935 mg sodium, 37 g carbo., 8 g fiber, 11 g pro. Daily Values: 2% vit. A, 3% vit. C, 8% calcium, 15% iron.

Hot dogs do it all. Served solo on a bun, they're a kid's idea of the perfect feast. Paired with grape tomato chutney, they switch into something-special mode, definitely appreciated by the over-10 crowd.

Hot Dogs and Texas Tomato Chutney

Hot Dogs and Texas Tomato Chutney

All-beef hot dogs are a good choice for this recipe, but also consider those made from turkey, tofu, and chicken.

PREP: 15 MINUTES **GRILL:** 20 MINUTES

- 3 cups grape or cherry tomatoes, halved
- 1 cup finely chopped red onion
- 6 cloves garlic, minced, or ½ tsp. garlic powder
- 2 Tbsp. honey mustard
- 2 Tbsp. snipped fresh marjoram, oregano, or parsley
- 1 Tbsp. water
- ½ tsp. salt
- ½ tsp. packed brown sugar
- ¼ tsp. ground black pepper
- 6 large hot dogs (about 1 lb. total)
- 1 cup seedless red grapes, halved or quartered
- 6 hot dog buns, split and toasted

1. For Texas Tomato Chutney, fold 36×18-inch heavy foil in half to 18 inches square. In a medium bowl combine 2 cups of the tomatoes, the onion, garlic, mustard, marjoram, water, salt, brown sugar, and pepper. Place mixture in center of foil. Bring up two opposite edges of foil; seal with double fold. Fold remaining edges to enclose mixture, leaving space for steam to build.

2. FOR A CHARCOAL GRILL: Place foil packet on grill rack directly over medium coals. Grill for 10 minutes; turn packet. Grill about 10 minutes more or until onion is tender. Carefully open packet.

FOR A GAS GRILL: Preheat grill. Reduce heat to medium. Place foil packet on grill rack directly over heat. Cover and grill as above.

3. Meanwhile, place hot dogs on grill rack around foil packet; grill for 5 to 7 minutes or until heated through, turning occasionally. Remove hot dogs from grill.

4. Stir remaining 1 cup tomato halves and the grapes into hot chutney mixture. Place hot dogs in toasted buns; serve Texas Tomato Chutney with the hot dogs. Makes 6 servings.

EACH SERVING: 567 cal., 39 g total fat (15 g sat. fat), 64 mg chol., 1,840 mg sodium, 36 g carbo., 3 g fiber, 19 g pro. Daily Values: 16% vit. A, 28% vit. C, 9% calcium, 19% iron.

Double-Berry Cooler

STRAWBERRIES, BLUEBERRIES, BLACKBERRIES—OH, MY! THIS COOL AND LUSCIOUS DESSERT WILL HAVE YOU SEEING TRIPLE (BERRIES, THAT IS).

Hello, gorgeous! This tall beauty is the best kind of summertime dessert—light, sweet, and refreshing.

Kid Friendly Double-Berry Cooler

Homemade gelatin desserts are a time-honored American tradition. This yummy, refreshing dessert is created from fruit juices and fresh fruit.

PREP: 20 MINUTES **CHILL:** 5 HOURS

- 2 envelopes unflavored gelatin
- ½ cup sugar
- 4 cups peach-white-cranberry juice or ginger ale*
- 1 Tbsp. lemon juice
- 2 cup blackberries and/or blueberries
- 2 cups small whole strawberries, halved
- 1 recipe Sweetened Whipped Cream

1. In a medium saucepan stir together gelatin and sugar. Add 1 cup of the juice. Cook over low heat, stirring constantly, about 5 minutes or until gelatin dissolves. Remove from heat. Slowly stir in remaining juice and the lemon juice (if using ginger ale, pour slowly so it doesn't fizz).

2. Spoon blackberries into a 2-quart glass bowl or straight-sided container. Add half the gelatin mixture. Cover and refrigerate for 2 hours or until set. After 1 hour of chilling, in a medium bowl stir together strawberries and remaining gelatin-juice mixture. Cover and chill 1 hour or just until partially set (consistency of unbeaten egg whites). Spoon strawberry mixture on set blueberry mixture. Cover and refrigerate 3 to 4 hours or until set. Serve with Sweetened Whipped Cream. Makes 8 to 10 side-dish servings.

SWEETENED WHIPPED CREAM: Chill a medium mixing bowl and beaters of an electric mixer. In the bowl beat ½ cup whipping cream, 1 tablespoon sugar, and ¼ teaspoon vanilla with an electric mixer on medium speed until soft peaks form. Makes about 1 cup.

***NOTE:** Liquid will be darker if using ginger ale.

EACH SERVING: 208 cal., 6 g total fat (3 g sat. fat), 21 mg chol., 27 mg sodium, 37 g carbo., 3 g fiber, 3 g pro. Daily Values: 7% vit. A, 114% vit. C, 3% calcium, 2% iron.

Firecracker Coconut Dip

Whip up an extra-large batch of this spirited dual-purpose dip and sauce. Try it one day with chips, veggies, and chicken; the next day, spoon it generously over grilled pork.

Firecracker Coconut Dip

Vary the heat of this dip with the amount of wasabi or horseradish. It's important to use unsweetened coconut milk; find it in the Asian food section of a supermarket or specialty store.

 START TO FINISH: 15 MINUTES

- 1 8-oz. pkg. cream cheese, softened
- 1 8-oz. carton dairy sour cream
- ½ cup unsweetened coconut milk or cream of coconut
- 1 to 2 Tbsp. wasabi paste or 2 Tbsp. prepared horseradish or Dijon-style mustard
- 1 Tbsp. grated fresh ginger
- 1 tsp. finely shredded lime peel
- 3 Tbsp. lime juice

  Raw vegetables such as sliced carrots, sugar snap peas, or sweet pepper strips

1. In a medium mixing bowl beat cream cheese with an electric mixer on medium speed 30 seconds. Beat in sour cream, coconut milk, wasabi paste, fresh ginger, lime peel, and lime juice until smooth.

2. Serve dip with carrots, sugar snap peas, sweet pepper strips, or other vegetables. Or serve with sesame sticks, grilled shrimp or pork, or spread on a hamburger. Makes 2½ cups dip (about 20 servings).

EACH SERVING: 102 cal., 8 g total fat (5 g sat. fat), 17 mg chol., 42 mg sodium, 6 g carbo., 2 g fiber, 3 g pro. Daily Values: 18% vit. A, 66% vit. C, 3% calcium, 5% iron.

Potato Salad with Fresh Stir-Ins

Surround a basic potato salad with bowls of flavorful stir-ins and let guest create their own versions of this summer classic.

PREP: 20 MINUTES **ROAST:** 40 MINUTES **STAND:** 15 MINUTES

Potato Salad with Fresh Stir-Ins

   5 lb. tiny new red potatoes or baby Yukon gold potatoes, halved
¼ cup olive oil
   1 tsp. salt
½ tsp. ground black pepper
   1 recipe Classic Potato Salad Dressing
      Milk (up to ⅓ cup)

STIR-INS:

   Snipped fresh sorrel, parsley, dill, and/or basil
   Crisp-cooked bacon, drained and crumbled
   Seeded and chopped jalapeño chile peppers and/or chopped bottled red cherry peppers*
   Mustard seeds, fennel seeds, and/or caraway seeds, toasted**
   Chopped peeled avocado (drizzled with lemon juice)
   Chopped radishes and/or celery
   Chopped red onion and/or green onion

1. Preheat oven to 425°F. Place potatoes in a greased large shallow roasting pan. Drizzle with the ¼ cup oil. Sprinkle with the salt and black pepper; toss to coat. Roast, uncovered, for 40 to 45 minutes or until just tender and browned, stirring occasionally.

2. Meanwhile, prepare Classic Potato Salad Dressing. Toss potatoes with dressing while potatoes are hot. Let stand for 15 minutes. Cover and refrigerate up to 24 hours.

3. To serve, stir up to ⅓ cup milk into potato mixture to desired consistency. Place potato salad in a large serving bowl. Arrange assorted fresh stir-ins and condiments in separate bowls around the potato salad. Makes 10 to 12 side-dish servings.

CLASSIC POTATO SALAD DRESSING: In a medium bowl stir together 1½ cups mayonnaise or salad dressing, 2 tablespoons prepared yellow mustard, 1 tablespoon white wine vinegar, ½ teaspoon salt, and ¼ teaspoon ground black pepper.

TEST KITCHEN TIP: If desired, cook potatoes in a microwave oven. To microwave potatoes, omit olive oil. Place half the potatoes in a microwave-safe 2-quart casserole dish. Add ¾ cup water and ½ teaspoon salt. Microwave, covered, on 100% power (high) for 10 to 14 minutes or until the potatoes are just tender, stirring twice. Drain potatoes; set aside. Repeat with remaining uncooked potatoes, using additional water and salt.

***NOTE:** Because chile peppers contain oils that can burn your skin and eyes, avoid direct contact. Wear plastic or rubber gloves. If your bare hands touch the chile peppers, wash them well with soap and water.

****NOTE:** To toast seeds, heat them in a small skillet over medium heat about 2 minutes or until fragrant and lightly browned, stirring frequently.

EACH SERVING (WITH PARSLEY, BACON, AND ONION STIR-INS): 466 cal., 36 g total fat (6 g sat. fat), 31 mg chol., 727 mg sodium, 29 g carbo., 3 g fiber, 6 g pro. Daily Values: 2% vit. A, 46% vit. C, 3% calcium, 15% iron.

Fourth of July Cherry-Cola Cake

Fourth of July Cherry-Cola Cake

This cola cake has extra spices that bring out the distinctive cola flavor. Though soft drink makers guard their flavor secrets, nearly every cola has touches of citrus and ginger.

PREP: 30 MINUTES **BAKE:** ACCORDING TO PACKAGE DIRECTIONS
COOL: 1 HOUR **CHILL:** 5 HOURS

> 1 pkg. 2-layer size German chocolate cake mix
> Cherry cola
> 1½ tsp. ground ginger
> 1 tsp. finely shredded lime peel
> 1 recipe Celebration Icing
> 10 to 12 dark sweet cherries with stems

1. Preheat oven to 350°F. Grease and flour a 13×9×2-inch baking pan; set aside. Prepare cake mix according to package directions, except substitute cherry cola for the liquid called for and add ground ginger and lime peel. Pour batter into prepared pan. Bake according to package directions. Cool for 10 minutes on a wire rack. Remove from pan; cool completely on wire rack.

2. Use a serrated knife to cut top of cake level. Trim edges of cake to make even. Discard trimmed pieces. Cut cake in half lengthwise into two 13×4½-inch rectangles. Place one rectangle on a serving platter. Spread with tinted icing. Top with second rectangle. Spread with white icing. Refrigerate cake for 1 hour or until icing is set. Wrap cake in plastic wrap. Refrigerate for 4 to 24 hours before serving. Top each slice with a cherry. Makes 10 to 12 servings.

CELEBRATION ICING: This recipe is based on a 1-lb. box of powdered sugar (about 4½ cups total). In a medium mixing bowl beat ⅓ cup butter with electric mixer until smooth. Gradually add 1 cup powdered sugar, beating well. Slowly beat in 3 tablespoons milk and 1 teaspoon vanilla. Gradually beat in 2 cups powdered sugar. Divide the mixture in half. To half of the mixture beat in 2 tablespoons cherry spreadable fruit and red food coloring to tint icing pink. Gradually beat in enough powdered sugar for spreading consistency. To remaining mixture add enough powdered sugar for spreading consistency. Makes about 2½ cups total icing.

EACH SERVING OF CAKE WITH ICING: 554 cal., 19 g total fat (6 g sat. fat), 81 mg chol., 457 mg sodium, 96 g carbo., 0 g fiber, 5 g pro. Daily Values: 6% vit. A, 1% vit. C, 6% calcium, 9% iron.

Watermelon Coolers

This refresher is watermelon in a glass.
PREP: 15 MINUTES **CHILL:** 2 HOURS

- 5 cups seeded and cubed watermelon (about 3½ lbs)
- ⅓ cup raspberry or cherry syrup
- 1 recipe Watermelon Ice Cubes or ice cubes
- 1 1-liter bottle carbonated water, chilled
  Raspberry or cherry syrup (optional)

1. In a blender container or food processor bowl combine the watermelon and the ⅓ cup syrup. Cover and blend or process until smooth. Press mixture through a fine-mesh sieve into a medium bowl; discard pulp. Cover and refrigerate mixture at least 2 hours or up to 24 hours.

2. To serve, add ice cubes to ten 12-ounce glasses. Pour enough watermelon mixture into glasses to fill half full. Add enough carbonated water to fill glasses. If desired, sweeten individual servings with additional syrup; stir to dissolve syrup. Makes ten 12-ounce servings.

WATERMELON ICE CUBES: Use these cubes to keep coolers cold without thinning out flavor. Cut 1-inch cubes from watermelon flesh. Place the melon cubes in a single layer in a 15×10×1-inch baking pan. Freeze for 1 to 2 hours or until firm. If storing longer than 4 hours, transfer cubes to a resealable plastic freezer bag or freezer container and freeze until ready to use.

EACH SERVING: 44 cal., 0 g total fat, 0 mg chol., 22 mg sodium, 11 g carbo., 0 g fiber, 0 g pro. Daily Values: 9% vit. A, 10% vit. C, 1% calcium, 1% iron.

Watermelon Coolers

In good taste
FOOD AND ENTERTAINING

FLOAT AWAY

Whip up this classic summer ice cream drink with a version for every family member. July is National Ice Cream Month—what better time to try out some new flavors. Ice Creams: Tangerine Sorbet, Froot Loop; Coldstone Creamery; www.coldstonecreamery.com for store locations. Cheesecake, Mud Pie; Breyers Ice Cream; 800/483-9939 or www.icecreamusa.com for availability.

MOM'S RED DREAMSICLE
Top a float of strawberry or Cheesecake ice cream and raspberry soda with raspberries, strawberries, or cherries.

GRANDMA AND GRANDPA'S TANGERINE TREAT
Float Tangerine Sorbet in ginger ale or cream soda. Add a dash of pineapple juice and a fresh pineapple spear.

DAD'S CHOCOLATE SECRET
Add chocolate or Mud Pie ice cream to chocolate stout. Finish with a drizzle of chocolate syrup.

KIDS' BUBBLE UP
Add a scoop of bubblegum or Froot Loop ice cream to bubblegum soda.

PHOTOGRAPHS BY **KIM CORNELISON**

KEEP IT COOL
Summer flowers seem to float in this refreshing, translucent serving bowl.
Use this frosty dish to serve sorbet, berries, cut vegetables, or seafood. To make one, bring about 2 quarts of water to room temperature. Place a layer of ice cubes in an 8-inch plastic or glass bowl. Nestle a 6-inch bowl inside. Use tape to secure the two bowls in four places, making sure the rims are level. Insert flowers, fresh herbs, or sliced fruit between the two bowls. Slowly fill the outer bowl with the water. Freeze at least 24 hours. Remove from freezer. Dip the outer bowl in warm water for a few seconds to loosen bowls. Stand ice bowl on a rimmed plate. Bowls: Bed Bath and Beyond; 800/462-3966; or visit www.bedbathandbeyond.com (product line varies).

How to do it.

DOG DAYS OF SUMMER

There's more than one way to dress up a hot dog. The Dogma Grill in Miami serves some summer toppers that keep vacation only a bite away year-round. Owner David Tunnell suggests the Greek Island mix of chopped cucumbers, tomatoes, onions, olives, oregano, and olive oil (photo, *left*); guacamole-style with avocado, bacon, and sour cream; or simplified with piles of coleslaw. Dogma Grill, 7030 Biscayne Boulevard, Miami, Florida; 305/759-3433.

BERRY POWERFUL

Blueberries have healthful magic packed in a tiny size. Mix up a power potion with wild blueberry juice, soda, and a squeeze of lemon. In addition to the wonderful taste and pretty color, health experts report blueberries may help reduce cholesterol, improve vision, and fight short-term memory loss. Wyman's Wild Blueberry Juice; 800/341-1758.

MAKING BUTTER BETTER

Add quick and easy flavor to grilled meats, chicken, fish, and vegetables with compound butters. Soften a stick of butter; then blend in fresh herbs, spices, wine, or other ingredients. Wrap the butter in parchment or waxed paper and freeze until ready to use. Thaw; then slice off equal measures to use on cooked foods. Try these combinations: olive oil, black pepper, and red wine; lemon zest, Parmesan cheese, and chile pepper; or rosemary, garlic, and parsley.

AUGUST

Anytime Calzones
page 155

STRIPEY SHAKES, SEARED PANCAKES, AND RAISIN
MEN COOKIES ARE JUST A FEW OF THE FABULOUS
RECIPES OUR FAVORITE AUSTRALIAN CHEF IS
COOKING UP IN HER KITCHEN. DINING DOWN
UNDER HAS NEVER BEEN THIS GOOD!

Downtime Down Under

Plus

Seared Peach Pancakes
page 152

Herb-Crusted Lamb and Tomato and Mint Salad
page 156

Downtime Down Under

WE SETTLED IN FOR A WEEKEND WITH
AUSTRALIA'S AWARD-WINNING COOK,
AUTHOR, AND FOOD STYLIST
DONNA HAY. HERE'S WHAT
WE LEARNED.

Raisin Men Cookies

PREP: 35 MINUTES **CHILL:** 1 HOUR **BAKE:** 15 MINUTES PER BATCH

- 1/2 cup raisins
- 1 cup boiling water
- 1/2 cup butter, softened
- 1/2 cup packed brown sugar
- 1/4 cup granulated sugar
- 1 egg
- 2 cups all-purpose flour
- 1/2 cup malted milk powder
- 1 tsp. ground cinnamon
- 1/2 tsp. baking soda
- 1/4 cup flaked coconut

1. Preheat oven to 325°F. Line 2 cookie sheets with parchment paper or foil; set aside. Place raisins in bowl; cover with boiling water. Let stand 15 minutes. Drain. Pat dry with paper towels; set aside.

2. Meanwhile, in mixing bowl beat butter with electric mixer on medium speed 30 seconds. Beat in sugars until well combined. Add egg; beat until combined. In small bowl combine flour, milk powder, cinnamon, and baking soda. Add to egg mixture, beating well (mixture will be crumbly). Stir in raisins and coconut. Knead dough until it holds together.

3. Divide dough in half. Cover; chill dough at least 1 hour. On floured surface roll half of dough at a time to 1/4 inch thick. Using 4-inch gingerbread man cutter, cut out dough;* place on prepared cookie sheets. Repeat with remaining half of dough and scraps.

4. Bake cookies about 15 minutes or until edges are just firm but centers appear slightly soft. Cool on sheet 1 minute; transfer to wire racks. Makes 12 to 14 (4-inch) cookies.

***NOTE:** Use a knife to cut through raisins around edges that cutter does not cut through.

EACH COOKIE: 288 cal., 11 g total fat (6 g sat. fat), 43 mg chol., 198 mg sodium, 45 g carbo., 1 g fiber, 5 g pro. Daily Values: 6% vit. A, 1% vit. C, 6% calcium, 8% iron.

BY SARA MULCAHY PHOTOGRAPHS BY CON POULOS FOOD STYLING BY DONNA HAY

Stripey Strawberry Shake (page 158) with Raisin Men Cookies

I

t's 6:30 p.m. on Friday and Donna Hay is home for the weekend. Closing the front gate of the light and airy Victorian terrace behind her, she drops her bags, kicks off her "vintage" loafers (she calls them that because she's had them for so long), and sweeps her 2 1/2-year-old son, Angus, into a huge hug. After a full-on week at the helm of her food publishing business, Friday night means family night, and she's more than ready to kick back and relax.

Award-winning cook, food stylist, best-selling book author, magazine editor-in-chief—these are just a few titles held by Donna Hay, Australia's favorite cook. With a bimonthly magazine, nationwide Sunday newspaper columns, and 10 cookbooks to her name, there aren't many people in her homeland who haven't "cooked a Donna." Nearly 2.5 million people worldwide own one of her cookbooks. Not bad for a working mum who's only 35.

For someone who creates recipes, cooks, and styles food for a living, cooking could be one of the last things she'd want to do with her precious time off. Not so. Donna loves preparing meals for the family. And as a couple, she and her partner, Bill, a rancher and butcher (they met when she bought meat from his shop), love to entertain.

Cooking for family and friends, according to Donna, should be simple, fresh, and fun. That's why her recipes are short, the ingredients are available from the supermarket, and the techniques are easy for even the most inexperienced cooks.

"My personal time is precious," says Donna, "which is why I don't go in for fancy recipes with obscure ingredients. And I'm a big believer in getting everyone to help out."

Donna's theory is that when cooking for a crowd, the more you can do ahead, the better, so by the time friends arrive, it's more a matter of assembly than cooking. She applies the same concept when cooking for her family during the week.

"We all have busy schedules, so I like to get organized on a Sunday evening," Donna says. "I might make something to pop in the freezer or a batch of soup—anything that means I don't have to be rushing about on weeknights. Those few hours we get to spend together are my favorite part of the day. I'm very driven when it comes to my business, but the important things in my life are right here at home."

Seared Peach Pancakes

Seared Peach Pancakes

Peaches will caramelize when they hit the skillet.

 PREP: 10 MINUTES **COOK:** 4 MINUTES PER BATCH

- 4 medium peaches, nectarines, or apples
- 2 cups all-purpose flour
- ¼ cup sugar
- 2 tsp. baking soda
- 3 eggs
- 1¾ cups milk
- 2 Tbsp. butter, melted
- 1 Tbsp. malt vinegar
  Butter
  Maple syrup

1. Slice fruit crosswise about ¼ inch thick, cutting around pit to form rings. For apples, core and slice crosswise; set aside. In a bowl combine flour, sugar, and baking soda. Make well in the center of flour mixture; set aside.

2. In another bowl whisk together eggs, milk, melted butter, and vinegar. Add egg mixture to flour mixture. Stir until moistened.

3. Add about 1 teaspoon *butter* to a hot large nonstick skillet or griddle. Place a peach slice on hot skillet. Pour or spread a scant ¼ cup batter over peach slice. Cook over medium heat about 2 minutes on each side until pancakes are golden brown, turning when pancakes have bubbly surfaces and edges are slightly dry. Repeat with remaining batter and peach slices; add butter to skillet as needed. Serve warm with maple syrup. Makes 8 servings.

EACH SERVING (2 PANCAKES): 409 cal., 14 g total fat (7 g sat. fat), 112 mg chol., 446 mg sodium, 64 g carbo., 2 g fiber, 8 g pro. Daily Values: 14% vit. A, 6% vit. C, 11% calcium, 14% iron.

To make the ring of fruit in the center of these pancakes, cut around the pit of the peach. Then gently pull the peach slice away. If using an apple, core the apple first, then slice crosswise to form a ring.

Anytime Calzones Dough

PREP: 20 MINUTES **RISE:** 40 MINUTES

- 1 Tbsp. active dry yeast
- 1 tsp. sugar
- 2 cups warm water (105°F to 115°F)
- 5 to 5½ cups all-purpose flour
- 1 Tbsp. olive oil
- 2 tsp. salt

1. In a very large bowl combine yeast and sugar. Pour warm water over all. Let stand 5 minutes. Using a wooden spoon stir in 2 cups of the flour, the olive oil, and salt. Stir in as much remaining flour as you can. Knead in enough remaining flour to make a moderately stiff dough that is smooth and elastic (6 to 8 minutes). Shape dough into a ball. Place in a greased bowl; turn to grease surface. Cover; let rise for 40 minutes or until double in size.

2. Punch dough down. Turn dough out onto a lightly floured surface. Divide dough into 10 equal portions. Cover and let rest for 10 minutes. Roll out each dough portion into a 7-inch round. Use dough to prepare Anytime Calzones (recipe, *page 155*) or freeze. Makes about 2½ pounds dough.

CALZONES DOUGH FOR ELECTRIC STAND MIXER: In a small bowl combine yeast and sugar. Pour warm water over all. Let stand 5 minutes. Place yeast mixture in large mixing bowl fitted with dough hook. Add 2 cups flour, olive oil, and salt. Mix on low speed until soft dough forms. Beat 3 minutes more. Slowly add 3½ to 4 cups additional flour. Continue to knead, on low speed, for 5 to 6 minutes more or until dough feels smooth and elastic (dough will be sticky). Transfer to well-floured surface; shape into a ball. Let rise and shape as above.

MAKE AHEAD: Place dough rounds between sheets of parchment paper. Freeze in airtight container up to 1 month. For Anytime Calzones, place frozen dough rounds on parchment paper on baking sheet(s). Let stand 30 minutes or until thawed.

EACH ROUND DOUGH: 226 cal., 2 g total fat (0 g sat. fat), 0 mg chol., 468 mg sodium, 45 g carbo., 2 g fiber, 6 g pro. Daily Values: 1% calcium, 16% iron.

Anytime Calzones Dough

TRY THIS Use Donna's Anytime Calzones Dough to make pizza too. Place a dough round on a baking sheet. Bake in a 400°F oven for 5 minutes. Spread pizza sauce and top with desired toppings. Bake 5 to 8 minutes more.

ANYTIME CALZONES ARE FOR JUST THAT—ANYTIME. SWITCH UP THE FILLINGS FOR A FAST AND FUN BREAKFAST, LUNCH, OR EVEN FOR A CASUAL GET-TOGETHER WITH FRIENDS.

Anytime Calzones

Anytime Calzones

One basic great-tasting dough and two flavor variations make a family night meal. Make these calzones one at a time, as follows, or by the batch.

PREP: 25 MINUTES **BAKE:** 25 MINUTES

- 4 or five ¼-inch-thick potato slices
- 1 round Anytime Calzones Dough (recipe, *page 153*)
- Olive oil

FETA AND PROSCIUTTO VARIATION:

- ¼ cup sliced roasted red sweet peppers
- 2 slices prosciutto
- ¼ cup crumbled feta cheese
- ½ tsp. snipped fresh dill

RICOTTA AND HAM VARIATION:

- ¼ cup ricotta cheese
- 2 Tbsp. grated Parmesan cheese
- 1 tsp. snipped fresh chives
- 1½ oz. good-quality smoked ham, thinly sliced

1. Preheat oven to 400°F. For each calzone, place potato slices in single layer on microwave-safe plate. Cover with plastic wrap; vent. Microwave on 100% power (high) 2 to 3 minutes or until tender. Remove wrap; cool.

2. On lightly floured surface place round of Anytime Calzones Dough. Layer potato slices on half of dough circle to within 1-inch of edges. For Feta and Prosciutto Variation, layer red sweet peppers, prosciutto, feta cheese, and fresh dill. For Ricotta and Ham Variation, in a small bowl combine ricotta, Parmesan cheese, and chives. Spread ricotta mixture evenly over potato slices. Top with ham.

3. Moisten edges with water. Fold dough in half over filling. Seal. Place calzone on lightly greased baking sheet. Brush with olive oil.

4. Bake for 25 minutes or until golden. Makes 1 calzone .

EACH CALZONE (FETA AND PROSCIUTTO VARIATION): 456 cal., 16 g total fat (7 g sat. fat), 46 mg chol., 1,372 mg sodium, 59 g carbo., 4 g fiber, 18 g pro. Daily Values: 3% vit. A, 187% vit. C, 20% calcium, 26% iron.

EACH CALZONE (RICOTTA AND HAM VARIATION): 533 cal., 21 g total fat (9 g sat. fat), 64 mg chol., 1,232 mg sodium, 59 g carbo., 3 g fiber, 26 g pro. Daily Values: 7% vit. A, 21% vit. C, 27% calcium, 25% iron.

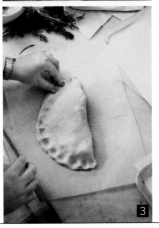

THREE STEPS AND YOU'RE FINISHED

"We love calzones. They're fast, fun, and perfect for using up little bits of leftovers that end up in the refrigerator. I always have a batch of dough waiting in the freezer," Donna says.

Step One: Thaw a round of the dough. Add a favorite cheese spread.

Step Two: Top with cooked potatoes, ham, prosciutto, and/or sweet peppers.

Step Three: Fold the dough over; seal.

Herb-Crusted Lamb

Tomato and Mint Salad

Tomato and Mint Salad

Fast! **START TO FINISH:** 30 MINUTES

- 2½ lb. assorted tomatoes (heirloom tomatoes, sliced; plum tomatoes, cut into wedges; yellow pear tomatoes, halved; and/or cherry tomatoes, halved)
- 1 cup shredded fresh mint or basil leaves
- 2 Tbsp. red wine vinegar
- 2 Tbsp. olive oil
- 1 clove garlic, minced
- 1 tsp. sugar
- ⅛ tsp. sea salt
- ⅛ tsp. cracked black pepper
- 8 oz. marinated feta cheese, undrained*
  Sea salt and cracked black pepper

1. In bowl combine tomatoes and mint. In small bowl whisk together vinegar, oil, garlic, sugar, salt, and pepper. Pour over tomatoes; toss.
2. To serve, divide tomatoes among individual plates. Top with undrained feta. Pass additional sea salt and pepper. Makes 6 servings.
***TEST KITCHEN TIP:** Find marinated feta in jars in the refrigerated section of some supermarkets and specialty stores.
EACH SERVING: 160 cal., 11 g total fat (5 g sat. fat), 16 mg chol., 462 mg sodium, 9 g carbo., 2 g fiber, 7 g pro. Daily Values: 32% vit. A, 55% vit. C, 4% calcium, 17% iron.

Herb-Crusted Lamb

PREP: 30 MINUTES **COOK:** 9 MINUTES

- 1½ cups fresh flat-leaf parsley
- 1 cup fresh dill
- 1 cup fresh mint leaves
- ⅔ cup olive oil
- ⅓ cup capers
- 1 Tbsp. Dijon-style mustard
- 2 cloves garlic, minced
- 6 lamb rib or sirloin chops, cut 1 inch thick
- 1 recipe Toasted Pita Wedges
- ½ of a 6-oz. pkg. baby spinach leaves

1. For sauce, in processor or mini chopper place parsley, dill, mint, oil, capers, mustard, and garlic. Cover; process until chopped.
2. Trim fat from chops. Remove about one-fourth of the sauce; use to brush on both sides of chops. In a large skillet cook chops over medium heat for 9 to 11 minutes for medium (160°F), turning once.
3. For each serving, place a wedge of toasted pita bread on serving plate. Top with some of the spinach leaves. Top with lamb chop. Spoon some of the remaining sauce over lamb. Makes 6 servings.
TO GRILL: Prepare sauce and lamb chops as above. For charcoal grill, arrange medium-hot coals around drip pan. Test for medium heat above pan. Place chops on rack over drip pan. Cover and grill to desired doneness: 16 to 18 minutes for medium rare (145°F); 18 to 20 for medium (160°F). (For gas grill, preheat grill. Reduce heat to medium. Adjust for indirect cooking. Grill as above.)
TOASTED PITA WEDGES: Place 6 pita bread wedges or flatbread wedges in single layer on baking sheet. Bake in 375°F oven 7 to 9 minutes or until toasted. Or place on grill rack directly over medium heat for 1 to 2 minutes, turning once.

Healthy **EACH SERVING:** 160 cal., 11 g total fat (5 g sat. fat), 16 mg chol., 462 mg sodium, 9 g carbo., 2 g fiber, 7 g pro. Daily Values: 32% vit. A, 55% vit. C, 4% calcium, 17% iron.

Prawn Fritters with Cucumbers and Peanuts
PREP: 50 MINUTES **COOK:** 4 MINUTES PER BATCH

- 2 small cucumbers (about 2 lb. total)
- 2 stalks celery
- 1 cup fresh mint or cilantro leaves
- 1/3 cup peanuts, chopped
- 2 lb. uncooked prawns, peeled, deveined, and halved lengthwise, or 2 lb. medium fresh shrimp in shells, peeled and deveined
- 8 oz. snow pea pods, sliced lengthwise (about 2 1/2 cups)
- 1/2 cup coarsely chopped fresh cilantro leaves
- 2 green onions, thinly sliced
- 1 Tbsp. finely shredded lime peel
- 6 Tbsp. lime juice
- 3 egg whites
- 1/4 cup rice flour
- 1 Tbsp. granulated sugar
- 1 tsp. sea salt
- 1/4 cup cooking oil
- 1 Tbsp. packed brown sugar
- Lime wedges

1. For salad, use vegetable peeler to remove a large strip of peel from cucumbers; discard. Using same peeler thinly slice cucumber and celery lengthwise into long thin strips; place in large bowl. Add mint and peanuts; set aside.

2. For prawn fritters, in a large bowl place the prawns, snow peas, 1/2 cup cilantro, onions, lime peel, 2 tablespoons of the lime juice, egg whites, rice flour, granulated sugar, and salt; stir gently to combine. Heat 2 tablespoons of the oil in a very large skillet over medium-high heat. For each fritter, place 1/2 cup of the prawn mixture into the skillet and flatten slightly, cooking 4 fritters at a time. Cook 2 to 3 minutes per side or until golden and prawns turn opaque. Turn carefully; if necessary, use spatula to reshape. Remove fritters; keep warm. Repeat with remaining oil and prawn mixture.

3. To serve, toss cucumber mixture with remaining lime juice and brown sugar. Divide among serving plates. Top with fritters. Pass lime wedges. Makes 6 servings.

EACH SERVING: 347 cal., 16 g total fat (2 g sat. fat), 172 mg chol., 516 mg sodium, 21 g carbo., 3 g fiber, 30 g pro. Daily Values: 18% vit. A, 42% vit. C, 14% calcium, 33% iron.

Prawn Fritters with Cucumbers and Peanuts

Overnight Oats with Fruit

PREP: 15 MINUTES **CHILL:** 6 HOURS

- 2 cups regular rolled oats
- 1 cup milk
- 1 cup apple juice
- ¼ cup honey
- 1 tsp. ground cinnamon
- ¾ cup blanched almonds, pecans, or walnuts, toasted and coarsely chopped
- 1 tart green apple, cored, seeded, and very thinly sliced crosswise
- 1 6-oz. container desired-flavor yogurt
- 1 cup fresh raspberries

1. In bowl stir together oats, milk, apple juice, honey, and cinnamon. Cover; chill 6 hours or overnight (until oats are soft). Stir in nuts. To serve, spoon oats mixture into 8-ounce serving glasses. Top with apple slices, yogurt, and raspberries. Makes 4 to 6 servings.

TEST KITCHEN TIP: The oats mixture will last 2 days in the refrigerator.

EACH SERVING: 530 cal., 18 g total fat (3 g sat. fat), 7 mg chol., 59 mg sodium, 81 g carbo., 11 g fiber, 17 g pro. Daily Values: 4% vit. A, 15% vit. C, 24% calcium, 22% iron.

Overnight Oats with Fruit

Raisin Men Cookies (page 151) with Stripey Strawberry Shake

 Kid Friendly
 ## Stripey Strawberry Shake

Fast! **START TO FINISH:** 20 MINUTES

- 1 lb. strawberries, hulled and chopped (about 3 cups)
- ⅔ cup sugar
- 4 tsp. cornstarch
- 2 Tbsp. water
  Cold milk or chocolate-flavored milk
  Vanilla ice cream

1. For syrup, in blender container combine strawberries and sugar. Cover; blend until smooth. Strain through sieve to remove seeds; place in saucepan. Combine cornstarch and water; whisk into strawberry mixture. Cook and stir until thickened and bubbly. Cook and stir 2 minutes longer. Remove from pan; cool. Makes 2 cups syrup.*

2. To make Stripey Shakes, pour a teaspoon of syrup down sides of glass, using 2 tablespoons total syrup for each glass. Fill glass with cold milk; top with scoops of ice cream.

*****TEST KITCHEN TIP:** Store remaining syrup in airtight container in refrigerator up to 2 weeks.

EACH SHAKE: 257 cal., 11 g total fat (6 g sat. fat), 54 mg chol., 138 mg sodium, 30 g carbo., 1 g fiber, 10 g pro. Daily Values: 14% vit. A, 29% vit. C, 32% calcium, 3% iron.

Roasted Plums with Frozen Vanilla Ice Cream

PREP: 45 MINUTES **FREEZE:** 6 HOURS **BAKE:** 40 MINUTES

- 1 vanilla bean, split*
- 3 eggs
- 2 egg yolks
- 2/3 cup sugar
- 1 tsp. vanilla*
- 1 3/4 cups whipping cream
- 12 ripe plums, halved and pitted
- 1 1/2 cups late-harvest Riesling or other dessert wine
- 2 Tbsp. sugar

1. For custard mixture, scrape seeds from vanilla bean; reserve seeds. In medium heatproof bowl combine eggs, egg yolks, the 2/3 cup sugar, vanilla seeds, and vanilla. Place bowl over saucepan of simmering water (bowl should not touch water). Whisk mixture constantly for 5 to 10 minutes or until egg mixture reaches 165°F on instant-read thermometer or mixture reaches and remains at 140°F for 3 minutes. Carefully remove bowl from saucepan. Discard vanilla seeds. Beat custard mixture with an electric hand mixer 3 to 5 minutes or until mixture is thick and pale colored. Rinse beaters.

2. In mixing bowl beat cream with electric mixer until soft peaks form (tips curl). Fold custard into cream. Pour into freezer-safe serving bowl; cover with plastic wrap. Freeze until firm (6 to 24 hours).

3. Preheat oven to 350°F. In 3-quart rectangular baking dish place plums, cut sides up, in single layer. Pour wine over plums. Sprinkle plums evenly with sugar. Bake, uncovered, for 40 to 50 minutes or until plums are soft and slightly browned. Serve warm plums with scoops of frozen vanilla ice cream. Makes 6 to 8 servings.

***TEST KITCHEN TIP:** Use 1 vanilla bean and 1 teaspoon vanilla or 2 teaspoons vanilla. Use only pure vanilla, not imitation.

EACH SERVING: 555 cal., 30 g total fat (17 g sat. fat), 270 mg chol., 70 mg sodium, 51 g carbo., 2 g fiber, 7 g pro. Daily Values: 32% vit. A, 17% vit. C, 8% calcium, 6% iron.

Roasted Plums with Frozen Vanilla Ice Cream

Sharing
the fruits of labor

BLUEBERRY BAY FARM
IS PLANTED WITH
NINE VARIETIES OF
BLUEBERRIES THAT RIPEN
AT DIFFERENT POINTS IN
THE SEASON; THE BEST
BERRIES ARE THE ONES
THAT ARE RIPEST ON ANY
GIVEN BUSH.

BY **KRISTINE KENNEDY** PHOTOGRAPHS BY **EDMUND BARR**

Blueberries—small, sweet, and innocuous—are instruments

of a profound life change for Ron and Lois Laurence. The couple's days are now long, filled with new challenges and experiences. One could hardly blame them if they never looked up from their work. But they do. "I've never noticed the moon like I notice it now," says Lois, who, at 63, sees the sky differently since she's been viewing it from the couple's Blueberry Bay Farm in Stratham, New Hampshire.

As of 2002 the Laurences have been the proud and passionate owners of these twelve gently sweeping acres. Toward the center of the property sits their 1726 home, the second-oldest in Stratham, flanked by rows and rows of head-high blueberry bushes. Traipsing a wide grassy path, U-pick customers outfitted in sun visors and sensible shoes head straight to the rustic sales shack to get their buckets for collection. It's easy to spot the regulars, who devise waist harnesses to hold the buckets—the better to double-fist it while picking. For those who choose not to roam the three acres of blueberries, there are another two acres of vegetables, fruit trees, and cutting garden flowers to harvest.

At an age when many lifelong workers are ready to hit a few balls around the golf course, Ron, now 67, bent backwards and sideways to buy the farm. Lois remembers telling him, "If this is something you want, you've got to do it now because in 10 years you'll be too old." Another factor weighed heavily on their decision: This small family farm would soon be sold to developers.

Their momentous decision to buy it meant selling two homes and having Lois return to 40-hour workweeks processing medical records so she would have insurance. After her day at the office, she rakes, weeds, and bakes blueberry cakes to sell in the shack. For Ron, the farm has meant intense and usually physical labor seven days a week, whether pruning bushes in knee-high snow, digging furrows for new beds, or making ambitious plans for the following year's crop. Despite the seeming hardships, the Laurences wake up every morning in excited anticipation of the tasks to be done. "I'm just not a person to slack off or hang around," Ron says. "I want to continue to produce something, to accomplish something, till the day I die."

Pineapple-Glazed Banana Blueberry Muffins

PREP: 20 MINUTES **BAKE:** 15 MINUTES **COOL:** 5 MINUTES

1³/₄ cups all-purpose flour
¹/₃ cup packed brown sugar
2 tsp. baking powder
¹/₂ tsp. ground cinnamon
¹/₄ tsp. salt
³/₄ cup mashed ripe banana
¹/₂ cup milk
¹/₄ cup butter, melted
1 egg, slightly beaten
1 tsp. vanilla
³/₄ cup fresh blueberries
¹/₄ cup pineapple jam
Pineapple jam (optional)

1. Preheat oven to 400°F. Grease twelve 2¹/₂-inch muffin cups; set aside.
2. In a large bowl combine flour, brown sugar, baking powder, cinnamon, and salt. Make a well in center of flour mixture; set aside.
3. In a medium bowl combine banana, milk, melted butter, egg, and vanilla. Add banana mixture all at once to flour mixture. Stir just until moistened (batter should be lumpy). Fold in blueberries.
4. Spoon batter into prepared muffin cups; fill each about three-fourths full. Spoon 1 teaspoon pineapple jam in batter in each muffin cup. Bake 15 to 20 minutes or until golden and a wooden toothpick inserted in centers comes out clean. Cool in muffin cups on wire rack for 5 minutes. Remove from muffin cups. If desired, serve warm with additional pineapple jam. Makes 12 muffins.
EACH MUFFIN: 174 cal., 5 g total fat (2 g sat. fat), 29 mg chol., 133 mg sodium, 30 g carbo., 2 g fiber, 3 g pro. Daily Values: 4% vit. A, 5% vit. C, 4% calcium, 6% iron.

Blueberry Pound Cake

STAND: 30 MINUTES **PREP:** 30 MINUTES **BAKE:** 70 MINUTES
COOL: 2¹/₂ HOURS

¹/₂ cup butter
3 eggs
3¹/₂ cups all-purpose flour
2 tsp. baking powder
¹/₄ tsp. salt
2 cups sugar
4 cups fresh blueberries
1 cup milk

1. Allow butter and eggs to stand at room temperature for 30 minutes. Meanwhile, grease a 10-inch tube pan with a removable bottom;* set aside.
2. Preheat oven to 325°F. In a large bowl sift together the flour, baking powder, and salt; set aside. In a very large mixing bowl beat the butter and sugar with an electric mixer on medium speed until mixture is crumbly. Beat in eggs. Stir blueberries into flour mixture. By hand, stir blueberry mixture into butter mixture. Stir in milk just until combined. Spread batter in prepared pan.
3. Bake for 70 to 80 minutes or until a wooden skewer inserted near center comes out clean. Cool on wire rack for 15 minutes. Loosen cake from pan with a narrow metal spatula. Lift tube from pan, leaving cake on tube. Cool cake completely on tube on wire rack. Using a serrated knife, cut cake into slices from the tube. Makes 10 to 12 servings.
*TIP: If your 10-inch tube pan does not have a removable bottom, cool cake completely in the pan. Loosen edges as directed above and invert onto a cooling rack.
EACH SERVING: 444 cal., 12 g total fat (6 g sat. fat), 91 mg chol., 209 mg sodium, 77 g carbo., 4 g fiber, 7 g pro. Daily Values: 9% vit. A, 9% vit. C, 7% calcium, 13% iron.

Kid Friendly
Fast!

Uncovered Blueberry Pie

PREP: 15 MINUTES **COOK:** 10 MINUTES

³/₄ cup sugar
3 Tbsp. cornstarch
¹/₈ tsp. salt
1 cup water
3 cups fresh blueberries
1 Tbsp. butter
1 9-inch baked pie shell
Sweetened whipped cream

1. In a medium saucepan combine sugar, cornstarch, and salt. Stir in water and 1 cup of the blueberries. Cook and stir over medium heat until thickened. Remove from heat. Stir in remaining 2 cups blueberries and butter until butter is melted. Cool completely. Pour into pie shell. If desired, cover and chill in refrigerator until ready to serve. Serve with whipped cream. Makes 8 servings.
EACH SERVING: 261 cal., 10 g total fat (3 g sat. fat), 4 mg chol., 122 mg sodium, 40 g carbo., 3 g fiber, 2 g pro. Daily Values: 2% vit. A, 9% vit. C, 1% calcium, 5% iron.

WITH THESE THREE EASY BLUEBERRY RECIPES, YOU'RE SURE TO FIND A SWEET TREAT FOR ALL THE DISCERNING TASTES IN YOUR FAMILY. BUT DON'T STOP THERE! MUFFINS, PIES, AND CAKES ARE JUST THE BEGINNING OF THE RECIPES BLUEBERRIES CAN BE USED FOR IN THE KITCHEN.

Blueberry Pound Cake

Pineapple-Glazed Banana Blueberry Muffins

Uncovered Blueberry Pie

Great Grilled Burgers

GRILLING THE PERFECT BURGER

Does it surprise you that when Americans fire up the grill,

93 percent will be grilling burgers? It's almost a national pastime. Grilling the perfect burger involves five steps—seasoning, shaping, cooking, flipping, and timing. Make the most flavorful burgers with 85 percent lean ground chuck, or for a little less fat, use 90 percent lean ground sirloin, which yields an equally juicy burger.

When you season ground beef, measure with a light hand so the herbs and spices add flavor without overpowering the meat. A bit of salt and pepper is often enough to bring out the meat's natural flavor. Loosen the ground beef with your fingers before adding the seasoning; then mix gently but thoroughly.

Shape burgers gently to form a 1-inch-thick patty. Don't overhandle the meat, and absolutely no smooshing! An overworked flat patty will be a tough burger.

Cook the burgers to 160°F (about 20 minutes total) for medium doneness. Flip patties once about halfway through cooking. Use a spatula for turning; piercing the burger with a fork lets juices escape. Resist the temptation to flatten the burger with the spatula; the resulting sizzle and smoke may have drama, but flattening squeezes flavorful juices from the meat, resulting in a dry burger.

Ketchup Stir-Ins

Kid Friendly Great Grilled Burgers

PREP: 25 MINUTES **GRILL:** 20 MINUTES

Basic Burger

- 1½ lb. 85% lean ground chuck or 90% lean ground sirloin
- ¾ tsp. kosher salt
- ½ tsp. freshly ground black pepper

For Stuffed Burger, add:

- ¼ cup finely chopped onion
- 4 oz. semi-firm cheese, such as cheddar, Edam, or Monterey Jack, shredded

Serve with:

- 4 hamburger buns
- Iceberg lettuce leaves
- 4 ¼-inch tomato slices
- 4 thin slices white onion
- Bread-and-butter pickles
- Ketchup and/or mustard

1. Place ground beef in bowl. Sprinkle with salt and pepper. Mix gently—do not overwork. Form beef into 4 patties about 1 inch thick. Grill on well-oiled rack of uncovered grill directly over medium coals for 10 minutes. Turn with spatula; grill 10 to 12 minutes more or until meat is no longer pink and meat thermometer registers 160°F internal temperature. Toast buns, cut sides down, on grill during last 1 to 2 minutes of grilling. To serve, top bun bottom with lettuce, burger, tomato, onion, and pickles. Spread top half of bun with ketchup and/or mustard; place top half of bun on sandwich.

2. For Stuffed Burger, place ground beef in bowl. Sprinkle with salt and pepper; add chopped onion. Mix gently—do not overwork. Divide cheese in 4 equal portions. Form beef around cheese into 4 patties about 1 inch thick. Continue as directed above. Makes 4 burgers.

BASIC BURGER: 460 cal., 23 g total fat (9 g sat. fat), 107 mg chol., 658 mg sodium, 24 g carbo., 2 g fiber, 37 g pro. Daily Values: 4% vit. A, 7% vit. C, 8% calcium, 26% iron.

STUFFED BURGER: 578 cal., 32 g total fat (15 g sat. fat), 137 mg chol., 835 mg sodium, 26 g carbo., 2 g fiber, 44 g pro. Daily Values: 10% vit. A, 8% vit. C, 28% calcium, 27% iron.

TRY THIS

Ketchup Stir-Ins. Start with ¾ cup ketchup.
- **Two-Tomato:** Stir in ¼ cup chopped, drained oil-packed dried tomatoes, 1 Tbsp. red wine vinegar, 1 Tbsp. packed brown sugar, dash salt and pepper.
- **Blueberry:** Stir in ¾ cup lightly mashed blueberries and/or raspberries, 2 Tbsp. cider vinegar, and 2 slices crisp-cooked crumbled bacon (stir in bacon just before use).
- **Sweet and Hot:** Stir in ¼ cup chopped, drained roasted red sweet peppers, 1 Tbsp. adobo sauce from canned chipotle chile peppers, 1 Tbsp. sherry vinegar, and 1 tsp. sugar.

Makes about 1 cup each. Cover and chill up to 1 week.

GROW A HEALTHY SALAD

BY **RICHARD SWEARINGER** PHOTOGRAPHS BY **PETE KRUMHARDT**

In late summer when most

crops slow down because of approaching fall, lettuce continues to make a wonderful contribution to the table. It won't surprise you to learn that most varieties of lettuce—especially dark green and red—are healthful. They're high in vitamins A, C, and folate—all nutrients that help keep the body's defenses working and help head off health problems such as heart disease and colds.

Garden-fresh lettuce has a sweetness and flavor that are quite different from many packaged greens. And here's good news about growing lettuce: from seed packet to table takes only a month, and lettuce isn't picky about the soil it grows in. Although full sun is best, lettuce will grow in a spot that has at least a half day of sun. A good time to plant your late-summer crop is the first Saturday in August. Sow additional crops every two weeks after that for fresh lettuce until frost comes to your area and brings the bounty to an end.

To get off to a successful start, look for seeds labeled "lea" or "loose leaf." Pick heat-tolerant varieties for fall crops, and improve your bounty and chance of success by planting several varieties. Lettuces sprout and flourish under a variety of conditions. If you're not sure which varieties your family likes, plant several so you can experience them all.

On the deck, grow lettuce in decorative pots. Three or four 18-inch pots will hold enough for a fall season of salads. Lettuces are so shallow rooted that they will also grow in window boxes.

Water seeds and sprouts lightly to keep the soil moist and cool but not wet. Mulch the plants to keep them from drying out, covering soil around young lettuces with 1 inch of compost, pine straw, shredded leaves, straw, or dry grass clippings. About every three days, check the soil by moving aside the mulch and touching the surface of the soil—it should feel damp.

Here are some flavor profiles of popular varieties to grow:
● Leaf lettuces, such as red and green, have a mild, somewhat sweet flavor.
● Many oak leaf lettuces (so-called for the shape of the leaves) taste slightly spicy.
● Romaines are known for juicy texture and slightly pungent bite; they add crunch to salads.
● Other greens—such as watercress, arugula, and mizuna—are peppery. Add a few leaves to salads for a flavor accent.

Fresh Herb Vinaigrette

A great salad deserves a flavorful dressing.

 START TO FINISH: 10 MINUTES

- ⅓ cup olive oil or salad oil
- ⅓ cup white or red wine vinegar,
- 1 Tbsp. snipped fresh thyme, oregano, or basil
- ¼ tsp. dry mustard or 1 tsp. Dijon-style mustard
- 1 clove garlic, minced
- ⅛ tsp. ground black pepper

1. In a screw-top jar combine all ingredients; cover and shake well. Serve immediately or cover and store in refrigerator up to 3 days. Shake before serving. Makes about ¾ cup.

EACH TABLESPOON: 57 cal., 6 g total fat (1 g sat. fat), 0 mg chol., 0 mg sodium, 1 g carbo., 0 g fiber, 0 g pro. Daily Values: 1% vit. C, 1% iron.

GETTING TO GREAT FLAVOR

BY **LISA GADDY FREDERICK** PHOTOGRAPHS BY **GREG SCHEIDEMANN, [N] HAUS FOTO**

The way Lauren Groveman

sees it, serving her family home-cooked, thoughtfully prepared meals is the highest expression of love. As the mom of three, with a thriving career and a packed schedule, she occasionally struggles to put that belief into practice. Lauren makes it mesh by relying on flavor-builders that help her get from-scratch goodies on the table in time for a sit-down dinner before family members slip out for various activities.

Food is the focus of Lauren's life, personally and professionally. "Cooking is the bridge that connects my life in a way that everyone is truly happy," says Lauren, a cooking teacher, cookbook author, and radio show host who lives in Larchmont, New York. She and husband Jon, along with children Benjamin, Julie, and Jessica, regularly gather for family dinners no matter how hectic the day.

The best time for her and Jon to reconnect with the kids and each other happens around the table during dinnertime. And a satisfying meal doesn't have to be elaborate—even something as basic as grilled cheese sandwiches can do the job.

"I don't care if you fix scrambled eggs. Turn off the TV and sit down at the table," Lauren says. In her kitchen, simple doesn't mean bland or boring. Far from it. A burst of flavor can take the easiest meal to a tasty new conclusion. "I never sacrifice anything when it comes to food for my family."

Lauren's favorite strategies for piling on flavors lie in versatile, easy-to-make toppings and embellishments. For example, she creates spreads and toppers from mixtures of sweet or savory ingredients. A caper, kalamata olive, and roasted red pepper trio complements chicken, fish, or cooked vegetables. Lauren also has ready a container of make-ahead Sweet-and-Sour Onions (recipe, *opposite*), glazed with brown sugar and balsamic vinegar, to pep up fajitas, grilled chops, omelets, and Brie cheese.

To squeeze in more time with her family at meals, Lauren does as much as possible ahead of time. "Organization is the key to preparing great meals with ease," she says. Veggies are blanched and stashed in the fridge until needed; blanching speeds the cooking time without diminishing freshness. On weekends, Lauren puts together dry mixes for pancakes, biscuits, or corn bread, which slashes the prep time right before meals to nearly nothing. Her book, *The I Love to Cook Book*, is full of big-flavor food ideas.

Despite her kitchen skills, Lauren insists that her family's meals wouldn't be as satisfying without that one special ingredient: love. Cooking with care keeps on-the-fly meals grounded in familiar flavors that families crave—and that draw them close, she says. In her words, "Family meals shape lives."

Browned Butter Topper

Try this on fish, chicken, pork, pasta, or polenta.

 Fast! **START TO FINISH:** 30 MINUTES

- ½ cup butter
- 12 cloves garlic, peeled
- 1 cup bottled roasted red sweet peppers, drained and cut into thin strips
- ⅓ cup pitted kalamata olives
- 2 Tbsp. capers, drained
- 2 Tbsp. snipped fresh sage, dill, or basil
- 2 Tbsp. lemon juice

1. In a large skillet heat butter and garlic over medium heat until butter is melted (butter will foam). Reduce heat to medium low (or low if butter browns too fast). Continue cooking for 15 minutes or until butter is light brown, stirring occasionally. Mash the garlic cloves, if desired.

2. Add pepper strips, olives, and capers to skillet. Cook for 4 minutes or until heated through. Stir in sage and lemon juice. Makes 1½ cups.

EACH ¼-CUP SERVING: 173 cal., 17 g fat (8 g sat. fat), 43 mg chol., 242 mg sodium, 5 g carbo., 1 g fiber, 1 g pro. Daily Values: 10% vit. A, 120% vit. C.

Sweet-and-Sour Onions

Cook onions a little longer—until they're golden brown—to caramelize them for sweeter flavor.

 Fast! **START TO FINISH:** 30 MINUTES

- 3 cups (about 13 oz.) pearl onions, peeled*
- 2 Tbsp. olive oil
- 2 large red onions, halved and sliced into thin strips (2 cups)
- ¼ cup balsamic vinegar or red wine vinegar
- 2 Tbsp. packed brown sugar
- ½ tsp. salt
- ¼ tsp. ground black pepper
  Brie cheese (optional)

1. In a large skillet cook pearl onions in hot oil over medium-low heat for 5 minutes, stirring occasionally. Add onion strips, vinegar, brown sugar, salt, and pepper. Cook and stir for 5 minutes more or until mixture thickens and pearl onions are crisp-tender. If desired, spoon onto Brie. Makes 2½ cups.

***NOTE:** To peel onions, cook in boiling water for 30 seconds; cool. Cut a thin slice off the root end and squeeze from other end to remove peel.

EACH ¼-CUP SERVING: 58 cal., 3 g total fat (0 g sat. fat), 119 mg sodium, 8 g carbo., 1 g fiber, 1 g pro. Daily Values: 5% vit. C, 1% calcium, 1% iron.

Browned Butter Topper

In good taste
FOOD AND ENTERTAINING

Urban (e) Accents

Add a surprise to summer entertaining. Use spice rubs or flavored sugars and salts, meant for rimming glassware, as dippers for fruits or marinated olives. Tom Knibbs, (*right*) and Jim Dygas (*below*), owners of the Chicago-based spice and condiment company Urban Accents, created "Cocktail Dippers" for at-home gatherings. The dippers include strawberries soaked in vanilla vodka and then dipped in Mandarin Orange Sugar. They each have a favorite. Visit them at www.urbanaccents.com.

Tom says:

"One of our most successful ideas was for a Sunday brunch— Bloody Mary on a Stick. Soak grape or cherry tomatoes in a bowl of vodka. Chill in the refrigerator for about 1 hour. To serve, set the bowl out and have guests spear the tomatoes with a toothpick then dip into our Bloody Mary Mix. It's the world's fastest Bloody Mary."

Jim says:

"My Rum Runners are just right to put on the table for everyone to nibble post-dessert. Soak small bunches of red grapes in dark rum for 1 hour. Remove them with a slotted spoon (reserve the rum), place on a tray, and freeze them overnight. Remove the tray about half an hour before serving. When the grapes have thawed a bit, place them in a bowl of reserved rum alongside Citrus Rimming Sugar for dipping."

Peachy Twist

Jonathan Rapp, owner of the River Tavern in Chester, Connecticut, makes the most of summer fruit by marinating halved peaches in olive oil, lemon juice, black pepper, salt, and a dash of cayenne. He serves them with thinly sliced prosciutto, fresh mint leaves, and a drizzle of the marinade. River Tavern, 23 Main St., Chester, Connecticut; 860/526-9417.

Market Math

When farmers' markets are brimming with tomatoes, making and freezing homemade tomato sauce is the best way to preserve the harvest into the winter months. Fifteen pounds of tomatoes (which sounds like more than it really is) will yield about 2 quarts of sauce. Cook chopped tomatoes down until the sauce coats the back of a wooden spoon. Portion and freeze. Add seasonings when you use the sauce for preparing pasta sauces, salsa, soup, or chili.

Quick Chill

Need to chill wine fast? Here's an easy trick that doesn't risk a cracked bottle in the freezer or force you to put ice cubes in the pinot grigio. Fill an ice bucket with half ice and half cold water, sprinkle with a handful of salt, and put the bottle in. The salt reduces the freezing point of the water, which becomes super chilled.

Can't Be Beat!

Cooked, peeled baby red beets are the latest news in packaged vegetables. They're convenient for speeding up dinner prep. Toss the beets right into a salad of greens, red onion, and carrots dressed with a squeeze of lemon. Beets: $10.70 for three packs; www.melissas.com.

SEPTEMBER

TECHNICALLY SUMMER IS STILL IN FULL SWING THIS MONTH, SO SOAK IT UP! PACK A SATURDAY AFTERNOON PICNIC AND ENJOY THE LAST FEW WARM DAYS OF THE SEASON IN STYLE.

Turkey on Leaf-Cutout Biscuits
Leaf-Peeking Slaw
Butternut Squash Kabobs
page 176

Peak of Autumn Picnic

Plus

Caramel Apple Crisp To Go
page 179

Berry-Ginger Cider
page 175

Cream of Pumpkin Soup
Pumpkin Seed Breadsticks
page 178

Peak of Autumn Picnic

PACK A FEAST, PILE INTO THE
VAN, AND EXPLORE FALL'S
SPLENDOR. ALONG THE WAY,
TAKE ADVANTAGE OF NATURE'S
BOUNTY FOR MUNCHING,
DECORATING, AND CRAFTING.

Kid Friendly

Berry-Ginger Cider

If you plan to buy a jug of cider from a roadside stand, take along the syrup to stir in.

Fast! **START TO FINISH:** 15 MINUTES

  1 12-oz. pkg. unsweetened frozen red raspberries, blackberries, or strawberries, thawed

  3 Tbsp. light-colored corn syrup

  ½ tsp. ground ginger

  8 cups (½ gallon) apple cider

    Ice cubes

    Fresh raspberries (optional)

1. In a blender container or food processor bowl combine berries, corn syrup, and ginger. Cover and blend or process until pureed. Press berry mixture through a fine-mesh sieve; discard seeds.* Transfer to a half-pint jar with lid. Cover and refrigerate up to 2 weeks.

2. To serve, combine the berry-ginger syrup with cider in a large pitcher or jug. For an individual serving, add 2 tablespoons of berry syrup to 8 ounces (1 cup) cider. Serve over ice. If desired, top with fresh berries. Makes 8 servings.

*TEST KITCHEN TIP: Because strawberry seeds are so much smaller than other berries, it is not necessary to sieve.

EACH SERVING: 158 cal., 0 g total fat (0 g sat. fat), 13 mg sodium, 0 mg chol., 39g carbo., 1 g fiber, 0 g pro. Daily Values: 5% vit. C, 2% calcium, 6% iron.

Berry-Ginger Cider

A

hint of fall in the air—a cool wind, the golden glow of leaves ...

These are signals to pack a picnic lunch, gather the family, and head out for a day devoted to outdoor fun. All too soon, weekends will be filled with chilly days, school activities, and homework. So carve out some family time to spend together at a park, lake, seashore, or the backyard.

Build the day around harvest fare of apples, pumpkins, and squash and pack up a picnic lunch the night before. In the morning, get out the door early enough so you have plenty of time to turn off at an orchard, pick some crisp apples to munch in the car, explore duck ponds, and scout hiking trails.

Once you arrive at your destination, fortify the group with homemade trail mix to tide them over until lunchtime.

As you unpack the picnic basket, your family will be dazzled with hearty sandwiches of turkey stacked between flaky leaf-shape biscuits; pumpkin soup that chases the chill from the day; and butternut squash kabobs, ready for the grill. Creamy, fruity cheesecake provides the crowning touch.

Great food is even better ...

when served on unexpectedly homey tableware. If you don't mind a wee bit of added weight, consider toting sturdy stoneware and chunky tumblers or, if it suits the mood, Mason jars. Hefty dishes add woodsy style to a meal served outdoors. Be sure to pack breakables between layers of blankets or towels to prevent chips and cracking. Although paper plates are a reliable choice, plastic plates have taken a leap forward—look for them in bright colors to enliven your picnic scene.

Pack most of the food in a cooler; keep the pumpkin soup piping hot in a vacuum container. If you have room, consider taking a small folding table for serving. Remember to take a supply of trash bags to collect all your leavings from the day.

Take nothing but pictures.

Before your family treks through the park, take time to check the rules. At most parks, collecting even so much as a twig or a pebble is prohibited. Instead, remember the day by assembling a memory-collecting kit with cameras, watercolors, paintbrushes, crayons, and art papers. Photograph or draw fall motifs—acorns, leaves, wildlife—to take home for decorations or scrapbooking.

Butternut Squash Kabobs

Think of it as veggies on a stick. This kabob is wonderful either hot or cold.

PREP: 30 MINUTES **ROAST:** 20 MINUTES

> 1 2-lb. butternut squash
> 3 Tbsp. butter, melted
> 1 tsp. curry powder
> 8 8-inch wooden or metal skewers

1. Preheat oven to 450°F. Cut squash in half lengthwise and remove seeds. Peel squash. Cut squash halves in 1- to 1½-inch pieces. Place in a 3-quart rectangular baking dish. In a small bowl combine butter and curry powder. Drizzle over squash, tossing to coat.

2. Roast squash, uncovered, for 20 to 25 minutes or until tender and lightly browned, stirring once or twice. Serve immediately or let cool to tote. Store in an airtight container in the refrigerator up to 2 days.

3. Serve squash at room temperature threaded on eight 8-inch skewers. Season to taste with *salt*. Makes 8 servings.

NOTE: To reheat kabobs, grill on a gas or charcoal grill directly over medium coals (or preheat gas grill to medium) about 10 minutes or until heated through, turning kabobs occasionally.

 EACH SERVING: 69 cal., 5 g total fat (2 g sat. fat), 12 mg chol., 36 mg sodium, 7 g carbo., 1 g fiber, 1 g pro. Daily Values: 24% vit. A, 14% vit. C, 3% calcium, 3% iron.

Leaf-Peeking Slaw

Golden Delicious apples hold their shape and color well after being sliced.

PREP: 25 MINUTES **CHILL:** 2 HOURS

> 4 cups 1-inch pieces red cabbage
> 2 medium Golden Delicious apples, cored and cubed
> 2 medium carrots, sliced
> ⅓ cup chopped red onion
> ¼ cup salad oil
> ¼ cup red wine vinegar
> 1 Tbsp. Dijon-style mustard
> 1 tsp. sugar
> ½ tsp. salt
> ½ tsp. ground black pepper

1. In a large bowl combine the cabbage, apples, carrots, and onion. For dressing, in a bowl whisk together the oil, vinegar, mustard, sugar, salt, and pepper until well combined. Add dressing to salad; toss to coat. Refrigerate, covered, for 2 to 24 hours. Makes 6 servings.

EACH SERVING: 131 cal., 9 g total fat (1 g sat. fat), 0 mg chol., 281 mg sodium, 13 g carbo., 3 g fiber, 2 g pro. Daily Values: 60% vit. A, 50% vit. C, 4% calcium, 3% iron.

Turkey on Leaf-Cutout Biscuits

Tuck this biscuit recipe away in your Thanksgiving recipe file; then bake a batch for your holiday meal.

 PREP: 20 MINUTES **BAKE:** 10 MINUTES

> 4 cups all-purpose flour*
> 4 tsp. baking powder
> ½ tsp. baking soda
> ½ tsp. salt
> 1⅓ cups buttermilk
> ½ cup cooking oil
> 2 Tbsp. butter, melted
> ½ tsp. paprika
> 1 recipe Pear-Sage Butter (recipe, *page 180*) or purchased apple butter
> 10 oz. shaved smoked turkey
> ¼ cup sliced almonds, toasted

1. Preheat oven to 450°F. In a medium bowl combine flour, baking powder, baking soda, and salt. In a small bowl stir together the buttermilk and oil. Pour into flour mixture; stir just until moistened.

2. On a lightly floured surface knead dough gently for 10 to 12 strokes. Roll out or pat dough to 1-inch thickness. Cut with a 3-inch leaf-shape cookie cutter, dipping cutter in flour between cuts. Transfer biscuits to an ungreased baking sheet. In a bowl combine melted butter and paprika. Brush biscuit tops with butter mixture.

3. Bake for 10 to 12 minutes or until bottoms are browned. Cool on a wire rack. With a serrated knife or a sharp knife, carefully split biscuits in half horizontally.

4. Prepare Pear-Sage Butter and spread bottom half of each biscuit with 2 tablespoons of butter mixture. Top with some of the smoked turkey and almonds; cover with biscuit top. Makes 8 to 10 sandwiches.

*NOTE: If desired, substitute ½ cup whole wheat flour or oat bran for ½ cup of the all-purpose flour.

EACH SANDWICH: 508 cal., 21 g total fat (4 g sat. fat), 28 mg chol., 769 mg sodium, 66 g carbo., 3 g fiber, 15 g pro. Daily Values: 4% vit. A, 4% vit. C, 12% calcium, 18% iron.

A LITTLE SHADE, A LITTLE LUNCH: THE FAMILY IS READY FOR AFTERNOON FUN.

Turkey on Leaf-Cutout Biscuits
Butternut Squash Kabobs
Leaf-Peeking Slaw

Cream of Pumpkin Soup
Pumpkin Seed Breadsticks

Cream of Pumpkin Soup

Shaking flour and half-and-half together prevents the flour mixture from lumping when it is stirred into the soup.

PREP: 15 MINUTES **COOK:** 20 MINUTES

- 3 Tbsp. butter
- 1 large onion, finely chopped (1 cup)
- 2 cloves garlic, minced
- ⅛ to ¼ tsp. crushed red pepper
- 2 14-oz. cans chicken broth
- ½ cup uncooked orzo or wild rice
- 1½ cups half-and-half, light cream, or milk
- 1 Tbsp. all-purpose flour
- 1 15-oz. can pumpkin
  Cracked black pepper (optional)

1. In a large saucepan melt butter over medium-high heat. Add onion and garlic; cook for 3 to 5 minutes or until tender, stirring occasionally. Stir in crushed red pepper; cook for 1 minute. Add broth; bring to boiling. Stir in orzo (or rice). Reduce heat and simmer, covered, about 10 minutes for orzo (40 minutes for wild rice) or until orzo (or rice) is tender.

2. In a screw-top jar combine half-and-half and flour. Cover; shake well to combine. Stir into orzo mixture; cook and stir until slightly thickened and bubbly. Stir in pumpkin; heat through. Transfer to an insulated container. If desired, sprinkle each serving with cracked black pepper. Makes 6 to 8 side-dish servings.

EACH SERVING: 234 cal., 14 g total fat (8 g sat. fat), 40 mg chol., 614 mg sodium, 23 g carbo., 3 g fiber, 6 g pro. Daily Values: 229% vit. A, 9% vit. C, 9% calcium, 9% iron.

Pumpkin Seed Breadsticks

Shelled pumpkin seeds are available in the Hispanic food section of many grocery stores.

PREP: 15 MINUTES **BAKE:** 8 MINUTES PER BATCH

- 1 13- to 14-oz. pkg. refrigerated pizza dough
- 1 egg, beaten
- 1 to 3 Tbsp. shelled pumpkin seeds, plain sesame seeds, and/or black sesame seeds
  Coarse salt or salt

1. Preheat oven to 425°F. Lightly grease two large baking sheets. Unroll pizza dough on a lightly floured surface. Using your hands, shape dough into a 12×9-inch rectangle. Brush the dough with some of the egg. Sprinkle with seeds and lightly sprinkle with salt. Use a floured long knife or floured pizza cutter to cut dough crosswise into ¼- to ½-inch-wide strips.

2. Place strips on prepared baking sheets. Bake, one sheet at a time, for 8 to 10 minutes or until golden brown. Cool on wire racks. Makes about 24 breadsticks.

EACH BREADSTICK: 39 cal., 1 g total fat (0 g sat. fat), 9 mg chol., 75 mg sodium, 6 g carbo., 0 g fiber, 1 g pro. Daily Values: 1% calcium, 3% iron.

Autumn Trail Mix

 Fast! **PREP:** 15 MINUTES **BAKE:** 10 MINUTES

Butter

2 cups mixed nuts

2 cups small checker pretzels or small pretzel twists

1 cup packed brown sugar

¼ cup water

½ to 1 tsp. ground nutmeg

2 cups miniature chocolate chip cookies and/or bite-size rich round sandwich crackers with peanut butter filling

1. Preheat oven to 300°F. Line a baking sheet with foil; butter the foil and set aside. In a large bowl combine nuts and pretzels; set aside.

2. In a medium skillet combine brown sugar, water, and nutmeg. Cook and stir over medium heat until sugar is dissolved. Heat to boiling. Reduce heat to medium and simmer about 5 minutes or until mixture is thickened and syrupy. Drizzle sugar mixture over nut mixture, tossing to coat. Spread onto prepared baking sheet. Bake 10 minutes. Stir; spread on another piece of foil. Allow nut mixture to cool.

3. Break nut mixture into small clusters. Stir in cookies Store in an airtight container up to 4 days. Makes about 16 (½-cup) servings.

EACH SERVING: 216 cal., 12 g total fat (2 g sat. fat), 0 mg chol., 233 mg sodium, 26 g carbo., 2 g fiber, 4 g pro. Daily Values: 3% calcium, 6% iron.

Autumn Trail Mix

Caramel Apple Crisp To Go

Caramel Apple Crisp To Go

A jar of this quick-to-make sauce is a welcome hostess gift.

PREP: 20 MINUTES **COOL:** 15 MINUTES **CHILL:** UP TO 2 WEEKS

½ cup whipping cream

½ cup butter

¾ cup packed dark brown sugar

2 Tbsp. light-colored corn syrup

1 tsp. vanilla

4 to 6 apples, cored and sliced

1 cup crushed cookies , such as biscotti, pecan shortbread, peanut butter, oatmeal, snickerdoodle, or chocolate chip (about 3 oz.)

1. For caramel sauce, in a heavy medium saucepan combine whipping cream, butter, brown sugar, and corn syrup. Bring to boiling over medium-high heat (about 5 to 6 minutes), whisking occasionally. Reduce heat to medium. Boil gently for 3 minutes more. Stir in vanilla. Transfer sauce to a storage jar with a lid. Let cool for 15 minutes. Cover and refrigerate up to 2 weeks. Let stand at room temperature 1 hour before serving.

2. To serve, place apple slices in individual bowls. Drizzle with caramel sauce. Top with crushed cookies. Makes 8 servings.

EACH SERVING: 339 cal., 19 g total fat (10 g sat. fat), 56 mg chol., 139 mg sodium, 42 g carbo., 2 g fiber, 2 g pro. Daily Values: 13% vit. A, 5% vit. C, 4% calcium, 4% iron.

Pear-Sage Butter

Also spread this flavored butter on muffins in the morning.

PREP: 15 MINUTES **COOK:** 20 MINUTES

>   2 cups peeled, finely chopped fresh pears or one
>   15-oz. can pear halves (juice pack)*
>   ½ cup sugar
>   1 Tbsp. snipped fresh sage or 1 tsp. dried sage, crushed

1. In a medium saucepan place chopped pears, ¼ cup *water*, sugar, and dried sage, if using. Cook and stir over medium-low heat until bubbly. Boil gently, uncovered, for 20 to 25 minutes or until mixture is very thick and liquid is nearly evaporated, mashing fruit after 15 minutes of cooking. Adjust heat to maintain a gentle boil.

2. Remove saucepan from heat. Stir in fresh sage, if using. Cool completely. Serve with Turkey on Leaf-Cutout Biscuits (recipe, *page 176*). Makes about 1 cup.

*NOTE: If using canned pears, drain pears, reserving ¼ cup of the liquid. Finely chop canned pear halves. Cook as above, using reserved liquid in place of water.

EACH 2-TABLESPOON SERVING: 71 cal., 0 g total fat, 0 mg chol., 0 mg sodium, 18 g carbo., 1 g fiber, 0 g pro. Daily Values: 3% vit. C, 1% calcium.

Out-and-About Cheesecake

An unexpected treat for the great outdoors.

PREP: 20 MINUTES **STAND:** 15 MINUTES

>   1 4-oz. round Brie cheese
>   1 8-oz. pkg. cream cheese
>   3 Tbsp. sugar
>   1 tsp. finely shredded lemon peel
>   1 Tbsp. lemon juice
>   4 cups fresh blueberries
>   ⅓ cup butter toffee-glazed sliced almonds or honey-roasted
>   almonds
>   8 purchased maple leaf candies (optional)

1. Remove and discard Brie rind. Let Brie and cream cheese stand at room temperature for 15 minutes to soften. In a medium mixing bowl beat Brie, cream cheese, sugar, lemon peel, and lemon juice with electric mixer on medium speed until smooth. Set aside.

2. Divide blueberries and cheese mixture among eight 10-ounce disposable drinking glasses, alternating layers of berries and cheese. Sprinkle almonds over cheese mixture. Cover each cup with plastic wrap; secure with decorative string. Serve immediately or refrigerate up to 4 hours before serving. If desired, top with maple leaf candies before serving. Makes 8 servings.

EACH SERVING: 225 cal., 16 g total fat (9 g sat. fat), 45 mg chol., 193 mg sodium, 15 g carbo., 4 g fiber, 6 g pro. Daily Values: 10% vit. A, 14% vit. C, 7% calcium, 3% iron.

TO MAKE ONE LARGE CHEESECAKE: Place blueberries in a shallow 2-quart rectangular plastic or glass storage container. Spoon cheese mixture over berries; spread to form an even layer. Sprinkle almonds over cheese mixture. Cover to tote.

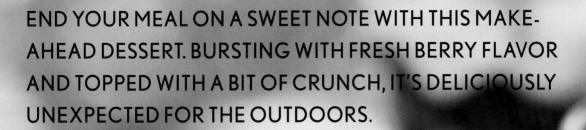

END YOUR MEAL ON A SWEET NOTE WITH THIS MAKE-AHEAD DESSERT. BURSTING WITH FRESH BERRY FLAVOR AND TOPPED WITH A BIT OF CRUNCH, IT'S DELICIOUSLY UNEXPECTED FOR THE OUTDOORS.

Out-and-About Cheesecake

Chipotle Apple Pecan Cake

Chipotle Apple Pecan Cake
PREP: 40 MINUTES **BAKE:** 1¼ HOURS

	Nonstick cooking spray
3	cups all-purpose flour
2	tsp. ground cinnamon
1½	tsp. ground nutmeg
1	tsp. baking soda
1	tsp. ground chipotle pepper
¾	tsp. ground ginger
½	tsp. ground white pepper
¼	tsp. salt
⅛	tsp. ground cloves
1½	cups cooking oil
1¾	cups sugar
3	eggs
1	Tbsp. vanilla
3	large (1¼ lb.) sweet-tart apples peeled, cored, and diced (3 cups)
1	cup chopped pecans, toasted
1	recipe Spicy Caramel Glaze

1. Preheat oven to 325°F. Lightly coat 10-inch fluted tube pan with cooking spray; lightly sprinkle with flour. Set aside. In a bowl combine the 3 cups flour, cinnamon, nutmeg, baking soda, chipotle, ginger, white pepper, salt, and cloves; set aside.

2. In a mixing bowl beat oil and sugar with electric mixer on medium speed until combined. Add eggs, one at a time; beat well after each addition. Beat in vanilla and as much flour mixture as you can. Stir in remaining flour mixture, apples, and pecans. Spoon batter into pan.

3. Bake 1¼ hours, until wooden toothpick inserted near center comes out clean. Meanwhile, prepare Spicy Caramel Glaze. Cool cake in pan 10 minutes; invert on rack. Place rack over baking sheet. Drizzle warm cake with Spicy Caramel Glaze, respooning glaze that drips on baking sheet over cake. Cool completely before serving. Makes 16 servings.

SPICY CARAMEL GLAZE: In a saucepan combine ½ cup packed brown sugar, ¼ cup butter, ¼ cup whipping cream, and ½ teaspoon ground chipotle pepper. Bring to boiling, stirring occasionally. Boil gently 2 minutes. Remove from heat. Stir in 1 teaspoon vanilla. Let stand ¼ hours until slightly thickened. Drizzle over warm cake.

EACH SERVING: 490 cal., 31 g total fat (7 g sat. fat), 53 mg chol., 165 mg sodium, 50 g carbo., 2 g fiber, 4 g pro. Daily Values: 7% vit. A, 3% vit. C, 3% calcium, 9% iron.

SWEET HEAT

Liven up desserts with a kick of heat!

For delightfully intense flavor, discover the complement of fiery and sweet in cakes and cookies and with cheese and fruit. Traditional spices used in these recipes offer a familiar taste with a twist and a bit of south-of-the-border flavor.

Two sources add culinary heat: chile peppers and peppercorns. Find ground chile peppers—chipotle, jalapeño, dried red chiles, or crushed red pepper flakes—in grocery stores and specialty markets. Chiles contain capsaicin, the compound that makes them hot. Colorful peppercorns—black, white, red, and green—contribute a wonderful pungency to desserts and fresh fruit. For the best flavor, use a peppermill to freshly grind peppercorns each time they're called for. Then experience the heat.

BY **ROBIN KLINE** PHOTOGRAPHS BY **JOYCE OUDKERK POOL**

Three-Pepper Spice Cookies

PREP: 40 MINUTES **CHILL:** 4 HOURS **BAKE:** 8 MINUTES PER BATCH

- ½ cup butter, softened
- 1 cup sugar
- 1½ tsp. baking powder
- ½ tsp. ground red chile
- ½ tsp. finely ground black pepper
- ½ tsp. ground ginger
- ½ tsp. ground cloves
- ½ tsp. ground cinnamon
- ¼ tsp. cayenne pepper
- 1 egg
- 1 Tbsp. milk
- 2 cups all-purpose flour
  Medium-grind black pepper
- 10 oz. bittersweet chocolate, coarsely chopped
- 1 Tbsp. shortening

1. In a mixing bowl beat butter with electric mixer on medium to high speed for 30 seconds. Add sugar, baking powder, ground red chile, the ½ teaspoon finely ground black pepper, ginger, cloves, cinnamon, and cayenne pepper. Beat until combined, scraping sides of bowl. Beat in egg and milk until combined. Beat in as much flour as you can. Stir in remaining flour. If necessary, knead dough slightly to blend. Shape dough into a ball. Divide dough in half. Shape each half into a 6½-inch-long roll. Wrap in plastic wrap; chill 4 to 24 hours.

2. Preheat oven to 375°F. Cut rolls in ¼-inch slices. Place slices 1 inch apart on ungreased cookie sheets. Sprinkle cookies with medium-grind black pepper. Bake 8 to 10 minutes or until edges are golden. Transfer cookies to wire rack to cool.

3. In small saucepan melt chocolate and shortening over low heat, stirring occasionally. Dip each cookie halfway in melted chocolate; shake off excess. Place chocolate-dipped cookies on waxed paper. Let stand until chocolate is set. Makes about 60 cookies.

EACH COOKIE: 67 cal., 4 g total fat (2 g sat. fat), 8 mg chol., 28 mg sodium, 9 g carbo., 0 g fiber, 1 g pro. Daily Values: 2% vit. A, 0% vit. C, 1% calcium, 2% iron.

Chile Nut Honey with Cheese

Chile Nut Honey with Cheese

 Fast! **PREP:** 10 MINUTES **BAKE:** 10 MINUTES **COOL:** 10 MINUTES

- ¼ cup walnuts
- ½ cup honey
- ¾ tsp. cayenne pepper, ¼ tsp. ground chipotle chile pepper, or 1 tsp. crushed red pepper
- 4 oz. soft pungent cheese (fresh goat cheese or blue cheese)
  Crusty bread or crackers

1. Preheat oven to 350°F. In shallow baking pan toast walnuts for 10 to 12 minutes, just until they start to brown and become aromatic. Cool slightly; chop coarsely.

2. In a bowl stir together nuts, honey, and cayenne pepper.

3. To serve, bring cheese to room temperature. Serve with honey mixture and crusty bread. Makes 4 servings.

EACH SERVING: 254 cal., 11 g total fat (5 g sat. fat), 13 mg chol., 106 mg sodium, 36 g carbo., 1 g fiber, 7 g pro. Daily Values: 3% vit. A, 1% vit. C, 5% calcium, 5% iron.

Three-Pepper Spice Cookies

CHEESE PIZZA SPREAD
Combine a 5-ounce jar of process cheddar cheese spread, 2 tablespoons chopped pepperoni, and 1 tablespoon chopped green sweet pepper or green onion. Spread on a tortilla, roll, and slice.

PEANUT FRUIT SPREAD
Combine 1/3 cup peanut butter; about 3 tablespoons snipped dried fruit, such as apricots, raisins, cranberries, and/or apples; and 1 tablespoon toasted coconut. Spread on slices of warm, toasted banana bread or whole grain bread.

CRUNCHY VEGGIE SPREAD
Combine one-half an 8-ounce tub cream cheese with 2 tablespoons each chopped celery and shredded carrot. Stir in a splash of milk and top with a generous sprinkling of shelled sunflower seeds. Spoon on a freshly sliced apple, or spread on bread and top with apple slices for a pleasantly sweet lunch.

SUPER SPREADS

Chunky concoctions are superb when slathered on bread or used
as dippers for healthful snacks of apple, celery, or carrot. Best of all, they can be stirred together in a jiffy, perfect for drop-in visitors or hungry after-school snackers. Kids love the pepperoni-cheese combo in the Cheese Pizza Spread.

These spreads tote well as take-along lunches for school and work. Spreads are easy to carry packed in plastic containers. Tote bread, crackers, or your favorite quick bread in a separate sealed plastic bag to keep foods fresh. Pretzels and breadsticks also make good dippers.

BY **JEANNE AMBROSE** PHOTOGRAPHS BY **GREG SCHEIDEMANN, [N] HAUS FOTO** FOOD STYLING BY **BROOKE LEONARD**

Orange Minted Barley Wrap

ORANGE MINTED BARLEY WRAP

Cook ³/₄ cup regular barley according to package directions, substituting 2 cups orange juice for 2 cups of the water; drain. Toss warm barley with thinly sliced radishes, a dash of cayenne pepper to taste, finely shredded orange peel, and snipped fresh mint and cilantro. For dressing, combine ¹/₄ cup orange juice, 3 tablespoons salad oil, 1 tablespoon toasted sesame oil, 2 tablespoons white wine vinegar, salt, and ground black pepper. Toss barley mixture with half the dressing; reserve remaining half for dipping sauce. Place on Bibb lettuce leaves, roll up, and serve.

BARLEY "RISOTTO"

Saute 1 cup chopped leeks in extra-virgin olive oil until softened; add 1¹/₂ cups quick-cooking barley. Cook and stir for 1 minute. Add 3³/₄ cups hot chicken stock, ¹/₂ cup at a time, stirring in each addition until the liquid is absorbed. When liquid is absorbed and mixture is creamy (about 25 minutes), remove saucepan from heat; stir in 1 cup finely shredded Parmesan cheese, ¹/₂ cup shredded carrots, and snipped fresh tarragon.

MANGO-BARLEY SALAD

Cook ¹/₃ cup regular barley in 2 cups water according to package directions. Toss warm barley with ¹/₂ cup toasted pecan pieces, one thinly sliced mango, and 2 tablespoons crumbled blue cheese. Toss with 6 cups field greens or mesclun. Drizzle with ¹/₄ cup balsamic vinaigrette.

CHOOSING BARLEY

Once hulled, this nutty-tasting grain becomes a polished pearl

with firm texture and sweet flavor. Toss versatile barley with grated cheese, steamed green vegetables, spicy vinaigrette, and/or cooked mushrooms and it becomes a nutritious substitute for rice or pasta.

BY **MARGE PERRY** PHOTOGRAPH BY **COLLEEN DUFFLEY**

In good taste
FOOD AND ENTERTAINING

PHOTOGRAPHS BY **KIM CORNELISON** (COLD BREW AND BROWNIES); **KELLER + KELLER** (PORTRAIT)

Cold Brew

That iced mocha from a coffee shop may be made with cold-brewed coffee. The brewing process, in which time replaces heat, starts by immersing ground coffee in cold water and produces a cold, rich coffee concentrate that can be stored in the refrigerator up to 14 days. Simply add hot water to the cold concentrate for a cup or pot of coffee prepared to your desired strength. Cold-brewing reduces coffee acidity by 50 percent and also eliminates about 20 percent of the caffeine. This brew is the perfect substitute in recipes that call for instant or brewed coffee. Try it in pumpkin pie, brownies, or cheesecake or stir it into barbecue or mole sauce. Toddy Cold Brew Coffee System; $34.95; 713/225-2066; www.toddycafe.com.

Make Mine Marshmallow

Gooey, oozy marshmallow creme still delights, just as it did on a peanut butter sandwich when you were a kid. Suzanne Lombardi, owner of Tiny Trapeze Confections, suggests using marshmallow creme for a decadent brownie dessert. Spoon the creme and sprinkle walnuts onto brownie batter the last 5 minutes of baking. Lombardi also suggests using marshmallow creme to top a cup of hot cocoa, spreading it on a graham cracker for a quick snack, filling and frosting cupcakes, or warming it with a few tablespoons of water to top ice cream, cake, or fruit. Tiny Trapeze Marshmallow Creme; $4.50; www.tinytrapeze.com.

Tiny Trapeze Confections produces old-fashioned, all-natural, no-preservatives candy. The company's factory in Hyde Park, Massachusetts, is home to vintage candy-making equipment that the owners have restored to working condition.

Pepper-Grinder Lowdown

"With freshly ground pepper, it's all in the grind. The finer the grind, the harder it works." says Vic Firth, creator of state-of-the-art peppermills. Firth is a former timpanist for the Boston Symphony and manufacturer of the standard bearer drumsticks that carry his name (he whittled the first pair in 1963). Firth makes sure that the grind mechanism—the part most people never see—can be removed, cleaned, and most important, locked for the grind of choice. "Freshly ground pepper should complement the food with which it's served. Use a bigger grind when you want a big hit of flavor, as in a salad or soup. When you want pepper to blend with food, such as in a vinaigrette, use a finer grind." Vic Firth peppermills; 800/894-5970; www.vicfirthgourmet.com.

GOOD TO KNOW

Vic Firth keeps his favorite blend of peppercorns in a 3-inch grinder on his desk for working lunches. The appetizing aroma of whole Madagascar and Jamaican black, white, and pink peppercorns is tantalizing, he says, and really adds to a lunch on the go.

SEASONED SALTS

Sprinkle on seasoned sea salts to add a final punch of flavor to salads, soups, stews, and vegetables.

CHILE SALT
Combine chopped chile pepper with salt for heating up chicken, fish, or steaks or to season a taco or tortilla soup.

STAR ANISE SALT
Ground star anise and sea salt add a marvelous hit of licorice flavor to melons and citrus fruits—even a milk chocolate bar.

FLORAL SALT
Scented geraniums (or other edible flowers) and sea salt are an elegant touch for pastas, salads, grilled fish, and vegetables. (Discard any unused mixed salt.)

FLUFFY MATZO BALLS

Two Jewish grandmas have some advice for you. (They thought you'd never ask!) Ruthie and Gussie, whose matzo ball batter is conveniently frozen, suggest adding 1 tablespoon of oil to the batter for fluffier matzo balls. Cook the matzo balls about 1 hour until they double in size. Fold parsley or dill into the batter before cooking for additional flavor. Ruthie & Gussie's Matzo Ball Batter; $20.95 for two 16 oz. tubs; 877-4LATKES (877-452-8537); http://store.ruthieandgussies.com.

OCTOBER

FALL IS BACK IN ALL ITS GLORY, AND WITH IT
COMES OUR FAVORITE SQUASH: THE PUMPKIN.
PUREE, GRILL, OR TOAST THESE FALL BEAUTIES FOR
SOME SURPRISINGLY DELICIOUS FLAVOR.

Grilled Pumpkin Bowl with Veggies
page 199

The Splendid Pumpkin

Plus

Peppery Pumpkin Seed Toffee
page 195

Roasted Red Pepper Lasagna
page 201

Roasted Pumpkin Kabob Salad
page 192

Pumpkin Pie Nog

WHAT BETTER WAY TO SERVE PUMPKIN NOG
THAN IN A PUMPKIN PUNCH BOWL? CARVE IN
LARGE SCALLOPED EDGES OR CREATE YOUR
OWN UNIQUE DESIGN!

The Splendid Pumpkin

Pumpkin Pie Nog

A serving of this autumn-perfect drink is like pumpkin pie in a glass.

Fast! **START TO FINISH:** 25 MINUTES

- 1 46 oz. bottle peach-mango smoothie drink or peach nectar (5½ cups)
- 2 cups Pumpkin Puree (recipe, *page 192*) or one 15-oz. can pumpkin
- 2 tsp. pumpkin pie spice
- 1 qt. vanilla or pumpkin ice cream
- 1 Pumpkin Punch Bowl (optional)

1. If using Pumpkin Puree, in a blender container combine 1 cup of the smoothie drink and the Pumpkin Puree; cover and blend until smooth.

2. In a 5- to 6-quart saucepan combine the remaining smoothie drink, the blended pumpkin mixture or the canned pumpkin, and pumpkin pie spice; heat about 10 minutes until warm. Add about three-fourths of the ice cream by spoonfuls. Heat and stir 3 to 5 minutes more just until melted. If desired, pour into Pumpkin Punch Bowl or into a large serving bowl. Top with scoops of remaining ice cream. Serve immediately; nog will be slightly warm. Makes 16 (⅔-cup) servings.

PUMPKIN PUNCH BOWL: To make a pumpkin bowl, cut off top of 1 pumpkin. Using a large, sturdy metal spoon, remove stringy pulp and seeds from pumpkin. With pumpkin carving saw or sharp paring knife, cut oversize scallops along edge.

EACH SERVING: 142 cal., 8 g fat (5 g. sat. fat), 43 mg chol., 39 mg sodium, 17 g carbo., 1 g fiber, 2 g pro. Daily Values: 62% vit. A, 35% vit. C, 6% calcium, 2% iron.

BY **NANCY BYAL** AND **RICHARD SWEARINGER** PHOTOGRAPHS BY **JAMES CARRIER** FOOD STYLING BY **POUKÉ** PROP STYLING BY **KAREN JOHNSON**

I t's time to give the noble pumpkin a promotion.

We love them as decorations for the doorstep and dinner table and as a velvety filling for Thanksgiving pies. In our country's early history, pumpkins fed Native Americans and pilgrims alike. Their lustrous orange skins and plump silhouettes symbolize everything captivating about autumn.

With so many merits, pumpkins deserve a place of honor at the table, so we set out to explore savory, unexpected, and easy ways to transform plain pumpkins into dishes that celebrate their potential.

The nine recipes featured here have no-fuss preparation methods (we grate pumpkins—peel and all—for the cake), and they make use of many of the sizes and varieties of pumpkins. Whole miniature pumpkins, for example, stand in for potatoes in Pumpkin-Cider Stew. Emptied of seeds and flesh, the sturdy attractive shell begs for the role of serving vessel—either whole to show off a holiday punch or in a wedge to hold a scoop of homemade pumpkin marmalade.

Every recipe includes instructions for using canned pumpkin, but don't be too quick to reach for the can opener. Fresh pumpkins are no harder to cook with than other hard-shell squashes, such as acorn and butternut squashes. And they share the same traits: They're versatile, sweet, and naturally nutritious. Pumpkins are low in calories, high in fiber, and a good source of vitamins and minerals, especially beta-carotene, vitamin C, and potassium—all three help fight cancer and chronic illnesses such as heart disease.

Even the seeds are edible and nutritious. We show you how to dry and roast pumpkin seeds and how to use them in place of nuts for snacks, as a salad topper, and in candies and baked goods.

Be aware that pumpkins are available in both cooking and decorating varieties. More than 40 varieties of pumpkins are grown just for cooking. You can decorate with cooking pumpkins but not vice versa. Culinary types are often labeled "sugar," "sweet," or "pie" pumpkins because they're higher in natural sugar and have less water content than carving types. Carvers have less flavor and a less-desirable texture.

Take advantage, too, of carving a few specimens into something extraordinary for the table or sideboard. Pumpkins can be turned into tabletop candleholders or bowls for soup or beverages. No special tools are needed— just a sharp kitchen knife and a little imagination. It's one more example of how autumn's most remarkable squash

PUMPKIN PUREE

For a delicious spark of fresh flavor, try this cooked puree for the featured recipes.

PREP: 50 MINUTES **ROAST:** 1 HOUR **STAND:** 1 HOUR

1. Preheat oven to 375°F. Scrub pumpkins thoroughly. Cut pumpkins into 5-inch-square pieces, discarding stems. Remove seeds and fibrous strings (if desired, save seeds for Toasted Pumpkin Seeds, *page 197*). Arrange pumpkin pieces in a single layer, skin sides up, in a foil-lined shallow baking pan.

2. Roast, covered, for 1 to 1 1/2 hours or until tender. When cool enough to handle, scoop pulp from rind. Place, in batches if necessary, in a blender container or food processor bowl. Cover and blend or process until smooth (for a chunkier puree, blend or process until slightly chunky).

3. Place puree in a 100%-cotton cheesecloth-lined fine-mesh sieve (use a double thickness of cheesecloth). Allow to stand for 1 hour to drain. Press lightly to remove any additional liquid (discard liquid).

PUMPKIN MATH

After cooking and draining, this is about what to expect from a typical cooking pumpkin.

2 1/2-lb.	pie pumpkin	1 3/4 cups puree
3 1/2-lb.	pie pumpkin	2 1/2 cups puree
6-lb.	carving pumpkin	2 3/4 cups puree
5-lb.	round pumpkin	3 1/3 cups puree

PUMPKIN PUREE STORAGE

Puree can be refrigerated in a tightly sealed container up to 3 days or stored in the freezer up to 6 months.

Roasted Pumpkin Kabob Salad
PREP: 45 MINUTES **ROAST:** 55 MINUTES

- 1 pie pumpkin (about 2 lb.) or 2-lb. butternut or acorn squash
- 1 recipe Garlic Brush-On
- 1 recipe Lemon Dressing
- 4 oz. semisoft goat cheese (chèvre) or 6 small fresh mozzarella balls (bocconcini)*
- 2 Tbsp. chopped Toasted Pumpkin Seeds (recipe, *page 197*), purchased pumpkin seeds, or toasted walnuts or pecans
- 1 Tbsp. snipped fresh sage
- 6 cups mesclun or arugula

1. Preheat oven to 325°F. Halve pumpkin; scoop out and discard fibrous strings and seeds. Peel with a vegetable peeler or sharp paring knife. Cut into 1 1/2- to 2-inch chunks. Thread onto six 8- to 10-inch wooden skewers. Place in a foil-lined shallow baking pan.

2. Prepare Garlic Brush-On; brush half over kabobs. Roast, uncovered, for 40 minutes. Raise oven temperature to 450°F. Brush kabobs with remaining Garlic Brush-On. Roast for 15 minutes more or until tender.

3. Meanwhile, prepare Lemon Dressing. Shape goat cheese into 6 balls; roll in Toasted Pumpkin Seeds and sage. Just before serving, place mesclun, kabobs, and prepared cheese balls in a serving bowl. Drizzle with Lemon Dressing. Makes 6 servings.

GARLIC BRUSH-ON: Combine 1/4 cup extra-virgin olive oil; 2 cloves garlic, minced; 2 teaspoons snipped fresh sage or flat-leaf parsley; 2 teaspoons finely shredded lemon peel; 1 teaspoon kosher salt or 1/2 teaspoon salt; and 1/4 teaspoon ground black pepper.

LEMON DRESSING: In a screw-top jar combine 1/3 cup extra-virgin olive oil or salad oil, 1/4 cup lemon juice, 1/4 teaspoon dry mustard, and 1/4 teaspoon ground black pepper. Cover and shake well; set aside.

***TEST KITCHEN TIP:** If using mozzarella balls, place in bowl with mesclun and kabobs; sprinkle salad with seeds and sage.

EACH SERVING: 289 ca., 27 g fat (6 g. sat. fat), 9 mg chol., 399 mg sodium, 10 g carbo., 1 g fiber, 6 g pro. Daily Values: 158% vit. A, 28% vit. C, 9% calcium, 11% iron.

Roasted Pumpkin Kabob Salad

THIS YEAR, CARVE YOUR PUMPKIN AND EAT IT TOO. WITH DOZENS OF VARIETIES, THERE'S A PERFECT PUMPKIN FOR EACH PROJECT AND RECIPE.

Pumpkin Marmalade

This traditional spread was originally made by cooking pumpkin with orange and lemon peel. It took forever. This recipe goes together in a mere 15 minutes by starting with cooked pumpkin puree and prepared marmalade.

PREP: 15 MINUTES   **COOL:** 1 HOUR

- 2 cups Pumpkin Puree (recipe, *page 192*) or one 15-oz. can pumpkin
- 1 cup orange marmalade
- 1 tsp. grated fresh ginger
- 2 Tbsp. lemon juice

  English cheddar cheese, white cheddar cheese, or Parmesan cheese (buy about 2 ounces per person) (optional)

  Assorted hearty breads (optional)

1. In a medium saucepan combine Pumpkin Puree, marmalade, and ginger. Bring to boiling. Reduce heat to medium-low. Simmer, uncovered, for 5 minutes, stirring occasionally. Remove from heat. Stir in lemon juice. Transfer to a serving bowl. Cover and cool. If desired, serve as a spread with cheese and bread. Makes about 3 cups or 24 (2-tablespoon) servings. Refrigerate up to 1 week.

EACH 2-TABLESPOON SERVING: 37 cal., 0 g fat, 0 mg chol., 8 mg sodium, 10 g carbo., 0 g fiber, 0 g pro. Daily Values: 21% vit. A, 4% vit. C, 1% calcium, 1% iron.

TRY THIS

Did you know that a wedge of cheese and a sensational spread like Pumpkin Marmalade make an innovative substitute for dessert? Chocolate cake they're not, but the combination is easy and light, especially accompanied by fruit.

Pumpkin Marmalade

Peppery Pumpkin Seed Toffee

A hint of spicy heat keeps this candy from seeming too sweet.

PREP: 20 MINUTES (PLUS TOASTING SEEDS) **COOK:** 15 MINUTES

- 1½ cups Toasted Pumpkin Seeds (recipe, *page 197*) or purchased pumpkin seeds
- 1 tsp. ground cumin
- ½ tsp. cayenne pepper
- ¾ cup butter
- 1 cup sugar
- 3 Tbsp. water
- 1 Tbsp. light-colored corn syrup

1. Prepare Toasted Pumpkin Seeds according to recipe, except add cumin and cayenne pepper to the oil mixture. Or use purchased pumpkin seeds and omit cumin and cayenne pepper.

2. Line a 13×9×2-inch baking pan with foil, extending it over edges.

3. Butter sides of a heavy 2-quart saucepan. In pan melt butter. Add sugar, water, and corn syrup. Cook and stir over medium-high heat until mixture boils. Clip a candy thermometer to side of pan. Reduce heat to medium; continue boiling at a moderate, steady rate, stirring frequently, until thermometer registers 290°F (soft-crack stage), about 15 minutes. Watch carefully after 280°F to prevent scorching.

4. Remove saucepan from heat; remove thermometer. Quickly stir in Toasted Pumpkin Seeds. Pour candy into prepared pan; spread evenly (mixture will be thick). Let candy stand until firm. When candy is cool and firm, use foil to lift from pan. Break into pieces. Store tightly covered. Makes about 1 pound (24 servings).

EACH SERVING: 138 cal., 11 g fat (4 g sat. fat), 16 mg chol., 82 mg sodium, 10 g carbo., 0 g fiber, 2 g pro. Daily Values: 4% vit. A, 1% calcium, 5% iron.

Peppery Pumpkin Seed Toffee

Pumpkin-Cider Stew

CHILLY AUTUMN DAYS ARE NO MATCH FOR THIS
HEARTY FALL-FLAVOR STEW.

Pumpkin-Cider Stew

Here, miniature edible pumpkins replace the traditional potatoes.

PREP: 30 MINUTES **COOK:** 1³/4 HOURS

  3   Tbsp. all-purpose flour
  2   tsp. fennel seeds, crushed
  2   tsp. kosher salt or 1¹/2 tsp. salt
 ¹/2   tsp. coarsely ground black pepper
  2   lb. beef chuck roast, cut into 1-inch cubes
  2   medium onions, halved, sliced, and broken into thin slivers
  2   Tbsp. olive oil
  1   14-oz. can beef broth
 1¹/2 cups apple cider
 ¹/4   cup cider vinegar
  6   or 7 miniature white and/or orange pumpkins, or half a
       5-lb. pie pumpkin, or 2 lb. potatoes
  2   medium parsnips or carrots, peeled and cut into 1-inch pieces, or
       8 oz. baby carrots with tops, scrubbed and trimmed
  2   Jonathan or Gala apples, cored and cut into wedges
       Pumpkin Bowls*
       Fennel seeds (optional)

1. In a resealable plastic bag combine flour, the 2 teaspoons crushed fennel seeds, the salt, and pepper. Add beef chunks. Close bag; shake to coat. In a Dutch oven brown half the beef and half the onion at a time in 1 tablespoon of the oil. Repeat with remaining beef, onion, and oil. Return all beef and onion to Dutch oven. Add broth, cider, and vinegar. Bring to boiling; reduce heat. Simmer, covered, for 1¹/4 hours.

2. Meanwhile, if using miniature pumpkins, cut a ¹/2-inch slice from the bottom of each; discard slice. Scoop out seeds and fibrous strings. If using pie pumpkin, peel, seed, remove strings, and cut into large chunks. If using potatoes, peel and cut into wedges.

3. Add pumpkins and parsnips to beef mixture. Return to boiling; reduce heat. Simmer, covered, for 25 minutes. Add apples; cover and simmer 5 to 10 minutes more or until vegetables and fruit are tender. Ladle into Pumpkin Bowls or soup bowls to serve. If desired, sprinkle with additional fennel seeds. Makes 8 servings.

***PUMPKIN BOWLS:** For each pumpkin bowl, cut a 1-inch slice from the stem end of a 1¹/4- to 2-lb. pumpkin; set aside stem. Scoop out seeds and fibrous strings. Ladle soup in bowl; replace stem. Or, if desired, place hollowed pumpkin with top in a shallow baking pan. Bake in a 350°F oven for 1 to 1¹/4 hours or until tender. Season inside of pumpkin with salt; serve.

TEST KITCHEN TIP: Miniature pumpkins can be hard and the skin tough. To make them easier to eat, remove the stem and carefully peel each pumpkin. You can cut large miniatures into wedges.

 EACH SERVING: 283 cal., 8 g fat (2 g sat. fat), 68 mg chol., 749 mg sodium, 27 g carbo., 4 g fiber, 27 g pro. Daily Values: 140% vit. A, 26% vit. C, 6% calcium, 25% iron.

Toasted Pumpkin Seeds

Kid Friendly

Use seeds from pie pumpkins or carving pumpkins; avoid decorative white pumpkins—their seeds tend to be tougher.

PREP: 15 MINUTES **STAND:** 24 HOURS **BAKE:** 30 MINUTES

  2   cups raw pumpkin seeds
  1   Tbsp. cooking oil
 ¹/2   tsp. salt

1. Rinse pumpkin seeds until pulp and strings are washed off; drain.

2. Spread seeds on a waxed paper-lined 15×10×1-inch baking pan. Let stand for 24 to 48 hours or until dry, stirring occasionally. In a medium bowl combine pumpkin seeds, cooking oil, and salt.

3. Preheat oven to 325°F. Remove waxed paper from baking pan. Return seeds to pan. Bake, uncovered, 30 to 35 minutes until lightly toasted and crisp, stirring twice. Cool on paper towels. Makes 2 cups.

EACH ¹/4-CUP SERVING: 202 cal., 21 g fat (3 g. sat. fat.), 0 mg chol., 152 mg sodium, 5 g carbo., 1 g fiber, 9 g pro. Daily Values: 1% vit. A, 1% vit. C, 2% calcium, 19% iron.

Chocolate Chunk Pumpkin Cake

Chocolate Chunk Pumpkin Cake

If you don't have a food processor, use the canned pumpkin option.
PREP: 45 MINUTES **BAKE:** 1 HOUR **COOL:** 30 MINUTES

	Nonstick spray for baking
3	cups all-purpose flour
2$^{1}/_{4}$	cups granulated sugar
$^{3}/_{4}$	cup packed brown sugar
1	Tbsp. pumpkin pie spice or apple pie spice
1$^{1}/_{2}$	tsp. baking powder
1$^{1}/_{2}$	tsp. baking soda
$^{1}/_{2}$	tsp. salt
6	oz. bittersweet or semisweet baking chocolate, chopped into chunks (1$^{1}/_{2}$ cups)
1	1$^{1}/_{2}$-lb. pie pumpkin, shredded,* or one 15-oz. can pumpkin
$^{3}/_{4}$	cup butter, melted
6	eggs, slightly beaten
1	recipe Molasses Glaze
1	recipe Molasses Whipped Cream

1. Preheat oven to 350°F. With the nonstick spray for baking, generously coat a 10-inch square tube pan without removable bottom or a 10-inch fluted tube pan. Set aside.

2. In a small bowl set aside $^{1}/_{2}$ cup of the flour. In a large bowl combine remaining flour, granulated sugar, brown sugar, pumpkin pie spice, baking powder, baking soda, and salt. To the reserved $^{1}/_{2}$ cup flour, stir in chocolate chunks; toss to coat.

3. In another bowl combine pumpkin, butter, and eggs. Add pumpkin mixture to flour mixture; stir until combined. Add chocolate mixture. Stir until combined. Pour batter into tube pan.

4. Bake for 60 to 70 minutes or until a wooden toothpick inserted near the center comes out clean. Cool in pan on a wire rack for 15 minutes. Gently remove cake from pan; cool 30 minutes.

5. Brush cake with Molasses Glaze; cool completely. Serve with Molasses Whipped Cream. Makes 12 to 16 servings.

MOLASSES GLAZE: In a small saucepan melt $^{1}/_{4}$ cup butter; stir in $^{1}/_{3}$ cup packed brown sugar, $^{1}/_{4}$ cup dark-colored corn syrup, and 2 tablespoons molasses. Bring to simmer. Cook, uncovered, 3 minutes or until slightly thickened. Cool 5 minutes; spoon over cake.

MOLASSES WHIPPED CREAM: In a chilled mixing bowl combine 1 cup whipping cream, 1 tablespoon powdered sugar, and 2 to 3 teaspoons molasses. Beat with electric mixer until soft peaks form. Spoon into serving bowl. Sprinkle lightly with pumpkin pie spice, apple pie spice, or ground cinnamon. Pass with cake.

*TEST KITCHEN TIP: To shred pumpkin without peeling, thoroughly wash the outside of the pumpkin. Cut off top and bottom; discard. Halve the pumpkin; remove seeds but do not peel pumpkin. Cut pumpkin into pieces that will fit through the feed tube of your food processor; shred pumpkin using food processor. Makes about 4$^{1}/_{2}$ cups.

EACH SERVING: 683 cal., 31 g fat (17 g sat. fat), 176 mg chol., 464 mg sodium, 98 g carbo., 2 g fiber, 8 g pro. Daily Values: 74% vit. A, 5% vit. C, 9% calcium, 18% iron.

Grilled Pumpkin Bowl with Veggies

To serve this bountiful bowlful as a main dish, stir in a 14-ounce package of frozen grilled chicken breast strips about 10 minutes before serving; heat through.

PREP: 30 MINUTES **BAKE:** 30 MINUTES **GRILL:** 17 MINUTES

- 2 3-lb. pie pumpkins, or four 1¹/₂-lb. striped white pumpkins, or a combination of both
- 1 recipe Toasted Pumpkin Seeds (recipe, *page 197*) (optional)
- ¹/₃ cup butter, melted
- 2 Tbsp. packed brown sugar
- 1 Tbsp. chili powder
- ¹/₄ tsp. ground cinnamon
- 4 large yellow, red, and/or orange sweet peppers, seeded and cut into 1-inch chunks
- 2 medium red onions, cut into wedges (3 cups)
- 2 Tbsp. cooking oil
- 1 tsp. kosher salt or salt
- ¹/₂ tsp. freshly ground black pepper
- 2 cups grape tomatoes, cherry tomatoes, or plum tomato wedges
Snipped fresh cilantro (optional)

1. Preheat oven to 325°F. To make pumpkin serving bowls, cut off the top one-fourth of the pumpkins; discard tops. Scoop out stringy pulp and seeds. (If desired, use seeds in recipe for Toasted Pumpkin Seeds.) Place pumpkin bowls, cut sides down, in 3-quart rectangular baking dish. Add 2 tablespoons *water*. Bake for 30 to 45 minutes or just until tender.

2. In a small bowl combine butter, brown sugar, chili powder, and cinnamon. To grill pumpkin bowls, brush insides and cut edges of pumpkins with some of the butter mixture. Set aside remaining butter mixture. Place pumpkins, cut sides down, directly on the rack of an uncovered grill over medium-hot coals. (For a gas grill, preheat grill 10 minutes, reduce heat to medium.) Grill for 10 to 15 minutes or until browned. Remove from grill to a platter. Cover loosely with foil to keep warm.

3. Meanwhile, in a bowl toss sweet peppers and onion with oil, salt, and black pepper. Heat a 12-inch cast-iron skillet or grill wok on grill over medium-hot coals (for a gas grill, use medium heat). Add vegetable mixture; cook and stir 6 to 8 minutes until vegetables are crisp-tender. Add tomatoes; cook and stir 1 to 2 minutes more or until tomatoes are heated through. Stir in reserved butter mixture (if using a grill wok, return vegetables to a large bowl before adding butter mixture). Toss gently.

4. To serve, place grilled pumpkin bowls on a serving platter. Spoon vegetable mixture into pumpkin bowls, scooping up some of the pumpkin pulp. If desired, sprinkle with snipped cilantro and Toasted Pumpkin Seeds. Makes 6 side-dish servings.

EACH SERVING: 314 cal., 16 g fat, (6 g. sat. fat), 28 mg chol., 423 mg sodium, 43 g carbo., 5 g fiber, 6 g pro. Daily Values: 453% vit. A, 529% vit. C, 11% calcium, 21% iron.

Grilled Pumpkin Bowl with Veggies

Roasted Red Pepper Lasagna

LASAGNA ON THE DOUBLE

Did you feel it? That hint of the

cool weather to come, a nip in the air that makes you want to savor something soul-soothing and body-warming for supper? Lasagna fills the bill; but in its traditional form, it requires lots of chopping, simmering, and stirring and has a long baking time (not to mention that it makes enough to feed the whole neighborhood). So what to do when you want to make fresh-from-the-oven lasagna—and eat it too—all before bedtime?

There's beauty in small things, so we scaled down the size and preparation and fired up the taste with fresh herbs, olives, citrus, capers, and full-flavored cheeses for three easy-to-assemble lasagnas. Each serves 4 to 6 and can be ready to bake in just 20 minutes. Add a crisp green salad and a glass of wine, and you're set.

BY **LISA KINGSLEY** PHOTOGRAPHS BY **GREG SCHEIDEMANN, [N] HAUS FOTO**

Roasted Red Pepper Lasagna

Tangy goat cheese and a splash of red wine make a simple dish special.

PREP: 20 MINUTES **BAKE:** 50 MINUTES **STAND:** 20 MINUTES

    Nonstick cooking spray
  2 cups red pasta sauce, such as portobello mushroom or
    garden vegetable
  6 no-boil lasagna noodles
½ container (15-oz.) ricotta cheese
  6 oz. goat cheese or shredded mozzarella cheese (1½ cups)
  1 Tbsp. Chianti or other red wine (optional)
¼ cup finely shredded Parmesan cheese
  1 cup roasted red sweet peppers, drained well and cut into strips

1. Preheat oven to 350°F. Lightly coat a 2-quart square baking dish with cooking spray. Spoon ⅓ cup of the sauce in the dish. Top with 2 lasagna noodles. In a small bowl stir together ricotta cheese, 1 cup of the goat cheese, and, if desired, the Chianti. Spoon half the mixture over the noodles in the dish. Sprinkle with 2 tablespoons Parmesan. Top with half the red pepper strips. Spoon half the remaining sauce on the pepper layer.

2. Top with 2 more noodles, the remaining ricotta mixture, and remaining peppers. Add remaining 2 noodles and remaining sauce. Dot with remaining goat cheese; sprinkle with remaining Parmesan.

3. Cover with foil. Bake for 50 minutes. Let stand, covered, on a wire rack for 20 minutes before serving. Makes 4 to 6 servings.

EACH SERVING: 415 cal., 21 g total fat (19 g sat. fat), 52 mg chol., 803 mg sodium, 32 g carbo., 4 g fiber, 23 g pro. Daily Values: 16% vit. A, 200% vit. C, 34% calcium, 17% iron.

Smoked Sausage Lasagna

Smoked Sausage Lasagna

Chicken-apple sausage and fresh fennel infuse this dish with fall flavors. Sweet or spicy Italian sausage would also be tasty.

PREP: 20 MINUTES **BAKE:** 50 MINUTES **STAND:** 20 MINUTES

> Nonstick cooking spray
> 2 cups red pasta sauce, such as tomato-basil or roasted garlic and onion
> 1/2 cup pitted kalamata olives, halved
> 6 no-boil lasagna noodles
> 1/2 container (15-oz.) ricotta cheese
> 6 oz. Monterey Jack cheese with jalapeño peppers or Monterey Jack cheese, shredded (1 1/2 cups)
> 1/4 cup finely shredded Parmesan cheese
> 8 oz. smoked chicken sausage with apple or Italian sausage, halved lengthwise and sliced
> 1 medium fennel bulb, trimmed, halved lengthwise, and thinly sliced

1. Preheat oven to 350°F. Lightly coat a 2-quart square baking dish with cooking spray; set aside. In a medium bowl stir together pasta sauce and olives. Spoon 1/3 cup of the sauce mixture in prepared dish. Top with 2 lasagna noodles. In a small bowl stir together ricotta cheese and 1 cup of the Monterey Jack cheese. Spoon half the cheese mixture on the noodles in the dish. Sprinkle with 2 tablespoons of the Parmesan. Top with half the sausage and half the fennel. Spoon half the remaining sauce over the sausage layer.

2. Top with 2 more lasagna noodles, remaining ricotta mixture, remaining sausage, and remaining fennel. Add 2 remaining noodles and remaining sauce. Sprinkle with remaining Monterey Jack and Parmesan cheeses.

3. Cover with foil. Bake for 50 minutes. Let stand, covered, on a wire rack for 20 minutes before serving. Makes 6 servings.

EACH SERVING: 541 cal., 33 g total fat (16 g sat. fat), 85 mg chol., 1,357 mg sodium, 29 g carbo., 8 g fiber, 32 g pro. Daily Values: 22% vit. A, 14% vit. C, 61% calcium, 11% iron.

Lemon Chicken Lasagna

To save a step, you can omit heating the sauce. Just add 10 minutes to the baking time.

PREP: 20 MINUTES **BAKE:** 40 MINUTES **STAND:** 20 MINUTES

Nonstick cooking spray
1 16-oz. jar roasted garlic Alfredo sauce
1 Tbsp. drained capers
6 no-boil lasagna noodles
½ container (15-oz.) ricotta cheese
6 oz. fontina cheese or mozzarella, shredded (1½ cups)
1½ tsp. finely shredded lemon peel
¼ cup finely shredded Parmesan cheese
1 9-oz. pkg. refrigerated or frozen cooked chicken breast strips (thawed, if frozen)

1. Preheat oven to 350°F. Lightly coat a 2-quart square baking dish with cooking spray; set aside. In a saucepan combine Alfredo sauce and capers. Bring to boiling over medium heat, stirring occasionally. Spoon ⅓ cup of sauce mixture into prepared dish. Top with 2 lasagna noodles. In a bowl stir together ricotta, 1 cup of the fontina cheese, and 1 teaspoon of the lemon peel. Spoon half the cheese mixture over noodles. Sprinkle with 2 tablespoons of the Parmesan. Top with half the chicken. Spoon half the remaining sauce over chicken layer.

2. Top with 2 more noodles, remaining cheese mixture, and remaining chicken. Add remaining 2 noodles, remaining sauce, and sprinkle with remaining fontina and Parmesan cheeses.

3. Cover with foil. Bake for 40 minutes. Let stand, covered, on wire rack for 20 minutes before serving. Sprinkle with remaining lemon peel. Makes 6 servings.

EACH SERVING: 529 cal., 34 g total fat (19 g sat. fat), 159 mg chol., 1,522 mg sodium, 20 g carbo., 0 g fiber, 35 g pro. Daily Values: 18% vit. A, 1% vit. C, 56% calcium, 5% iron.

Lemon Chicken Lasagna

SNACK-SIZE MEALS

To entice her nine nephews and

nieces to eat healthy food, TV personality and cookbook author Sandra Lee downsizes, making miniature versions of the kids' favorite main courses.

"They think they're getting something naughty, but it's really nice," says Sandra, whose latest work is *Sandra Lee Semi-Homemade Cooking 2* (Meredith Books).

Scaled-down food makes memorable party appetizers. Served at dinner, small versions bring fun to family mealtime and eliminate the temptation of full-size burgers, for example—a big help for dieters.

Other mini versions of food to consider are grilled cheese and peanut butter sandwiches, as well as beverages. Berry Frothy Burst (recipe, *opposite*) is charming served small. Each glassful contains a healthful serving of fruit and includes one of Sandra's favorite hunger fighters—a dose of protein from tofu.

BY **RICHARD SWEARINGER** PHOTOGRAPHS BY **CAMERON SADEGHPOUR**

Kid Friendly Mini Burgers on Toast Rounds

Bake these ahead and freeze; then at snacktime, pull a few out and microwave for a novel snack.

PREP: 20 MINUTES **BAKE:** 19 MINUTES

    8   slices white bread
        Olive oil nonstick cooking spray
    1   lb. lean ground beef
    1   packet (1-oz.) meat loaf seasoning, fajita seasoning, or other meat
        seasoning blend
    1   egg, lightly beaten
    2   Tbsp. Worcestershire sauce
        Ketchup and/or mustard

1. Preheat oven to 400°F. From bread slices, use a 1³⁄₄-inch round pastry cutter to cut 32 circles for Toast Rounds. Arrange rounds on baking sheet; spray lightly with cooking spray. Bake rounds 7 minutes or until toasted. Cool completely on baking sheet.

2. In a large bowl combine beef, seasoning, egg, and Worcestershire sauce. Form 1-inch balls using 1 tablespoon of beef mixture per ball. Place balls 1 inch apart on a baking sheet. Gently press index finger into the center of each ball to make an indentation, which will hold condiments after burgers are cooked. Bake 12 minutes or until brown. Remove from oven.

3. Immediately transfer burgers to Toast Rounds. Fill indentation in each burger with ketchup and/or mustard. Serve warm. Makes 32 appetizer burgers or enough for about 6 main-dish servings.

MAKE AHEAD: For Toast Rounds, prepare and bake as directed in Step 1. Transfer to freezer container. Cover and freeze for up to 1 month. For Mini Burgers, prepare and bake burgers as directed in Step 2. Remove from oven; cool completely. Transfer to a freezer container. Cover and freeze for up to 1 month. To serve, place burgers, 4 at a time, on a small microwave-safe plate in single layer. Microwave on 50% power (medium) for 1 to 2 minutes or until heated through. Place 4 Toasted Rounds on a microwave-safe plate in a single layer. Microwave on 100% power (high) for 10 seconds. Continue as directed in Step 3.

EACH BURGER: 41 cal., 2 g total fat (1 g sat. fat), 16 mg chol., 93 mg sodium, 3 g carbo., 0 g fiber, 3 g pro. Daily Values: 1% calcium, 3% iron.

Poker Potato Chips

Kid Friendly Poker Potato Chips

PREP: 15 MINUTES **CHILL:** 20 MINUTES **COOK:** ABOUT 15 MINUTES

- 1 cup all-purpose flour
- 4 packets (0.6 ounces each) roasted garlic or zesty Italian dressing mix
- 4 small sweet potatoes or red-skinned potatoes
  Vegetable oil for frying
  Salt and ground black pepper

1. In a large resealable plastic bag combine flour and dressing mix; set aside.

2. Scrub potatoes under running water and pat dry with paper towels. Using a sharp knife or a mandoline slicer, thinly slice potatoes into round disks. Add about half of the slices to the seasoned flour. Seal bag and shake. Arrange slices in an even layer on a baking sheet; repeat with remaining potatoes. Chill seasoned potatoes about 20 minutes.

3. Fill a large, heavy-bottom Dutch oven a little less than half full of oil. If using a deep-fat fryer, fill according to manufacturer's instructions. Heat oil to 375°F. Using a spoon carefully add potato slices a few at a time; fry until crisp and golden, about 3 minutes. Remove with a slotted spoon and drain on paper towels. Season to taste with salt and pepper. Repeat with remaining potato slices. Makes 6 to 8 servings.

EACH 1-CUP SERVING: 258 cal., 12 g total fat (2 g sat. fat), 0 mg chol., 686 mg sodium, 33 g carbo., 3 g fiber, 4 g pro. Daily Values: 126% vit. A, 30% vit. C, 2% calcium, 11% iron.

Berry Frothy Burst

Kid Friendly **Fast!** Berry Frothy Burst

PREP: 5 MINUTES

- 1 cup frozen mixed berries
- 1 cup orange juice
- 3½ oz. (about one-fourth of a 14-oz. package) silken (soft) tofu
- ½ banana, peeled

1. Place all ingredients in a blender jar. Cover and blend until smooth. Makes 2 servings. If desired, top with fresh berries.

EACH 1½-CUP SERVING: 145 cal., 2 g total fat (0 g sat. fat), 0 mg chol., 14 mg sodium, 29 g carbo., 4 g fiber, 4 g pro. Daily Values: 5% vit. A, 108% vit. C, 3% calcium, 6% iron.

Poker Potato Chips and Mini Burgers on Toast Rounds

In good taste
FOOD AND ENTERTAINING

SWEPT AWAY

Hold onto your broomsticks. Create clever party skewers by tying snipped natural straw from a crafts store around 10-inch bamboo skewers. Then layer dried fruits, bits of candy, and cream-filled cookies.

Seasonal Dressing

Autumn inspires new salad combinations: fruits and nuts, red and deep green leaf lettuces, and hearty cheeses such as cheddar and blue. Dress these robust flavors with equally intriguing vinaigrettes. Create homemade pear and honey vinaigrette by cooking down peeled, cored pears in water with a cinnamon stick. Add honey, cider vinegar, olive oil, salt, and pepper to taste; cook until drizzling consistency. Spoon over a salad of pears, walnuts, and autumn lettuce. Or let blue cheese and pecan, fig and port, or Merlot and walnut complement the lineup of fall salad favorites. *Left to right:* Blue Cheese Balsamic Pecan Vinaigrette, $9.49, Entertain with Ease; entertainwithease.com. Fig and Port Vinaigrette, $7.95, The Girl & the Fig; www.thegirlandthefigcom. Merlot Vinaigrette, $8, Tulocay's Made in Napa Valley; www.madeinnapavalley.com.

Harvest Wines

Brian Duncan, owner and wine director of Bin 36 in Chicago, gives us his matches for wines for fall foods. In addition to selecting the wines on Bin 36's wine list, Duncan also blends the restaurant's private label wines. Bin 36's menu suggests "flights" of wines—three to four tastings based on region, varietal, and taste. Bin 36 information and locations can be found at http://bin36.com.

ZINFANDELS: "In fall, I look forward to creamy textured blue-vein cheeses, which work wonderfully with Zinfandels. The deep black fruit and toasty oak spice provide a delicious contrast to the mildly salty, pungent quality of the cheese. It also eliminates the need for fruit. Spiced nuts and raisin bread will suffice."

CHARDONNAYS: "For a hearty starter, I love butternut squash soup with a touch of cream and honey. Full-bodied Chardonnays work really well here because of the rich texture and smoky notes in the wine. Both the soup and the wine share hints of vanilla, nutmeg, and cinnamon."

SYRAHS: "My favorite main courses include braised lamb or pork shanks with cumin, star anise, cardamom, chiles, and turmeric. These spice elements marry beautifully with the ripe berry and plum flavors in Syrah."

FLIGHTS FOR KIDS: Bin 36's Lincolnshire, Illinois, location—recognized for its family clientele—offers a witty take on flights with kid-friendly offerings of milk and juice flavors.

PHOTOGRAPHS BY **TYLLIE BARBOSA** (PROTRAIT); **KING AU/AU STUDIO** (WINE GLASSES)

NOVEMBER

IT'S TURKEY TIME AGAIN, AND THE BIRD IS READY
FOR ITS STARRING ROLE ON THE FEASTING TABLE.
PICK UP SOME NEW TRICKS FOR OTHER SPECIAL
THANKSGIVING TREATS.

Maple-Tarragon Glazed Turkey
with Orange Gravy
page 223

Potluck Thanksgiving

Citrus Marinated Turkey Breast with Cilantro Dipping Sauce
page 217

Apple, Bacon, and Leek Bread Pudding
page 219

Plus

Potluck Thanksgiving

THIS YEAR, DISPERSE THE HOLIDAY COOKING DUTIES AMONG THE GUESTS. KICK THE STRESS OF COOKING BY YOURSELF BUT STILL GET ALL YOUR THANKSGIVING FOOD FAVORITES.

Arugula and Roasted Cauliflower Salad

Arugula and Roasted Cauliflower Salad

PREP: 30 MINUTES **ROAST:** 30 MINUTES

 2 medium heads cauliflower,
   cut in bite-size florets (about 10 cups)
 3 Tbsp. extra-virgin olive oil
 ¾ tsp. salt
 ¼ tsp. ground black pepper
 2 Tbsp. champagne vinegar or white wine vinegar
 1 Tbsp. Dijon-style mustard
 ⅓ cup extra-virgin olive oil
 2 5-oz. pkg. arugula (8 cups lightly packed) or two 5-oz. pkg. baby
   spinach
 1 large red onion, thinly sliced
 4 oz. shaved Parmesan cheese

1. Preheat oven to 425°F. In shallow roasting pan combine cauliflower, the 3 tablespoons olive oil, ½ teaspoon of the salt, and the pepper; toss. Roast, uncovered, 30 to 35 minutes, stirring twice. Remove from oven; cool.

2. In a small bowl combine vinegar, mustard, and the remaining ¼ teaspoon salt. Whisk in the ⅓ cup olive oil until combined. In a large bowl combine cauliflower mixture, arugula, and onion. Add vinegar mixture; toss. Top with shaved Parmesan. Makes 12 servings.

EACH SERVING: 143 cal., 11 g total fat (2 g sat. fat), 5 mg chol., 321 mg sodium, 7 g carbo., 3 g fiber, 5 g pro. Daily Values: 12% vit. A, 71% vit. C, 14% calcium, 5% iron.

Arugula and Roasted Cauliflower Salad

BY **ELIZABETH SCHATZ PASSARELLA** PHOTOGRAPHS BY **TINA RUPP** FOOD STYLING BY **WILLIAM SMITH**

Thanksgiving is all about giving thanks and sharing

whether you're swapping family stories or passing potatoes across the table. But how do you preserve tradition when your "family" is eight single friends throwing a potluck-style meal? The answer: Add your own spin on Thanksgiving Day.

Serving appetizers in the kitchen—whether
you prepare them yourself, buy favorites, or delegate the making to your friends—encourages everyone to catch up with one another. It also allows for last-minute preparation and reheating of the foods for the big feast. Plan on two to three "starter" options for a gathering of 10 to 12 guests.

Turkey is the star of Thanksgiving, but roasting and
carving a full-size bird isn't your only option. Try something different—roast two or more turkey breasts. They're readily available, easier to prepare (no special roasting pans required), and extremely versatile. They're also perfect for a small gathering (and eliminate the flood of turkey-themed leftovers), or you can cook as many as you need to accommodate a crowd. On average, they're ready in half the time it takes to roast a 12-pound turkey. There's no tricky carving—just slice and serve.

If you're a guest who's charged with taking a side dish or two, consider making one that's
traditional, such as cranberry relish or green bean casserole, and another that's innovative, such as a savory bread pudding instead of traditional stuffing.

Side-dish possibilities are endless and can steal the spotlight, especially when they include familiar ingredients prepared in new and different ways.

An eclectic, flavorful meal
deserves desserts that are special and comforting. Of course someone will want the much-loved pumpkin pie—it's a requisite. If no one knows how to prepare the classic, pick up one at a bakery; then slice and serve it with fresh whipped cream. In addition, offer some new and inventive sweet treats. Dust cinnamon or cardamom over ice cream or custard, or add a surprise hit of chile pepper heat to a chocolate cake, torte, or mousse. For a change of pace, try a dessert accented with refreshing lemon or lime. For friends who can't linger, pack up individualized portions for them to enjoy later at home.

Sweet and Spicy Nuts

PREP: 10 MINUTES **BAKE:** 35 MINUTES

- 1 egg white
- 1 Tbsp. water
- 1 lb. raw whole cashews, whole almonds, walnut halves, and/or pecan halves (about 4 cups)
- ⅓ cup sugar
- 2 tsp. salt
- 1½ tsp. ground cumin
- 1 tsp. paprika
- 1 tsp. ground coriander
- ½ tsp. cayenne pepper*
- ¼ tsp. ground ginger

1. Preheat oven to 300°F. In a medium bowl beat egg white and water until frothy. Add nuts and toss to coat. Transfer to a wire-mesh sieve; drain nuts for 5 minutes.

2. Meanwhile, in a large plastic bag combine sugar, salt, cumin, paprika, coriander, cayenne pepper, and ginger. Add the nuts; shake well to coat with the spice mixture. Spread nuts evenly in an ungreased 15×10×1-inch baking pan.

3. Bake for 35 to 40 minutes until nuts are toasted and spice mixture is dry, stirring every 10 minutes. Remove from oven; transfer to a sheet of foil. Cool completely. Break apart. Store in airtight bag or container at room temperature up to 5 days or freeze up to 3 months. Makes 12 (⅓-cup) servings or 4 cups total.

*TEST KITCHEN TIP: To vary spiciness of these nuts, increase or decrease the cayenne pepper.

EACH SERVING: 242 cal., 18 g fat (3 g sat. fat), 0 mg chol., 399 mg sodium, 18 g carbo., 1 g fiber, 6 g pro. Daily Values: 2% vit. A, 2% calcium, 13% iron.

Celery Root and Sweet Potato Cakes
Olive Focaccia
Sweet and Spicy Nuts
Fresh Grape Chutney

Celery Root and Sweet Potato Cakes

PREP: 30 MINUTES **COOK:** 5 MINUTES PER BATCH

- 1½ tsp. cumin seeds
- 3 Tbsp. olive oil
- 2 eggs, slightly beaten
- 2 cloves garlic, minced
- ½ tsp. salt
- 12 oz. celery root or parsnips (1 small celery root or 2 medium parsnips), peeled and shredded
- 12 oz. sweet potato (2 small), peeled and shredded
- 2 to 4 Tbsp. olive oil
- Dairy sour cream or applesauce (optional)

1. In a small dry skillet toast cumin seeds over medium heat for 2 to 3 minutes or until lightly toasted. Remove from heat; cool. Crush seeds slightly with a mortar and pestle.

2. In a large bowl combine the 3 tablespoons olive oil, the eggs, garlic, salt, and crushed cumin seeds. Stir in shredded celery root and sweet potato until combined. Form mixture into 16 cakes, stirring mixture frequently to keep egg mixture well distributed.

3. Preheat oven to 300°F. In a large skillet heat 1 tablespoon of the olive oil over medium-high heat. Carefully place some of the cakes in hot skillet. Cook over medium-high heat 5 to 6 minutes or until cakes are golden brown, turning once. Repeat with remaining vegetable mixture, adding additional oil as needed during cooking. If necessary, reduce heat to medium to prevent overbrowning. Drain on paper towels.

4. Place cooked cakes on baking sheet in oven to keep warm while cooking remaining batches. If desired, serve with sour cream or applesauce. Makes 16 cakes.

TEST KITCHEN TIP: For quicker preparation, use shredding blade of food processor to shred peeled celery root and sweet potatoes.

EACH CAKE: 62 cal., 5 g fat (1 g sat. fat), 26 mg chol., 93 mg sodium, 3 g carbo., 1 g fiber, 1 g pro. Daily Values: 37% vit A, 6% vit C, 1% calcium, 2% iron.

Fresh Grape Chutney

You can also serve the grape chutney with a purchased focaccia or your favorite crusty bread.

Fast! **START TO FINISH:** 10 MINUTES

- 4 cups red seedless grapes (about 1¼ lb.)
- 1 Tbsp. butter
- ½ cup chopped red onion
- 1 tsp. snipped fresh rosemary or ¼ tsp. dried rosemary, crushed
- ¼ tsp. dried oregano, crushed
- 2 Tbsp. red wine vinegar

1. Place grapes in food processor bowl. Process with 3 or 4 on and off turns until chopped; set aside. In large skillet melt butter; add onion and cook just until tender. Add rosemary and oregano; cook for 1 minute. Add chopped grapes and vinegar; cook 1 to 2 minutes more or until heated through. Serve with a slotted spoon. Makes 24 (2-tablespoon) servings.

EACH SERVING: 24 cal., 1 g fat (0 g sat. fat), 1 mg chol., 4 mg sodium, 5 g carbo., 0 g fiber, 0 g pro. Daily Values: 1% vit. A, 5% vit. C, 1% iron.

Olive Focaccia

PREP: 30 MINUTES **RISE:** 1½ HOURS **BAKE:** 20 MINUTES
COOL: 20 MINUTES

- 1⅓ cups warm water (105° to 115°F)
- 1 pkg. active dry yeast
- 4 Tbsp. extra-virgin olive oil
- 1 tsp. sugar
- 4¼ to 4¾ cups all-purpose flour
- 1 Tbsp. chopped fresh rosemary or 1 tsp. dried rosemary, crushed
- 1 tsp. dried oregano, crushed
- 2 tsp. coarse sea salt or kosher salt
- 1 cup pitted kalamata olives, sliced
- 1 recipe Fresh Grape Chutney (recipe, *left*)

1. In a small bowl combine warm water, yeast, 3 tablespoons of the olive oil, and the sugar. Let stand about 5 minutes until bubbly. In a large bowl combine 4 cups of the flour, the rosemary, oregano, and 1 teaspoon of the salt. Add olives and yeast mixture to flour mixture. Stir until a dough forms. Turn dough out onto lightly floured surface and knead in enough of the remaining flour to make a moderately stiff dough (5 to 8 minutes total). Place dough in a lightly oiled bowl, turning once. Cover; let rise in a warm place until double in size (1 to 1½ hours).

2. Turn dough out onto a lightly oiled 15×10×1-inch baking pan. Press dough to fit pan. Brush dough with remaining 1 tablespoon olive oil. Sprinkle with remaining sea salt. Cover and let rise 30 minutes. Meanwhile, prepare Fresh Grape Chutney.

3. Preheat oven to 425°F. Bake focaccia for 20 to 25 minutes or until golden. Remove to wire rack; cool at least 20 minutes. Cut into squares. Serve with Fresh Grape Chutney. Makes 24 servings.

EACH SERVING: 105 cal., 3 g fat (0 g sat. fat), 0 mg chol., 197 mg sodium, 16 g carbo., 1 g fiber, 2 g pro. Daily Values: 6% iron.

Onion-Thyme Gravy

This delicious gravy goes great with all three of the turkey breast recipes in this chapter—Walnut and Sage Pesto Turkey Breast, BBQ Spice-Rubbed Turkey Breast, and Citrus Marinated Turkey Breast with Cilantro Dipping Sauce.

PREP: 15 MINUTES **COOK:** 20 MINUTES

- 2 Tbsp. butter
- 1 cup chopped onion (about 1 large)
- 3 shallots, chopped (about ⅔ cup)
- 1 tsp. snipped fresh thyme or ¼ tsp. dried thyme, crushed
- 2 Tbsp. all-purpose flour
- 1 14-oz. can reduced-sodium chicken broth
- 1 Tbsp. reduced-sodium soy sauce
- 1 Tbsp. Worcestershire sauce
- ¼ tsp. freshly ground black pepper
- ⅛ tsp. salt

1. In a medium saucepan melt butter over medium-high heat; add the onion, shallots, and thyme. Cook, stirring occasionally, for 10 to 12 minutes or until vegetables are tender and browned.

2. Stir in flour; cook and stir for 1 minute. Add broth, soy sauce, and Worcestershire sauce. Cook and stir until mixture comes to boiling; reduce heat to medium. Simmer, uncovered, for 8 to 9 minutes or until slightly thickened. Stir in pepper and salt. Makes 9 (¼-cup) servings or 2¼ cups total.

EACH SERVING: 52 cal., 3 g fat (1 g sat. fat), 7 mg chol., 244 mg sodium, 6 g carbo, 0 g fiber, 1 g pro. Daily Values: 5% vit. A, 3% vit. C, 1% calcium, 2% iron.

BBQ Spice-Rubbed Turkey Breast
with Cranberry Barbecue Sauce (page 216)
Walnut and Sage Pesto Turkey Breast (page 216)
Fingerling Potatoes (page 217)
Aromatic Parsnips and Carrots (page 218)
Onion-Thyme Gravy (opposite)

Walnut and Sage Pesto Turkey Breast

PREP: 25 MINUTES **ROAST:** 1 HOUR 35 MINUTES **STAND:** 10 MINUTES

- 2 3- to 3½-lb. fresh or frozen bone-in turkey breast halves
   Nonstick cooking spray
- 2 7-oz. containers refrigerated basil pesto or 10-oz. jar purchased pesto
- ⅓ cup finely chopped fresh sage
- ¼ cup finely chopped walnuts
- ½ tsp. salt
- ½ tsp. freshly ground black pepper
- 1 recipe Onion-Thyme Gravy (optional) (recipe, *page 214*)

1. Thaw turkey, if frozen. Preheat oven to 400°F. Coat a large shallow roasting pan and rack with cooking spray. Place turkey breast halves, bone sides down, on rack in prepared pan; set aside.

2. In medium bowl combine pesto, sage, walnuts, salt, and pepper; mix well. Reserve half the pesto mixture to pass with turkey breast halves. Cover; chill until serving time.

3. Starting at the breast bone, slip your fingers between skin and meat to loosen skin, leaving skin attached at top. Rub about two-thirds of the remaining pesto mixture under the skin over the breast meat halves. Rub remaining pesto mixture over the skin of each half. Insert an oven-going meat thermometer into thickest part of turkey breast, without touching bone. Roast for 20 minutes. Reduce oven temperature to 350°F and roast for 1¼ to 1½ hours longer or until thermometer registers 170°F, juices run clear, and turkey is no longer pink. If necessary, cover with foil last 30 to 45 minutes to prevent overbrowning. Let stand, covered with foil, 10 minutes before slicing. Serve with remaining pesto mixture and, if desired, Onion-Thyme Gravy. Makes 10 to 12 servings.

EACH SERVING: 519 cal., 27 g total fat (2 g sat. fat), 171 mg chol., 419 mg sodium, 6 g carbo., 0 g fiber, 61 g pro. Daily Values: 4% calcium, 16% iron.

BBQ Spice-Rubbed Turkey Breast

PREP: 25 MINUTES **ROAST:** 1 HOUR 20 MINUTES **STAND:** 10 MINUTES

   Nonstick cooking spray
- 2 Tbsp. packed dark brown sugar
- 2 tsp. paprika
- 2 tsp. garlic powder
- 1½ tsp. salt
- 1 tsp. ground cumin
- 1 tsp. chili powder
- ¾ tsp. freshly ground black pepper
- 2 3- to 3½-lb. fresh or frozen bone-in turkey breast halves
- 1 recipe Cranberry Barbecue Sauce (recipe, *below*)

1. Thaw turkey, if frozen. Preheat oven to 400°F. Coat a large shallow roasting pan and rack with cooking spray. In a small bowl combine brown sugar, paprika, garlic powder, salt, cumin, chili powder, and pepper. Place turkey breast halves, bone sides down, on roasting rack in prepared pan.

2. Starting at breast bone, slip fingers between skin and meat to loosen skin, leaving skin attached at top. Lift skin and spread spice mixture evenly under skin over breast meat. Insert oven-going meat thermometer into thickest part of breast, without touching bone.

3. Roast, uncovered, on lower rack of oven for 20 minutes. Reduce oven temperature to 350°F and roast for 1 to 1½ hours longer or until thermometer registers 170°F, juices run clear, and turkey is no longer pink, occasionally spooning pan juices over turkey. Let stand, covered with foil, for 10 minutes before slicing. Serve with Cranberry Barbecue Sauce. Makes 10 to 12 servings.

TEST KITCHEN TIP: To simplify, you can rub the spice mixture onto the outside of turkey breast for a crusty spice appearance. Place foil over turkey breast last 30 minutes of roasting to prevent burning.

EACH SERVING: 311 cal., 6 g total fat (2 g sat. fat), 167 mg chol., 440 mg sodium, 4 g carbo., 0 g fiber, 57 g pro. Daily Values: 6% vit. A, 1% vit. C, 4% calcium, 16% iron.

Cranberry Barbecue Sauce

 Fast! **PREP:** 5 MINUTES **COOK:** 10 MINUTES

- 1 cup chopped onion (about 1 large)
- 1 Tbsp. cooking oil
- 1 16-oz. can whole cranberry sauce
- ⅓ cup bottled chili sauce
- 1 Tbsp. cider vinegar
- 1 tsp. Worcestershire sauce
- ¼ tsp. freshly ground black pepper

1. In a medium saucepan cook onion in hot oil over medium heat 5 minutes. Add cranberry sauce, chili sauce, vinegar, Worcestershire sauce, and pepper. Bring to boiling; reduce heat. Simmer, uncovered, stirring occasionally, 5 minutes or until thickened. If desired, serve with BBQ Spice-Rubbed Turkey Breast. Makes 10 to 12 (¼-cup) servings.

EACH SERVING: 93 cal., 1 g total fat (0 g sat. fat), 0 mg chol., 16 mg sodium, 20 g carbo., 1 g fiber, 0 g pro. Daily Values: 16% vit. A, 6% vit. C, 1% iron.

BBQ Spice-Rubbed Turkey Breast
Onion-Thyme Gravy (page 214)
Fingerling Potatoes

Citrus Marinated Turkey Breast with Cilantro Dipping Sauce

PREP: 30 MINUTES **MARINATE:** 8 HOURS **ROAST:** 1 HOUR 20 MINUTES
STAND: 10 MINUTES

 2 3- to 3½-lb. fresh or frozen bone-in turkey breast halves
 2 cups lightly packed fresh cilantro leaves (about 1¼ oz.)
1⅓ cups orange juice
 ½ cup fresh lemon juice
 12 cloves garlic, halved
 1 fresh jalapeño chile pepper, seeded and cut up (see note, *page 143*)
 2 tsp. salt
 2 tsp. ground cumin
 ½ tsp. freshly ground black pepper
1½ cups olive oil
    Nonstick cooking spray

1. Thaw turkey, if frozen. Using tip of a sharp knife, prick turkey breast in several spots. Place turkey breast halves, skin sides down, in very large resealable plastic bag set in a baking dish; set aside.

2. For Cilantro Dipping Sauce, in a food processor bowl or blender container combine cilantro, orange juice, lemon juice, garlic, jalapeño, salt, cumin, and black pepper. Cover and process until almost smooth. With processor or blender running, slowly add oil in thin stream. Pour 2 cups sauce into covered container; refrigerate until serving time. Pour remaining cilantro sauce over turkey breast halves; marinate in refrigerator at least 8 hours or up to 24 hours, turning occasionally.

3. Preheat oven to 400°F. Coat shallow roasting pan and roasting rack with cooking spray. Remove the turkey from marinade; discard marinade. Place turkey breasts, bone sides down, on rack in the prepared roasting pan. Insert an oven-going meat thermometer into the thickest part of the turkey breast halves, without touching bone. Roast for 20 minutes. Reduce oven temperature to 350°F. Roast turkey 1 to 1½ hours longer or until thermometer registers 170°F, juices run clear, and turkey is no longer pink. If necessary, cover with foil to prevent overbrowning. Let stand, covered, 10 minutes before slicing. Stir remaining refrigerated sauce; pass with turkey. Makes 10 to 12 servings.

EACH SERVING (WITH 2 TABLESPOONS SAUCE): 578 cal., 35 g total fat (5 sat. fat), 167 mg chol., 504 mg sodium, 6 g carbo., 1 g fiber, 58 g pro. Daily Values: 21% vit. A, 47% vit. C, 6% calcium, 18% iron.

Fingerling Potatoes

PREP: 20 MINUTES **ROAST:** 1 HOUR 10 MINUTES

 6 lb. fingerling potatoes or small red potatoes
 ⅓ cup olive oil
 2 tsp. sea salt or salt
 1 tsp. freshly ground black pepper
 1 recipe Aïoli Sauce

1. Scrub potatoes. Cut large potatoes in half or thirds lengthwise. In a large bowl combine potatoes, oil, salt, and pepper; toss to coat potatoes.

2. If roasting potatoes with turkey, add potatoes in single layer to roasting pan with turkey for the last 1 hour and 10 minutes of roasting.* Place any extra potatoes in a 15×10×1-inch baking pan. Place baking pan on another oven rack and roast potatoes for 1 to 1¼ hours or until potatoes are tender and browned. Serve potatoes with Aïoli Sauce. Makes 12 (1-cup) servings plus leftovers.

AÏOLI SAUCE: In a medium bowl combine 1½ cups mayonnaise or salad dressing; ¾ cup Parmesan cheese; ⅓ cup lemon juice; 3 cloves garlic, minced; ⅛ teaspoon salt; and ⅛ teaspoon ground black pepper. Stir until mixture is well combined. Serve with Fingerling Potatoes.

*TEST KITCHEN TIP: If not roasting potatoes with turkey breasts, preheat oven to 350°F. Divide potatoes between two 15×10×1-inch baking pans. Roast as directed above.

MAKE AHEAD: Aïoli Sauce may be prepared up to 3 days ahead. Cover and chill in refrigerator until serving time.

EACH SERVING: 296 cal., 20 g fat (3 g sat. fat), 16 mg chol., 369 mg sodium, 26 g carbo., 2 g fiber, 5 g pro. Daily Values: 41% vit. C, 6% calcium, 12% iron.

Aromatic Parsnips and Carrots

Aromatic Parsnips and Carrots
START TO FINISH: 50 MINUTES

1½	lb. small parsnips, peeled and halved lengthwise
1½	lb. small carrots, peeled and halved lengthwise
3	tablespoons olive oil
¾	tsp. fennel seeds, crushed
½	tsp. ground coriander (optional)
¼	tsp. ground cinnamon
4	cloves garlic, thinly sliced
2	tablespoons chopped fresh cilantro
1	tsp. finely shredded lemon peel
2	Tbsp. lemon juice
½	tsp. salt
⅛	tsp. freshly ground black pepper
1	Tbsp. olive oil

1. Cut any long carrots and parsnips in half crosswise. In a very large skillet cook parsnips, covered, in small amount of boiling salted water 2 minutes. Add carrots; return to a boil. Cook 4 minutes more. Drain; set aside. Carefully wipe skillet dry.

2. Heat the 3 tablespoons olive oil in same skillet over medium heat. Add fennel seeds, coriander, if desired, and cinnamon. Cook about 1 minute or until fragrant, stirring occasionally.

3. Add the carrots, parsnips, and garlic. Cook 10 to 12 minutes or until vegetables are tender, turning occasionally. Remove from heat. Stir in cilantro, lemon peel and juice, salt, and pepper. Drizzle with the remaining 1 tablespoon olive oil. Makes 10 to 12 servings.

MAKE AHEAD: Prepare through Step 2. Transfer to 2½- or 3-quart microwave-safe casserole. Cover; refrigerate up to 24 hours. To serve, microwave, covered with lid or vented plastic wrap, on 100% power (high) 7 to 8 minutes, stirring once. Serve as above.

EACH SERVING: 130 cal., 6 g total fat (1 g sat. fat), 0 mg chol., 171 mg sodium, 20 g carbo., 6 g fiber, 2 g pro. Daily Values: 149% vit. A, 25% vit. C, 5% calcium, 4% iron.

Apple, Bacon, and Leek Bread Pudding

PREP: 45 MINUTES **BAKE:** 1½ HOURS **COOL:** 10 MINUTES **CHILL:** 3 HOURS
STAND: 50 MINUTES

- 1 1-lb. herbed country bread or other crusty country bread, cut into ¾-inch cubes
- 8 oz. bacon
- 2 8-oz. pkg. sliced fresh mushrooms
- 4 large leeks, white and tender green parts only, cut into ¾-inch pieces
- 4 cloves garlic, minced
- 3 Granny Smith apples (1 lb.) or pears, cored and cut into wedges
- 6 eggs, lightly beaten
- 5 cups milk
- 6 oz. aged provolone cheese, shredded
- ½ tsp. salt
- ½ tsp. freshly ground black pepper

1. Preheat oven to 400°F. Place bread cubes in two 15×10×1-inch baking pans or shallow roasting pans. Bake 15 to 20 minutes or until crisp, rotating and stirring once. Set aside.

2. Heat a very large skillet over medium-high heat. Add bacon and cook until crisp; drain bacon on paper towels, reserving 3 tablespoons drippings in skillet. Crumble bacon; set aside. Add mushrooms to skillet; cook about 7 minutes or just until brown. Stir in leeks and garlic; cook until just tender. Add apples; cook for 1 to 2 minutes or until apples begin to soften. Remove from heat; add bacon and set aside to cool for 10 minutes.

3. In a 4-quart casserole or Dutch oven combine eggs, milk, cheese, salt, pepper, bread cubes, and leek mixture; toss well. Cover and chill 3 hours or overnight.

4. Remove from refrigerator. Let stand 30 minutes. Preheat oven to 400°F. Bake, covered, 45 minutes. Uncover and bake 30 minutes more or until an instant-read thermometer inserted into center registers 170°F. Let stand 20 minutes before serving. Makes 12 servings.

EACH SERVING: 380 cal., 18 g total fat (7 g sat. fat), 144 mg chol., 923 mg sodium, 35 g carbo., 3 g fiber, 21 g pro. Daily Values: 19% vit. A, 11% vit. C, 28% calcium, 15% iron.

Apple, Bacon, and Leek Bread Pudding

Chile Chocolate Torte and Cinnamon Whipped Cream

Chile Chocolate Torte and Cinnamon Whipped Cream
PREP: 30 MINUTES **BAKE:** 35 MINUTES **COOL:** 1 HOUR **CHILL:** 3 HOURS

	Nonstick cooking spray
1	cup whole blanched almonds
2	Tbsp. granulated sugar
2	Tbsp. all-purpose flour
1	lb. Mexican chocolate, such as Ibarra, or 1 lb. semisweet chocolate, coarsely chopped
3	oz. semisweet chocolate, coarsely chopped
1	cup butter
6	egg yolks
¼	cup strong brewed coffee, cooled
1	tsp. vanilla
¼	tsp. almond extract
⅛	tsp. salt
½	tsp. chipotle chile powder or ¼ tsp. cayenne pepper
½	tsp. ground cinnamon
6	egg whites
¼	cup granulated sugar
1	cup whipping cream
¼	cup powdered sugar
	Whole blanched, unblanched, or candied almonds
	Crushed chipotle chile pepper (optional)

1. Preheat oven to 325°F. Lightly coat a 9-inch springform pan with nonstick cooking spray; line bottom with parchment paper. Coat with cooking spray; sprinkle with flour; shake excess; set aside.

2. In a food processor bowl combine the 1 cup almonds, sugar, and 2 tablespoons flour. Cover; process until ground, 1 to 2 minutes.

3. In a large heavy saucepan combine Mexican chocolate, semisweet chocolate, and butter. Cook over low heat, stirring occasionally, until chocolate and butter are melted; cool 5 minutes.

4. Meanwhile, in a large bowl combine egg yolks, coffee, vanilla, almond extract, and salt. Stir in almond mixture, chocolate mixture, chile powder, and ¼ teaspoon of the cinnamon. In another large bowl beat egg whites with electric mixer on high speed until soft peaks form. Gradually add the ¼ cup granulated sugar, beating until stiff peaks form, 1 to 2 minutes. Fold whites into chocolate mixture. Pour into prepared pan.

5. Bake 35 to 40 minutes or just until set. Transfer pan to rack; cool 1 hour. (Center will sink as cake cools.) Chill at least 3 hours.

6. To unmold cake, use a sharp small knife to loosen cake from sides of pan; remove sides of pan. Invert cake onto plate and remove pan bottom and parchment paper. Invert cake again onto platter.

7. In a chilled bowl combine whipping cream, powdered sugar, and remaining ¼ teaspoon of the cinnamon. Beat until soft peaks form. Top cake with whipped cream. Sprinkle with almonds and, if desired, crushed chipotle chile pepper. Makes 12 to 16 servings.

EACH SERVING: 553 cal., 40 g fat (19 g sat. fat), 173 mg chol, 184 mg sodium, 46 g carbo., 3 g fiber, 8 g pro. Daily Values: 19% vit. A, 7% calcium, 11% iron.

Earl Grey Pound Cake with Lemon Curd

STAND: 30 MINUTES **PREP:** 25 MINUTES **BAKE:** 25 MINUTES
COOL: 10 MINUTES

Earl Grey Pound Cake with Lemon Curd

1½	cups butter
6	eggs
1½	cups dairy sour cream
3⅓	cups all-purpose flour
4	tsp. finely ground Earl Grey tea leaves*
1½	tsp. baking powder
½	tsp. salt
¼	tsp. baking soda
1½	cups granulated sugar
1½	tsp. vanilla
1½	cups purchased lemon or orange curd (about one and a half 10-oz. jars)
	Powdered sugar

1. Let butter, eggs, and sour cream stand at room temperature 30 minutes. Preheat oven to 350°F. Grease and flour 12 individual fluted tube pans; set aside.

2. In a large bowl combine flour, ground tea leaves, baking powder, salt, and baking soda; set aside. In very large mixing bowl beat butter with an electric mixer on medium-high speed 1 to 2 minutes. Add granulated sugar; continue beating 5 minutes. Beat in eggs, 1 at a time, scraping sides of bowl after each addition. Beat in vanilla. (Mixture may appear curdled.) Alternately add flour mixture and sour cream to butter mixture, beating on low speed after each addition until combined. Spoon batter into prepared pans, filling two-thirds full.

3. Bake 25 minutes or until pick inserted near center comes out clean. Cool in pans on wire racks 10 minutes. Remove from pans; cool on racks.

4. Split cakes in half. Place bottoms on plates; spread with curd. Replace cake tops. Sprinkle with powdered sugar. Makes 24 servings or 12 cakes total .

*TEST KITCHEN TIP: For 4 teaspoons ground Earl Grey tea leaves, open 5 tea bags with finely ground tea leaves; measure 4 teaspoons. (If using loose Earl Grey tea leaves, use a mortar and pestle to finely grind the leaves.)

EACH SERVING: 329 cal., 17 g fat, (9 g sat. fat), 105 mg chol., 202 mg sodium, 42 g carbo., 3 g fiber, 4 g pro. Daily Values: 10% vit. A, 3% calcium, 6% iron.

20 Delicious solutions
to your Thanksgiving questions

HOW TO MAKE THE MOST HEALTHFUL GRAVY, THE CREAMIEST MASHED POTATOES, THE QUICKEST CRANBERRY RELISH, AND 17 MORE WAYS TO MAKE THIS THE BEST HOLIDAY YET.

1. When I serve the turkey, I want "oohs" and "ahhs." How do I do it?

● Brush the turkey with a syrup of orange juice and herbs. The resulting gleam on the bird will win you all the applause you deserve.

Maple-Tarragon Glazed Turkey with Orange Gravy

Tarragon is used both in the bird and in the glaze. You'll need one 1-ounce package for both recipes. Start by chopping the ¼ cup for the glaze; use the remainder in the bird.

START TO FINISH: 4 HOURS

- 1   10- to 12-lb. turkey
     Salt and freshly ground black pepper
- 2   or 3 sprigs fresh tarragon or 2 tsp. dried tarragon, crushed
- 1   Tbsp. butter or margarine, melted
- 1   recipe Maple-Tarragon Glaze
- 2   blood oranges or regular oranges, quartered
- 2   large bunches seedless purple or red grapes
- 1   recipe Orange Gravy

1. Preheat oven to 325°F. Rinse turkey; dry with paper towels. Sprinkle turkey with salt and pepper. Place fresh tarragon sprigs in body cavity (if using dry tarragon, rub in cavity). Pull neck skin to back; fasten with skewer. Tuck ends of drumsticks under band of skin across tail. If there is no band of skin, tie drumsticks to tail. Twist wing tips under back.

2. Place turkey, breast side up, on a rack in a shallow roasting pan. Brush with butter. Insert oven-going meat thermometer into center of an inside thigh muscle (don't let thermometer touch bone). Loosely cover turkey with foil.

3. Roast turkey until internal temperature registers 160°F (2 to 2½ hours). Prepare Maple-Tarragon Glaze.

4. When thermometer registers 160°F, remove foil and cut band of skin or string between drumsticks so thighs cook evenly. Add quartered oranges to roasting pan; brush orange wedges and turkey with half of the glaze. Roast for 30 minutes more.

5. Add grapes to roasting pan; brush fruit and turkey with remaining glaze. Roast about 15 minutes more or until the thermometer registers 180°F. (The juices should run clear and drumsticks should move easily in their sockets.)

6. Remove turkey from oven; reserve drippings. Transfer turkey to a serving platter. Cover turkey with foil; let stand for 15 to 20 minutes before carving. Prepare Orange Gravy. Arrange on a platter with roasted oranges and grapes and remaining fresh tarragon. Serve with Orange Gravy. Makes 10 (6-ounce) servings plus 1 to 2 pounds of leftovers.

MAPLE-TARRAGON GLAZE: In a medium saucepan combine ¼ cup chopped fresh tarragon or 1½ teaspoons dried tarrago, 1½ teaspoons finely shredded orange peel, 1½ cups orange juice, ¾ cup maple syrup, ⅓ cup tarragon vinegar, 1 teaspoon dry mustard, ½ teaspoon salt, and ¼ teaspoon ground black pepper. Bring to boiling, stirring frequently (watch carefully as mixture will bubble up); reduce heat. Boil gently, uncovered, for 30 to 35 minutes or until mixture reaches a glazing consistency, stirring occasionally. (You should have about 1 cup.)

ORANGE GRAVY: Place the drippings from roasted turkey in a 2-cup glass measure. Add enough orange juice to equal 1½ cups. Place in a medium saucepan. Combine one 14-ounce can chicken broth and 2 tablespoons cornstarch; stir into orange juice mixture in saucepan. Cook and stir over medium heat until thickened and bubbly. Cook and stir 2 minutes more. Season to taste with salt and ground black pepper. Makes about 12 (¼-cup) servings.

EACH SERVING (TURKEY, 3 OUNCES GRAPES, AND ¼ CUP GRAVY): 384 cal., 8 g total fat (3 g sat. fat), 141 mg chol., 379 mg sodium, 36 g carbo., 1 g fiber, 39 g pro. Daily Values: 5% vit. A, 67% vit. C, 7% calcium, 17% iron.

BY RICHARD SWEARINGER AND NANCY BYAL PHOTOGRAPHS BY ALEXANDRA ROWLEY FOOD STYLING BY ANNE DISRUDE PROP STYLING BY BARB FRITZ

Maple-Tarragon Glazed Turkey with Orange Gravy

2. How can I transform my pre-dinner cheese plate into something special?

Replace the traditional cheese assortment with just one cheese so guests can really focus on its unique character. Partner it with fresh pears and a crock of homemade mustard apple butter to spread on the cheese and pears.

Cheese, Pears, and Mustard-Laced Apple Butter

Fast! **PREP:** 10 minutes

- 2 cups apple butter
- 2 Tbsp. Dijon-style mustard
- 2 Tbsp snipped fresh sage or rosemary or 1½ tsp. dried sage, crushed
- 2 Tbsp. champagne vinegar, pomegranate vinegar, or lemon juice
- 1 1- to 2-lb. round semisoft cheese, such as Tomme De Savoie or Brie
  Fresh or dried pears
  Fresh sage sprigs

1. In a small saucepan combine apple butter, mustard, and sage; bring to boiling. Stir in champagne vinegar; remove from heat. Place apple butter mixture in a small bowl. Serve warm or at room temperature.
2. Serve with cheese and pears. Garnish with sage sprigs. Store apple butter in the refrigerator up to 1 week. Makes 24 servings.

EACH SERVING (1 TABLESPOON APPLE BUTTER AND 1 OUNCE OF CHEESE): 232 cal., 7 g total fat (4 g sat. fat), 20 mg chol., 280 mg sodium, 37 g carbo., 2 g fiber, 6 g pro. Daily Values: 5% vit. A, 4% vit. C, 13% calcium, 2% iron.

3. I need a great all-occasion wine. Where do I start?

The holidays bring together such a delightfully wide variety of foods—and people—that the best bet is a wine that's subtle yet delicious. Good choices: Mirassou Monterey County Pinot Noir, $11, www.mirassou.com; Red Knot Shiraz, $12, www.redknotwine.com; Smoking Loon Chardonnay, $9, www.donandsons.com; Little Penguin White Shiraz, $8, www.thelittlepenguin.com.

Cheese, Pears, and Mustard-Laced Apple Butter

5. Have any festive, easy salad ideas?

Try this no-measure version, and keep your eye out for candy cane beets, a striped variety that shows up in some grocery store produce sections during the holidays.

No-Measure Spinach Salad

Candy cane beets can be ordered from Melissa's World Variety Produce by calling 800/588-0151.

Fast! START TO FINISH: 30 minutes

18-oz. bottle honey-mustard salad dressing
- ½ can (16-oz.) jellied cranberry sauce
- 1 lemon or lime
- 2 Tbsp. water
- 2 apples, cored and very thinly sliced crosswise (use a very sharp knife or mandoline slicer)
- 1 16-oz. bag baby spinach leaves or 4 bunches watercress (thick stems discarded), rinsed and dried
- 2 small beets or candy cane (chioggia) beets (about 12 oz.), trimmed, peeled, and thinly sliced

1. For dressing, in a blender container or food processor bowl combine salad dressing and jellied cranberry sauce; cover and blend until smooth. Pour into a small serving bowl; set aside. (Dressing may be made ahead and stored in refrigerator until serving time.)
2. Squeeze juice from lemon into medium bowl; add 2 tablespoons water. Add apple slices to juice mixture. Turn slices to coat well; set aside.
3. In a large serving bowl arrange spinach and sliced beets. Drain the apples; add to bowl. Serve with dressing. Cover and refrigerate any remaining dressing up to 1 week; stir before using. Makes 8 servings.
EACH SERVING: 190 cal., 9 g total fat (1 g sat. fat), 0 mg chol., 310 mg sodium, 28 g carbo., 3 g fiber, 1 g pro. Daily Values: 40% vit. A, 19% vit. C, 5% calcium, 5% iron.

No-Measure Spinach Salad

4. What's a fast way to make cranberry relish?

Use this no-cook recipe and a food processor; you'll be done in 10 minutes. Save any leftover relish; it's delicious on sandwiches.

Fresh Cranberry-Fig Relish

Fast! PREP: 10 MINUTES CHILL: 2 HOURS

- 4 cups fresh cranberries*
- 1 cup dried figs, stems removed
- 2 Tbsp. snipped fresh mint leaves
- 1 cup orange marmalade
- 2 Tbsp. balsamic vinegar

1. Using a food processor or hand food chopper, process or chop cranberries and dried figs until coarsely chopped. Transfer to a bowl; add mint. Stir together marmalade and balsamic vinegar. Add to cranberry mixture; stir well. Cover and chill at least 2 hours or up to 1 week. Or freeze up to 6 months; thaw overnight in refrigerator before serving. Makes 16 (¼-cup) servings.
***TEST KITCHEN TIP:** If cranberries are frozen, measure while frozen. Let stand at room temperature about 15 minutes to thaw slightly before processing.
EACH SERVING: 96 cal., 0 g total fat, 0 mg chol., 13 mg sodium, 25 g carbo., 3 g fiber, 1 g pro. Daily Values: 1% vit. A, 9% vit. C, 3% calcium, 3% iron.

6. How do I make great mashed potatoes?

Use a potato ricer (photo, *below*); the lever mechanism pushes cooked potatoes through the tiny holes in the metal cylinder, ensuring there are no lumps and that potatoes are fluffy. (Don't have one? Try www.oxo.com, www.surlatable.com, or www.cooking.com.) The other secret: Cook the potatoes in evaporated milk.

Best-Ever Mashed Potatoes
PREP: 15 MINUTES **COOK:** 30 MINUTES

- 1   Tbsp. juniper berries
- 4   lb. Yukon gold potatoes or russet potatoes
- 2   12-oz. cans evaporated milk or 3 cups half-and-half
- 1   14-oz. can chicken broth
- ¼   cup Worcestershire sauce for chicken
- 6   bay leaves
- ½   tsp. salt
- ¼   tsp. ground white pepper or ground black pepper

1. Place juniper berries in a small piece of 100%-cotton cheesecloth; tie closed with 100%-cotton kitchen string. Scrub, peel, and cut potatoes into 1½-inch pieces. Place potatoes, cheesecloth bag, and remaining ingredients in a 6-quart Dutch oven or large saucepan. Bring to boiling; reduce heat. Simmer, covered, for 30 minutes or until potatoes are tender. Drain, reserving cooking liquid. Use tongs to remove juniper berries and bay leaves.

2. Push potatoes through a ricer into a large bowl (or place potatoes in a large bowl and mash with potato masher until smooth). Gently stir in 1 cup of the reserved cooking liquid, 1 teaspoon additional *salt*, and ½ teaspoon additional *pepper* until combined. Season to taste with additional *salt* and *pepper*, if necessary. Makes 8 to 10 servings.

MAKE AHEAD: Potatoes can be prepared and kept warm up to 2 hours in a slow cooker on low-heat setting.

EACH SERVING: 252 cal., 7 g total fat (4 g sat. fat), 25 mg chol., 566 mg sodium, 41 g carbo., 3 g fiber, 10 g pro. Daily Values: 4% vit. A, 43% vit. C, 23% calcium, 8% iron.

7. Glazed acorn squash is wonderful to eat but tricky to cut. What's the best way?

For every 4 guests, cut off both ends of squash, pierce it all over with a fork, then precook it on 100% power (high) in a microwave oven for 10 minutes or until soft. Allow to cool, cut in half, remove seeds, and slice into 8 wedges. Then, create a sweet, herb-scented glaze by combining ⅓ cup each of lemon juice, honey, and olive oil; then whisking in 1 teaspoon of dried rosemary, crushed, and ¼ teaspoon of ground nutmeg. Arrange the wedges, skin sides down, in a large baking pan. Drizzle with the glaze and bake in a preheated 375°F oven for 20 minutes or until tender.

8. My family loves green bean casserole, but how can I give it a new twist?

Use the same basic flavors in a new way. Instead of french fried onions, use a fresh onion cut into generous wedges; in place of mushroom soup, use fresh baby portobello mushrooms. Though it has some new ingredients, it can still be made ahead.

Green Bean Bake Revisited

PREP: 50 MINUTES **ROAST:** 20 MINUTES

- 1 large sweet onion (white, yellow, or red), cut in 1-inch wedges, or 4 cups cipollini (wild onions), halved
- ¼ cup cooking oil
- 3 Tbsp. packed brown sugar
- 2 lb. fresh or frozen whole green beans, trimmed
- 6 oz. baby portobello (cremini) or button mushrooms, halved
- 2 Tbsp. olive oil
- 1 Tbsp. soy sauce
- 2 tsp. balsamic vinegar
- 6 oz. goat cheese or cream cheese, softened
- 2 to 3 Tbsp. milk

1. In a large skillet cook onions, covered, in hot oil over medium-low heat for 13 to 15 minutes or until onions are tender. Uncover; add brown sugar. Cook and stir over medium-high heat for 3 to 5 minutes or until onions are golden and caramelized. Set aside.

2. Preheat oven to 400°F. In a large saucepan cook green beans, covered, in a small amount of boiling water for 3 minutes. Drain. In a 3-quart au gratin or baking dish combine green beans and mushrooms. Combine olive oil, soy sauce, and balsamic vinegar. Pour over vegetables, tossing to coat. Roast for 15 to 20 minutes, stirring once, until crisp tender.

3. Meanwhile, in a medium mixing bowl beat cheese and milk with an electric mixer on medium speed. Spoon cheese in lengthwise mounds along center of baking dish. Top with caramelized onions. Return to oven; heat 5 to 8 minutes or until cheese and onions are heated through. Makes 10 to 12 servings.

MAKE AHEAD: Prepare onions as directed in Step 1; refrigerate until ready to assemble. Prepare vegetables and mushrooms as directed in Step 2; refrigerate until ready to assemble. Remove onions and vegetables from refrigerator 30 minutes before using. To reheat, assemble dish as directed in Step 3, omitting cheese mixture. Heat in a 400°F oven for 30 minutes. The last 5 minutes of baking time, spoon cheese mixture over onions.

EACH SERVING: 173 cal., 12 g total fat (4 g sat. fat), 8 mg chol., 163 mg sodium, 12 g carbo., 3 g fiber, 6 g pro. Daily Values: 10% vit. A, 18% vit. C, 6% calcium, 8% iron.

Green Bean Bake Revisited

Turkey Roasting Guide

9. Which is better, a fresh or frozen turkey?

They're about equal, so base your choice on personal preference. Fresh turkeys take up shelf space in the fridge for a day or two; frozen birds take up to a week to thaw there. Around Thanksgiving, fresh and frozen birds are available in grocery stores.

10. What do I do when it's Thanksgiving morning and the bird is not thawed?

Place the turkey in a clean sink full of cold water; change the water every 30 minutes. For food safety, don't thaw the turkey at room temperature, in the microwave oven, or in warm water. When thawed, remove giblets and neck. Rinse bird, if desired. Pat dry with paper towels.

11. Where do I place the meat thermometer?

Push the thermometer probe into the center of an inside thigh muscle so that it does not touch any bone.

12. How do I know when the turkey is done?

When a meat thermometer registers 180°F and the stuffing is at least 160°F. The drumsticks will move easily in their sockets and the thickest parts feel soft when pressed.

13. What if the turkey is done but the stuffing is not?

Remove the bird from the oven, spoon the stuffing into a baking dish, cover with foil, and return immediately to the oven. Or consider baking stuffing outside the bird.

14. What is standing time?

After the bird is out of the oven, a 20-minute "rest" makes the meat easier to carve.

15. Where can I get more info?

Try the Butterball Turkey Talk-Line: 800/288-8372 or the U.S. Department of Agriculture Meat and Poultry Hot Line: 800/535-4555.

16. What's an easy, stylish way to serve the turkey?

Carve it in the kitchen; then serve it artfully arranged on a pretty platter. First, remove the whole legs by pulling them away from the body of the turkey; cut loose the joints that hold the thighs to the body. Place on cutting board and cut drumsticks from the thighs at the joints. Place drumsticks on a serving platter. As you hold each thigh firmly with a meat fork, cut slices away from the bone. Arrange slices on platter. Hold turkey firmly with the meat fork and carve each breast meat section away from the rib cage. Slice each breast section crosswise and arrange on platter. Cut wings away from the body, cutting at the joints, and arrange with the rest of the turkey on the platter.

17. Roasting Times?

READY-TO-COOK TURKEY WEIGHT	ROASTING TIME
8 to 12 lb.	2¾ to 3 hours
12 to 14 lb.	3 to 3¾ hours
14 to 18 lb.	3¾ to 4¼ hours
18 to 20 lb.	4¼ to 4½ hours
20 to 24 lb.	4½ to 5 hours

FOR STUFFED TURKEYS OF THE SAME WEIGHT: INCREASE TOTAL COOKING TIME BY 15 TO 45 MINUTES.

18. How can I make a rich gravy that's healthy?

Imagine an almost fat-free combo of broth, sweet potato, and carrots with the rich flavor of molasses and allspice. The amazing part? Instead of drippings and flour, the thickening comes from the carrots and sweet potatoes.

Molasses-Spice Gravy

PREP: 20 MINUTES **COOK:** 30 MINUTES

- 2 14-oz. cans reduced-sodium chicken broth
- ½ of a large sweet potato, peeled and coarsely chopped (8 oz.)
- ⅔ cup peeled, sliced fresh carrot (about 1 large)
- ½ cup chopped onion
- 1 to 2 Tbsp. full-flavor molasses
- ½ tsp. ground allspice
- ¼ tsp. salt
- ⅛ tsp. freshly ground black pepper

1. In a medium saucepan combine chicken broth, sweet potato, carrot, and onion. Bring to boiling. Reduce heat; simmer, covered, for 20 minutes or until vegetables are tender. Remove from heat; cool slightly.

2. Pour half the vegetable mixture into a deep bowl or blender container. Blend with immersion blender or in blender container until smooth. Repeat with remaining mixture. Return all to saucepan. Bring to boiling; reduce heat. Simmer, uncovered, for 10 minutes, stirring occasionally. Remove from heat; stir in molasses, allspice, salt, and pepper. Makes about 12 (¼-cup) servings or 3 cups total.

EACH SERVING: 25 cal., 0 g total fat, 1 mg chol., 183 mg sodium, 5 g carbo., 1 g fiber, 1 g pro. Daily Values: 53% vit. A, 6% vit. C, 1% calcium, 1% iron.

19. Can lumpy gravy be rescued?

As soon as you notice lumps, stop cooking and pour the gravy through a mesh strainer into a clean bowl. Return the lump-free gravy to the heat and resume cooking. If the gravy isn't thick enough, place 2 tablespoons of flour in a screw-top jar, add 2 tablespoons of cold water, cover, and shake. Add the liquid about 1 tablespoon at a time to gravy, cooking and stirring after each addition until gravy is the thickness you prefer.

20. How can I jazz up pumpkin pie yet still keep it simple to make?

Instead of the classic, offer Pumpkin Gingerbread Pie. The marbling is created by gingerbread mix swirled into the pumpkin.

Pumpkin Gingerbread Pie

PREP: 25 MINUTES **BAKE:** 50 MINUTES

-    Nonstick cooking spray
- 1 cup canned pumpkin
- ⅓ cup sugar
- 1 tsp. pumpkin pie spice
- 1 egg, slightly beaten
- ½ cup half-and-half or light cream
- 1 14½-oz. pkg. gingerbread mix
-    Whipped cream (optional)

1. Preheat oven to 350°F. Coat a 10-inch deep-dish pie plate or an 8×8×2-inch baking dish with cooking spray; set aside. In a small mixing bowl combine pumpkin, sugar, and pumpkin pie spice. Add egg. Beat lightly with a rotary beater or fork just until combined. Gradually stir in half-and-half; mix well.

2. Prepare gingerbread mix according to package directions. Pour batter into prepared pie plate or dish. Lightly spoon pumpkin mixture over gingerbread batter; swirl gently using a table knife. Bake for 50 minutes for pie plate or 60 minutes for baking dish or until a toothpick inserted into gingerbread portion comes out clean. Cool slightly. Serve warm or at room temperature and, if desired, with whipped cream. Makes 8 servings.

EACH SERVING: 304 cal., 10 g total fat (3g sat. fat), 59 mg chol., 363 mg sodium, 50 g carbo., 2g fiber, 5 g pro. Daily Values: 98% vit. A, 3% vit. C, 81% calcium, 17% iron.

Pumpkin Gingerbread Pie

PASSIONATE ABOUT SQUASH

BY **STEPHEN EXEL** PHOTOGRAPHS BY **ROBERT PELLETIER**

Pascale Coutu, seventh generation owner of La Courgerie farm near Montreal, is known to family and friends as the "Queen of Squash." She should be. She grows more than 200 varieties of squash at the picturesque 250-year-old farm. It's Pascale's love of the lumpy, bumpy, colorful fruit that energizes her life. An avid cook, she develops squash recipes for the culinary classes she teaches on-site. She also teaches home decor using squash as a focal point.

At the first pick each fall Pascale's family goes on a treasure hunt to survey the new varieties that have grown. "They are so original, the way they are colored and shaped. Sometimes so strange," she says. "The potential for cooking and decorating is so varied. I discover new possibilities each year, and every year I have a new crush. Squash are nutritious and easy to preserve, therefore a good choice for the family."

Pascale confesses a partiality for squash that has an interesting taste as well a special look for a gorgeous autumnal table. Large squat squash can be used for unexpected serving pieces; others, such as 'Sweet Dumpling' and 'Délicata,' are excellent for stuffing with meat and vegetable combinations.

As Pascale, who had a career in tourism management, crossed into her thirties, she re-evaluated her priorities. Her mother gave her a piece of advice that put a new perspective on the farm she grew up on. "My wonderful, wise mother told me something that really clicked inside me. She said, 'Find a project that will have your colors.' And what colors!"

Wanting to start a family and change the rhythm of her life helped Pascale make the decision to purchase La Courgerie from her parents. She studied agriculture by working on the farm for five years and eventually purchased it in 2003.

Pascale balances work and family so that life objectives dictate professional projects, rather than the opposite. She runs the family farm with her husband, Pierre Tremblay, and her parents, Ghislaine and André. Even 3-year-old son, François, gets in the act; his walks through fields are opportunities to learn about farming, harvesting, and the cycle of the seasons.

"He sowed his first garden this spring, and this has helped him connect with Mom's work in the fields," Pascale says. "He's found out that Mom's garden is huge."

Note: La Courgerie is located at 2321 Grand rang St-Pierre, Ste-Élisabeth, Québec, Canada, J0K 2J0. For information: 800/711-2021 or www.lacourgerie.com. (Website is in French.)

Pascale Coutu (second from left, *opposite*) gathers with her family. "The people I love inspire me daily," she says. Some of the farm's more unusual squash (*above*, clockwise from top) include fagtoon, cushaw, jarrahdale, courge de Siam, and patisson.

Potimarron Bread

Potimarron Bread

PREP: 25 MINUTES **BAKE:** 55 MINUTES FOR SQUASH, 55 MINUTES FOR BREAD **STAND:** OVERNIGHT **COOL:** 2 HOURS

1	2-lb. potimarron or butternut squash
¼	cup milk
2	cups all-purpose flour
1	tsp. baking soda
½	tsp. salt
½	tsp. cracked black pepper
1	3-oz. pkg. cream cheese, softened
¼	cup butter, softened
1¼	cups packed brown sugar
2	eggs
1	Tbsp. maple sugar or granulated sugar
½	tsp. ground sage
¼	tsp. coarse sea salt or kosher salt or ⅛ tsp. salt
1	recipe Squash Butter

1. Preheat oven to 350°F. Halve squash lengthwise and remove seeds. Place squash halves, cut sides down, in a shallow baking dish. Bake, uncovered, for 55 to 60 minutes or until tender. Cool squash completely. Scoop squash pulp from shell using a spoon. Using a potato masher or fork, mash pulp until smooth. Or place squash in a food processor bowl; cover and process until smooth. Measure 1 cup pulp into a small bowl; stir in milk. Set aside. Reserve remaining squash pulp for Squash Butter (about ⅔ cup).

2. Meanwhile, grease the bottom and ½ inch up the sides of a 9×5×3-inch loaf pan; set aside. In a medium bowl combine flour, baking soda, the ½ teaspoon salt, and the cracked black pepper; set aside. In a large mixing bowl beat together cream cheese and butter with an electric mixer on medium speed for 30 seconds. Add brown sugar; beat until well combined. Beat in eggs.

3. Alternately add flour mixture and squash mixture to brown sugar mixture, beating on low speed after each addition just until combined. Spoon batter into prepared pan. In a small bowl stir together maple sugar, sage, and the ¼ teaspoon sea salt. Sprinkle over batter in pan. Bake for 55 to 60 minutes or until a wooden toothpick inserted near center comes out clean. Cool in pan on wire rack for 10 minutes. Remove from pan. Cool completely on wire rack. Wrap and store overnight before slicing. Serve with Squash Butter. Makes 16 servings.

SQUASH BUTTER: In a small saucepan combine ⅔ cup mashed squash pulp, ⅓ cup packed brown sugar, 2 tablespoons honey, 1 tablespoon lemon juice, and ½ teaspoon ground sage. Bring to boiling, stirring to mix well; reduce heat. Cook, uncovered, over medium-low heat for 40 minutes or until very thick, stirring often. Remove from heat; cool. Serve with Potimarron Bread. To store, place in an airtight container and chill in refrigerator up to 1 month. Makes ⅔ cup.

EACH SERVING: 235 cal., 6 g total fat (3 g sat. fat), 41 mg chol., 235 mg sodium, 44 g carbo., 2 g fiber, 4 g pro. Daily Values: 122% vit. A, 17% vit. C, 6% calcium, 10% iron.

PHOTOGRAPHS BY **GREG SCHEIDEMANN** (SWEET MAMA SOUP AND POTIMARRON BREAD); **ROBERT PELLETIER** (SQUASH)

Sweet Mama Soup

Sweet Mama Soup

PREP: 30 MINUTES **BAKE:** 1 HOUR **COOK:** 25 MINUTES

- 2 to 2½ pounds Sweet Mama or butternut squash
- 1 medium onion, chopped
- 1 tablespoon olive oil
- 5 cups chicken broth
- 2 medium cooking apples, peeled, cored, and quartered
- ¼ cup pure maple syrup
- 1 cup whipping cream
  Salt and ground black pepper
  Chopped red and/or green apple

1. Preheat oven to 350°F. If using Sweet Mama squash, use half to three-fourths of the squash. If using butternut squash, cut in half lengthwise. Remove and discard seeds. Arrange squash, cut sides down, in a 3-quart rectangular baking dish. Bake for 1 to 1¼ hours for Sweet Mama squash, 45 to 60 minutes for butternut squash, or until squash is tender. Remove from oven; cool slightly. Scoop pulp from squash halves. Place cooked pulp in a bowl; mash with a potato masher or fork (you should have about 2 cups pulp).

2. Meanwhile, in a saucepan cook the onion in oil for 5 minutes or until onion is tender. Stir in chicken broth, apples, and maple syrup. Bring to boiling, reduce heat. Simmer, covered, for 20 minutes or until apple is very tender. Remove from heat. Cool slightly. Stir in mashed squash.

3. Transfer half of the mixture to a blender container or one-fourth of the mixture to a food processor bowl. Cover; blend or process until smooth. Repeat with remaining mixture.

4. Return the blended mixture to the saucepan over low heat. Stir in whipping cream (if necessary, add additional chicken broth to make desired consistency). Heat through. Season to taste with salt and pepper. Sprinkle each serving with chopped apple. Makes 8 side-dish servings.

EACH SERVING: 235 cal., 6 g total fat (3 g sat. fat), 41 mg chol., 235 mg sodium, 44 g carbo., 2 g fiber, 4 g pro. Daily Values: 122% vit. A, 17% vit. C, 6% calcium, 10% iron.

SQUASH IN THE KITCHEN

Choose squash with firm, unblemished peduncles (stalks). Squash will last several months in fresh, ventilated places. Squash that are preserved for several months lose their brightness but gain flavor and are easier to cut.

GOOD TO KNOW Pascale Couto suggests using these squash for certain dishes: SOUPS: acorn, Hubbard, Blue Banana, Pink Jumbo Banana. PUREES: butternut, buttercup, Hubbard. TARTS: buttercup. RATATOUILLE: butternut, summer squash. SALADS: Délicata, summer squash, Red Kuri.

FROZEN GRAPES

Create a gorgeous display with frosty frozen grapes and watch the colors emerge as they defrost. Freeze bunches of red or globe grapes for 6 hours. For the centerpiece, stack 2 pedestal cake stands. Tuck snipped bunches between layers with a whole bunch at the top.

TRY THIS

Stir a delicious change into your cranberry sauce recipe; add a bay leaf or a few whole cloves wrapped in cheesecloth while cooking, substitute sliced kumquats for orange peel in the recipe, or mash raspberries into the cooled, cooked sauce.

PHOTOGRAPHS BY KIM CORNELISON

Morning After Thanksgiving

What to do for the weekend crowd's Friday breakfast? Lisa Santos, owner of Southport Grocery and Cafe, one of Chicago's favorite breakfast stops, suggests using leftover mashed potatoes as a side dish to scrambled eggs. Reheat the mashed potatoes with a little milk to make them creamy and then stir in sautéed leeks, snipped rosemary, and shredded cheddar cheese. Top with crispy-cooked bacon. Breakfast at Southport Grocery and Cafe is something of a treat. When a menu item features a specialty food item, you'll find it available for purchase in the small yet well-stocked grocery portion of Santos' establishment. Southport Grocery and Café, 3552 N. Southport, Chicago; 773/665-0100; www.southportgrocery.com.

Best Friends and Brownies

The golden rules of friendship also apply to brownies. This is especially true as we give thanks for friends, according to the three women who own Simply Divine Brownies. To bake seasonal brownies for your best friends, the Brownie Ladies suggest adding flavored liqueur, such as hazelnut, to the batter; spreading warm jelly over the top; or layering brownie batter with your favorite cookie dough. Mother and daughter, Sue Rand and Melissa Rand, at left and middle, with best friend Trina Beaulier pack their brownies with ingredients because "a friend is always generous," layer them with frostings and toppings because "friendship is multilayered," and make them extra thick because "a friend stands by you through thick and thin." Simply Divine Brownies; 207/729-0111; www.simplydivinebrownies.com.

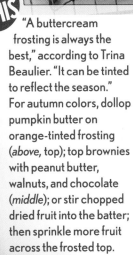

TRY THIS

"A buttercream frosting is always the best," according to Trina Beaulier. "It can be tinted to reflect the season." For autumn colors, dollop pumpkin butter on orange-tinted frosting (*above, top*); top brownies with peanut butter, walnuts, and chocolate (*middle*); or stir chopped dried fruit into the batter; then sprinkle more fruit across the frosted top.

PHOTOGRAPHS BY GREG SCHEIDEMANN (BREAKFAST); JEFF KAUCK (PORTRAIT); KIM CORNELISON (BROWNIES); JAMIE SALOMON (PORTRAIT)

DECEMBER

WHEN FRIENDS AND FAMILY GATHER, 'TIS THE OCCASION FOR A JOLLY BUFFET. THE MORE THE MERRIER REALLY DOES HOLD TRUE WHEN HOLIDAY COOKING IS SO EASILY ACCOMPLISHED.

White Chocolate Snowdrift Cake
page 250

3 Easy Holiday Buffets

Buffet 1: Casual Appetizers with Friends

Buffet 2: A Family Feast, Fast

Buffet 3: Decadent Desserts After the Show

Fluffy Cranberry Mousse
page 251

**White Cheddar Shortbread Sandwiches
with Red Onion Marmalade**
page 243

**No-Fuss Blue Cheese and Pear Salad with
Apricot Nectar Dressing**
page 247

3 easy

Holiday Buffets

WHEN YOU'RE FEEDING FRIENDLY CROWDS, BUFFETS ARE THE BEST. WITH FESTIVE FOOD OUT IN THE OPEN, THE PARTY STARTS WITH A "WOW" AND SPIRITS STAY MERRY ALL NIGHT. GUESTS MINGLE MORE; YOU FUSS LESS.

BY WINIFRED MORANVILLE RECIPES BY CHARLES WORTHINGTON PHOTOGRAPHS BY NGOC MINH NGO FOOD STYLING BY ALISON ATTENBOROUGH PROP STYLING BY CHRISTINA WRESSELL (FAUCHER ARTISTS)

One-Step Artichoke Bean Dip with Roasted Red Peppers

PREP: 20 MINUTES **STAND:** 2 HOURS

1 19-oz. can cannellini beans (white kidney beans), rinsed and drained
1 14-oz. can artichoke hearts, drained
¼ cup extra-virgin olive oil
2 to 3 cloves garlic, quartered
3 Tbsp. lemon juice
¼ tsp. coarse sea salt or kosher salt
¼ tsp. cayenne pepper
Coarse sea salt or kosher salt
¼ cup roasted red sweet pepper strips
1 Tbsp. snipped fresh basil
Assorted crackers, toasted baguette slices, or toasted pita chips

1. In a food processor bowl combine beans, artichokes, oil, garlic, lemon juice, the ¼ teaspoon salt, and the cayenne pepper. Cover and process until almost smooth, scraping sides as necessary. Transfer to a serving bowl; cover and let stand at room temperature until ready to serve (up to 2 hours). For longer storage, cover and chill up to 24 hours. Let stand at room temperature about 1 hour before serving. To serve, sprinkle lightly with additional sea salt. Top with sweet pepper strips and basil. Serve with crackers, baguette slices, or pita chips. Makes 12 to 14 (3-tablespoon) servings.

EACH SERVING: 76 cal., 5 g total fat (1 g sat. fat), 0 mg chol., 207 mg sodium, 8 g carbo., 3 g fiber, 3 g pro. Daily Values: 1% vit. A, 18% vit. C, 2% calcium, 7% iron.

One-Step Artichoke Bean Dip with Roasted Red Peppers

1. Casual Appetizers with Friends

Whether you're having an after-work get-together, a post-caroling fete, or a New Year's Eve spread, these tips work for all kinds of occasions. Here's how to set the scene with style:

• Keep garnishes minimal. Instead, let the clean lines of plates and platters do the work to achieve the look you want.

• Serve the soups in small vessels or demitasse cups that are handy for guests to grab and sip (no spoons needed).

• There are endless no-cook variations on the appetizer sandwich, all involving purchased spreads served on high-quality crackers, savory scones, or crustless breads.

• For a heartier appetizer spread, add an array of cheeses. A blue cheese, such as Stilton, would go well with the Red Onion Marmalade, while Parmigiano-Reggiano would pair nicely with the Mediterranean influences of the artichoke bean dip.

2. A Family Feast, Fast

Whether hosting the family's holiday event or catering to old friends, this menu can do it. Here's what it takes:

• Some of the ingredients—such as the pears and the cheeses in the salad—are cut into large pieces for guests to see what's in the dish and grab more of what they like.

• You can switch in choices your family loves. Substitute apples for the pears, bacon for the prosciutto, green beans for the Brussels sprouts, Brie for the blue cheese. It's up to you.

• Grandma made mashed potatoes and gravy. You make Herb Butter Mashed Potatoes. Both are loved, but your version requires no potato peeling or gravy making. Hint: You could even start with refrigerated mashed potatoes.

3. Decadent Desserts After the Show

This buffet is for the Sugar Plum Fairy in all of us:

• Add drama to the Fluffy Cranberry Mousse by serving the billowy drift in a footed glass bowl.

• Consider making the White Chocolate Snowdrift Cake into cupcakes. Guests will love having their own cakes.

• Round out the spread with ready-made lovelies, such as candy-coated almonds and chocolate truffles. It's a good idea to have a surplus of such items waiting in the wings so you can easily replenish the buffet.

• What to drink? For the adults, Moscato d'Asti, a lightly sweet, softly sparkling wine from Italy, will go well with this selection. For the kids, you can't go wrong with hot chocolate. Keep it warm in a slow cooker on low-heat setting for up to two hours.

Green Pea Soup

PREP: 20 MINUTES **COOK:** 20 MINUTES **COOL:** 10 MINUTES

- ½ cup chopped onion
- 2 Tbsp. butter
- 2 14-oz. cans reduced-sodium chicken broth
- 1 16-oz. pkg. frozen baby sweet peas
- 1 head butterhead lettuce, torn (about 4 cups)
- 1 Tbsp. snipped fresh oregano or 1 tsp. dried oregano, crushed
- 2 oz. goat cheese (chèvre), or cream cheese plus 1 tablespoon lemon juice

1. In a 4-quart Dutch oven cook onion in hot butter over medium heat about 5 minutes or until onion is tender, stirring occasionally.

2. Add chicken broth and peas to the Dutch oven. Bring to boiling; reduce heat. Simmer, uncovered, about 5 minutes or until peas are tender. Add lettuce; cook 1 minute more or until lettuce is wilted. Remove from heat; stir in oregano. Cool slightly, about 10 minutes.

3. Transfer half of the pea mixture to a blender container or food processor bowl. Cover and blend until smooth. Repeat with remaining pea mixture. Return all to Dutch oven. Break apart goat cheese and add to soup (or cut up cream cheese and stir into soup with the lemon juice). Heat and whisk until cheese is melted. Season to taste with *sea salt* or *kosher salt* and *freshly ground black pepper.*

4. Serve at once in small heatproof glasses or demitasse cups. Cover and chill leftovers up to 2 days. Makes about 18 (⅓-cup) servings or 6 cups total.

EACH SERVING: 46 cal., 2 g total fat (1 g sat. fat), 5 mg chol., 166 mg sodium, 5 g carbo., 1 g fiber, 2 g pro. Daily Values: 19% vit. A, 9% vit. C, 2% calcium, 3% iron.

Tomato Bisque Sip Soup

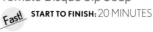 **START TO FINISH:** 20 MINUTES

- 3 14½-oz. cans diced tomatoes with garlic and onion
- 1 Tbsp. balsamic vinegar
- 1 Tbsp. packed brown sugar
- 1½ tsp. finely shredded orange peel
- ¼ tsp. cracked black pepper
- ¾ cup whipping cream
- 1 to 2 oz. Parmesan cheese, shaved (optional)
  Cracked black pepper (optional)

1. Place 2 cans of the tomatoes in a blender container. Cover and blend until very smooth. Transfer to a large saucepan. Cover and blend remaining tomatoes, vinegar, brown sugar, orange peel, and the ¼ teaspoon pepper until very smooth. Transfer to the saucepan. Bring to a simmer over medium-low heat. Simmer, uncovered, for 5 minutes; remove from heat. (At this point, soup can be covered and chilled until ready to serve or up to 24 hours.)

2. When ready to serve, return soup to a simmer and stir in cream until combined. Serve in small heatproof glasses or demitasse cups. If desired, sprinkle each serving with cheese and additional pepper. Makes about 10 (½-cup) appetizer servings, 4 (1-cup) main-dish servings, or 5½ cups total.

EACH (½-CUP) SERVING: 109 cal., 7 g total fat (4 g sat. fat), 25 mg chol., 605 mg sodium, 10 g carbo., 1 g fiber, 2 g pro. Daily Values: 5% vit. A, 16% vit. C, 3% calcium, 8% iron.

**Green Pea Soup and
Tomato Bisque Sip Soup**

15-Minute Zesty Smoked Trout Spread

15-Minute Zesty Smoked Trout Spread
PREP: 15 MINUTES **CHILL:** 1 HOUR **STAND:** 15 MINUTES

  8 oz. smoked trout fillets (or other smoked whitefish), skin and bones removed and flaked

  2 3-oz. pkg. cream cheese, softened

  ¼ cup dairy sour cream

  3 Tbsp. finely chopped shallot or onion

1½ tsp. finely shredded lemon peel

  3 Tbsp. lemon juice

  ¼ tsp. freshly ground black pepper

     Fresh chives or chopped green onion (optional)

  3 medium red sweet peppers, seeded and cut into 1-inch-wide strips

     Assorted crackers or flatbreads (optional)

1. In a medium bowl stir together trout, cream cheese, sour cream, shallot, lemon peel, lemon juice, and pepper until well combined, smearing the trout against the sides of the bowl with the back of the spoon while stirring.

2. Transfer spread to a small serving bowl; cover and refrigerate for 1 hour or until ready to serve. Remove spread from refrigerator about 15 minutes before serving. If desired, top with chives. Serve with sweet pepper strips and, if desired, crackers. (Leftover spread can be covered and refrigerated up to 3 days.) Makes 16 (2-tablespoon) servings or 1¾ cups total.

EACH SERVING: 75 cal., 5 g total fat (3 g sat. fat), 29 mg chol., 84 mg sodium, 4 g carbo., 0 g fiber, 3 g pro. Daily Values: 18% vit. A, 74% vit. C, 3% calcium, 1% iron.

**White Cheddar Shortbread Sandwiches
with Red Onion Marmalade**

White Cheddar Shortbread Sandwiches
PREP: 35 MINUTES **CHILL:** 30 MINUTES **BAKE:** 20 MINUTES

- 8 oz. white cheddar cheese, finely shredded
- ½ cup butter
- 1½ cups all-purpose flour
- ¼ tsp. sea salt or salt
- ¼ tsp. coarsely ground black pepper
  Sea salt or salt
- 1 recipe Red Onion Marmalade

1. Preheat oven to 350°F. In a large mixing bowl place cheese, butter, flour, the ¼ teaspoon salt, and the pepper; let stand 30 minutes at room temperature. Beat with an electric mixer on medium speed until combined. Using your hands, work dough until it holds together. Divide dough in half.
2. Line two 8×8×2-inch baking pans or 2-qt. square baking dishes with plastic wrap. Press half the dough evenly into each prepared pan. Cover and chill about 30 minutes. Invert one pan onto a very large ungreased baking sheet. Remove pan and carefully peel off plastic wrap. Use a floured knife to cut dough into eight 1-inch-wide strips. Cut strips crosswise into four 2-inch-long rectangles to make 32 (2×1-inch) rectangles (do not separate rectangles). Repeat with remaining dough. With a floured fork, prick each rectangle 2 or 3 times. Sprinkle very lightly with sea salt.
3. Bake for 20 to 25 minutes or until light brown. Cut the rectangles again while shortbread is still warm. Transfer to a wire rack and cool. Serve immediately or store in an airtight container in the refrigerator up to 2 days or in the freezer up to 3 months.
4. To serve, top half of the crackers each with about 1 teaspoon of the Red Onion Marmalade. Top with remaining crackers to make sandwiches. If desired, top with additional marmalade. Makes 32 sandwiches.
TEST KITCHEN TIP: To make in a food processor, combine the cheese, butter (cut up), flour, the ¼ teaspoon salt, and the pepper in a food processor bowl. Let stand at room temperature for 30 minutes. Cover and process until mixture holds together. Continue as above.
EACH SANDWICH: 110 cal., 5 g total fat (3 g sat. fat), 16 mg chol., 132 mg sodium, 13 g carbo., 0 g fiber, 3 g pro. Daily Values: 3% vit. A, 2% vit. C, 6% calcium, 3% iron.

Red Onion Marmalade
PREP: 15 MINUTES **COOK:** 45 MINUTES

- 2 large red onions, chopped (4 cups)
- 1 cup packed brown sugar
- 1 cup red wine vinegar
- 2 tsp. snipped fresh thyme or ½ teaspoon dried thyme, crushed
- 2 tsp. bottled minced garlic or 4 cloves garlic, minced

1. In a medium saucepan combine onion, sugar, vinegar, dried thyme (if using), and garlic. Bring mixture to boiling over medium heat; reduce heat. Simmer, uncovered, about 45 minutes until onions are tender and liquid is nearly evaporated. (Mixture will thicken more as it cools.) Stir in fresh thyme (if using); remove from heat and allow to cool. Use immediately or chill, tightly covered, up to 2 weeks. Makes about 36 (2-teaspoon) servings or 1½ cups total.
EACH SERVING: 31 cal., 0 g total fat (0 g sat. fat), 0 mg chol., 3 mg sodium, 8 g carbo., 0 g fiber, 0 g pro. Daily Values: 2% vit. C, 1% calcium, 1% iron.

One-Hour Pork Tenderloin with Cranberry Chutney

PREP: 30 MINUTES **ROAST:** 25 MINUTES **COOK:** 20 MINUTES

- 3   1- to 1¼-lb. pork tenderloins
- 1   Tbsp. ground allspice
- 2   to 3 tsp. cracked black pepper
- 1   tsp. salt
- 2   Tbsp. cooking oil
- 1   Tbsp. butter
- 1   large onion, quartered and thinly sliced
- 1   12-oz. pkg. cranberries (3 cups)
- 1   10-oz. jar currant jelly (about 1 cup)
- 1   cup cranberry juice
- ¼   cup packed brown sugar
- 3   Tbsp. cider vinegar
- 1   Tbsp. grated fresh ginger or ½ teaspoon ground ginger
- ½   tsp. curry powder
- 2   bunches watercress

1. Preheat oven to 425°F. Trim fat from tenderloins. In a small bowl combine allspice, pepper, and salt; rub on all sides of tenderloins.*

2. In a 12-inch skillet brown tenderloins in hot oil over medium heat, turning to brown all sides. Transfer tenderloins to a shallow roasting pan. Roast for 25 minutes or until internal temperature registers 160°F on an instant-read thermometer and juices run clear. Remove from oven and keep warm until ready to serve.

3. Meanwhile, for Cranberry Chutney, add butter and onion to the same 12-inch skillet. Cook about 5 minutes until nearly tender, stirring occasionally. Add cranberries, jelly, cranberry juice, brown sugar, vinegar, ginger, and curry powder to skillet. Bring to boiling; reduce heat and boil gently but steadily for 20 to 25 minutes or until thickened to desired consistency and reduced to about 3 cups.

4. To serve, line a serving platter with watercress. Slice pork and arrange on top of watercress; spoon some of the sauce over the pork. Serve remaining sauce on the side. Makes 12 to 16 servings.

Kid Friendly *KID-FRIENDLY VERSION:* Lightly sprinkle one of the tenderloins with the spice mixture. Continue as directed above, except serve with the Raspberry-Barbecue Sauce (recipe, *below*) instead of the Cranberry Chutney.

RASPBERRY-BARBECUE SAUCE: In a medium saucepan combine 1 cup raspberry applesauce, 1 cup whole berry cranberry sauce, 1 cup bottled barbecue sauce, and 2 tablespoons lemon juice. Cook over low heat until heated through, stirring occasionally. Serve with the pork as an option to or in place of the Cranberry Chutney (skip step 3 above).

MAKE AHEAD: Prepare pork and Cranberry Chutney; allow pork and chutney to cool for 30 minutes. Cover and refrigerate pork up to 3 days or sauce up to 1 week. Warm pork in a 350°F oven for 20 to 25 minutes or until heated through. Heat sauce in a medium saucepan over medium-low heat until heated through, stirring occasionally. Serve as above.

Healthy **EACH SERVING:** 277 cal., 7 g total fat (2 g sat. fat), 76 mg chol., 260 mg sodium, 30 g carbo., 2 g fiber, 24 g pro. Daily Values: 7% vit. A, 26% vit. C, 3% calcium, 10% iron.

One-Hour Pork Tenderloin with Cranberry Chutney (opposite)
Brussels Sprouts with Frizzled Prosciutto (page 246)
Herb Butter Mashed Potatoes (page 247)
No-Fuss Blue Cheese and Pear Salad with
Apricot Nectar Dressing (page 247)

Brussels Sprouts with Frizzled Prosciutto

PREP: 30 MINUTES **COOK:** 20 MINUTES

- 2½ lb. Brussels sprouts
- 1 Tbsp. olive oil
- 4 oz. thinly sliced prosciutto*
- 3 Tbsp. butter
- ½ cup thinly sliced shallots or chopped onion
- ½ tsp. salt
- ¼ tsp. freshly ground black pepper
- 1 Tbsp. red wine vinegar

1. Trim stems and remove any wilted outer leaves from Brussels sprouts; wash. Cut any large sprouts in half lengthwise.

2. In a large Dutch oven bring a large amount of salted water to boiling. Carefully add Brussels sprouts and cook for 6 to 8 minutes just until tender (centers should still be slightly firm). Drain and spread out in a shallow baking pan. (At this point, the Brussels sprouts can be stored in an airtight container to contain the cabbage odor and chilled up to 24 hours.)

3. When ready to serve, heat oil in a 12-inch skillet over medium-high heat. Add prosciutto to skillet, half at a time, and cook until crisp; remove from skillet. Reduce heat to medium. Add butter and shallots to skillet. Cook and stir about 2 minutes or until shallots begin to soften.

4. Add Brussels sprouts, salt, and pepper to skillet. Cook and stir Brussels sprouts about 6 minutes (8 minutes, if chilled) or until heated through. Add vinegar and stir to coat. Transfer Brussels spouts to a serving bowl. Top with prosciutto and serve. Makes 12 (¾-cup) servings.

*****NOTE:** If desired, omit the prosciutto and oil and substitute 4 slices of chopped bacon; cook bacon until crisp. Discard drippings.

EACH SERVING: 92 cal., 5 g total fat (2 g sat. fat), 15 mg chol., 391 mg sodium, 8 g carbo., 3 g fiber, 5 g pro. Daily Values: 13% vit. A, 79% vit. C, 3% calcium, 7% iron.

Brussels Sprouts with Frizzled Prosciutto

Herb Butter Mashed Potatoes

PREP: 25 MINUTES **COOK:** 25 MINUTES **STAND:** 30 MINUTES

 1 recipe Herb Butter, softened
 ¾ cup half-and-half, light cream, or whole milk
3½ lb. red-skinned potatoes, peeled, if desired, and cut into
     2- to 3-inch pieces
 1 tsp. salt

1. Prepare and chill Herb Butter. Let half-and-half stand at room temperature 30 minutes. Meanwhile, place potatoes in a 4-quart Dutch oven with enough lightly salted water to cover. Bring to boiling; reduce heat. Cover and cook for 25 minutes or until potatoes are very tender.

2. Drain potatoes. Return to pan with half-and-half, Herb Butter, and salt. With a large wooden or other sturdy spoon, carefully stir potatoes, smashing lightly by pressing pieces of potatoes against the side of the pan with the back of the spoon, leaving mixture slightly chunky. Makes 8 to 10 (¾-cup) servings.

HERB BUTTER: In a small bowl stir together ½ cup butter, softened; 1 tablespoon snipped fresh flat-leaf parsley; 2 teaspoons snipped fresh oregano or ½ teaspoon dried oregano, crushed; 2 teaspoons snipped fresh thyme or ½ teaspoon dried thyme, crushed; and ¼ teaspoon cracked black pepper until well combined. Cover and chill at least 3 hours before using to allow flavors to blend. Chill butter up to 1 week or place in an airtight freezer container and freeze up to 3 months. Thaw before using. Makes ½ cup.

TEST KITCHEN TIP: To soften butter before making Herb Butter and to soften the Herb Butter before adding to potatoes, let stand at room temperature for 1 hour or place in a microwave-safe bowl and microwave on 100% power (high) for 10 to 15 seconds, watching carefully so the butter does not melt.

MAKE AHEAD: Place prepared potatoes in a covered 1½- to 2-quart casserole. Place covered casserole in a 12-inch skillet with 1-inch of simmering water. Hold over very low heat up to 2 hours.

EACH SERVING: 248 cal., 15 g total fat (8 g sat. fat), 41 mg chol., 397 mg sodium, 26 g carbo., 2 g fiber, 4 g pro. Daily Values: 10% vit. A, 3% vit. C, 5% calcium, 11% iron.

No-Fuss Blue Cheese and Pear Salad with Apricot Nectar Dressing

PREP: 30 MINUTES **CHILL:** 30 MINUTES

 ½ cup apricot nectar
 ⅓ cup extra-virgin olive oil
 ⅓ cup white wine vinegar
 1 Tbsp. Dijon-style mustard
 ½ tsp. salt
 3 green onions, finely chopped
 ½ cup snipped dried apricots
 6 ripe red-skinned Seckel and/or Bartlett pears, cored
     and cut into wedges
10 cups mesclun mix or torn mixed salad greens (about 9 ounces)
 ½ of a large head radicchio, finely shredded (about 2 cups)
 8 to 10 oz. Cambozola or other blue cheese, cut into wedges,
     or goat cheese, cut into rounds
 ¾ cup coarsely chopped almonds, toasted

1. For dressing, in a very large bowl whisk together apricot nectar, oil, vinegar, mustard, and salt. Stir in green onions and dried apricots. Add pears to dressing and toss to coat. Cover and chill until ready to serve, 30 minutes to 3½ hours.

2. When ready to serve, place mesclun on a very large serving platter. Sprinkle with shredded radicchio. Use a slotted spoon to remove pear wedges from dressing and place pears on the radicchio, reserving dressing. Arrange cheese wedges on the salad and sprinkle almonds over all. Drizzle with reserved dressing or pass dressing with salad. Makes 12 servings.

EACH SERVING: 242 cal., 16 g total fat (5 g sat. fat), 14 mg chol., 397 mg sodium, 21 g carbo., 4 g fiber, 7 g pro. Daily Values: 12% vit. A, 10% vit. C, 14% calcium, 5% iron.

Good Cheer Holiday Crunch

 PREP: 20 MINUTES

- 1½ cups powdered sugar
- ½ tsp. ground nutmeg
- 8 cups bite-size corn or rice square cereal
- 1 cup white baking pieces
- ½ cup cashew butter
- ¼ cup butter, cut up
- ¼ tsp. vanilla
- 1½ cups lightly salted cashews
- 1⅓ cups dried cherries or cranberries and/or chopped dried apricots (about 6 oz.)

1. In a very large plastic bag combine powdered sugar and nutmeg; set aside. Place cereal in a very large bowl; set aside.

2. In a medium saucepan combine white baking pieces, cashew butter, and butter. Stir over low heat until baking pieces and butter are melted. Remove from heat. Stir in vanilla.

3. Pour butter mixture over cereal and carefully stir until cereal is evenly coated. Cool slightly. Add cereal mixture, half at a time, to powdered sugar mixture in bag and shake to coat. Add nuts and fruit. Shake just until combined. Pour onto a waxed paper-lined shallow baking pan to cool. Store in an airtight container up to 2 days. Makes about 28 (½-cup) servings or 14 cups total.

KID-FRIENDLY VERSION: Prepare as above, except substitute ¼ cup unsweetened cocoa powder for the nutmeg, peanuts for the cashews, dried fruit bits for the dried cherries, and peanut butter for the cashew butter.

EACH SERVING: 186 cal., 9 g total fat (3 g sat. fat), 6 mg chol., 140 mg sodium, 24 g carbo., 1 g fiber, 3 g pro. Daily Values: 8% vit. A, 3% vit. C, 4% calcium, 18% iron.

Ginger and Apple Sled Tarts

PREP: 25 MINUTES **BAKE:** 20 MINUTES

- ½ of a 17.3-oz. pkg. frozen puff pastry sheets (1 sheet), thawed
- 1 egg, slightly beaten
- 1 Tbsp. water
- 2 Tbsp. coarse or granulated sugar
- 2 Tbsp. finely chopped crystallized ginger
- 2 small baking apples, cored, halved, and thinly sliced
  Crabapple sprigs (optional)

1. Preheat oven to 400°F. Line a large baking sheet with parchment paper; set aside. Unfold pastry onto a lightly floured surface. Roll pastry into a 12-inch square. If desired, trim a ½-inch strip from one side and use to make Leaf Garnishes.* Place pastry square on prepared baking sheet. Cut in half to form 2 rectangles; separate slightly. Prick pastry rectangles all over with a fork.

2. In a small bowl combine egg and water; brush pastry with egg mixture. Fold in all edges of each rectangle about ¼ inch, pressing lightly as you fold to form a rim. Brush folded edges with egg mixture; set aside.

3. In a small bowl stir together sugar and ginger. Arrange apple slices over pastry, overlapping as necessary. Sprinkle with sugar mixture.

4. Bake for 20 to 25 minutes or until pastry is deep golden brown and crisp. Cool on baking sheet on a wire rack. When cool, transfer to a cutting board or platter. Cut crosswise into rectangles. If desired, garnish platter with crabapple sprigs. Makes 12 servings.

*LEAF GARNISHES: Cut leaf-shape cutouts from the strip of puff pastry. Brush bottoms of cutouts with egg mixture and attach to sides of tarts. Brush tops of cutouts with egg mixture before baking.

EACH SERVING: 120 cal., 7 g total fat (0 g sat. fat), 18 mg chol., 83 mg sodium, 14 g carbo., 1 g fiber, 1 g pro. Daily Values: 1% vit. A, 1% vit. C, 1% iron.

Good Cheer Holiday Crunch

Ginger and Apple Sled Tarts

White Chocolate Snowdrift Cake

The melted chocolate mixture must be thoroughly chilled or it will not make a successful frosting.

PREP: 35 MINUTES **CHILL:** 2 HOURS **BAKE:** SEE PACKAGE DIRECTIONS*
COOL: 1 HOUR

 ¾ cup whipping cream
 8 oz. white baking chocolate, chopped
 1 pkg. 2-layer-size white cake mix
 ⅓ cup unsweetened cocoa powder
 1 8-oz. pkg. cream cheese, cut up and softened
 1 cup powdered sugar
  Sugared Rosemary and Cranberries (optional)
  Crushed purchased chocolate-cranberry biscotti or your favorite biscotti (optional)

1. For frosting, combine whipping cream and white chocolate in a medium saucepan. Cook, stirring occasionally, over low heat until chocolate is completely melted and smooth. Transfer to a large bowl; cover and refrigerate until completely chilled, at least 2 hours.

2. Meanwhile, grease and flour two 9×1½-inch or 8×1½-inch round cake pans; set aside. Prepare cake mix according to package directions using egg whites. Spoon about 1½ cups of batter into each cake pan. Sift cocoa over batter remaining in bowl; stir until blended. Spoon on top of cake mix in pans and swirl gently to marble and spread evenly. Bake according to package directions, except check cakes several minutes before minimum package time.* Cool cakes in pans on wire rack 10 minutes. Remove cakes from pans; cool completely on wire racks.

3. Add cream cheese to chilled white chocolate mixture and beat with an electric mixer until smooth. Gradually add powdered sugar, beating until sugar is completely combined. (Mixture should hold soft peaks; do not overbeat.) Use immediately.

4. Place one cake layer on a serving platter. Frost with about ¾ cup frosting. Top with second cake layer. Frost top and sides of cake.

5. Serve immediately or cover and chill until serving time, up to 4 hours. If desired, garnish cake with Sugared Rosemary and Cranberries and crushed biscotti. Makes 12 servings.

SUGARED ROSEMARY AND CRANBERRIES: Spray several rosemary sprigs and cranberries lightly with nonstick cooking spray. Sprinkle granulated sugar over rosemary; roll cranberries in a small amount of granulated sugar to coat. Place on waxed paper for 1 hour. For decoration only.

*NOTE: The added cocoa will make the cakes bake in a shorter time than instructed on the cake package.

EACH SERVING: 458 cal., 25 g fat total (13 g sat. fat), 45 mg chol., 382 mg sodium, 55 g carbo., 0 g fiber, 7 g pro. Daily Values: 41% vit. C, 6% calcium, 12% iron.

White Chocolate Snowdrift Cake

Fluffy Cranberry Mousse

 PREP: 20 MINUTES

- ½ of an 8-oz. pkg. cream cheese, softened
- 2 Tbsp. sugar
- ½ tsp. vanilla
- ½ cup frozen cranberry juice concentrate, thawed
- 1 16-oz. can whole cranberry sauce
- 1½ cups whipping cream
- 1 recipe Sweetened Cranberries

1. In a large mixing bowl beat cream cheese with an electric mixer on medium speed for 30 seconds. Beat in sugar and vanilla until smooth. Slowly add cranberry juice concentrate, beating until very smooth. In a small bowl stir cranberry sauce to remove any large lumps; set aside.

2. In a chilled large mixing bowl beat whipping cream with an electric mixer on low to medium speed until soft peaks form. Fold about half of the cranberry sauce and half of the whipped cream into the cream cheese mixture until combined. Fold in the remaining cranberry sauce and whipped cream until combined.

3. Serve immediately or cover and refrigerate up to 24 hours (if chilled, stir before serving). To serve, spoon fluff into a large serving bowl, 24 chilled demitasse cups, or 12 chilled small dessert dishes. Spoon Sweetened Cranberries on top just before serving. Makes 24 (¼-cup) servings or 12 (½-cup) servings.

SWEETENED CRANBERRIES: In a medium skillet combine 1 cup fresh cranberries, ⅓ cup sugar, and 2 tablespoons water. Cook and stir over medium heat until sugar dissolves and cranberries just begin to pop. Remove from heat. Cover and chill until serving time.

FROZEN CRANBERRY MOUSSE: Prepare as above through step 2. Spoon cranberry mixture into 24 freezer-safe demitasse cups or 12 freezer-safe small dessert dishes. Cover and freeze 24 hours or until firm. To serve, uncover and let stand 1 to 2 minutes. Top with Sweetened Cranberries.

EACH (¼-CUP) SERVING: 109 cal., 7 g fat total (4 g sat. fat), 26 mg chol., 24 mg sodium, 11 g carbo., 0 g fiber, 1 g pro. Daily Values: 41% vit. C, 6% calcium, 12% iron.

Fluffy Cranberry Mousse

Prize Tested
RECIPES®

HERE'S THE BEST OF THE BEST FROM 2005! SEE
WHAT OUR TALENTED READERS HAVE BEEN
COOKING UP IN THEIR OWN KITCHENS ALL YEAR.

Deep Chocolate Brownies
page 264

Raspberry-Rhubarb Pie
page 260

Blackberry Salad with Pork
page 262

Summer Fresh Salsa
page 254

Summer Fresh Salsa

PREP: 25 MINUTES **CHILL:** 4 HOURS

- 2 cups frozen whole kernel corn, thawed
- 1 medium jicama, peeled and chopped
- 1 medium cucumber, seeded and chopped (about 1 1/2 cups)
- 1 large tomato, seeded and chopped
- 2 small limes, peeled, sectioned, and seeds removed (about 1/3 cup)
- 3 Tbsp. stone-ground mustard
- 1 Tbsp. honey
- 1 1/2 tsp. dry mustard
- 1 tsp. salt
- 1 tsp. soy sauce
- 2 cloves garlic, cut up
- 1/4 tsp. cayenne pepper
- 1/3 cup olive oil
  Tortilla chips or assorted crackers (optional)

1. In a large bowl combine corn, jicama, cucumber, and tomato.
2. For dressing, in a blender container or food processor bowl combine lime sections, stone-ground mustard, honey, dry mustard, salt, soy sauce, garlic, and cayenne pepper. Cover and blend or process until dressing is smooth. With blender or processor running, slowly drizzle in oil until combined.
3. Stir dressing into vegetable mixture. Cover and chill up to 4 hours. If desired, serve with tortilla chips or crackers. Makes about 5 1/4 cups salsa.

EACH SERVING SALSA (1/4 CUP): 59 cal., 4 g total fat (0 g sat. fat), 0 mg chol., 178 mg sodium, 6 g carbo., 1 g fiber, 1 g pro. Daily Values: 2% vit. A, 11% vit. C, 1% iron.

Pesto-Provolone Terrine

PREP: 15 MINUTES **CHILL:** OVERNIGHT

- 1 8-oz. pkg. cream cheese, softened
- 1/2 cup purchased basil or dried tomato pesto
- 6 thin slices provolone cheese (about 6 oz.)
  Thin baguette slices, toasted, or crackers (optional)
  Fresh basil leaves (optional)

1. Line a 7 1/2 × 3 1/2 × 2-inch loaf pan with plastic wrap, extending wrap beyond edges of pan; set aside.
2. In a medium mixing bowl beat cream cheese and pesto with an electric mixer on medium speed until smooth. Lay 2 slices of the provolone cheese in bottom and slightly up sides of pan. Spread with half of the pesto mixture. Repeat layers; top with remaining 2 slices of provolone cheese. Cover surface with plastic wrap. Weight terrine down with a can of soup or vegetables. Chill overnight.
3. To serve, remove plastic wrap from top of terrine. Invert onto serving plate and remove plastic wrap. Cut terrine lengthwise in half. Cut crosswise into 1/2-inch slices. If desired, serve with baguette slices and garnish with basil leaves. Makes 24 to 28 servings.

EACH SERVING (TERRINE ONLY): 94 cal., 9 g total fat (3 g sat. fat), 16 mg chol., 128 mg sodium, 1 g carbo., 0 g fiber, 3 g pro. Daily Values: 4% vit. A, 6% calcium, 1% iron.

Barbecue and Blue Dip with Peppery Pita Crisps

PREP: 25 MINUTES **BAKE:** 12 MINUTES

- 1 8-oz. pkg. cream cheese, softened
- 1/4 cup bottled barbecue sauce
- 2 Tbsp. milk
- 1 tsp. garlic salt
- 1/2 tsp. celery seeds
- 1/4 tsp. bottled hot pepper sauce
- 4 oz. blue cheese, crumbled
- 1/2 cup finely chopped celery
- 4 pita bread rounds
- 3 Tbsp. cooking oil
- 2 teaspoons black, pink, and/or white peppercorns, coarsely crushed

1. Preheat oven to 350°F. In a medium mixing bowl beat together cream cheese, barbecue sauce, milk, 1/2 teaspoon of the garlic salt, the celery seeds, and bottled hot pepper sauce until combined. Stir in blue cheese and celery. Cover and chill.

2. Split pita breads horizontally. Brush rough sides with oil. Combine peppercorns and remaining garlic salt; sprinkle on pita rounds. Cut each pita round into wedges. Arrange wedges, pepper sides up, in a single layer on baking sheets. Bake for 12 to 15 minutes or until crisp. Cool on wire rack.

3. Serve dip with pita crisps.

MAKE AHEAD: Dip may be stored in refrigerator for up to 3 days. Peppery Pita Crisps may be stored in an airtight container for up to 5 days. Makes 16 appetizer servings.

EACH SERVING (2 TABLESPOONS DIP AND 3 CHIPS): 144 cal., 10 g total fat (5 g sat. fat), 21 mg chol., 318 mg sodium, 10 g carbo., 1 g fiber, 4 g pro. Daily Values: 5% vit. A, 1% vit. C, 7% calcium, 4% iron.

Basil-Peanut Wonton Toss

Fast! **PREP:** 20 MINUTES **BAKE:** 6 MINUTES

- 2 Tbsp. grated Parmesan cheese
- 2 tsp. dried basil, crushed
- 1/2 tsp. ground black pepper
- 12 wonton wrappers
  Nonstick cooking spray
- 1 cup peanuts
- 2 cups bite-size sesame sticks

1. Preheat oven to 350°F. In a large bowl combine Parmesan cheese, basil, and pepper; set aside. Cut the stack of wonton wrappers in half crosswise, then cut into 6 lengthwise strips. Keep covered with plastic wrap while you work so they won't dry out. Lightly coat a baking sheet with cooking spray. Arrange wonton strips in a single layer on the prepared baking sheet. Lightly coat wonton strips with more cooking spray. Sprinkle with Parmesan mixture. Bake for 6 to 8 minutes or until crisp and lightly browned. Cool completely.

2. In a large bowl combine wonton strips, peanuts, and sesame sticks. Toss gently to mix. Makes about 5 cups (10 appetizer servings).

MAKE AHEAD: Prepare mix and store, covered, for up to 3 days.

EACH SERVING: 247 cal., 17 g total fat (3 g sat. fat), 2 mg chol., 348 mg sodium, 18 g carbo., 2 g fiber, 8 g pro. Daily Values: 6% calcium, 5% iron.

Savory Balkan Bean Salad

PREP: 25 MINUTES **CHILL:** 2 HOURS

- 1 15-oz. can garbanzo beans (chickpeas), rinsed and drained
- 1/2 of a 15-oz. can black beans, rinsed and drained (1 cup)
- 2 6-oz. jars marinated artichoke hearts, drained and coarsely chopped (1 1/2 cups)
- 2 medium tomatoes, chopped (2 cups)
- 1/2 cup crumbled feta cheese (2 oz.)
- 1/4 cup finely chopped Vidalia or red onion
- 1/4 cup snipped fresh cilantro
- 1/4 cup olive oil
- 2 Tbsp. lemon juice
- 3 cloves garlic, minced
  Sliced baguette-style French bread, toasted

1. In a large bowl combine garbanzo beans, black beans, artichoke hearts, tomatoes, feta cheese, onion, and cilantro. For dressing, in a small bowl whisk together olive oil, lemon juice, and garlic. Pour dressing over the bean mixture and toss gently to coat. Cover and chill for 2 to 8 hours. Serve with toasted baguette slices. Makes 12 appetizer servings.

EACH SERVING: 151 cal., 8 g total fat (1 g sat. fat), 4 mg chol., 354 mg sodium, 17 g carbo., 3 g fiber, 5 g pro. Daily Values: 6% vit. A, 19% vit. C, 6% calcium, 6% iron.

Spinach-Artichoke Slices

PREP: 25 MINUTES **CHILL:** UP TO 6 HOURS

- 1/2 of an 8-oz. tub cream cheese with chive and onion (1/2 cup)
- 1/3 cup finely shredded Parmesan cheese
- 1/4 cup dairy sour cream
- 1/4 tsp. ground black pepper
- 1 6- to 6 1/2-oz. jar marinated artichoke hearts, drained and chopped
- 4 8- to 10-inch spinach-herb-flavored or plain flour tortillas
- 2 cups loosely packed fresh spinach leaves
- 1 medium red sweet pepper, cut into thin bite-size strips

1. In a medium bowl stir together cream cheese, Parmesan cheese, sour cream, and black pepper until combined. Stir in artichoke hearts.

2. Spread one side of each tortilla with cream cheese mixture. Arrange spinach leaves in a single layer over cream cheese mixture. Arrange red pepper strips over spinach. Roll up and wrap tightly in clear plastic wrap. Cover and chill up to 6 hours.

3. To serve, cut into 1-inch pieces (trim and discard ends, if necessary). Makes about 32 slices.

EACH SLICE: 70 cal., 4 g total fat (2 g sat. fat), 8 mg chol., 174 mg sodium, 6 g carbo., 0 g fiber, 3 g pro. Daily Values: 8% vit. A, 15% vit. C, 9% calcium, 1% iron.

Sweet and Hot Black Bean Dip

Fast! **PREP:** 20 MINUTES **COOK:** 5 MINUTES

- 1 15-oz. can black beans, rinsed and drained
- 1/2 cup chopped onion
- 1 Tbsp. grated fresh ginger
- 1 clove garlic, minced
- 1 Tbsp. olive oil
- 1/2 cup bottled hot picante sauce
- 2 plum tomatoes, chopped
- 2 Tbsp. bottled black bean sauce
- 1/4 cup maple syrup
- 1 Tbsp. balsamic vinegar
- 1/2 tsp. salt
- 1/4 tsp. cayenne pepper
  Assorted dippers, such as cooked shrimp, baby carrots, red sweet pepper strips, and/or tortilla chips

1. In a medium bowl slightly mash beans; set aside. In a medium saucepan cook onion, ginger, and garlic in hot oil until onion is tender. Stir in beans, picante sauce, tomatoes, black bean sauce, maple syrup, balsamic vinegar, salt, and cayenne pepper. If serving at once, heat through; or cover and chill.

2. To reheat, transfer to a medium saucepan and heat over medium-low heat, stirring occasionally.

3. Serve with dippers. Makes 2 3/4 cups dip.

EACH SERVING DIP (1/4 CUP): 72 cal., 2 g total fat (0 g sat. fat), 0 mg chol., 359 mg sodium, 13 g carbo., 2 g fiber, 3 g pro. Daily Values: 4% vit. A, 5% vit. C, 3% calcium, 4% iron.

DESSERTS FOR A CROWD

Black Forest Bread Pudding

PREP: 30 MINUTES **CHILL:** 2 HOURS **BAKE:** 70 MINUTES
COOL: 45 MINUTES

- 1/3 cup butter, softened
- 12 oz. black rye bread, sliced 1/2 inch thick
- 1 12- or 16-oz. pkg. frozen pitted dark sweet cherries
- 2 12-oz. pkg. semisweet chocolate pieces
- 1/2 tsp. ground cinnamon
- 3 1/4 cups whipping cream
- 3/4 cup sugar
- 8 eggs
- 1/2 tsp. almond extract
  Whipped cream (optional)
  Sliced almonds, toasted (optional)

1. Butter a 3-quart rectangular baking dish with some of the butter; spread remaining butter on bread slices. Place bread slices in baking dish, overlapping as necessary to fit. Sprinkle with frozen cherries, half of the chocolate pieces, and the cinnamon; set aside.

2. In a medium saucepan combine remaining chocolate pieces, 1 cup of the whipping cream, and the sugar; heat and stir just until chocolate is melted. Gradually stir in remaining cream. Beat eggs in a very large bowl; stir in melted chocolate mixture and almond extract. Slowly pour over bread in dish. Cover and chill 2 hours or overnight.

3. Preheat oven to 325°F. Uncover baking dish and place on a foil-lined baking sheet. Bake for 70 to 80 minutes or until an instant-read thermometer inserted in center registers 160°F. Cool on a wire rack at least 45 minutes. Serve warm. If desired, top with whipped cream and almonds. Makes 16 to 20 servings.

EACH SERVING: 546 cal., 38 g total fat (22 g sat. fat), 183 mg chol., 229 mg sodium, 51 g carbo., 4 g fiber, 8 g pro. Daily Values: 20% vit. A, 3% vit. C, 8% calcium, 14% iron.

Apple-Cranberry Dessert

PREP: 30 MINUTES **BAKE:** 1 HOUR **COOL:** 30 MINUTES

- 2 12-oz. pkg. fresh or frozen cranberries or two 16-oz. pkg. frozen unsweetened pitted tart red cherries*
- 2 cups chopped, peeled cooking apples
- 2 Tbsp. butter, cut up
- 1 1/4 cups sugar
- 3/4 cup chopped walnuts or pecans
- 2 eggs, slightly beaten
- 3/4 cup butter, melted
- 1 cup sugar
- 3/4 cup all-purpose flour
  Vanilla ice cream

1. Preheat oven to 325°F. Grease the bottom of a 13×9×2-inch baking pan. Toss cranberries and apples together in the pan. Dot fruit mixture with 2 tablespoons butter. Sprinkle evenly with 1 1/4 cups sugar and the chopped nuts.

2. In a medium mixing bowl whisk together eggs, melted butter, 1 cup sugar, and flour until well combined. Pour evenly over top of fruit mixture.

3. Bake, uncovered, for 1 to 1 1/4 hours or until top is golden brown. Serve warm (cool about 30 minutes) or at room temperature with vanilla ice cream. Makes 15 servings.

*NOTE: If using frozen cranberries, do not thaw before tossing with the apples. If using frozen cherries, let stand at room temperature for 30 minutes before tossing with the apples.

EACH SERVING: 312 cal., 16 g total fat (6 g sat. fat), 58 mg chol., 91 mg sodium, 42 g carbo., 3 g fiber, 3 g pro. Daily Values: 8% vit. A, 12% vit. C, 2% calcium, 4% iron.

Banana Cake with Strawberries and Peppered Pecans

PREP: 40 MINUTES **BAKE:** 30 MINUTES

- 1 cup butter, softened
- 1½ cups sugar
- 4 eggs
- 1 large banana, mashed (½ cup)
- ½ cup dairy sour cream
- ½ cup milk
- 1 tsp. vanilla
- 3 cups all-purpose flour
- 2 tsp. baking powder
- ½ tsp. salt
- ¼ tsp. baking soda
- 2 cups sliced strawberries
- 1 Tbsp. sugar (optional)
- 1 recipe Peppery-Spiced Pecans
  Sweetened whipped cream

1. Preheat oven to 350°F. Grease a 13×9×2-inch baking pan; set aside.

2. In a large mixing bowl beat butter and 1½ cups sugar until well combined. Add eggs, 1 at a time, beating well after each addition. In a medium bowl combine mashed banana, sour cream, milk, and vanilla. In another bowl combine flour, baking powder, salt, and baking soda. Alternately add flour mixture and banana mixture to butter mixture, beating on low speed after each addition just until combined.

3. Spread batter into the prepared pan. Bake for 30 to 35 minutes or until a toothpick inserted near center comes out clean. Cool completely on a wire rack.

4. If desired, combine strawberries and 1 tablespoon sugar in a medium bowl. Top cake servings with strawberries, Peppery-Spiced Pecans, and whipped cream. Makes 15 servings.

PEPPERY-SPICED PECANS: Line a 9×9×2-inch baking pan with foil; lightly coat with nonstick cooking spray. In a medium bowl combine 1 cup broken pecans, 2 tablespoons light-colored corn syrup, 3 tablespoons sugar, ½ teaspoon apple pie or pumpkin pie spice, and ¼ teaspoon cayenne pepper. Spread nuts in prepared pan. Bake in a 325°F oven for 15 minutes, stirring twice. Turn out onto a buttered piece of foil; cool. Break into clusters.

EACH SERVING: 455 cal., 27 g total fat (12 g sat. fat), 116 mg chol., 259 mg sodium, 49 g carbo., 2 g fiber, 6 g pro. Daily Values: 16% vit. A, 21% vit. C, 6% calcium, 9% iron.

Crunchy Caramel Apple Cake

PREP: 30 MINUTES **BAKE:** 45 MINUTES

- 1 cup plain granola, crushed
- 1 cup chopped walnuts or pecans
- ¼ cup butter, softened
- 3 cups all-purpose flour
- 1 tsp. baking soda
- 1 tsp. ground cinnamon
- ½ tsp. salt
- 2 eggs
- 1½ cups cooking oil
- 1 cup granulated sugar
- 1 cup packed brown sugar
- 3 cups finely chopped, peeled apples
- 1 recipe Caramel Sauce

1. Grease a 13×9×2-inch baking pan; set aside. In a medium bowl combine granola and ½ cup of the nuts. Use your fingers or a fork to combine the softened butter with the granola mixture until crumbly; set aside.

2. Preheat oven to 325°F. In a medium bowl stir together flour, baking soda, cinnamon, and salt; set aside. In a very large mixing bowl beat eggs slightly with a fork; stir in oil, granulated sugar, and brown sugar. Add flour mixture; stir just until combined. Fold in apples and remaining nuts (mixture will be thick). Spoon batter into prepared pan, spreading evenly. Sprinkle with granola mixture.

3. Bake for 45 to 55 minutes or until a wooden toothpick inserted near the center comes out clean. Cool cake completely on a wire rack. Serve with warm Caramel Sauce. Makes 16 servings.

CARAMEL SAUCE: In a small saucepan melt ½ cup butter over medium heat. Stir in 1 cup packed brown sugar and ½ cup whipping cream. Bring to boiling, stirring constantly; reduce heat. Simmer, uncovered, for 5 minutes or until mixture is slightly thickened. Stir in 1 teaspoon vanilla. Cool about 10 minutes. Serve warm.

EACH SERVING: 630 cal., 39 g total fat (10 g sat. fat), 61 mg chol., 240 mg sodium, 68 g carbo., 3 g fiber, 6 g pro. Daily Values: 9% vit. A, 2% vit. C, 5% calcium, 13% iron.

Kid Friendly Peanut Butter Cupcakes

PREP: 45 MINUTES **BAKE:** 18 MINUTES
COOL: 20 MINUTES

- 1⅓ cups all-purpose flour
- ⅔ cup graham cracker crumbs
- 1 Tbsp. baking powder
- 1 cup creamy peanut butter
- ⅓ cup shortening
- 1⅓ cups sugar
- 2 eggs
- 1 tsp. vanilla
- 1 cup milk
- 24 bite-size chocolate-covered peanut butter cups
- 1 recipe Chocolate Frosting
  Bite-size chocolate-covered peanut butter cups, halved (optional)

1. Preheat oven to 350°F. Line 24 muffin cups with paper bake cups; set aside. In a medium bowl combine flour, graham cracker crumbs, and baking powder; set aside.

2. In a very large mixing bowl beat peanut butter and shortening with an electric mixer until combined. Add sugar, beating until well combined. Beat in eggs and vanilla. Alternately add flour mixture and milk to beaten mixture, beating on low speed after each addition just until combined.

3. Spoon about 2 tablespoons batter into each prepared muffin cup. Unwrap peanut butter cups and place 1 in each muffin cup on top of batter. Spoon remaining batter into muffin cups to cover peanut butter cups.

4. Bake about 18 minutes or until a wooden toothpick inserted near edges comes out clean (some cupcakes may have a slight indentation). Cool cupcakes in muffin cups on wire rack for 5 minutes. Remove cupcakes from muffin cups; cool thoroughly on racks about 15 minutes. Frost with Chocolate Frosting. If desired, top each cupcake with a peanut butter cup half. Makes 24 cupcakes.

CHOCOLATE FROSTING: In a large saucepan melt 3 ounces unsweetened chocolate and 2 tablespoons butter over low heat, stirring frequently. Cool for 5 minutes. Gradually add 3 cups powdered sugar and 4 to 5 tablespoons milk, beating until smooth and of spreading consistency.

EACH CUPCAKE: 295 cal., 15 g total fat (5 g sat. fat), 21 mg chol., 139 mg sodium, 38 g carbo., 2 g fiber, 6 g pro. Daily Values: 2% vit. A, 4% calcium, 7% iron.

LASAGNA

Ham and Cheese Lasagna

PREP: 1 HOUR **BAKE:** 50 MINUTES **STAND:** 20 MINUTES

- 1 large onion, chopped (1 cup)
- 4 stalks celery, thinly sliced (2 cups)
- 4 carrots, chopped (2 cups)
- 2 cloves garlic, minced
- 2 Tbsp. olive oil
- 8 oz. cremini mushrooms or other small brown mushrooms, sliced (3 cups)
- 2 cups cubed cooked ham
- 2 cups whipping cream
- 1 14 1/2-oz. can diced tomatoes with basil, garlic, and oregano, undrained
- 1/2 cup water
- 1/4 cup dry red wine
- 1 cup grated Parmesan cheese
- 1 1/2 cups shredded Swiss cheese (6 oz.)
- 12 no-boil lasagna noodles

1. Preheat oven to 350°F. For sauce, in a 12-inch skillet or Dutch oven cook and stir onion, celery, carrots, and garlic in hot oil over medium heat for 10 minutes until vegetables are just tender. Add mushrooms and ham. Cook, uncovered, for 10 minutes, stirring occasionally. Stir in cream, undrained tomatoes, water, and wine. Bring to boiling; reduce heat. Simmer, uncovered, 5 minutes. Season to taste with *salt* and *ground black pepper*.

2. In a bowl combine cheeses. Spoon 1 1/2 cups of the sauce into a 3-quart rectangular baking dish. Sprinkle with 2/3 cup of the cheese mixture. Top with 4 lasagna noodles, overlapping as needed. Repeat twice. Spoon on remaining sauce and sprinkle with remaining cheese mixture. Cover tightly with foil. Bake about 50 minutes or until heated through and noodles are tender when pierced with a fork. Let stand, covered, 20 minutes before serving. Makes 12 servings.

EACH SERVING: 376 cal., 25 g total fat (14 g sat. fat), 86 mg chol., 671 mg sodium, 22 g carbo., 2 g fiber, 15 g pro. Daily Values: 64% vit. A, 10% vit. C, 26% calcium, 8% iron.

Greek-Style Lasagna

PREP: 45 MINUTES **BAKE:** 35 MINUTES **STAND:** 10 MINUTES

- 9 dried lasagna noodles (about 8 oz.)
- 1 lb. ground lamb or beef
- 1 medium onion, chopped (1/2 cup)
- 2 cloves garlic, minced
- 1 8-oz. can tomato sauce
- 1/4 cup dry red wine or beef broth
- 1 tsp. dried oregano, crushed
- 1/4 tsp. ground cinnamon
- 1 egg, beaten
- 3 Tbsp. butter
- 3 Tbsp. all-purpose flour
- 1 3/4 cups milk
- 1/2 cup grated Parmesan cheese
- 2 eggs, beaten
- 1 2 1/4-oz. can sliced pitted ripe olives, drained
- 8 oz. crumbled feta cheese
- 1 cup shredded white cheddar cheese (4 oz.)

1. Preheat oven to 350° F. Cook noodles according to package directions; drain and rinse. In large skillet cook lamb, onion, and garlic until lamb is brown. Drain off fat. Stir in tomato sauce, wine, oregano, and cinnamon. Heat to boiling; reduce heat. Simmer, uncovered, 10 minutes. Gradually stir lamb mixture into 1 beaten egg; set aside.

2. In medium saucepan melt butter; stir in flour and 1/4 teaspoon *ground black pepper*. Add milk. Cook and stir until thickened and bubbly; cook and stir 1 minute more. Stir in 1/4 cup of the Parmesan cheese; set aside. Combine 2 eggs and remaining Parmesan cheese. To assemble, spread 2 tablespoons cheese sauce in 3-quart rectangular baking dish. Top with 3 noodles, one-third each of the meat sauce, remaining cheese sauce, and olives. Drizzle with one-third of egg-Parmesan mixture; sprinkle with one-third of each cheese. Repeat layers twice. Bake, uncovered, 35 to 40 minutes or until hot. Let stand 10 minutes. Makes 12 servings.

EACH SERVING: 372 cal., 22 g total fat (12 g sat. fat), 128 mg chol., 588 mg sodium, 21 g carbo., 1 g fiber, 21 g pro. Daily Values: 11% vit. A, 1% vit. C, 33% calcium, 11% iron.

Bacon Cheeseburger Lasagna

PREP: 45 MINUTES **BAKE:** 40 MINUTES
STAND: 10 MINUTES

Nonstick cooking spray
9 dried lasagna noodles
1 lb. lean ground beef
1 large onion, chopped (1 cup)
1 Tbsp. prepared mustard
2 1.3- to 1.5-oz. envelopes cheddar cheese or four-cheese sauce mix
2 1/2 cups milk
1 cup shredded mozzarella cheese (4 oz.)
1 cup shredded cheddar cheese (4 oz.)
8 oz. bacon, crisp-cooked, drained, and crumbled
Chopped fresh tomato (optional)

1. Preheat oven to 350°F. Lightly coat a 2-quart rectangular baking dish with cooking spray; set aside. Cook noodles according to package directions; drain. Rinse with cold water; drain well and set aside.
2. In a large skillet cook ground beef and onion until beef is brown. Drain fat. Stir in mustard and cheese sauce mix. Add milk; cook and stir until thickened and bubbly. In a small bowl combine mozzarella and cheddar cheeses.
3. Spread about 1/2 cup of the sauce over bottom of prepared baking dish. Top with 3 noodles, one-third of the remaining sauce, one-third of the bacon, and one-third of the cheese mixture. Repeat layers twice, setting aside the remaining one-third cheese.
4. Bake, covered, for 35 minutes or until heated through. Sprinkle with remaining cheese. Bake, uncovered, 5 minutes more or until cheese is melted. If desired, sprinkle with tomatoes. Let stand 10 minutes before serving. Makes 8 servings.
EACH SERVING: 446 cal., 23 g total fat (11 g sat. fat), 83 mg chol., 762 mg sodium, 28 g carbo., 1 g fiber, 26 g pro. Daily Values: 8% vit. A, 2% vit. C, 29% calcium, 11% iron.

Brunch Lasagna

PREP: 50 MINUTES **BAKE:** 25 MINUTES

Nonstick cooking spray
6 dried lasagna noodles
4 Tbsp. butter
3 Tbsp. all-purpose flour
1 Tbsp. Dijon-style mustard
1/4 tsp. ground black pepper
2 cups milk
6 oz. process Swiss or Gruyère cheese, torn or cut up
6 eggs
1/4 tsp. salt
4 oz. Canadian-style bacon, chopped (1 cup)
1 10-oz. pkg. frozen chopped spinach, thawed and drained
1 oz. Parmesan cheese, shaved or shredded

1. Preheat oven to 375°F. Coat six 10- to 12-ounce au gratin dishes or individual casseroles with nonstick cooking spray. Set aside. Cook noodles according to package directions; drain. Rinse with cold water; drain well and set aside.
2. Meanwhile, for sauce, in a large skillet melt 3 tablespoons of the butter over medium heat. Stir in flour, mustard, and pepper until combined. Add 1 3/4 cups of the milk all at once; cook and stir until thickened and bubbly. Reduce heat to low; stir in Swiss cheese until melted. Remove sauce from skillet.
3. In the same skillet melt remaining 1 tablespoon butter. Beat together eggs, remaining 1/4 cup milk, and salt in a medium bowl; pour into hot skillet. Cook, without stirring, until mixture begins to set on the bottom and around the edges. Using a large spatula, lift and fold partially cooked egg mixture so that the uncooked portion flows underneath. Continue cooking until egg mixture is cooked through but still glossy and moist. Remove from heat. Stir in 1/4 cup of the sauce and the Canadian-style bacon.
4. Stir 1/2 cup of the remaining sauce into the spinach. Divide spinach mixture evenly among the au gratin dishes. Spread about 1/2 cup of the egg mixture over the whole length of each lasagna noodle; roll up. Place one roll in each dish, seam side down. Spoon remaining sauce over rolls.
5. Cover dishes and place on a large baking sheet. Bake for 20 minutes. Uncover and top with Parmesan cheese. Bake, uncovered, 5 minutes more or until heated through. Makes 6 servings.
MAKE AHEAD: Prepare as above through Step 4. Cover dishes and chill up to 24 hours. Place dishes on a large baking sheet. Bake, covered, for 40 minutes. Uncover and top with Parmesan cheese; bake, uncovered, 5 minutes more or until heated through.
EACH SERVING: 436 cal., 25 g total fat (12 g sat. fat), 276 mg chol., 1,123 mg sodium, 25 g carbo., 2 g fiber, 26 g pro. Daily Values: 155% vit. A, 6% vit. C, 44% calcium, 14% iron.

Salmon-Asparagus Lasagna Rolls

PREP: 45 MINUTES **BAKE:** 45 MINUTES
STAND: 10 MINUTES

8 dried lasagna noodles
12 oz. fresh asparagus or one 8-ounce package frozen asparagus spears
1 8-oz. tub cream cheese with chive and onion
1 cup finely shredded Pecorino Romano or Parmesan cheese
2 Tbsp. milk
4 oz. smoked salmon, skinned and flaked
1 10 3/4-oz. can condensed cream of celery soup
1/4 cup milk
1 tsp. finely shredded lemon peel

1. Preheat oven to 350°F. Cook noodles in a large pot according to package directions. Meanwhile, snap off and discard woody bases from fresh asparagus, if using. If desired, scrape off scales. Add fresh or frozen asparagus to pot with noodles the last 3 minutes of cooking. Using tongs, remove asparagus from water to a colander to drain. Rinse with cold water; drain again. Transfer asparagus to a cutting board; chop and set aside. Drain noodles. Rinse with cold water; drain well and set aside.
2. In a medium bowl stir together cream cheese, 1/2 cup of the shredded cheese, and the 2 tablespoons milk until combined. Fold in asparagus and salmon. Spread about 1/4 cup salmon mixture over the whole length of each noodle. Roll up noodles and arrange, seam sides down, in a lightly greased 2-quart rectangular baking dish.
3. For sauce, in another medium bowl stir together soup, the 1/4 cup milk, and lemon peel. Pour over lasagna rolls in dish. Sprinkle with remaining cheese.
4. Bake, covered, for 35 minutes. Uncover and bake 10 minutes more or until heated through. Let stand 10 minutes before serving. Makes 4 to 6 servings.
EACH SERVING: 564 cal., 31 g total fat (17 g sat. fat), 80 mg chol., 1,347 mg sodium, 44 g carbo., 3 g fiber, 23 g pro. Daily Values: 26% vit. A, 5% vit. C, 33% calcium, 17% iron.

Seafood Lasagna

PREP: 40 MINUTES **BAKE:** 40 MINUTES
STAND: 15 MINUTES

9 dried lasagna noodles
1 8-oz. tub cream cheese with garden vegetables
1 12-oz. carton cottage cheese
3 eggs, beaten
1/2 cup milk
1 Tbsp. Worcestershire sauce
1/4 tsp. salt
1 6- or 8-oz. pkg. flake-style imitation crabmeat, chopped
4 oz. smoked salmon or trout, skinned, boned, and flaked
Nonstick cooking spray
1 8-oz. pkg. shredded mozzarella and Parmesan cheese blend
1 10-oz. container refrigerated light Alfredo sauce

1. Preheat oven to 325°F. Cook noodles according to package directions; drain. Rinse with cold water; drain well and set aside. In a large bowl combine cream cheese and cottage cheese; stir in eggs, 1/4 cup of the milk, the Worcestershire sauce, and salt. Fold in seafood; set aside.
2. Lightly coat a 2-quart rectangular baking dish with cooking spray. Place 3 lasagna noodles in the dish. Top with half of the cheese-seafood mixture and half of the shredded cheese. Repeat layers. Top with remaining noodles. In a small bowl combine Alfredo sauce and remaining 1/4 cup milk. Spread evenly over top of lasagna.
3. Bake, covered, for 30 minutes. Uncover and bake 10 to 20 minutes more or until heated through. Let stand 15 minutes before serving. Makes 12 servings.
EACH SERVING: 305 cal., 17 g total fat (9 g sat. fat), 120 mg chol., 733 mg sodium, 18 g carbo., 0 g fiber, 18 g pro. Daily Values: 11% vit. A, 19% calcium, 6% iron.

Raspberry-Rhubarb Pie

PREP: 40 MINUTES **BAKE:** 1 HOUR **STAND:** 45 MINUTES

- 1¼ cups sugar
- 3 Tbsp. cornstarch
- ¼ tsp. five-spice powder
- 3 cups fresh raspberries or one 12-oz. pkg. frozen lightly sweetened red raspberries
- 2 cups fresh or frozen unsweetened sliced rhubarb
- ¼ cup orange marmalade
- 1 recipe Pastry for Double-Crust Pie
  Milk

1. Combine sugar, cornstarch, and five-spice powder. Stir in fruit and marmalade. Toss until coated. If using frozen fruit, let mixture stand 45 minutes or until fruit is partially thawed but still icy. If using all fresh fruit, let stand while preparing pastry. Preheat oven to 375°F.

2. Ease 1 pastry round into a 9×2-inch heart-shape baking pan or dish or 9-inch pie plate; do not stretch pastry. Add fruit mixture to pastry-lined pan. Trim bottom pastry to edge of pan. Roll out second ball of dough; cut slits in pastry and place pastry on filling. Trim ½ inch beyond edge of pan. Fold top pastry under bottom pastry; crimp edge. Brush with milk. If desired, cut small hearts out of pastry scraps; place on pie. Brush cutouts with milk. If desired, sprinkle with additional *sugar*. Bake 60 to 70 minutes or until filling is bubbly and pastry is golden. Cool on a wire rack. Serve warm or cool. Makes 8 servings.

PASTRY FOR DOUBLE-CRUST PIE: In a bowl combine 2¼ cups all-purpose flour and ¾ teaspoon salt. Cut in ⅔ cup shortening until pieces are pea-size. Sprinkle 1 tablespoon cold water over part of mixture; toss with fork. Push moistened dough to side. Using a total of 8 to 10 tablespoons, repeat until all the dough is moistened. Divide in half; form each into a ball. On lightly floured surface, flatten 1 dough ball. Roll into a 13-inch circle.

EACH SERVING: 443 cal., 18 g total fat (4 g sat. fat), 0 mg chol., 226 mg sodium, 69 g carbo., 5 g fiber, 4 g pro. Daily Values: 2% vit. A, 20% vit. C, 9% calcium, 11% iron.

Oaty Doodle Hearts

PREP: 30 MINUTES **BAKE:** 8 MINUTES PER BATCH

- 2 cups rolled oats
- 1½ cups all-purpose flour
- ½ cup whole wheat flour
- 4 tsp. ground cinnamon
- 1 tsp. baking soda
- ½ tsp. cream of tartar
- ¼ tsp. salt
- ½ cup butter, softened
- ½ cup butter-flavored shortening
- 1½ cups sugar
- 2 eggs
- 1 tsp. vanilla
- ⅓ cup sugar

1. Preheat oven to 400°F. Line cookie sheets with parchment paper or foil; set aside. In a food processor bowl process the oats until finely ground. In a medium bowl combine ground oats, all-purpose flour, whole wheat flour, cinnamon, baking soda, cream of tartar, and salt; set aside.

2. In a large mixing bowl beat butter and shortening with an electric mixer on medium to high speed for 30 seconds. Add the 1½ cups sugar and beat until combined. Beat in eggs and vanilla. Beat or stir in flour mixture. Using a heaping teaspoon for each cookie, roll dough into balls; roll in ⅓ cup sugar. Place on prepared cookie sheets 2 inches apart. Flatten to a little less than ½ inch thick. Use your fingers to shape into hearts by forming a point and two rounded shapes. Bake for 8 to 10 minutes or until set and lightly browned. Cool 1 minute on cookie sheet. Transfer to wire racks and let cool completely. Makes about 60 cookies.

EACH COOKIE: 82 cal., 4 g total fat (1 g sat. fat), 11 mg chol., 45 mg sodium, 11 g carbo., 1 g fiber, 1 g pro. Daily Values: 1% vit. A, 1% calcium, 2% iron.

Chocolate-Raspberry Shortcakes

PREP: 30 MINUTES **BAKE:** 12 MINUTES
STAND: 1 HOUR

- 2 cups all-purpose flour
- 1/2 cup packed brown sugar
- 1/2 cup unsweetened cocoa powder
- 2 tsp. baking powder
- 1/2 tsp. salt
- 1/2 cup butter
- 2 oz. bittersweet or semisweet chocolate, finely chopped
- 1/2 cup buttermilk
- 1 egg, beaten
- 1 Tbsp. buttermilk
- 1 Tbsp. coarse sugar
- 3 cups fresh raspberries and/or sliced strawberries
- 2 Tbsp. granulated sugar
- 1 cup whipping cream
- 1/4 cup dairy sour cream
- 1 Tbsp. granulated sugar
- 1/2 tsp. vanilla

1. Preheat oven to 400°F. Line a baking sheet with parchment paper or grease baking sheet; set aside. In a large bowl stir together flour, brown sugar, cocoa powder, baking power, and salt. Using a pastry blender, cut in butter until mixture resembles coarse crumbs. Add chopped chocolate; toss to coat. Make a well in the center of the dry mixture. In a small bowl combine 1/2 cup buttermilk and the egg; add all at once to dry mixture. Using a fork, stir just until moistened.

2. Turn dough out onto a well-floured surface. Gently knead dough for 10 to 12 strokes or until nearly smooth. Pat or lightly roll dough to 1/2-inch thickness. Cut the dough with a floured 3-inch heart-shape or round cookie cutter, rerolling scraps as necessary. Place shortcakes on prepared baking sheet. Brush tops with the 1 tablespoon buttermilk and sprinkle with coarse sugar. Bake for 12 to 15 minutes or until bottoms are lightly browned. Cool shortcakes on a wire rack.

3. Meanwhile, in a medium bowl combine berries and the 2 tablespoons granulated sugar. Cover and let stand for 1 hour. In a medium bowl combine whipping cream, sour cream, the 1 tablespoon granulated sugar, and the vanilla. Beat with an electric mixer on medium speed until soft peaks form.

4. To assemble, split shortcakes in half. Place bottoms on dessert plates. Divide whipped cream mixture and berry mixture among shortcake bottoms. Replace shortcake tops. Makes 6 to 8 servings.

EACH SERVING: 660 cal., 38 g total fat (21 g sat. fat), 137 mg chol., 454 mg sodium, 71 g carbo., 6 g fiber, 10 g pro. Daily Values: 25% vit. A, 22% vit. C, 22% calcium, 22% iron.

Decadently Delicious Dark Chocolate Cookies

PREP: 45 MINUTES
BAKE: 10 MINUTES PER BATCH
STAND: 2 MINUTES

- 1 1/2 cups all-purpose flour
- 1/4 cup unsweetened cocoa powder
- 1 tsp. baking soda
- 1 tsp. salt
- 3/4 cup butter, softened
- 1 1/4 cups packed brown sugar
- 3 eggs
- 1 tsp. vanilla
- 6 oz. semisweet chocolate, melted and cooled slightly
- 4 oz. unsweetened chocolate, melted and cooled slightly
- 1 12-oz. pkg semisweet chocolate pieces
- 3 oz. white chocolate baking squares or white baking pieces
- 1 tsp. shortening

1. Preheat oven to 350°F. In a medium bowl combine flour, cocoa powder, baking soda, and salt; set aside.

2. In a very large bowl beat butter with an electric mixer on medium speed for 30 seconds. Add brown sugar and beat until well combined. Beat in eggs and vanilla until combined. Beat in the 6 ounces melted semisweet chocolate and the melted unsweetened chocolate until well combined. Add flour mixture and beat on low speed just until combined. Stir in semisweet chocolate pieces.

3. Drop dough by rounded tablespoons 2 inches apart onto ungreased cookie sheets. Bake about 10 minutes or until edges are set but center appears soft. Let stand on cookie sheets 2 minutes. Transfer to a wire rack and let cool.

4. In a small saucepan combine white chocolate and 1 teaspoon shortening; heat and stir over low heat just until melted. Let cool about 5 minutes. Place melted white chocolate in a resealable plastic bag. Snip a small hole in the corner of the bag. Pipe white chocolate across entire surface of each cookie in a crisscross or heart pattern. Makes about 36 cookies.

EACH COOKIE: 191 cal., 11 g total fat (6 g sat. fat), 29 mg chol., 141 mg sodium, 23 g carbo., 1 g fiber, 2 g pro. Daily Values: 3% vit. A, 2% calcium, 7% iron.

Rice Pudding Sundae "Flirtini"

Fast! **PREP:** 15 MINUTES **STAND:** 10 MINUTES

- 1 1/4 cups unsweetened coconut milk
- 1 cup instant white rice
- 2 Tbsp. sugar
- 1 Tbsp. finely chopped crystallized ginger
- 1/4 cup orange marmalade
- 1 tsp. finely shredded lime peel
- 1 cup raspberries or 1 mango, pitted, peeled, and chopped
- 2 Tbsp. flaked coconut, toasted
  Lime wedges (optional)

1. In a medium saucepan combine coconut milk, rice, sugar, and crystallized ginger. Bring to boiling. Remove from heat; cover and let stand 10 minutes. Stir in orange marmalade and lime peel.

2. Divide mixture among 4 martini glasses. Top with raspberries or mango. Sprinkle with coconut. If desired, garnish with a lime wedge. Makes 4 servings.

EACH SERVING: 416 cal., 15 g total fat (14 g sat. fat), 0 mg chol., 44 mg sodium, 65 g carbo., 3 g fiber, 5 g pro. Daily Values: 1% vit. A, 13% vit. C, 4% calcium, 10% iron.

Saffron Sweethearts

PREP: 30 MINUTES
BAKE: 18 MINUTES PER BATCH

- 1 cup all-purpose flour
- 1 cup yellow cornmeal
- 2 Tbsp. sugar
- 1 tsp. ground cardamom
- 1/4 tsp. saffron threads, crushed
- 1/8 tsp. salt
- 3/4 cup butter
- 1/4 cup chopped pine nuts or almonds

1. Preheat oven to 325°F. In a large bowl stir together flour, cornmeal, sugar, cardamom, saffron, and salt. Using a pastry blender, cut in butter until mixture resembles fine crumbs. Using your hands, shape dough into a ball. (Mixture may seem dry at first but should come together as you gently knead.)

2. On a lightly floured surface, roll dough until 1/2 inch thick. Cut out dough using a 1 1/4-inch heart-shape cutter. Place cutouts 1 inch apart on ungreased cookie sheets. Gently press nuts into the top of each cutout.

3. Bake for 18 to 20 minutes or until edges are light golden brown. Transfer to wire racks and cool completely. Makes about 40 cookies.

EACH COOKIE: 63 cal., 4 g total fat (2 g sat. fat), 10 mg chol., 33 mg sodium, 6 g carbo., 0 g fiber, 1 g pro. Daily Values: 2% vit. A, 2% iron.

PORK AND ...

Blackberry Salad with Pork

PREP: 25 MINUTES **ROAST:** 25 MINUTES **STAND:** 5 MINUTES

- 1 12- to 16-oz. pork tenderloin
- ¼ cup olive oil
- ¼ cup honey
- ¼ cup lemon juice
  Salt and ground black pepper
- 4 oz. Brie cheese
- 6 cups packaged mixed baby greens (spring mix)
- 2 cups blackberries, raspberries, and/or sliced strawberries
- 1 cup grape tomatoes (halved, if desired)
- 1 recipe Toasted Pine Nuts

1. Preheat oven to 425°F. Place pork on a rack in a shallow roasting pan. Sprinkle with *salt* and *ground black pepper*. Roast, uncovered, for 25 to 35 minutes or until an instant-read thermometer inserted in center registers 155°F. Remove from oven. Cover roast with foil and let stand 5 minutes until thermometer registers 160°F. Cool slightly. Slice pork ¼ inch thick. If desired, place pork in a covered storage container; chill up to 3 days.

2. For dressing, in a screw-top jar combine oil, honey, lemon juice, and salt and pepper to taste; cover and shake well. If desired, remove rind from Brie; cut cheese into thin wedges.

3. To serve, place greens in salad bowls or on individual plates; top with berries, tomatoes, Toasted Pine Nuts, Brie, and pork slices. Drizzle with dressing. Serve immediately. Makes 4 servings.

TOASTED PINE NUTS: Place ½ cup pine nuts in a shallow baking pan. Bake in a 350°F oven for 5 to 7 minutes, shaking pan once or twice. Watch closely so nuts don't burn.

EACH SERVING: 569 cal., 36 g total fat (10 g sat. fat), 95 mg chol., 308 mg sodium, 32 g carbo., 5 g fiber, 37 g pro. Daily Values: 19% vit. A, 53% vit. C, 11% calcium, 24% iron.

Pork with Raisin Sauce

PREP: 15 MINUTES **ROAST:** 30 MINUTES **STAND:** 5 MINUTES

- 1 1- to 1¼-lb. peppercorn pork tenderloin
  Creole or Cajun seasoning
- 1 cup raisins
- ⅓ cup water
- 1 tsp. finely shredded orange peel
- ⅓ cup orange juice
- 1 tsp. finely shredded lemon peel
- 3 Tbsp. lemon juice
- ¼ cup white wine vinegar
- ¼ cup sugar
- 1 Tbsp. dry mustard
- 1 Tbsp. Worcestershire sauce
- ¼ tsp. ground allspice
- ¼ tsp. ground ginger
- 1 2-inch piece stick cinnamon

1. Preheat oven to 425°F. Place pork on a rack in a shallow roasting pan. Sprinkle lightly with seasoning. Roast, uncovered, for 30 to 35 minutes or until an instant-read thermometer inserted in center registers 155°F. Remove from oven. Cover with foil and let stand 5 minutes until thermometer registers 160°F.

2. Meanwhile, for sauce, in a medium saucepan combine raisins, water, orange peel and juice, lemon peel and juice, vinegar, sugar, mustard, Worcestershire, allspice, ginger, and cinnamon. Bring to boiling; reduce heat. Simmer, uncovered, for 8 to 10 minutes or until desired consistency. Remove cinnamon stick. Slice pork; serve sauce with pork. Makes 4 servings.

Healthy **EACH SERVING:** 304 cal., 5 g total fat (2 g sat. fat), 50 mg chol., 685 mg sodium, 47 g carbo., 2 g fiber, 20 g pro. Daily Values: 1% vit. A, 30% vit. C, 3% calcium, 7% iron.

Citrus-Chile Glazed Pork Chops with Rice and Posole Pilaf

PREP: 30 MINUTES **MARINATE:** 20 MINUTES
COOK: 8 MINUTES

- 2 to 3 canned chipotle peppers in adobo sauce
- 5 cloves garlic
- 1 tsp. finely shredded orange peel
- ³/₄ cup orange juice
- ¹/₂ cup canola oil
- ¹/₃ cup soy sauce
- 2 Tbsp. honey
- ¹/₂ cup snipped fresh parsley
- 4 6- to 8-oz. pork chops, cut ¹/₂ to ³/₄ inch thick
- 1 cup uncooked long grain white rice
- 2 cups chicken broth
- 1 15¹/₂-oz. can white hominy, drained
  Nonstick cooking spray
  Orange wedges (optional)

1. For marinade, in a blender container combine chipotle peppers, garlic, orange peel and juice, canola oil, soy sauce, and honey. Cover and blend until finely chopped. Stir in parsley. Set aside ¹/₂ cup of the marinade for the rice; cover and chill. Place pork chops in a resealable plastic bag set in a shallow dish; pour remaining marinade over pork chops. Seal bag and refrigerate at least 20 minutes or overnight.

2. In a medium saucepan combine rice and chicken broth. Bring to boiling; reduce heat. Simmer, covered, about 20 minutes or until rice is tender and liquid is absorbed. Stir in hominy and reserved ¹/₂ cup marinade. Heat through.

3. Lightly coat a grill pan or large skillet with cooking spray; heat over medium-high heat until very hot. Drain pork chops and discard marinade; pat meat dry with paper towels. Add pork chops to grill pan. Reduce heat to medium and cook 8 to 12 minutes or until centers are no longer pink (160°F), turning once. (If pork chops brown too quickly, reduce heat to medium-low). Serve chops with rice and, if desired, orange wedges. Makes 4 servings.

EACH SERVING: 517 cal., 14 g total fat (2 g sat. fat), 79 mg chol., 1,421 mg sodium, 56 g carbo., 4 g fiber, 39 g pro. Daily Values: 14% vit. A, 31% vit. C, 5% calcium, 22% iron.

Pork and Mushroom Skillet Cobbler

PREP: 25 MINUTES **BAKE:** 35 MINUTES
STAND: 15 MINUTES

- 1 lb. bulk pork sausage
- 1 medium onion, chopped (¹/₂ cup)
- 2 cups mushrooms, quartered
- 1 10³/₄-oz. can reduced-fat and reduced-sodium condensed cream of mushroom soup or condensed cream of mushroom soup

- 1 cup milk
- ¹/₄ tsp. ground black pepper
- 1¹/₄ cups all-purpose flour
- ¹/₄ cup grated Parmesan cheese
- 1 Tbsp. snipped fresh sage
- 1¹/₂ tsp. baking powder
- ³/₄ cup milk
  Fresh sage leaves (optional)

1. Preheat oven to 375°F. In a 10-inch cast-iron or oven-going skillet cook pork and onion until meat is brown; drain off fat. Add mushrooms; cook and stir just until mushrooms are tender. Stir soup, the 1 cup milk, and the pepper into pork mixture. Set aside.

2. In a medium bowl combine flour, cheese, sage, and baking powder. Stir in the ³/₄ cup milk until combined. Spoon over pork mixture in skillet.

3. Bake, uncovered, about 35 minutes or until top is golden brown. Let stand on wire rack 15 minutes before serving. If desired, garnish with additional sage. Makes 4 to 6 servings.

EACH SERVING: 614 cal., 36 g total fat (12 g sat. fat), 97 mg chol., 1,250 mg sodium, 42 g carbo., 2 g fiber, 29 g pro. Daily Values: 6% vit. A, 4% vit. C, 23% calcium, 20% iron.

Pork with Hot Pear Relish

PREP: 30 MINUTES **COOK:** 12 MINUTES
ROAST: 1¹/₄ HOURS **STAND:** 15 MINUTES

- 1 large sweet onion, peeled and finely chopped
- 1 medium red sweet pepper, finely chopped
- 1 jalapeño chile pepper, seeded and finely chopped*
- 1 Tbsp. olive oil
- 2 firm ripe pears, peeled and chopped
- ¹/₂ cup sugar
- ¹/₂ cup white balsamic vinegar
- 1 tsp. dry mustard
- ¹/₄ tsp. salt
- 1 2- to 2¹/₂-lb. boneless pork top loin roast (single loin)
  Salt and ground black pepper

1. In a large skillet cook and stir onion, sweet pepper, and jalapeño pepper in hot oil over medium heat for 2 minutes. Stir in pears, sugar, vinegar, mustard, and salt. Bring to boiling over medium-high heat, stirring occasionally. Reduce heat; simmer, uncovered, 10 minutes or until pears are soft and transparent.

2. Meanwhile, preheat oven to 350°F. Place pork on a rack in a shallow roasting pan. Sprinkle with salt and pepper. Roast, uncovered, for 1 hour. Top with ¹/₂ cup of the pear sauce. Roast 15 to 30 minutes more or until an instant-read thermometer inserted in center registers 150°F.

3. Remove roast from oven. Cover with foil and let stand 15 minutes until thermometer registers 160°F. Slice roast and serve with remaining pear sauce. Makes 8 servings.

*NOTE: Because hot chile peppers, such as jalapeños, contain volatile oils that can burn your skin and eyes, avoid direct contact with chiles as much as possible. When working with chile peppers, wear plastic or rubber gloves. If your bare hands do touch the chile peppers, wash your hands well with soap and water.

 Healthy **EACH SERVING:** 309 cal., 11 g total fat (3 g sat. fat), 74 mg chol., 174 mg sodium, 26 g carbo., 2 g fiber, 25 g pro. Daily Values: 9% vit. A, 47% vit. C, 4% calcium, 8% iron.

Roast Pork Tenderloin with Apple Cider Pecan Salsa

PREP: 15 MINUTES **ROAST:** 25 MINUTES
STAND: 5 MINUTES

- ¹/₂ tsp. salt
- ¹/₂ tsp. ground allspice
- ¹/₄ tsp. cayenne pepper
- 2 16-oz. pork tenderloins
- ¹/₂ cup chopped celery
- 2 Tbsp. butter
- 2 large tart cooking apples, peeled, cored, and chopped (2 cups)
- ¹/₄ cup apple cider vinegar
- 1 tsp. bottled minced garlic (2 cloves)
- ¹/₄ to ¹/₂ tsp. crushed red pepper
- ¹/₂ tsp. salt
- 1 cup chopped pecans, toasted
- ¹/₄ cup pure maple syrup or maple-flavor syrup

1. Preheat oven to 425°F. In a small bowl combine ¹/₂ teaspoon salt, the allspice, and cayenne pepper. Sprinkle over tenderloins and rub into meat with your fingers. Place pork on a rack in a shallow roasting pan. Roast, uncovered, for 25 to 35 minutes or until an instant-read thermometer inserted in center registers 155°F. Cover and let stand 5 minutes until thermometer registers 160°F.

2. Meanwhile, for salsa, in a large skillet cook celery in hot butter until tender. Stir in apples, vinegar, garlic, crushed red pepper, and ¹/₂ teaspoon salt. Bring mixture to boiling; reduce heat. Simmer, uncovered, about 10 minutes or until apples are tender and most of the liquid has evaporated. Remove from heat. Stir in pecans and maple syrup.

3. To serve, slice tenderloin and spoon salsa over top. Makes 8 servings.

EACH SERVING: 296 cal., 16 g total fat (4 g sat. fat), 81 mg chol., 365 mg sodium, 12 g carbo., 2 g fiber, 25 g pro. Daily Values: 4% vit. A, 4% vit. C, 3% calcium, 11% iron.

THE BEST BROWNIES EVER

Deep Chocolate Brownies
PREP: 25 MINUTES **BAKE:** 35 MINUTES

  1 egg
  1 cup butterscotch-flavor ice cream topping
  2 cups coarsely chopped pecans
  2 cups flaked coconut
$3/4$ cup butter, softened
$1^1/2$ cups packed dark brown sugar
  8 oz. bittersweet chocolate, melted and cooled
  2 eggs
  2 tsp. vanilla
  2 cups all-purpose flour
  1 tsp. baking powder
$1/2$ tsp. baking soda
$1/2$ tsp. salt
  1 12-oz. pkg. semisweet chocolate pieces (2 cups)

1. Preheat oven to 350°F. Lightly grease a 13×9×2-inch baking pan; set aside.

2. In a small mixing bowl beat 1 egg with an electric mixer on medium speed until fluffy and light colored. Stir in ice cream topping. Fold in pecans and coconut; set aside.

3. In a large mixing bowl beat butter with an electric mixer on medium to high speed for 30 seconds. Beat in brown sugar until combined. Beat in cooled chocolate, 2 eggs, and vanilla. Stir together flour, baking powder, baking soda, and salt; beat or stir into chocolate mixture. Stir in chocolate pieces. Spread in prepared pan; spread nut mixture over batter.

4. Bake about 35 minutes or until golden and set. Cool in pan on a wire rack. Cut into bars. Makes 24 bars.

EACH BAR: 404 cal., 23 g total fat (11 g sat. fat), 43 mg chol., 221 mg sodium, 50 g carbo., 4 g fiber, 5 g pro. Daily Values: 5% vit. A, 4% calcium, 10% iron.

Shortbread Brownies
PREP: 20 MINUTES **BAKE:** 48 MINUTES

  1 cup all-purpose flour
$1/4$ cup packed brown sugar
$1/2$ cup butter
$1/4$ cup miniature semisweet chocolate pieces
$1^1/3$ cups granulated sugar
$3/4$ cup all-purpose flour
$1/2$ cup unsweetened cocoa powder
$1^1/2$ tsp. baking powder
$1/2$ tsp. salt
  3 eggs
$1/3$ cup butter, melted
  1 Tbsp. vanilla
$1/2$ cup miniature semisweet chocolate pieces

1. Preheat oven to 350°F. Line a 9×9×2-inch baking pan with foil; set aside. In a medium bowl stir together 1 cup flour and the brown sugar. Cut in the $1/2$ cup butter until mixture resembles coarse crumbs. Stir in the $1/4$ cup chocolate pieces. Press into prepared pan. Bake for 8 minutes.

2. Meanwhile, in a large bowl stir together granulated sugar, $3/4$ cup flour, the cocoa powder, baking powder, and salt. Add eggs, melted butter, and vanilla; beat by hand until smooth. Stir in the $1/2$ cup chocolate pieces. Carefully spread over crust in pan.

3. Bake 40 minutes more. Cool in pan on a wire rack. Lift brownies out of pan by lifting up on foil. Cut into bars. Makes 24 bars.

EACH BAR: 180 cal., 9 g total fat (4 g sat. fat), 44 mg chol., 121 mg sodium, 23 g carbo., 1 g fiber, 3 g pro. Daily Values: 5% vit. A, 3% calcium, 5% iron.

Black Forest Brownies

PREP: 30 MINUTES **BAKE:** 35 MINUTES

2 10-oz. jars maraschino cherries, drained
1 cup semisweet chocolate pieces
1/2 cup butter
3 eggs, slightly beaten
1 1/4 cups granulated sugar
1 1/4 cups all-purpose flour
1 tsp. vanilla
3/4 tsp. salt
1/2 tsp. baking powder
1 cup white baking pieces
1/2 cup slivered almonds, toasted
1 3-oz. pkg. cream cheese, softened
2/3 cup powdered sugar

1. Preheat oven to 350°F. Grease a 13×9×2-inch baking pan; set aside. Remove stems from 1 cup of the cherries. Coarsely chop cherries. Drain on paper towels. Set aside with remaining cherries.
2. Place chocolate pieces and butter in a large microwave-safe bowl. Microwave on 100% power (high) for 1 minute; stir. Cook 10 to 20 seconds more or until mixture is melted and smooth. Add eggs, granulated sugar, flour, vanilla, salt, and baking powder. Stir until combined. Fold in white baking pieces, chopped cherries, and almonds. Spread batter in prepared pan.
3. Bake for 35 minutes. Cool in pan on a wire rack. Cut into bars.
4. Just before serving, in a medium mixing bowl beat cream cheese and powdered sugar with an electric mixer until smooth. Pipe on top of cooled brownies. Remove stems from remaining cherries; coarsely chop cherries and sprinkle on top of brownies. Makes 24 bars.
EACH BAR: 240 cal., 11 g total fat (5 g sat. fat), 40 mg chol., 128 mg sodium, 33 g carbo., 1 g fiber, 3 g pro. Daily Values: 4% vit. A, 3% calcium, 4% iron.

Chocolate Brownies with Peanut Butter Swirl

PREP: 25 MINUTES **BAKE:** 45 MINUTES

8 oz. semisweet chocolate, chopped
3 Tbsp. butter
4 eggs
1 1/4 cups sugar
1/3 cup water
1 tsp. vanilla
1 cup all-purpose flour
1 tsp. baking powder
1/4 tsp. salt
1 3-oz. pkg. cream cheese, softened
1/2 cup peanut butter
2/3 cup sugar
2 Tbsp. all-purpose flour
1/2 cup semisweet chocolate pieces
1 tsp. shortening

1. Preheat oven to 350°F. Line a 13×9×2-inch baking pan with foil, extending foil over edges of pan. Grease foil; set pan aside.
2. In a large heavy saucepan cook and stir chocolate and butter over low heat until chocolate melts. Remove from heat; cool for 15 minutes.
3. In a large mixing bowl beat 2 of the eggs with an electric mixer on medium speed until foamy. Add 1 1/4 cups sugar, the water, and the vanilla; beat on medium speed for 5 minutes or until mixture thickens. Beat in cooled chocolate mixture. Stir in 1 cup flour, baking powder, and salt. Spread half of the batter in prepared pan; set pan and remaining batter aside.
4. In a medium bowl beat remaining 2 eggs, cream cheese, peanut butter, 2/3 cup sugar, and 2 tablespoons flour until smooth. Spread evenly over batter in pan. Spoon remaining batter evenly over cream cheese mixture. Swirl batter with a knife to marble. Bake for 45 minutes. Cool in pan on a wire rack.
5. In a small saucepan heat and stir semisweet chocolate pieces and shortening over low heat until chocolate is melted and smooth. Drizzle over cooled brownies. Let stand until chocolate is firm. Lift from pan using foil and cut into bars. Makes 32 bars.
EACH BAR: 160 cal., 8 g total fat (3 g sat. fat), 32 mg chol., 71 mg sodium, 21 g carbo., 1 g fiber, 3 g pro. Daily Values: 2% vit. A, 1% calcium, 5% iron.

Heavenly Peanut Butter 'n' Fudge Truffle Brownies

PREP: 20 MINUTES **BAKE:** 25 MINUTES
COOL: 1 HOUR **CHILL:** 1 HOUR

1 1/3 cups semisweet chocolate pieces
1/4 cup butter
3/4 cup peanut butter
1 cup packed brown sugar
2 eggs, slightly beaten
2 tsp. vanilla
3/4 cup all-purpose flour
1/2 tsp. baking powder
1 8-oz. pkg. cream cheese, softened
1/2 cup powdered sugar

1. Preheat oven to 350°F. Lightly grease a 9×9×2-inch baking pan; set aside. In a medium saucepan heat and stir 1/3 cup of the chocolate pieces, the butter, and 1/4 cup of the peanut butter over low heat until melted and smooth. Remove from heat. Stir in brown sugar until combined. Add eggs and 1 teaspoon of the vanilla; beat lightly with a wooden spoon just until combined. Stir in flour and baking powder until combined. Spread batter into prepared pan. Bake for 25 minutes. Cool in pan on a wire rack, about 1 hour.

2. Meanwhile, for frosting, in a small saucepan heat and stir the remaining 1 cup chocolate pieces and 1/2 cup peanut butter over low heat until melted and smooth. Remove from heat and cool slightly. In a medium mixing bowl beat cream cheese with an electric mixer on medium speed for 30 seconds. Add powdered sugar and remaining 1 teaspoon vanilla. Beat until combined. Beat in chocolate mixture until combined. Spread over cooled brownies. Cover and chill at least 1 hour. Cut into bars. Makes 16 to 20 bars.
EACH BAR: 314 cal., 19 g total fat (9 g sat. fat), 50 mg chol., 144 mg sodium, 34 g carbo., 2 g fiber, 6 g pro. Daily Values: 6% vit. A, 4% calcium, 8% iron.

Kid Friendly Malted Fudge Brownies

PREP: 40 MINUTES **BAKE:** 35 MINUTES

1 1/2 cups all-purpose flour
1/3 cup malted milk powder
1/2 tsp. salt
1 cup butter
4 oz. unsweetened chocolate, cut up
2 cups sugar
4 eggs
1 tsp. vanilla
1 cup chopped walnuts, toasted
4 oz. malted milk balls, coarsely crushed (about 1 cup)
1/2 of a 15- to 16-oz. can chocolate fudge frosting

1. Preheat oven to 325°F. Lightly grease a 13×9×2-inch baking pan; set aside. In a medium bowl combine flour, malted milk powder, and salt; set aside.
2. In a medium saucepan melt butter and chocolate over low heat, stirring occasionally. Remove from heat; stir in sugar. Beat in eggs, 1 at a time, using a wooden spoon. Add vanilla. Stir in flour mixture, walnuts, and half of the malted milk balls. Spread in prepared pan.
3. Bake for 35 minutes. Cool in pan on a wire rack. Spread cooled brownies with frosting and sprinkle with remaining malted milk balls. Cut into bars. Makes 30 bars.
EACH BAR: 245 cal., 14 g total fat (5 g sat. fat), 47 mg chol., 140 mg sodium, 29 g carbo., 1 g fiber, 3 g pro. Daily Values: 5% vit. A, 3% calcium, 7% iron.

MAKE-AHEAD MAIN COURSES

Grilled Thai Leg of Lamb

PREP: 30 MINUTES **MARINATE:** OVERNIGHT **GRILL:** 50 MINUTES
STAND: 15 MINUTES

- 1 13 1/2-oz. can unsweetened coconut milk
- 1/2 cup snipped fresh basil
- 1/2 cup snipped fresh mint
- 1/2 cup sliced green onions
- 1 Tbsp. finely shredded lime peel
- 1/4 cup lime juice
- 2 Tbsp. fish sauce
- 1 Tbsp. packed brown sugar
- 1 tsp. red curry paste
- 1 1/2 tsp. each coarse salt and ground black pepper
- 1 Tbsp. grated fresh ginger
- 1 Tbsp. minced garlic
- 1 3- to 3 1/2-lb. boneless lamb leg, rolled and tied

1. For sauce, in a bowl combine coconut milk, basil, mint, onions, lime peel and juice, fish sauce, brown sugar, curry paste, 1 teaspoon of the coarse salt, and 1/2 teaspoon of the ground black pepper. Set aside. For rub, in a bowl combine ginger, garlic, and the remaining salt and ground black pepper. Untie and unroll lamb. Trim fat. Using flat side of meat mallet, pound lamb to an even thickness (1 1/2 to 2 inches thick). Rub ginger mixture over lamb. Place in large resealable plastic bag set in shallow dish. Add 1/2 cup of the sauce. Seal bag; turn to coat. Refrigerate overnight. Cover and refrigerate remaining sauce.

2. Remove lamb from marinade. To keep lamb from curling, insert 2 long metal skewers through meat forming an X. To grill, arrange medium coals around drip pan. Test for medium-low heat above pan. Place lamb on rack over pan. Cover; grill 50 to 60 minutes or until instant-read thermometer registers 135°F for medium rare. Let chilled sauce stand at room temperature 30 minutes. Remove lamb. Cover with foil; let stand 15 minutes. (Temperature should rise 10 degrees during standing.) Thinly slice lamb against grain; serve with sauce. Makes 8 to 10 servings.

EACH SERVING: 315 cal., 15 g total fat (10 g sat. fat), 108 mg chol., 947 mg sodium, 7 g carbo., 1 g fiber, 36 g pro. Daily Values: 4% vit. A, 15% vit. C, 5% calcium, 28% iron.

Dried Tomato Casserole

PREP: 25 MINUTES **CHILL:** OVERNIGHT **BAKE:** 40 MINUTES
STAND: 10 MINUTES

- 2 9-oz. pkg. refrigerated four-cheese or beef ravioli
- 1/2 to one 8-oz. jar oil-packed dried tomatoes, drained and chopped
- 1 1/2 cups shredded cheddar cheese (6 oz.)
- 1 1/2 cups shredded Monterey Jack cheese (6 oz.)
- 1/2 cup grated Parmesan cheese
- 8 eggs, beaten
- 2 1/2 cups milk
- 1 to 2 Tbsp. snipped fresh basil or flat-leaf parsley

1. Grease a 3-quart rectangular or oval baking dish. Place uncooked ravioli evenly in dish. Sprinkle evenly with tomatoes. Top evenly with cheeses; set aside. Whisk eggs and milk together until combined. Pour over layers in dish. Cover; chill overnight. Preheat oven to 350°F. Bake, uncovered, about 40 minutes or until top is golden and center is set. Let stand 10 minutes before serving. Sprinkle with basil just before serving. Makes 12 servings.

EACH SERVING: 353 cal., 21 g total fat (11 g sat. fat), 213 mg chol., 490 mg sodium, 20 g carbo., 1 g fiber, 21 g pro. Daily Values: 13% vit. A, 17% vit. C, 42% calcium, 10% iron.

Fiesta Mañana

PREP: 30 MINUTES **BAKE:** 45 MINUTES
CHILL: OVERNIGHT **STAND:** 20 MINUTES

- 1 lb. bulk hot pork sausage or bulk pork sausage
- 1/2 cup chopped onion
- 2 cloves garlic, minced
- 2 4-oz. cans diced green chile peppers
- 8 6-inch corn tortillas, cut into 1-inch strips
- 4 cups shredded Monterey Jack cheese (1 lb.)
- 8 eggs, beaten
- 1/2 cup milk
- 3/4 tsp. ground cumin
- 1/2 tsp. ground black pepper
- 1/4 tsp. salt
- 3 large tomatoes, sliced
- 1 tsp. paprika
  Dairy sour cream, salsa, and/or guacamole (optional)

1. In a large skillet cook sausage, onion, and garlic until sausage is brown. Remove from skillet and drain.
2. In bottom of a greased 3-quart rectangular baking dish spread half of the chile peppers. Top with half of the tortilla strips, half of the cooked sausage mixture, and half of the cheese. Repeat layers.
3. In a large bowl whisk together eggs, milk, cumin, black pepper, and salt. Carefully pour over layers in dish. Top with tomato slices and sprinkle with paprika. Cover and chill overnight.
4. Preheat oven to 350°F. Bake, uncovered, for 45 to 50 minutes or until set. Let stand for 20 minutes before serving. If desired, serve warm with sour cream, salsa, and/or guacamole. Makes 12 servings.
EACH SERVING: 354 cal., 23 g total fat (11 g sat. fat), 200 mg chol., 537 mg sodium, 14 g carbo., 2 g fiber, 21 g pro. Daily Values: 20% vit. A, 22% vit. C, 36% calcium, 14% iron.

Indian-Spiced Shepherd's Pie

PREP: 45 MINUTES **CHILL:** OVERNIGHT
BAKE: 1 HOUR **STAND:** 15 MINUTES

- 1 1/2 lb. potatoes, peeled and quartered
- 1 lb. ground lamb or beef
- 2 large carrots, chopped (1 cup)
- 2 medium onions, chopped (1 cup)
- 1 Tbsp. curry powder
- 1 cup beef broth
- 1/3 cup mango chutney
- 1/4 cup tomato paste
- 1 Tbsp. snipped fresh parsley
- 1/4 cup butter
- 3 medium leeks, sliced 1/2 inch thick (1 cup)
- 1/4 tsp. salt
- 1/8 tsp. ground black pepper
- 1/2 cup crumbled feta cheese
- 2 Tbsp. snipped fresh parsley

1. In a large saucepan cook potatoes in lightly salted boiling water about 25 minutes or until tender; drain and set aside.
2. Meanwhile, in a large skillet cook ground meat, carrots, and onions until meat is no longer pink; drain off fat. Stir in curry powder; cook and stir 1 minute. Stir in broth, chutney, and tomato paste. Bring to boiling; reduce heat. Simmer, uncovered, for 5 minutes (most of the liquid will evaporate). Stir in 1 tablespoon parsley. Transfer mixture to a 2-quart rectangular baking dish; set aside.
3. Meanwhile, melt butter in large saucepan over medium heat. Add leeks; cook until tender, stirring occasionally. Add drained potatoes, salt, and pepper; mash potatoes with a potato masher. Add cheese; stir until melted. Spoon on top of meat mixture in dish. Cover and chill overnight.
4. Preheat oven to 375°F. Bake, covered, for 1 hour or until heated through. Let stand, uncovered, for 15 minutes before serving. Sprinkle with 2 tablespoons parsley. Makes 6 servings.
EACH SERVING: 382 cal., 21 g total fat (10 g sat. fat), 81 mg chol., 524 mg sodium, 32 g carbo., 4 g fiber, 18 g pro. Daily Values: 82% vit. A, 41% vit. C, 10% calcium, 16% iron.

Kid Friendly Make-Ahead Chili-Cheese Hoagies

PREP: 25 MINUTES **CHILL:** 2 HOURS
BAKE: 25 MINUTES

- 1 lb. lean ground beef
- 1 large onion, chopped (1 cup)
- 2 small green and/or red sweet peppers, seeded and chopped (1 cup)
- 2 cloves garlic, minced
- 1 14.5-oz. can diced tomatoes for chili, undrained
- 1 15-oz. can chili beans in chili gravy, undrained
- 1/2 tsp. ground cumin
- 1/4 tsp. ground black pepper
- 8 hoagie buns or French-style rolls
- 8 thin slices Monterey Jack cheese or Monterey Jack cheese with jalapeño peppers (8 oz.)
- 8 thin slices cheddar cheese (8 oz.)
  Pickled jalapeños (optional)

1. In a large skillet cook ground beef, onion, sweet peppers, and garlic over medium heat until beef is brown; drain off fat. Add undrained tomatoes, undrained chili beans, cumin, and black pepper. Bring to boiling; reduce heat. Simmer, uncovered, for 15 minutes or until thick, stirring occasionally.
2. Split rolls lengthwise. Hollow out roll bottoms leaving a 1/4-inch-thick shell. Place a Monterey Jack cheese slice, cut to fit, on bottom half of roll. Spoon beef mixture on top of cheese. Place a slice of cheddar cheese on top of beef. If desired, sprinkle with pickled jalapeños. Top with roll top. Repeat with remaining rolls. Wrap each roll in nonstick foil or foil that has been coated with nonstick cooking spray. Refrigerate for 2 to 24 hours.

3. Preheat oven to 375°F. Place foil-wrapped sandwiches on a baking sheet. Bake for 25 to 30 minutes or until hot. Makes 8 sandwiches.
EACH SANDWICH: 785 cal., 32 g total fat (15 g sat. fat), 90 mg chol., 1,407 mg sodium, 88 g carbo., 8 g fiber, 39 g pro. Daily Values: 15% vit. A, 30% vit. C, 55% calcium, 34% iron.

Spicy Sicilian Strata

PREP: 40 MINUTES **CHILL:** 2 HOURS
BAKE: 50 MINUTES **STAND:** 10 MINUTES

- 1 8-oz. loaf French bread, cut into 1-inch cubes (10 cups)
- 1 3.5-oz. pkg. sliced pepperoni, coarsely chopped
- 1/2 cup pepperoncini salad peppers, drained, stemmed, and chopped
- 1 10-oz. pkg. frozen chopped spinach, thawed and well drained
- 1/2 cup oil-packed dried tomatoes, drained and chopped
- 2 cups shredded Italian-blend cheeses (8-oz. pkg.)
- 6 eggs, slightly beaten
- 3 cups milk
- 2 tsp. dried Italian seasoning, crushed
- 1/4 tsp. salt
- 1/8 tsp. cayenne pepper
- 1/4 cup grated Parmesan cheese

1. Preheat oven to 350°F. Place bread cubes in a 15×10×1-inch baking pan. Bake, uncovered, for 10 minutes, stirring once.
2. In a greased 3-quart rectangular baking dish place half of the bread cubes. Top with half of the pepperoni, half of the pepperoncini peppers, all of the spinach, and all of the tomatoes. Sprinkle with 1 cup of the Italian-blend cheeses. Repeat layers with remaining bread, pepperoni, pepperoncini peppers, and Italian blend cheeses.
3. In a large bowl whisk together eggs, milk, Italian seasoning, salt, and cayenne pepper. Slowly pour over layers in dish; press down lightly on top layer using the back of a large spoon. Sprinkle with Parmesan cheese. Cover and chill for 2 to 24 hours.
4. Preheat oven to 350°F. Bake, uncovered, for 40 to 45 minutes or until a knife inserted near the center comes out clean (170°F). Let stand for 10 minutes before serving. Makes 10 to 12 servings.
EACH SERVING: 290 cal., 16 g total fat (7 g sat. fat), 162 mg chol., 811 mg sodium, 18 g carbo., 2 g fiber, 18 g pro. Daily Values: 90% vit. A, 13% vit. C, 29% calcium, 10% iron.

NUTTY DESSERTS

Three Nut Upside-Down Cake

PREP: 30 MINUTES **BAKE:** 45 MINUTES **COOL:** 10 MINUTES

- 1/4 cup butter
- 1/4 cup packed dark brown sugar
- 2/3 cup light-colored corn syrup
- 1/4 cup whipping cream
- 1/2 cup chopped pecans
- 1/2 cup chopped walnuts
- 1/2 cup chopped macadamia nuts
- 1 1/3 cups all-purpose flour
- 1/3 cup unsweetened cocoa powder
- 1 tsp. baking powder
- 1/2 tsp. baking soda
- 1/2 tsp. salt
- 1/3 cup butter, softened
- 1 cup granulated sugar
- 2 eggs
- 1 tsp. vanilla
- 2/3 cup milk

1. Preheat oven to 350°F. Line a 9×9×2-inch baking pan with foil; grease foil. In a small saucepan melt 1/4 cup butter over medium heat. Stir in brown sugar. Cook and stir until sugar is dissolved. Stir in corn syrup and cream. Bring just to boiling. Stir in all nuts. Spread in pan.
2. Combine flour, cocoa powder, baking powder, baking soda, and salt; set aside. In a large mixing bowl beat 1/3 cup butter with electric mixer on medium to high speed for 30 seconds. Gradually add granulated sugar, beating on medium speed until well combined, scraping sides of bowl. Add eggs, 1 at a time, beating after each (about 1 minute total). Beat in vanilla. Alternately add flour mixture and milk to butter mixture, beating on low speed after each addition just until combined. Pour into pan, being careful not to disturb nuts. Bake for 45 to 50 minutes or until a wooden toothpick inserted near center comes out clean. Cool in pan on wire rack 10 minutes. Remove from pan. Carefully peel off foil. Place nut side up on plate. Serve at room temperature. Makes 9 servings.
EACH SERVING: 551 cal., 31 g total fat (10 g sat. fat), 91 mg chol., 393 mg sodium, 65 g carbo., 2 g fiber, 7 g pro. Daily Values: 12% vit. A, 10% calcium, 12% iron.

Nutty Biscotti

PREP: 35 MINUTES **BAKE:** 45 MINUTES **COOL:** 1 HOUR

- 1/2 cup butter, softened
- 1 1/2 cups sugar
- 1 tsp. baking soda
- 1 tsp. baking powder
- 1/2 tsp. salt
- 2 eggs
- 1 tsp. finely shredded lemon peel
- 1 Tbsp. lemon juice
- 1 tsp. lemon extract
- 3 cups all-purpose flour
- 1 cup coarsely chopped lightly salted pistachio nuts
- 1 cup coarsely chopped macadamia nuts
- 1 recipe Nut Coating

1. Preheat oven to 350° F. Line cookie sheet with parchment paper. Beat butter with mixer on medium to high speed 30 seconds. Add sugar, baking soda, baking powder, and salt; beat until combined. Add eggs, lemon peel and juice, and extract. Beat until combined. Add flour; beat until combined. Stir in nuts. Divide dough in half. Shape each into a 12-inch roll. Place at least 3 inches apart on baking sheet. Bake 35 to 40 minutes or until beginning to brown (logs will spread). Cool completely on a rack. Use a serrated knife to cut each roll into 3/4-inch slices. Place, cut sides down, on ungreased cookie sheet. Bake in 350°F oven for 5 minutes. Turn slices over; bake 5 minutes more or until dry and crisp. Cool on wire rack for 1 hour. Prepare and follow directions for Nut Coating. Makes 36 biscotti.
NUT COATING: Combine 1/4 cup finely chopped pistachio nuts and 1/4 cup finely chopped macadamia nuts. In small saucepan melt 8 to 10 ounces white chocolate baking squares over low heat. Stir in 1 teaspoon finely shredded lemon peel and 1 tablespoon shortening. Add additional shortening, 1 teaspoon at a time, until of drizzling consistency. Dip 1 end of biscotti into white chocolate; sprinkle with nuts. Dry completely.
EACH BISCOTTI: 181 cal., 10 g total fat (4 g sat. fat), 20 mg chol., 128 mg sodium, 20 g carbo., 1 g fiber, 3 g pro. Daily Values: 2% vit. A, 1% vit. C, 2% calcium, 4% iron.

Four-Nut Caramel-Chocolate Tart

PREP: 30 MINUTES **BAKE:** 18 MINUTES
CHILL: 1 HOUR

- 1 cup all-purpose flour
- 1/3 cup ground almonds or pecans
- 1/4 cup granulated sugar
- 1 oz. semisweet chocolate, grated
- 1/4 tsp. salt
- 1/4 cup butter
- 1 egg, beaten
- 1/2 cup salted cashews, coarsely chopped
- 1/2 cup pecans, coarsely chopped
- 1/2 cup macadamia nuts, coarsely chopped
- 1/2 cup slivered blanched almonds
- 1/2 cup packed brown sugar
- 1/3 cup butter
- 4 Tbsp. whipping cream
- 1 oz. semisweet chocolate, coarsely chopped

1. Preheat oven to 400°F. In a bowl combine flour, ground nuts, granulated sugar, grated chocolate, and salt. Using a pastry blender, cut in butter until pieces are pea-size. Stir in beaten egg. Toss until moist, adding 1 tablespoon *water*, if necessary.

2. Form dough into a ball; press evenly onto bottom and up sides of a 10-inch tart pan. Bake for 10 minutes. Cool completely in pan on a wire rack. Reduce oven temperature to 375°F.

3. In a shallow baking pan place cashews, pecans, macadamia nuts, and almonds. Bake for 8 minutes or until lightly toasted. In a medium saucepan combine brown sugar and 1/3 cup butter. Cook and stir over low heat until sugar dissolves. Bring mixture to boiling over medium heat, stirring often. Boil, uncovered, for 1 minute; remove from heat. Stir in 2 tablespoons of the whipping cream and the toasted nuts. Spoon mixture into prepared crust.

4. In a small saucepan combine remaining whipping cream and chopped chocolate. Cook and stir over low heat until melted. If necessary, add 1 teaspoon additional *whipping cream* to reach drizzling consistency. Drizzle over nut filling. Chill 1 hour or until set. Makes 12 servings.

EACH SERVING: 371 cal., 28 g total fat (9 g sat. fat), 49 mg chol., 176 mg sodium, 28 g carbo., 3 g fiber, 6 g pro. Daily Values: 8% vit. A, 5% calcium, 10% iron.

Nutty Apricot Bars

PREP: 25 MINUTES **BAKE:** 40 MINUTES

- 3/4 cup all-purpose flour
- 2/3 cup packed brown sugar
- 1/2 cup slivered almonds, toasted
- 1/2 tsp. salt
- 1/2 cup butter, cut up
- 1 1/4 cups granulated sugar
- 2 eggs, beaten

- 2 Tbsp. milk
- 1 tsp. finely shredded lemon peel
- 1 tsp. vanilla
- 2/3 cup finely snipped dried apricots
- 1/2 cup finely chopped slivered almonds
- 1/2 cup finely chopped walnuts or pecans
- 2 qt. vanilla ice cream
- 1 recipe Apricot-Lemon Sauce

1. Preheat oven to 350°F. In a food processor bowl combine flour, brown sugar, 1/2 cup toasted slivered almonds, and salt. Process until almonds are finely ground. Add butter; process with on/off turns until mixture resembles coarse crumbs. Press flour mixture into the bottom of an ungreased 13×9×2-inch baking pan. Bake for 10 to 15 minutes or until crust is lightly browned around the edges.

2. Meanwhile, in a mixing bowl combine granulated sugar, eggs, milk, lemon peel, and vanilla. Beat until combined. Stir in dried apricots. Carefully pour over hot crust, spreading evenly. Sprinkle with remaining almonds and walnuts.

3. Bake 30 minutes or until golden. Cool slightly in pan on a wire rack. Score into rectangles. Cool completely in pan.

4. To serve, top with ice cream and drizzle with Apricot-Lemon Sauce. Makes 18 bars.

APRICOT-LEMON SAUCE: In a food processor bowl combine 2/3 cup purchased lemon curd and 1/2 cup apricot preserves; process until combined.

EACH BAR: 462 cal., 23 g total fat (11 g sat. fat), 107 mg chol., 167 mg sodium, 60 g carbo., 2 g fiber, 6 g pro. Daily Values: 16% vit. A, 2% vit. C, 12% calcium, 7% iron.

Quick Walnut Mousse

PREP: 10 MINUTES **BAKE:** 5 MINUTES
FREEZE: 2 HOURS

- 1 1/2 cups chopped walnuts
- 2 cups whipping cream
- 1 cup packed brown sugar
- 1/2 tsp. salt
- 1/4 tsp. ground black pepper

1. Preheat oven to 350°F. In a shallow baking pan spread walnuts in a single layer. Bake for 5 to 10 minutes or until light golden brown; set aside to cool.

2. In a blender container or food processor bowl combine whipping cream, brown sugar, salt, and pepper. Cover and blend or process for 30 seconds. Fold in walnuts.

3. Divide mixture among 6 individual serving dishes. Cover and freeze or chill for 2 hours or until set. Makes 6 servings.

EACH SERVING: 611 cal., 49 g total fat (20 g sat. fat), 110 mg chol., 239 mg sodium, 42 g carbo., 2 g fiber, 6 g pro. Daily Values: 24% vit. A, 1% vit. C, 11% calcium, 9% iron.

Very-Almond Cheesecake

PREP: 30 MINUTES **CHILL:** 5 HOURS
BAKE: 1 HOUR **COOL:** 45 MINUTES

- 2 cups shortbread or butter cookie crumbs (about 7 1/2 ounces)
- 1/2 cup ground toasted almonds
- 2 Tbsp. sugar
- 1/2 cup butter, melted
- 1 8-oz. can almond paste
- 3/4 cup sugar
- 2 Tbsp. amaretto
- 3 tsp. vanilla
- 4 8-oz. pkg. cream cheese, softened
- 4 eggs
- 2 egg yolks
- 1 8-oz. carton dairy sour cream
- 1/4 cup sugar
- 1 Tbsp. amaretto
- 1/3 cup sliced almonds, toasted

1. For crust, in a medium bowl stir together cookie crumbs, ground almonds, 2 tablespoons sugar, and butter until combined. Press mixture into the bottom and 1 1/2 inches up the sides of a 10-inch springform pan. Cover and chill for 1 hour.

2. Preheat oven to 350°F. For filling, in a very large bowl beat almond paste, 3/4 cup sugar, 2 tablespoons amaretto, and 2 teaspoons of the vanilla with an electric mixer on medium speed until combined. Add cream cheese and beat until combined. Beat in eggs and egg yolks just until combined. Pour mixture into crust-lined pan. Place filled pan in a 15×10×1-inch baking pan.

3. Bake about 55 minutes or until center is almost set when gently shaken. Meanwhile, in a small bowl stir together sour cream, 1/4 cup sugar, 1 tablespoon amaretto, and remaining 1 teaspoon vanilla. Spread mixture over hot cheesecake. Bake for 5 minutes.

4. Cool in pan on a wire rack for 15 minutes. Using a sharp small knife, loosen the crust from the sides of pan; cool for 30 minutes more. Remove the sides of the pan; cool cheesecake completely on rack. Cover and chill at least 4 hours before serving. Sprinkle with sliced almonds before serving. Makes 16 servings.

EACH SERVING: 540 cal., 41 g total fat (19 g sat. fat), 166 mg chol., 298 mg sodium, 33 g carbo., 2 g fiber, 10 g pro. Daily Values: 23% vit. A, 11% calcium, 11% iron.

Mediterranean Pizza Skillet

 PREP: 20 MINUTES **COOK:** 10 MINUTES

- 3 medium skinless, boneless chicken breast halves, cut into ³⁄₄-inch pieces
- 2 cloves garlic, minced
- 2 Tbsp. olive oil
- 4 plum tomatoes, chopped
- 1 14-oz. can artichoke hearts, drained and quartered
- 1 2 ¹⁄₄-oz. can sliced pitted ripe olives, drained
- ¹⁄₂ tsp. dried Italian seasoning, crushed
- ¹⁄₄ tsp. ground black pepper
- 2 cups romaine lettuce or hearty mesclun, chopped
- 1 cup crumbled feta cheese (4 oz.)
- ¹⁄₃ cup fresh basil leaves, shredded or torn
  Sliced crusty Italian or French bread

1. In a large skillet cook and stir chicken and garlic in hot oil over medium-high heat until chicken is browned. Stir in tomatoes, artichokes, olives, seasoning, and pepper. Bring to boiling; reduce heat. Simmer, covered, for 10 minutes or until chicken is no longer pink. Top with lettuce and cheese. Cook, covered, for 1 to 2 minutes more or until lettuce starts to wilt. Sprinkle with basil and serve on or with bread. Makes 4 servings.

EACH SERVING: 395 cal., 17 g total fat (6 g sat. fat), 82 mg chol., 1,003 mg sodium, 27 g carbo., 6 g fiber, 33 g pro. Daily Values: 57% vit. A, 34% vit. C, 25% calcium, 28% iron.

Moroccan Lamb

PREP: 30 MINUTES **COOK:** 1 HOUR

- 2 lb. boneless lamb shoulder roast
- 2 Tbsp. olive oil
- 1 medium onion, chopped (¹⁄₂ cup)
- 2 cloves garlic, minced
- 1 Tbsp. grated fresh ginger
- 2¹⁄₂ cups water
- 1 6-oz. pkg. long grain and wild rice mix (with seasoning packet)
- ¹⁄₂ tsp. coarsely ground black pepper
- ¹⁄₄ tsp. ground cinnamon
- ¹⁄₈ to ¹⁄₄ tsp. cayenne pepper
- 2 medium yellow summer squash, cut into 1-inch pieces (2¹⁄₂ cups)
- 1 8-oz. pkg. fresh mushrooms, halved or quartered (about 3 cups)
- ³⁄₄ cup dried apricots
- ¹⁄₂ cup raisins
- ¹⁄₂ cup dried tart cherries

1. Trim fat from lamb; cut meat into 1-inch pieces. In a very large skillet heat oil over medium heat. Add half of the lamb and brown on all sides; remove lamb from skillet using a slotted spoon. Add remaining lamb, the onion, garlic, and ginger to skillet. Cook until meat is brown and onion is tender, stirring occasionally. Return all lamb to skillet. Add water. Bring mixture to boiling; reduce heat. Simmer, covered, for 25 minutes.

2. Add rice mix and seasoning packet from rice mix, black pepper, cinnamon, and cayenne pepper to lamb mixture. Return mixture to boiling; reduce heat. Simmer, covered, for 20 minutes. Add squash, mushrooms, apricots, raisins, and cherries to lamb mixture. Simmer, covered, about 10 minutes or just until squash is tender. Makes 6 to 8 servings.

EACH SERVING: 610 cal., 31 g total fat (12 g sat. fat), 102 mg chol., 490 mg sodium, 54 g carbo., 4 g fiber, 32 g pro. Daily Values: 14% vit. A, 18% vit. C, 8% calcium, 22% iron.

Chicken, Vegetables, and Tortellini

 START TO FINISH: 30 MINUTES

- 1 lb. skinless, boneless chicken breast halves, cut into 1-inch pieces
- 2 Tbsp. olive oil
- 1 medium onion, thinly sliced (1 cup)
- 1 14.5-oz. can diced tomatoes with basil, garlic, and oregano
- 1 cup chicken broth
- 1 large green sweet pepper, cut into 3/4-inch pieces
- 1 large red sweet pepper, cut into 3/4-inch pieces
- 1 cup sliced cremini mushrooms
- 1 lb. asparagus, trimmed and cut into 2-inch pieces
- 1 9-oz. pkg. refrigerated tortellini
- 1 oz. Parmesan cheese, shaved into large strips

1. In a 12-inch skillet cook chicken in hot oil until brown, stirring often. Remove chicken from skillet. Add onion to skillet; cook and stir until tender. Drain any excess fat. Return chicken to skillet. Add undrained tomatoes, broth, sweet peppers, and mushrooms. Bring to boiling. Add asparagus and tortellini. Return to boiling; reduce heat. Simmer, covered, for 5 to 8 minutes or until tortellini is tender.
2. Uncover and simmer about 3 minutes or until juices thicken slightly. Top with shaved Parmesan cheese. Makes 6 servings.

 EACH SERVING: 335 cal., 11 g total fat (3 g sat. fat), 68 mg chol., 796 mg sodium, 32 g carbo., 2 g fiber, 29 g pro. Daily Values: 32% vit. A, 125% vit. C, 20% calcium, 20% iron.

Indian Chicken and Rice

START TO FINISH: 45 MINUTES

- 2 tsp. ground cardamom
- 1 tsp. salt
- 1/2 tsp. ground black pepper
- 1 lb. skinless, boneless chicken thighs, cut into 1-inch pieces
- 2 Tbsp. cooking oil
- 2 medium onions, cut into wedges
- 1 Tbsp. grated fresh ginger
- 4 cloves garlic, minced
- 3/4 cup basmati or long grain rice
- 2 tsp. garam masala*
- 1/4 tsp. crushed red pepper
- 1 13 1/2- or 14-oz. can unsweetened coconut milk
- 1 14-oz. can chicken broth
- 2 cups fresh sugar snap peas, strings and tips removed, or 2 cups frozen sugar snap peas, thawed
- 1 medium red, green or yellow sweet pepper, chopped
- 2 Tbsp. lime juice
- 1/2 cup chopped fresh cilantro

1. In a large bowl combine cardamom, salt, and black pepper. Add chicken and toss with cardamom mixture. In an extra large skillet cook chicken in hot oil over medium heat for 5 minutes, turning occasionally. Remove chicken from skillet with a slotted spoon. Add onion, ginger, and garlic to skillet; cook until onion is tender. Add rice, garam masala, and crushed red pepper; cook and stir for 2 minutes.
2. Return chicken to skillet; add coconut milk and chicken broth. Bring to boiling; reduce heat. Simmer, covered, for 15 minutes. Add peas and sweet pepper. Cook, covered, for 5 minutes more.
3. Drizzle chicken with lime juice and sprinkle with cilantro. Makes 6 servings.
*NOTE: If you don't wish to purchase garam masala, you can make your own. In an 8×8×2-inch baking pan combine 2 tablespoons whole black peppercorns; 4 teaspoons cumin seeds; 2 teaspoons whole cloves; 1 teaspoon coriander seeds; 1 teaspoon whole cardamom seeds, pods removed; and 3 inches broken stick cinnamon. Roast in a 350°F oven for 15 minutes. Transfer roasted spices to a blender container. Cover tightly; blend until very fine. Cool to room temperature and store in a covered container in a cool, dry place.
EACH SERVING: 370 cal., 20 g total fat (12 g sat. fat), 61 mg chol., 735 mg sodium, 28 g carbo., 3 g fiber, 20 g pro. Daily Values: 35% vit. A, 87% vit. C, 7% calcium, 14% iron.

Shrimp with Vermicelli

START TO FINISH: 35 MINUTES

- 12 oz. fresh or frozen medium shrimp, peeled and deveined
- 6 oz. dried vermicelli pasta
- 1 large onion, halved and thinly sliced
- 2 Tbsp. butter
- 1/4 to 1/2 tsp. crushed red pepper
- 1 8-oz. can tomato sauce with basil, garlic, and oregano
- 1 medium yellow summer squash or zucchini, halved lengthwise and sliced
- 1/8 tsp. salt
- 4 cups prewashed baby spinach
- 1 cup cherry tomatoes, halved
- 2 Tbsp. finely shredded Parmesan cheese

1. Thaw shrimp, if frozen. Cook vermicelli according to package directions; drain.
2. Meanwhile, in an extra large skillet cook onion in butter until tender. Add shrimp and crushed red pepper; cook and stir for 1 minute. Add tomato sauce, squash, and salt. Bring to boiling; reduce heat. Simmer, covered, for 5 minutes.
3. Stir drained vermicelli, spinach, and cherry tomatoes into skillet. Toss gently over medium heat until heated through. Sprinkle with Parmesan cheese. Makes 4 servings.
EACH SERVING: 341 cal., 9 g total fat (4 g sat. fat), 115 mg chol., 580 mg sodium, 44 g carbo., 4 g fiber, 22 g pro. Daily Values: 77% vit. A, 48% vit. C, 12% calcium, 23% iron.

Zesty Mexican Porcupine Balls with Black Bean Salsa

PREP: 30 MINUTES **COOK:** 15 MINUTES
STAND: 2 MINUTES

- 1 lb. lean ground beef
- 1 small onion, finely chopped (1/3 cup)
- 1/2 cup uncooked instant rice
- 1/2 teaspoon chili powder
- 1 1/2 cups shredded Mexican blend cheese (6 oz.)
- 2 Tbsp. water
- 2 Tbsp. cooking oil
- 1/2 cup chopped red or green sweet pepper
- 1 16-oz. jar black bean and corn salsa
- 1/2 cup tomato juice
- 1 cup crushed corn or tortilla chips (optional)
  Hot cooked rice (optional)

1. In a large bowl combine beef, onion, rice, chili powder, 1/2 cup of the cheese, and the water. Shape into 16 large meatballs. In a 12-inch skillet brown meatballs in hot oil over medium heat for 5 minutes, turning to brown evenly. Carefully drain excess fat from skillet. Add sweet pepper, salsa, and tomato juice to skillet. Bring to boiling; reduce heat. Simmer, covered, for 10 to 15 minutes or until a thermometer inserted in meatballs registers 160°F.
2. Sprinkle with remaining cheese and, if desired, crushed chips. Let stand 2 minutes before serving. If desired, serve with hot cooked rice. Makes 4 servings.
EACH SERVING: 521 cal., 31 g total fat (13 g sat. fat), 109 mg chol., 1,278 mg sodium, 26 g carbo., 1 g fiber, 34 g pro. Daily Values: 23% vit. A, 90% vit. C, 26% calcium, 15% iron.

SPINACH FROM SALAD TO SOUFFLÉ

Easy Florentine Soufflé Rolls

PREP: 25 MINUTES **BAKE:** 18 MINUTES **STAND:** 2 MINUTES

    4 green onions, finely chopped
    2 cloves garlic, minced
    1 Tbsp. olive oil
    1 6-oz. pkg. fresh baby spinach
  1/4 cup snipped fresh basil
  1/2 tsp. salt
  1/4 tsp. ground black pepper
    1 13.8-oz. pkg. refrigerated pizza dough
    1 Tbsp. olive oil
  1/4 cup crumbled feta cheese (1 oz.)
    2 Tbsp. toasted pine nuts
    1 Tbsp. butter, melted
  1/4 cup finely shredded Parmesan cheese

1. Preheat oven to 375° F. Grease twelve 2½-inch muffin cups; set aside. In a large skillet cook green onions and garlic in 1 tablespoon of oil until tender. Add spinach and basil; cook and stir over medium heat just until wilted. Drain off excess liquid. Stir in salt and pepper. Set aside to cool.

2. On a well-floured surface, unroll pizza dough and shape into a 12×8-inch rectangle. Brush surface of dough with 1 tablespoon oil. Spread spinach mixture to within 1 inch of the edges of dough. Sprinkle with feta cheese and pine nuts. Starting with one of the long sides, roll dough into a spiral.

3. Slice roll into 12 pieces. Place cut sides up in prepared muffin cups. Brush with butter and sprinkle with Parmesan cheese. Bake for 18 to 20 minutes or until golden brown. Let stand in muffin cups for 2 minutes. Carefully remove from cups and serve warm. Makes 12 rolls.

EACH ROLL: 165 cal., 9 g total fat (4 g sat. fat), 13 mg chol., 443 mg sodium, 14 g carbo., 1 g fiber, 7 g pro. Daily Values: 31% vit. A, 9% vit. C, 18% calcium, 9% iron.

Chilled Spinach Couscous Salad

PREP: 15 MINUTES **STAND:** 30 MINUTES **CHILL:** 2 HOURS

  2 1/4 cups water
    1/2 tsp. salt
      1 10-oz. pkg. quick-cooking couscous
    1/3 cup olive oil
      3 Tbsp. lemon juice
      4 cups torn fresh spinach
    1/4 cup sliced green onions
      3 Tbsp. snipped fresh dill
    1/3 cup crumbled feta cheese
         Lemon wedges
         Fresh dill sprigs (optional)

1. In a large saucepan bring water and salt to boiling. Remove from heat. Stir in couscous; cover and let stand for 5 minutes. Fluff couscous with a fork.

2. Meanwhile, combine oil and lemon juice. Add oil mixture to couscous, stirring to coat. Let stand until completely cool about 25 minutes.

3. Stir in spinach, green onions, and snipped dill. Cover and refrigerate for 2 to 12 hours or until thoroughly chilled. Sprinkle with feta cheese before serving. Serve with lemon wedges and , if desired, top with fresh dill sprigs. Makes 8 to 10 servings.

EACH SERVING: 235 cal., 11 g total fat (2 g sat. fat), 5 mg chol., 231 mg sodium, 29 g carbo., 2 g fiber, 6 g pro. Daily Values: 29% vit. A, 15% vit. C, 6% calcium, 5% iron.

Blue and Green Salad

START TO FINISH: 20 MINUTES

1 cup fresh or frozen blueberries
1/4 cup fresh or frozen huckleberries or blueberries
1 6-oz. pkg. fresh baby spinach (about 8 cups)
2 kiwifruits, peeled and chopped
1/2 cup pistachio nuts
1/4 cup crumbled blue cheese (1 oz.)
1/4 cup raspberry vinegar
2 Tbsp. honey
1/4 cup olive oil or salad oil

1. Thaw berries, if frozen. In a large salad bowl toss together spinach, the 1 cup blueberries, kiwi, pistachios, and blue cheese; set aside.
2. For dressing, in a blender container or food processor bowl combine huckleberries, vinegar, and honey. Cover and blend or process until smooth. With blender running, add oil in a thin, steady stream.
3. Drizzle about half of the dressing over spinach mixture; toss lightly to coat. Pass remaining dressing with salad. Cover remaining dressing and store in refrigerator for up to 1 week. Makes 6 to 8 servings.
EACH SERVING: 216 cal., 15 g total fat (3 g sat. fat), 4 mg chol., 91 mg sodium, 17 g carbo., 4 g fiber, 5 g pro. Daily Values: 56% vit. A, 60% vit. C, 8% calcium, 9% iron.

Spicy Spinach Salmon Salad

PREP: 30 MINUTES **COOK:** 7 MINUTES

4 fresh or frozen salmon fillets, 3/4 to 1 inch thick
1 tsp. garlic powder
1 tsp. salt
1/8 tsp. cayenne pepper
1 Tbsp. peanut oil
1 10-oz. pkg. prewashed fresh spinach
1 cup packaged julienned carrots
1 medium red sweet pepper, thinly sliced
1 medium yellow sweet pepper, thinly sliced
1/2 cup sliced green onions
1/4 cup snipped fresh cilantro
1 recipe Peanut Dressing
Toasted sesame seeds

1. Thaw salmon, if frozen. Rinse salmon; pat dry with paper towels. In a small bowl combine garlic powder, salt, and cayenne pepper. Sprinkle mixture over both sides of salmon. In a large skillet cook salmon in hot oil over medium-high heat for 4 minutes. Carefully turn salmon. Reduce heat to medium; cook 3 minutes more or until fish flakes easily when tested with a fork. Remove from pan; set aside.
2. In a large bowl toss together spinach, carrots, sweet peppers, green onions, and cilantro.
3. Divide spinach mixture among 4 plates. Break salmon into bite-size pieces. Top each salad with salmon pieces. Drizzle with Peanut Dressing and sprinkle with toasted sesame seeds. Makes 4 servings.

PEANUT DRESSING: In a blender container combine 1/4 cup creamy peanut butter; 1/4 cup soy sauce; 3 tablespoons orange juice; 2 tablespoons toasted sesame seeds; 2 tablespoons rice vinegar; 1 tablespoon packed brown sugar; 1 tablespoon bottled pickled sushi ginger; 2 cloves garlic, minced; 1 teaspoon crushed red pepper; and 1 teaspoon sesame oil. Cover and blend until smooth.
EACH SERVING: 453 cal., 22 g total fat (4 g sat. fat), 88 mg chol., 1,783 mg sodium, 22 g carbo., 6 g fiber, 44 g pro. Daily Values: 241% vit. A, 291% vit. C, 19% calcium, 29% iron.

Spinach-Blue Cheese Cheesecake

PREP: 30 MINUTES **BAKE:** 28 MINUTES
COOL: 45 MINUTES **CHILL:** 4 HOURS
STAND: 30 MINUTES

1 cup chopped walnuts, toasted
1/4 cup all-purpose flour
2 Tbsp. butter, melted
2 Tbsp. grated Parmesan cheese
1 shallot, finely chopped (2 Tbsp.)
2 cloves garlic, minced
1 Tbsp. olive oil or cooking oil
1 10-oz. pkg. frozen chopped spinach, thawed and well drained
2 8-oz. pkg. cream cheese, softened
2 Tbsp. all-purpose flour
Few dashes bottled hot pepper sauce
2 eggs
4 oz. blue cheese, finely crumbled (1 cup)
Assorted crackers
Pear or apple slices (optional)

1. Preheat oven to 375°F. In a food processor bowl or blender container combine walnuts, 1/4 cup flour, the butter, and Parmesan cheese. Cover and process or blend until very finely chopped. Press mixture evenly in the bottom of a 9-inch springform pan. Bake for 8 minutes or until lightly browned; cool.
2. In a small skillet cook shallot and garlic in hot oil until tender. Remove from heat; stir in spinach.
3. In a large mixing bowl beat cream cheese, 2 tablespoons flour, 1/4 teaspoon *salt*, 1/4 teaspoon *ground black pepper*, and hot pepper sauce with an electric mixer on medium speed until combined. Add eggs; beat on low speed just until combined. Stir in spinach mixture and blue cheese. Transfer mixture to the crust-lined pan. Set pan in a 15×10×1-inch baking pan.
4. Bake for 20 minutes or until mixture appears nearly set when shaken. Cool on wire rack for 15 minutes; loosen sides of pan. Cool 30 minutes more. Remove sides of pan. Cool completely. Transfer to a serving plate. Cover and chill for 4 hours or overnight.
5. Let stand at room temperature for 30 minutes before serving. Slice with a warm damp knife, wiping blade between slices. Serve with assorted crackers and, if desired, pear slices. Makes 16 to 20 servings.
EACH SERVING: 221 cal., 20 g total fat (9 g sat. fat), 69 mg chol., 273 mg sodium, 5 g carbo., 1 g fiber, 7 g pro. Daily Values: 62% vit. A, 3% vit. C, 9% calcium, 5% iron.

Spinach-Filled Crepes

START TO FINISH: 45 MINUTES

3 cups lightly packed fresh baby spinach leaves
1 cup milk
1 egg
1/4 tsp. salt
1/4 tsp. ground black pepper
1/2 cup all-purpose flour
1 recipe Creamy Cheese Sauce
4 eggs, beaten
1 Tbsp. butter
4 slices bacon, crisp-cooked and crumbled

1. In a blender container or food processor bowl combine 1 cup of the spinach, 3/4 cup of the milk, 1 egg, salt, and pepper. Cover and blend or process until smooth. Add flour; process just until combined. Transfer to a medium bowl.
2. Heat a lightly greased 6-inch skillet over medium heat; remove from heat. Spoon in 2 to 3 tablespoons batter; lift and tilt skillet to spread batter. Return to heat and cook for 1 minute or until top is completely set. (Or cook on a crepe maker according to manufacturer's directions.) Invert pan over paper towels; remove crepe. Repeat with remaining batter, greasing skillet occasionally (you should have 8 crepes).
3. Prepare Creamy Cheese Sauce. Transfer to a measuring cup and keep warm.
4. In a medium bowl combine 4 eggs and remaining 1/4 cup milk. In the medium saucepan melt butter; add egg mixture. Cook over medium heat, without stirring, until mixture begins to set on the bottom and around edge. With a spatula or large spoon, lift and fold the partially cooked egg mixture so that the uncooked portion flows underneath. Continue cooking until egg mixture is cooked through but is still glossy and moist. Stir in 1/2 cup of the Creamy Cheese Sauce, bacon, and remaining spinach. Remove from heat.
5. Spoon mixture onto the unbrowned sides of prepared crepes. Roll up. Place 2 crepes on each serving plate; drizzle with remaining warm Creamy Cheese Sauce. Serve immediately. Make 4 servings.
CREAMY CHEESE SAUCE: In a medium saucepan melt 2 tablespoons butter; stir in 2 tablespoons all-purpose flour, 1/4 teaspoon salt, 1/4 teaspoon nutmeg, and 1/8 teaspoon cayenne pepper. Add 1 1/4 cups milk all at once. Cook and stir until thickened and bubbly. Add half of an 8-ounce tub cream cheese with chive and onion; cook and stir until cheese melts.
EACH SERVING: 459 cal., 31 g total fat (16 g sat. fat), 334 mg chol., 777 mg sodium, 23 g carbo., 1 g fiber, 18 g pro. Daily Values: 67% vit. A, 11% vit. C, 25% calcium, 16% iron.

SIZZLING KABOBS

ANASTASSIA SKARLINSKI, JOHNS ISLAND, S.C.

AMY OLIVER, BANGOR, MAINE

Thai Shrimp Kabobs

PREP: 20 MINUTES **MARINATE:** 30 MINUTES **GRILL:** 5 MINUTES

- 1 lb. fresh or frozen large shrimp, peeled and deveined (about 26 to 30)
- 1 13 1/2- or 14-oz. can unsweetened coconut milk
- 1 1/2 tsp. finely shredded lime peel
- 3 Tbsp. lime juice
- 1 1/2 tsp. sugar
- 1 1/2 tsp. green curry paste
- 1 1/2 tsp. fish sauce
- 1 tsp. grated fresh ginger
- 2 to 3 cups hot cooked rice
  Lime wedges (optional)

1. If using wooden skewers, soak in water for 30 minutes. Thaw shrimp, if frozen. In a small bowl stir together coconut milk, lime peel, lime juice, sugar, curry paste, fish sauce, and ginger. Place shrimp in a medium bowl. Pour 1/2 cup of the coconut milk mixture over the shrimp. Cover shrimp and chill for 30 minutes. Cover and chill remaining milk mixture.

2. Drain shrimp, discarding marinade. Thread shrimp onto pairs of metal or wooden skewers, leaving a 1/4-inch space between pieces.

3. For a charcoal grill, place skewers on the rack of an uncovered grill directly over medium coals. Grill for 5 to 8 minutes or until shrimp turn opaque, turning skewers once. (For a gas grill, preheat grill. Reduce heat to medium. Place skewers on grill rack. Cover and grill as above.)

4. Meanwhile, heat reserved coconut milk mixture over medium heat until boiling. Reduce heat; simmer, uncovered, for 5 minutes (mixture will be thin). Serve milk mixture with shrimp and rice. If desired, garnish with lime wedges. Makes 4 to 6 servings.

EACH SERVING: 420 cal., 21 g total fat (16 g sat. fat), 172 mg chol., 350 mg sodium, 30 g carbo., 0 g fiber, 27 g pro. Daily Values: 4% vit. A, 10% vit. C, 8% calcium, 26% iron.

Hoisin Beef and Broccoli Kabobs

PREP: 30 MINUTES **GRILL:** 20 MINUTES

- 1/2 cup bottled hoisin sauce
- 3 Tbsp. water
- 2 Tbsp. cooking oil
- 1 Tbsp. soy sauce
- 1 clove garlic, minced
- 1/4 to 1/2 tsp. crushed red pepper
- 1 red sweet pepper, cut into 1-inch pieces
- 2 to 3 cups large broccoli florets and/or 1-inch pieces of yellow summer squash
- 1 lb. beef steak, such as tenderloin, sirloin, or top loin, cut into 1-inch pieces
- 1 Tbsp. finely chopped peanuts (optional)

1. Soak 4 to 8 wooden skewers in water for 30 minutes. In a small bowl combine hoisin sauce, water, oil, soy sauce, garlic, and crushed red pepper; set aside.

2. Alternately thread sweet pepper, broccoli, and steak pieces onto skewers, leaving a 1/4-inch space between pieces. Brush with some of the hoisin sauce mixture.

3. For a charcoal grill, arrange medium-hot coals around a drip pan. Test for medium heat above pan. Place skewers on grill rack over drip pan. Cover and grill for 20 to 25 minutes or until meat is desired doneness, turning and brushing with remaining hoisin sauce mixture halfway through grilling. (For a gas grill, preheat grill. Reduce heat to medium. Adjust for indirect cooking. Grill as above, except omit drip pan.) If desired, sprinkle with peanuts. Makes 4 servings.

EACH SERVING: 326 cal., 18 g total fat (4 g sat. fat), 70 mg chol., 715 mg sodium, 14 g carbo., 2 g fiber, 27 g pro. Daily Values: 27% vit. A, 136% vit. C, 6% calcium, 20% iron.

Grilled Italian Meatball Kabobs

PREP: 1 HOUR **GRILL:** 15 MINUTES

  1 medium onion, cut into thin wedges
  1 medium yellow, red, or green sweet
    pepper, cut into 1/2-inch strips
  1 medium zucchini or yellow summer
    squash, cut into 1-inch pieces
  1/2 of a small eggplant, peeled and cut into
    1-inch pieces
  1/3 cup extra virgin olive oil
  1/4 cup balsamic vinegar
  3 cloves garlic, minced
  3/4 teaspoon salt
  3/4 teaspoon dried Italian seasoning, crushed
  1/2 teaspoon ground black pepper
  1 egg, slightly beaten
  1/3 cup Italian-seasoned fine dry bread
    crumbs
  1/4 cup grated Parmesan cheese
  2 Tbsp. snipped fresh flat-leaf parsley
  2 tsp. dried Italian seasoning, crushed
  1/4 tsp. salt
  1/4 tsp. garlic powder
  12 oz. bulk hot or sweet Italian sausage
  8 oz. lean ground beef
  8 oz. dried linguine or fettuccine
    Shaved Parmesan cheese (optional)

1. Soak six 12-inch wooden skewers in water for 1 hour. Tear off a 36×18-inch piece of heavy-duty foil; fold in half to form an 18-inch square.

2. In a large bowl combine onion, sweet pepper, zucchini, and eggplant. In a small bowl whisk together olive oil, balsamic vinegar, garlic, 3/4 teaspoon salt, 3/4 teaspoon Italian seasoning, and 1/2 teaspoon black pepper. Pour half of the oil mixture over vegetables. Reserve remaining oil mixture. Place vegetable mixture in center of foil. Bring up two opposite edges of foil and seal with a double fold. Fold remaining edges together to completely enclose vegetables, leaving space for steam to build.

3. In a large bowl combine egg, bread crumbs, cheese, parsley, 2 teaspoons Italian seasoning, 1/4 teaspoon salt, and garlic powder. Add sausage and ground beef; mix well. Form meat mixture into thirty 1 1/2-inch meatballs. Thread meatballs onto skewers, leaving a 1/4-inch space between meatballs.

4. For a charcoal grill, arrange medium-hot coals around a drip pan. Test for medium heat above the pan. Place vegetable packet directly over coals. Place kabobs on grill rack over drip pan. Cover and grill for 15 minutes for kabobs or until meatballs are cooked through and 15 to 20 minutes for vegetable packet or until vegetables are tender, turning vegetable packet once. (For a gas grill, preheat grill. Reduce heat to medium. Adjust for indirect cooking. Grill as above.)

5. Meanwhile, cook pasta according to package directions. Drain pasta and return to pan. Carefully open vegetable packet and add to pasta along with reserved oil mixture; toss to combine. Divide among 6 serving plates. Add a kabob to each plate. If desired, garnish with shaved Parmesan cheese. Makes 6 servings.

EACH SERVING: 563 cal., 31 g total fat (9 g sat. fat), 100 mg chol., 947 mg sodium, 43 g carbo., 3 g fiber, 24 g pro. Daily Values: 6% vit. A, 109% vit. C, 9% calcium, 19% iron.

Middle Eastern Chicken Kabobs

PREP: 25 MINUTES **MARINATE:** 1 HOUR
BROIL: 8 MINUTES

  1 lb. skinless, boneless chicken breast
    halves, cut into 1-inch pieces
  1/4 cup plain low-fat yogurt
  1 Tbsp. lemon juice
  1 tsp. dry mustard
  1 tsp. ground cinnamon
  1 tsp. curry powder
  1/2 tsp. salt
  1/4 to 1/2 tsp. crushed red pepper
  1 large red sweet pepper, cut into 1-inch
    pieces
  1 medium yellow summer squash, halved
    lengthwise and cut into 1/2-inch-thick
    slices
    Pita breads, warmed (optional)
  1 recipe Tomato Relish (optional)

1. Place chicken in a resealable plastic bag set in a shallow dish. For marinade, in a small bowl combine yogurt, lemon juice, mustard, cinnamon, curry powder, salt, and crushed red pepper. Pour over chicken. Seal bag and shake to coat chicken. Marinate in the refrigerator for 1 to 4 hours.

2. On 6 long metal skewers, alternately thread chicken, sweet pepper, and squash, leaving a 1/4-inch space between pieces.

3. Broil 4 to 5 inches from the heat for 8 to 10 minutes or until chicken is no longer pink, turning once.

4. If desired, serve kabobs with warm pita bread and Tomato Relish. Makes 6 servings.

 EACH SERVING: 107 cal., 2 g total fat (0 g sat. fat), 44 mg chol., 254 mg sodium, 4 g carbo., 1 g fiber, 19 g pro. Daily Values: 18% vit. A, 92% vit. C, 4% calcium, 6% iron.

TOMATO RELISH: In a medium bowl combine 2 plum tomatoes, coarsely chopped; 1/2 cup yellow or red grape tomatoes, halved; 1 teaspoon snipped fresh oregano or 1/4 teaspoon dried oregano, crushed; 1 teaspoon snipped fresh thyme or 1/4 teaspoon dried thyme, crushed; 1 clove garlic, minced; 1 tablespoon white balsamic or balsamic vinegar; and 1 teaspoon honey. Season to taste with salt and ground black pepper. Cover and chill for up to 4 hours.

Pork and Potatoes with Pomegranate Glaze

PREP: 25 MINUTES **MARINATE:** 4 HOURS
COOK: 20 MINUTES **GRILL:** 12 MINUTES

  1 lb. pork tenderloin
  1 cup bottled pomegranate juice or
    cranberry juice
  1/4 cup soy sauce
  4 cloves garlic, minced
  1 1/2 tsp. ground ginger
  3/4 tsp. salt
  1/2 tsp. ground black pepper
  12 tiny new potatoes or 6 small new
    potatoes, halved (about 1 pound)
  1 1/2 tsp. cornstarch
  2 Tbsp. pomegranate seeds (optional)
  2 Tbsp. snipped Italian flat-leaf or regular
    parsley

1. Trim fat from pork; cut pork into 1-inch cubes. Place pork in a resealable plastic bag set in a shallow dish. For marinade, in a small bowl combine pomegranate juice, soy sauce, garlic, ginger, salt, and pepper. Pour marinade over pork. Seal bag and refrigerate for 4 to 24 hours, turning bag occasionally.

2. Meanwhile, in a medium saucepan cook potatoes in lightly salted boiling water for 10 minutes; drain. Cover and chill.

3. Drain pork, reserving marinade. On six 10- to 12-inch metal skewers, alternately thread pork and potatoes, leaving a 1/4-inch space between pieces. In a small saucepan combine marinade and cornstarch. Cook and stir over medium heat until thickened and bubbly; cook and stir 2 minutes more. Set aside.

4. For a charcoal grill, grill kabobs on the rack of an uncovered grill directly over medium coals for 12 to 15 minutes or until pork is no longer pink and juices run clear, turning occasionally and brushing with some of the glaze for the last 5 minutes of grilling. (For a gas grill, preheat grill. Reduce heat to medium. Place kabobs on grill rack over heat. Cover; grill as above.)

5. Transfer kabobs to a serving platter. Combine pomegranate seeds, if desired; and parsley. Sprinkle over kabobs. Pass with remaining glaze. Makes 6 servings.

EACH SERVING: 184 cal., 2 g total fat (1 g sat. fat), 49 mg chol., 943 mg sodium, 20 g carbo., 1 g fiber, 19 g pro. Daily Values: 3% vit. A, 33% vit. C, 3% calcium, 14% iron.

BERRY DESSERTS

JULIANA GOODWIN, SPRINGFIELD, MO.

JACQUELINE J. ANDERSON, BAKERSFIELD, CALIF.

Blueberry-Brie Quesadillas

PREP: 15 MINUTES **BAKE:** 8 MINUTES

- 5 7- to 8-inch flour tortillas
- 1 Tbsp. butter, melted
- 4 oz. Brie cheese, cut in ¼-inch-thick slices (remove rind, if desired)
- 1 cup fresh blueberries
- 1 cup fresh raspberries
- ¼ cup honey
- 1 cup quartered fresh strawberries

1. Preheat oven to 400°F. For quesadillas, brush one side of each tortilla with melted butter. Place tortillas, buttered sides down, on a large baking sheet. Place Brie slices on one half of each tortilla. Sprinkle blueberries over Brie. Fold other half of each tortilla over berries. Bake for 8 to 10 minutes or until golden brown and cheese is melted.

2. Meanwhile, for sauce, in a blender container or food processor bowl combine raspberries and honey. Cover and blend or process until smooth. Serve quesadillas with raspberry sauce and strawberries. Makes 5 servings.

EACH SERVING: 269 cal., 11 g total fat (6 g sat. fat), 29 mg chol., 280 mg sodium, 37 g carbo., 4 g fiber, 7 g pro. Daily Values: 5% vit. A, 42% vit. C, 9% calcium, 8% iron.

Chocolate-Berry Meringue

PREP: 40 MINUTES **BAKE:** 1 HOUR **COOL:** 1 HOUR

- 1 recipe Chocolate Meringue
- 1 recipe Raspberry Puree
- 1 cup whipping cream
- 1 Tbsp. sugar
- ½ tsp. vanilla
- 6 cups fresh blueberries, raspberries, blackberries, and/or sliced strawberries
  Bittersweet chocolate curls or shavings

1. Prepare Chocolate Meringue and Raspberry Puree. In chilled bowl beat cream, sugar, and vanilla until soft peaks form; spread onto meringue. Top with berries and chocolate. Drizzle raspberry puree onto plates. Serve meringue wedges on top of puree. Makes 10 servings.

CHOCOLATE MERINGUE: Allow 6 egg whites to stand at room temperature for 30 minutes. Preheat oven to 350°F. Cover a very large baking sheet with parchment paper or foil. Draw a 10-inch-diameter circle on paper, leaving a 1- to 2-inch margin outside the circle; set aside. In large mixing bowl beat egg whites with electric mixer on medium to high speed until soft peaks form (tips curl). Add 1 cup sugar, 1 tablespoon at a time, beating on high speed until stiff peaks form (tips stand straight) and sugar is dissolved. Gently fold in 3 ounces bittersweet chocolate, finely shredded; 3 tablespoons unsweetened cocoa powder; and 1 teaspoon balsamic vinegar. Spread meringue on circle on prepared baking sheet. Place in oven. Immediately reduce oven temperature to 300°F. Bake for 1 hour. Remove from oven; cool completely on baking sheet on rack for about 1 hour. Carefully remove meringue from parchment; transfer to a serving platter.

RASPBERRY PUREE: In a blender container place 1½ cups fresh raspberries. Cover and blend until pureed; sieve, if desired. Transfer to a small bowl. Stir in 1 tablespoon sugar.

EACH SERVING: 274 cal., 12 g total fat (7 g sat. fat), 33 mg chol., 44 mg sodium, 39 g carbo., 6 g fiber, 4 g pro. Daily Values: 9% vit. A, 21% vit. C, 5% calcium, 5% iron.

Marzipan Cheese Tart with Warm Berry Sauce

PREP: 20 MINUTES **BAKE:** 1¼ HOURS
COOL: 1 HOUR **CHILL:** 3 HOURS

- 1 18- to 20-oz. pkg. brownie mix
- 1 7- to 8-oz. tube marzipan
- 2 15-ounce containers ricotta cheese
- 3 eggs
- ½ tsp. almond extract
- ⅓ cup orange marmalade
- 1 tablespoon balsamic vinegar
- 3 cups fresh raspberries, blueberries, blackberries, and/or sliced strawberries

1. Preheat oven to 350°F. Grease bottom and sides of a 10½×2- or 11×2-inch tart pan with removable bottom. Set aside.
2. Prepare brownie mix according to package directions. Spread in prepared pan.
3. Crumble marzipan into a large food processor bowl. Add 1 container of ricotta cheese; process until smooth. Add eggs, remaining ricotta, and almond extract; process just until combined. Spoon on top of brownie batter. Place tart on a baking sheet.
4. Bake for 1¼ hours or until center appears just set when shaken. Cool in pan on wire rack for 1 hour. Cover and chill for 3 hours. Just before serving, remove sides of pan. Transfer tart to a serving plate.
5. In a medium saucepan combine orange marmalade and vinegar; heat and stir until marmalade is melted. Remove from heat. Gently fold in berries to coat. Just before serving, slice tart and top with berry mixture. Makes 12 servings.
EACH SERVING: 417 cal., 20 g total fat (8 g sat. fat), 109 mg chol., 190 mg sodium, 46 g carbo., 2 g fiber, 13 g pro. Daily Values: 8% vit. A, 17% vit. C, 22% calcium, 10% iron.

Blueberry Danish Cobbler

PREP: 25 MINUTES **BAKE:** 25 MINUTES
COOL: 30 MINUTES

- Nonstick cooking spray
- 1 8½-oz. pkg. corn muffin mix
- 2 3-oz. pkg. cream cheese, softened
- ¼ cup sugar
- 1 tsp. lemon juice
- 1½ cups fresh blueberries
- Sweetened whipped cream or vanilla ice cream (optional)

1. Preheat oven to 350°F. Lightly coat a 2-quart square baking dish with cooking spray. Set aside.
2. Prepare muffin mix according to package directions; set aside ½ cup of batter. Spoon remaining batter into bottom of prepared baking dish.
3. In a medium mixing bowl stir together cream cheese, sugar, and lemon juice until combined. Gently fold in berries. Spoon berry mixture evenly over muffin mixture in dish; gently spread. Drop reserved batter in small mounds onto filling.

4. Bake, uncovered, for 25 minutes or until edges are golden brown. Cool on wire rack about 30 minutes before serving. If desired, top each serving with whipped cream or ice cream. Makes 6 to 8 servings.
EACH SERVING: 334 cal., 17 g total fat (6 g sat. fat), 58 mg chol., 404 mg sodium, 42 g carbo., 2 g fiber, 6 g pro. Daily Values: 8% vit. A, 6% vit. C, 9% calcium, 7% iron.

Triple Berry Pudding Cake

PREP: 25 MINUTES **BAKE:** 40 MINUTES
BROIL: 1 MINUTE **COOL:** 30 MINUTES

- 1 cup fresh or frozen blueberries, thawed
- 1 cup fresh or frozen raspberries, thawed
- ½ cup cranberries
- 1 cup all-purpose flour
- ⅔ cup granulated sugar
- 1½ tsp. baking powder
- ¼ tsp. salt
- ½ cup milk
- 2 Tbsp. butter, melted
- 1 tsp. vanilla
- ¾ cup boiling water
- ⅓ cup granulated sugar
- ⅓ cup packed brown sugar
- ¼ cup butter, melted
- ½ cup sliced almonds

1. Preheat oven to 350°F. Grease a 9×9×2-inch baking pan. Arrange blueberries, raspberries, and cranberries in pan; set aside.
2. In a medium mixing bowl combine flour, the ⅔ cup granulated sugar, baking powder, and salt. Add milk, 2 tablespoons melted butter, and vanilla; stir well. Spoon batter over berries in pan; carefully spread batter over berries.
3. In a small bowl combine boiling water and the ⅓ cup granulated sugar; pour evenly over batter. Bake for 40 minutes or until top is browned and edges are bubbly.
4. Meanwhile, in a small bowl combine brown sugar, ¼ cup melted butter, and almonds.
5. Remove cake from oven. Preheat broiler and carefully adjust oven rack so cake will be 4 to 5 inches from heat. Spoon almond mixture evenly over cake; broil for 1 to 2 minutes just until golden. Cool on wire rack for 30 minutes. Spoon warm pudding into dessert dishes. Makes 8 servings.
EACH SERVING: 335 cal., 14 g total fat (5 g sat. fat), 25 mg chol., 194 mg sodium, 50 g carbo., 4 g fiber, 4 g pro. Daily Values: 7% vit. A, 10% vit. C, 7% calcium, 8% iron.

Mixed Berry Cream Pie

PREP: 40 MINUTES **BAKE:** 50 MINUTES
CHILL: 3 HOURS

- 1 Baked Pastry Shell
- 6 cups fresh blackberries, blueberries, and/or raspberries*
- 1 cup granulated sugar
- 2 Tbsp. all-purpose flour
- 1 Tbsp. lemon juice
- 1 8-oz. carton dairy sour cream
- 3 Tbsp. all-purpose flour
- ¼ tsp. salt
- ½ cup fine dry bread crumbs
- 3 Tbsp. packed brown sugar
- 2 Tbsp. butter, melted

1. Prepare Baked Pastry Shell. Reduce oven temperature to 375°F. In a large bowl toss berries with ¼ cup of the granulated sugar, 2 tablespoons flour, and lemon juice. Transfer berry mixture to baked pastry shell. In a medium bowl combine sour cream, remaining granulated sugar, 3 tablespoons flour, and salt. Spread sour cream mixture over berries.
2. In a small bowl combine bread crumbs, brown sugar, and melted butter. Sprinkle crumb mixture over sour cream mixture. Cover edge of pie with foil. Place pie on a baking sheet. Bake about 50 minutes or until juices are clear. Cool completely on wire rack; chill 3 hours or until serving time. Makes 8 servings.
BAKED PASTRY SHELL: Preheat oven to 450°F. In a large bowl stir together 1¼ cups all-purpose flour and ¼ teaspoon salt. Using a pastry blender, cut in ⅓ cup shortening until pieces are pea-size. Sprinkle 1 tablespoon water over part of the mixture; gently toss with a fork. Push moistened dough to the side of the bowl. Repeat moistening dough, using 1 tablespoon water at a time, until all dough is moistened, using 4 to 5 tablespoons of water total. Form dough into a ball. On a lightly floured surface, use your hands to flatten dough. Roll dough into a 12-inch circle. Wrap pastry around the rolling pin. Unroll pastry into a 9-inch pie plate. Ease pastry into pie plate. Trim to ½ inch beyond edge of pie plate. Fold under extra pastry. Crimp edge as desired. Generously prick bottom and sides of pastry in pie plate with a fork. Prick all around where bottom and sides meet. Line pastry with a double thickness of foil. Bake for 8 minutes. Remove foil. Bake 5 to 6 minutes more or until golden. Cool on a wire rack.
***TIP:** Do not use more than 3 cups raspberries because they are juicier than the other berries listed.
EACH SERVING: 463 cal., 23 g total fat (10 g sat. fat), 47 mg chol., 361 mg sodium, 62 g carbo., 7 g fiber, 5 g pro. Daily Values: 13% vit. A, 31% vit. C, 6% calcium, 11% iron.

FAMILY GRILLING

Garlic-Chili-Rubbed Lamb

PREP: 15 MINUTES **MARINATE:** 4 HOURS **GRILL:** 16 MINUTES

- 4 large cloves garlic, minced
- 1/2 tsp. salt
- 1 Tbsp. chili powder
- 1 tsp. ground cumin
- 1/2 tsp. sugar
- 1/2 tsp. ground black pepper
- 1/2 tsp. dried thyme, crushed
- 1/4 tsp. ground cinnamon
- 1/4 tsp. ground allspice
- 2 to 3 tsp. olive oil
- 8 lamb rib or loin chops, cut 1 inch thick
  Grilled tomatoes (optional)

1. On a cutting board rub together garlic and salt with the flat side of a chef's knife until a paste forms. Transfer garlic paste to a small bowl. Stir in chili powder, cumin, sugar, pepper, thyme, cinnamon, and allspice. Stir in enough of the oil to make a paste.

2. Rub paste over all sides of lamb chops. Cover lamb and chill for 4 to 24 hours.

3. For a charcoal grill, arrange medium-hot coals around a drip pan. Test for medium heat above the pan. Place chops on grill rack over drip pan. Cover and grill to desired doneness, turning once halfway through grilling. Allow 16 to 18 minutes for medium rare (145°F) or 18 to 20 minutes for medium (160°F). (For a gas grill, preheat grill. Reduce heat to medium. Adjust for indirect cooking. Grill as above.) If desired, serve with grilled tomatoes. Makes 4 servings.

Healthy **EACH SERVING:** 119 cal., 7 g total fat (2 g sat. fat), 32 mg chol., 342 mg sodium, 3 g carbo., 1 g fiber, 10 g pro. Daily Values: 12% vit. A, 4% vit. C, 3% calcium, 9% iron.

Grilled Avocados

 PREP: 10 MINUTES **GRILL:** 10 MINUTES

- 1 Tbsp. olive oil
- 1 Tbsp. lime juice
- 2 large ripe avocados, halved, seeded, and peeled (about 1 pound total)
- 1/4 tsp. kosher salt or 1/8 tsp. salt
- 1/4 cup bottled picante sauce
- 1 oz. Monterey Jack or farmer cheese, shredded or crumbled (1/4 cup)
  Snipped fresh cilantro
  Salad greens (optional)
  Bottled picante sauce (optional)
  Dairy sour cream (optional)

1. Stir together oil and lime juice. Brush oil mixture over all sides of avocados. Sprinkle cut sides of avocados with salt.

2. For a charcoal grill, grill avocado halves, cut sides down, on the rack of an uncovered grill directly over medium coals for 5 minutes or until browned. Turn avocado halves cut sides up. Fill centers of avocado halves with the 1/4 cup picante sauce and shredded cheese. Cover grill and grill about 5 minutes more or until cheese begins to melt. (For a gas grill, preheat grill. Reduce heat to medium. Place avocado halves on grill rack over heat. Cover and grill as above.)

3. Remove from grill. Sprinkle tops of avocado halves with cilantro. If desired, serve on a bed of salad greens with additional picante sauce and sour cream. Makes 4 servings.

EACH SERVING: 204 cal., 19 g total fat (4 g sat. fat), 6 mg chol., 292 mg sodium, 9 g carbo., 6 g fiber, 4 g pro. Daily Values: 6% vit. A, 15% vit. C, 7% calcium, 4% iron.

Apricot-Mustard Barbecue Sauce
PREP: 15 MINUTES **COOK:** 20 MINUTES

   1 medium onion, finely chopped (1/2 cup)
   1 Tbsp. cooking oil
   1 cup apricot preserves
   2/3 cup bottled salsa
   1/4 cup Dijon-style mustard
   1/4 cup white balsamic or white wine vinegar
   1 Tbsp. Worcestershire sauce
   1/2 tsp. ground black pepper
      Beef, pork, or chicken

1. In a medium saucepan cook onion in hot oil over medium heat until tender. Stir in preserves, salsa, mustard, vinegar, Worcestershire sauce, and pepper. Bring to boiling, stirring constantly; reduce heat. Simmer, uncovered, for 20 minutes or until desired consistency, stirring occasionally. Use as a barbecue sauce for beef, pork, or chicken, brushing on the last 10 minutes of grilling or broiling. Makes 1 3/4 cups.
EACH SERVING SAUCE (1/4 CUP): 176 cal., 2 g total fat (0 g sat. fat), 0 mg chol., 304 mg sodium, 38 g carbo., 1 g fiber, 2 g pro. Daily Values: 2% vit. A, 11% vit. C, 3% calcium, 5% iron.

Gone Bananas
PREP: 30 MINUTES **GRILL:** 11 MINUTES

   2 bananas, sliced 1/2 inch thick
   2 oranges, peeled and sectioned
   2/3 cup dark sweet cherries, pitted and halved, or 1/3 cup dried tart cherries
   1/4 cup chopped walnuts or pecans, toasted
   1 Tbsp. butter
   1/4 cup honey
   1 cup shredded coconut
   1 quart vanilla, cherry vanilla, or butter brickle ice cream

1. Tear off a 36×12-inch piece of heavy foil; fold in half to make an 18×12-inch rectangle. Place bananas, oranges, cherries, and nuts in center of foil. Dot with butter. Drizzle with honey. Bring up two opposite edges of foil; seal with a double fold. Fold remaining edges together to completely enclose the mixture, leaving space for steam to build; set aside.
2. Tear off another 36×12-inch piece of heavy foil; fold in half to make another 18×12-inch rectangle. Fold up edges slightly. Spread coconut evenly over the foil. For a charcoal grill, arrange medium-hot coals around the edge of the grill. Test for medium heat in center of grill. Place coconut on foil on grill rack in center of grill. Grill, uncovered, for 4 to 6 minutes or until golden brown, stirring coconut occasionally to brown evenly (coconut will toast faster toward the end of grilling time). (For a gas grill, preheat grill. Reduce heat to medium; adjust for indirect cooking. Place coconut on foil on grill rack. Grill as directed above.) Carefully remove coconut and foil from heat; set aside.

3. Place fruit packet on grill rack in center of grill. Cover and grill about 7 minutes or until fruit mixture is hot (do not turn packet upside down). (For a gas grill, place packet on grill rack. Cover and grill as above.) Remove packet from grill.
4. Meanwhile, use a large ice cream scoop to place 6 to 8 mounds of ice cream onto coconut in foil. Using two forks or large spoons, roll ice cream in coconut to coat, shaping ice cream into balls as you roll. Place ice cream balls in serving dishes; cover and freeze until ready to serve.
5. To serve, carefully open foil packet of fruit. Let cool slightly. Spoon warm fruit and juices over ice cream balls. Serve immediately. Makes 6 to 8 servings.
EACH SERVING: 487 cal., 28 g total fat (18 g sat. fat), 96 mg chol., 136 mg sodium, 56 g carbo., 4 g fiber, 6 g pro. Daily Values: 16% vit. A, 26% vit. C, 13% calcium, 4% iron.

Grilled Florentine Flank Steak Sandwiches
PREP: 30 MINUTES **MARINATE:** OVERNIGHT **GRILL:** 17 MINUTES

   2 Tbsp. balsamic vinegar
   2 Tbsp. olive oil
   2 Tbsp. lemon juice
   2 cloves garlic, minced
   2 tsp. Dijon-style mustard
   1 tsp. fennel seeds, crushed
   1 lb. beef flank steak
   1 15-oz. can Great Northern beans, rinsed and drained
   1/4 cup dairy sour cream
   2 Tbsp. shredded Parmesan cheese
   1 Tbsp. finely chopped red onion
   1 Tbsp. snipped fresh parsley
   1 Tbsp. capers
   1/2 tsp. lemon-pepper seasoning
   12 slices Italian sandwich bread, toasted
   1 cup shredded fresh spinach
   1/2 cup roasted red sweet peppers, cut into strips

1. For marinade, in a small bowl whisk together vinegar, oil, lemon juice, garlic, mustard, and fennel seeds. Place steak in a large resealable plastic bag set in a shallow dish. Reserve 2 tablespoons of marinade. Pour remaining marinade over the steak; seal bag. Marinate in the refrigerator overnight, turning bag occasionally.
2. For bean spread, in a medium bowl use a potato masher to mash beans. Add the 2 tablespoons reserved marinade, sour cream, Parmesan cheese, onion, parsley, capers, and lemon-pepper seasoning. Stir to combine. Set aside.
3. Drain steak. For a charcoal grill, grill steak on the rack of an uncovered grill directly over medium coals for 17 to 21 minutes for medium (160°F), turning halfway through grilling. (For a gas grill, preheat grill. Reduce heat to medium. Place steak on grill rack over heat. Cover and grill as above.)

4. To serve, thinly slice steak diagonally across the grain. Spread one side of each bread slice with bean spread. Arrange steak on top of half of the bread slices, spread sides up. Top with spinach, roasted peppers, and remaining bread slices, spread sides down. Makes 6 servings.
EACH SERVING: 425 cal., 15 g total fat (5 g sat. fat), 35 mg chol., 778 mg sodium, 45 g carbo., 6 g fiber, 27 g pro. Daily Values: 12% vit. A, 65% vit. C, 16% calcium, 26% iron.

Stuffed Turkey Burgers
PREP: 30 MINUTES **GRILL:** 20 MINUTES

   1/2 cup finely chopped onion
   1/2 tsp. five-spice powder
   1 1/2 lb. uncooked ground turkey
   2 oz. Monterey Jack cheese with jalapeño peppers, shredded (1/2 cup)
   1/4 cup walnuts, toasted and chopped
   1/4 cup dried cranberries
   1/3 cup low-fat mayonnaise dressing
   1/4 cup bottled salsa
   6 kaiser buns, split and toasted
   6 romaine leaves

1. In a large bowl combine onion and five-spice powder. Add turkey; mix to combine. Shape turkey mixture into twelve 1/4-inch-thick patties. In a small bowl combine cheese, walnuts, and cranberries; spoon some of mixture on top of half of the patties, leaving a 1/2-inch border around the filling. Top with remaining patties; press edges to seal.
2. For a charcoal grill, arrange medium-hot coals around a drip pan. Test for medium heat above the pan. Place burgers on grill rack over drip pan. Cover and grill for 20 to 24 minutes or until meat is done (160°F). (For a gas grill, preheat grill. Reduce heat to medium. Adjust for indirect cooking. Grill as above.)
3. Meanwhile, in a small bowl combine mayonnaise and salsa. Spread cut sides of buns with mayonnaise mixture. Serve burgers on toasted buns with mayonnaise mixture and romaine. Makes 6 servings.
EACH SERVING: 472 cal., 22 g total fat (6 g sat. fat), 102 mg chol., 544 mg sodium, 39 g carbo., 2 g fiber, 29 g pro. Daily Values: 3% vit. A, 3% vit. C, 16% calcium, 20% iron.

NOT YOUR ORDINARY SALSA

SHERRY LITTLE, SHERWOOD, ARK.

CAROL SCHEDER, JASPER, GA.

Ginger-Pear Salsa

PREP: 20 MINUTES **CHILL:** 1 HOUR

- 2 medium ripe pears, peeled (if desired), cored, and chopped
- 1 small red sweet pepper, seeded and chopped ($^2/_3$ cup)
- 1 medium fresh jalapeño pepper, seeded and finely chopped*
- $^1/_4$ cup snipped fresh parsley
- 1 Tbsp. lime juice
- 1 tsp. minced, peeled** fresh ginger
- $^1/_8$ tsp. salt
  Cooked chicken, turkey, or pork (optional)
  Lime wedges (optional)

1. In a medium bowl combine pears, sweet pepper, jalapeño pepper, parsley, lime juice, ginger, and salt. Cover and chill for 1 to 6 hours, stirring once or twice.

2. If desired, serve with cooked chicken, turkey, or pork. If desired, accompany with lime wedges to squeeze over each serving. Makes 8 ($^1/_4$-cup) servings.

*NOTE: Because hot chile peppers, such as jalapeños, contain volatile oils that can burn your skin and eyes, avoid direct contact with chiles as much as possible. When working with chile peppers, wear plastic or rubber gloves. If your bare hands do touch the chile peppers, wash your hands well with soap and water.

**NOTE: To peel the ginger, use a spoon to scrape off the peel.

EACH SERVING: 29 cal., 0 g total fat (0 g sat. fat), 0 mg chol., 38 mg sodium, 8 g carbo., 2 g fiber, 0 g pro. Daily Values: 12% vit. A, 49% vit. C, 1% calcium, 1% iron.

Avocado-Feta Salsa

PREP: 20 MINUTES **CHILL:** 2 HOURS

- 2 plum tomatoes, chopped
- 1 avocado, halved, seeded, peeled, and chopped
- $^1/_4$ cup finely chopped red onion
- 1 clove garlic, minced
- 1 Tbsp. snipped fresh parsley
- 1 Tbsp. snipped fresh oregano
- 1 Tbsp. olive oil
- 1 Tbsp. red or white wine vinegar
- 4 oz. feta cheese, coarsely crumbled
  Pita chips or tortilla chips (optional)

1. In a medium bowl combine tomatoes, avocado, onion, garlic, parsley, oregano, oil, and vinegar. Stir gently to mix. Gently stir in feta cheese. Cover and chill for 2 to 6 hours. If desired, serve with pita or tortilla chips. Makes 12 ($^1/_4$-cup) servings.

EACH SERVING: 63 cal., 5 g total fat (2 g sat. fat), 8 mg chol., 106 mg sodium, 3 g carbo., 1 g fiber, 2 g pro. Daily Values: 4% vit. A, 7% vit. C, 5% calcium, 1% iron.

Berry Berry Salsa

PREP: 20 MINUTES **CHILL:** 2 HOURS

- 1 cup fresh blackberries
- 1 cup fresh raspberries
- 1/2 cup chopped tomato
- 1/2 cup chopped green sweet pepper
- 1/4 cup chopped red sweet pepper
- 2 Tbsp. finely chopped red onion
- 1 small fresh jalapeño pepper, seeded and finely chopped*
- 1 clove garlic, minced
- 2 Tbsp. snipped fresh cilantro
- 2 Tbsp. olive oil
- 2 Tbsp. red wine vinegar
- 1 tsp. ancho chile powder
- 1/2 tsp. ground cumin
- 1/4 tsp. salt
- 1/4 tsp. ground black pepper
  Grilled fish, chicken, or pork (optional)

1. In a medium bowl combine berries, tomato, green and red sweet peppers, onion, jalapeño, garlic, and cilantro.
2. In a small bowl combine oil, vinegar, ancho chile powder, cumin, salt, and black pepper; stir into berry mixture. Cover and chill for 2 to 8 hours.
3. If desired, serve with grilled fish, chicken, or pork. Makes 10 (3/4-cup) servings.
*NOTE: Because hot chile peppers, such as jalapeños, contain volatile oils that can burn your skin and eyes, avoid direct contact with chile peppers as much as possible. When working with chile peppers, wear plastic or rubber gloves. If your bare hands do touch the chile peppers, wash your hands well with soap and water.
EACH SERVING: 41 cal., 3 g total fat (0 g sat. fat), 0 mg chol., 63 mg sodium, 4 g carbo., 2 g fiber, 1 g pro. Daily Values: 8% vit. A, 35% vit. C, 1% calcium, 2% iron.

Black Bean and Jicama Salsa

PREP: 25 MINUTES **COOK:** 10 MINUTES

- 1 15.5-oz. can black-eyed peas with bacon and jalapeño, rinsed and drained
- 1 15-oz. can black beans, rinsed and drained
- 1 10-oz. can tomatoes and jalapeño peppers, drained
- 1 medium green or red sweet pepper, chopped
- 1 medium onion, chopped
- 1 cup bottled Italian salad dressing
- 1 tsp. ground cumin
- 1 1/2 cups finely chopped, peeled jicama
- 1/2 cup snipped fresh cilantro
  Tortilla chips (optional)

1. In a 4-quart Dutch oven combine black-eyed peas, black beans, tomatoes, sweet pepper, onion, salad dressing, and cumin. Bring to boiling; reduce heat. Simmer, uncovered, for 10 minutes. Stir in the jicama. Sprinkle with cilantro. If desired, serve warm with tortilla chips. Makes 20 (1/4-cup) servings.
EACH SERVING: 79 cal., 4 g total fat (1 g sat. fat), 0 mg chol., 422 mg sodium, 10 g carbo., 2 g fiber, 3 g pro. Daily Values: 5% vit. A, 15% vit. C, 2% calcium, 5% iron.

Melon-Berry Salsa

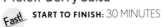 **START TO FINISH:** 30 MINUTES

- 1 1/2 cups chopped, seeded watermelon, honeydew, and/or cantaloupe
- 1 cup chopped strawberries
- 1/4 cup fresh blueberries
- 1/4 cup chopped, seeded cucumber
- 1 green onion, thinly sliced
- 1 Tbsp. finely chopped crystallized ginger
- 1 Tbsp. lemon juice
- 1 Tbsp. honey
- 1/2 tsp. toasted sesame oil
  Dash salt
  Dash cayenne pepper
  Grilled chicken, ham, or pork (optional)

1. In a medium bowl combine melon, strawberries, blueberries, cucumber, green onion, and ginger. In a small bowl combine lemon juice, honey, sesame oil, salt, and cayenne pepper; toss with fruit mixture. Serve at once or cover and chill for up to 2 hours.
2. Serve with a slotted spoon, if necessary. If desired, serve with grilled chicken, ham, or pork. Makes 10 (1/4-cup) servings.
EACH SERVING: 27 cal., 0 g total fat (0 g sat. fat), 0 mg chol., 15 mg sodium, 6 g carbo., 1 g fiber, 0 g pro. Daily Values: 3% vit. A, 20% vit. C, 1% calcium, 1% iron.

Peach and Pepper Salsa

 START TO FINISH: 30 MINUTES

- 1 large peach, peeled, pitted, and chopped, or 1 large nectarine, pitted and chopped
- 1 medium red, yellow, or green sweet pepper, chopped
- 1/4 cup cherry tomatoes, quartered, or grape tomatoes, halved
- 2 Tbsp. finely chopped celery
- 2 Tbsp. finely chopped red onion
- 1 small fresh jalapeño pepper, seeded and finely chopped*
- 1/2 of an Anaheim pepper, seeded and chopped* (1/4 cup)
- 1 Tbsp. cider vinegar
- 1 Tbsp. lime juice
- 1 1/2 tsp. sugar

- 1/4 tsp. salt
- 1/8 tsp. crushed red pepper
- 1/8 tsp. ground allspice
  Grilled beef, pork, chicken, or tortilla chips (optional)

1. In a medium bowl combine peaches, sweet pepper, tomatoes, celery, onion, jalapeño, and Anaheim pepper. In a small bowl combine vinegar, lime juice, sugar, salt, crushed red pepper, and allspice; toss with peach mixture. Serve at once or cover and chill for up to 6 hours.
2. Serve with a slotted spoon, if necessary. If desired, serve with grilled beef, pork, or chicken, or with tortilla chips. Makes 10 (1/4-cup) servings.
*NOTE: Because hot chile peppers, such as jalapeños, contain volatile oils that can burn your skin and eyes, avoid direct contact with chile peppers as much as possible. When working with chile peppers, wear plastic or rubber gloves. If your bare hands do touch the chile peppers, wash your hands well with soap and water.
EACH SERVING: 16 cal., 0 g total fat (0 g sat. fat), 0 mg chol., 60 mg sodium, 4 g carbo., 1 g fiber, 0 g pro. Daily Values: 11% vit. A, 49% vit. C, 1% iron.

Stone Fruit Salsa

PREP: 30 MINUTES **CHILL:** 30 MINUTES

- 2 large peaches, peeled, pitted, and chopped, and/or nectarines, pitted and chopped
- 1 medium avocado, halved, seeded, peeled, and chopped
- 2 medium apricots, pitted and chopped
- 2 medium plums, pitted and chopped
- 1/4 cup snipped fresh cilantro
- 1 medium fresh jalapeño pepper, seeded and finely chopped*
- 2 Tbsp. lime juice
- 1 clove garlic, minced
- 1/4 tsp. salt
  Tortilla chips, cooked fish, or chicken (optional)

1. In a medium bowl combine peaches, avocado, apricots, plums, cilantro, jalapeño pepper, lime juice, garlic, and salt. Cover and chill for at least 30 minutes before serving. If desired, serve with tortilla chips, fish, or chicken. Makes 16 (1/4-cup) servings.
*NOTE: Because hot chile peppers, such as jalapeños, contain volatile oils that can burn your skin and eyes, avoid direct contact with chile peppers as much as possible. When working with chile peppers, wear plastic or rubber gloves. If your bare hands do touch the chile peppers, wash your hands well with soap and water.
EACH SERVING: 42 cal., 2 g total fat (0 g sat. fat), 0 mg chol., 38 mg sodium, 7 g carbo., 2 g fiber, 1 g pro. Daily Values: 8% vit. A, 11% vit. C, 1% iron.

CHICKEN

Grilled Chicken Sandwiches

PREP: 35 MINUTES **MARINATE:** 1 HOUR **COOK:** 16 MINUTES
GRILL: 8 MINUTES

- 4 medium skinless, boneless chicken breast halves
- 1 recipe Marinade
- 2 medium onions, cut into ¹⁄₂-inch slices (about 4 cups)
- 2 medium red sweet peppers, cut in bite-size strips (about 2 cups)
- 2 Tbsp. olive oil
- 2 cloves garlic, minced
- 2 Tbsp. balsamic vinegar
- 3 Tbsp. butter, softened
- 1 clove garlic, minced
- 4 sandwich rolls, split
- 4 thin slices provolone cheese

1. Between two pieces of plastic wrap, pound chicken to ¹⁄₂-inch thickness. Place in resealable plastic bag set in shallow dish. Add Marinade; seal bag. Refrigerate 1 to 2 hours.
2. Drain chicken; discard Marinade. In a large skillet cook onions and sweet peppers, covered, in hot oil over medium-low heat 13 to 15 minutes or until tender; stir occasionally. Uncover; add 2 cloves minced garlic; cook and stir over medium-high heat 3 to 5 minutes more or until onions are golden. Stir in vinegar and ¹⁄₄ teaspoon each *salt* and *ground black pepper.* Cook until vinegar evaporates. Remove from heat; set aside.
3. Grill chicken on rack of uncovered grill directly over medium coals for 8 to 11 minutes or until no longer pink; turn once. Combine butter and 1 clove minced garlic. Spread on cut sides of rolls. Grill rolls, cut sides down, 1 to 2 minutes until golden. Place cheese on bottom halves of rolls. Top with chicken and vegetables. Add tops. Makes 4 servings.
MARINADE: Combine 3 tablespoons each lemon juice and olive oil; 1 tablespoon dried Greek or Italian seasoning, crushed; ¹⁄₂ teaspoon salt; and ¹⁄₄ teaspoon ground black pepper.
EACH SERVING: 627 cal., 33 g total fat (12 g sat. fat), 109 mg chol., 1,007 mg sodium, 42 g carbo., 3 g fiber, 40 g pro. Daily Values: 48% vit. A, 198% vit. C, 30% calcium, 18% iron.

Skillet Coconut Chicken

PREP: 25 MINUTES **COOK:** 20 MINUTES

- 6 medium skinless, boneless chicken breast halves
- ¹⁄₂ tsp. salt
- ¹⁄₂ tsp. ground black pepper
- 2 Tbsp. butter
- 1 14-oz. can unsweetened coconut milk
- ¹⁄₃ cup cold water
- 1 Tbsp. cornstarch
- ¹⁄₂ cup coarsely chopped almonds, toasted
- ¹⁄₂ cup snipped dried apricots
- 1 tsp. finely shredded lemon peel
- 2 Tbsp. lemon juice
- ¹⁄₄ tsp. salt
- ¹⁄₈ tsp. cayenne pepper
- 3 cups hot cooked rice
- ¹⁄₃ cup golden raisins
- 2 green onions, thinly bias-sliced

1. Place a chicken breast half between 2 pieces of plastic wrap. Using the flat side of a meat mallet, pound chicken lightly until ¹⁄₂ inch thick. Repeat with remaining chicken. Sprinkle chicken with ¹⁄₂ teaspoon salt and the black pepper.
2. In a large skillet cook chicken, half at a time, in hot butter over medium heat about 8 minutes or until no longer pink, turning once. Remove chicken from skillet; cover and keep warm.
3. Add coconut milk to skillet, stirring to scrape up any brown bits. Bring to a simmer. In a small bowl combine water and cornstarch. Add to skillet, stirring constantly. Cook and stir until thickened. Stir in almonds, apricots, lemon peel, lemon juice, ¹⁄₄ teaspoon salt, and the cayenne pepper. Serve chicken with hot cooked rice and sauce. Sprinkle with raisins and green onions. Makes 6 servings.
EACH SERVING: 556 cal., 24 g total fat (14 g sat. fat), 98 mg chol., 423 mg sodium, 43 g carbo., 3 g fiber, 41 g pro. Daily Values: 12% vit. A, 7% vit. C, 7% calcium, 20% iron.

Chicken and Spinach Salad with Avocado Dressing

START TO FINISH: 40 MINUTES

- 1 6-ounce pkg. fresh baby spinach (about 6 cups)
- 4 cups chopped or shredded cooked chicken
- 1 medium cucumber, halved lengthwise, seeded, and sliced
- 1 cup cherry tomatoes, halved
- 2 medium red, yellow, and/or green sweet peppers, cut into thin strips
- 1 small red onion, thinly sliced
- ¼ cup snipped fresh cilantro
- 1 large ripe avocado, halved, seeded, peeled, and cut up
- 2 cloves garlic, minced
- 2 Tbsp. lime juice
- 2 tsp. finely shredded lime peel
- ²/₃ cup dairy sour cream
- 2 Tbsp. snipped fresh cilantro
- ½ tsp. salt
- ⅛ tsp. ground black pepper
  Bottled hot pepper sauce

1. In a large serving bowl toss together spinach, chicken, cucumber, cherry tomatoes, sweet peppers, half of the sliced red onion, and the cilantro. Set aside.
2. For dressing, in a food processor bowl* combine avocado, remaining red onion, garlic, and lime juice. Cover and process until mixture is smooth. Stir in lime peel, sour cream, cilantro, salt, and black pepper. Season to taste with bottled hot pepper sauce. If desired, stir in 1 to 2 tablespoons *water* to make dressing of desired consistency.
3. Spoon dressing over spinach mixture. Toss gently to combine. Makes 8 servings.
*****NOTE:** If you don't have a food processor, mash avocado with a fork or a potato masher. Finely chop the onion. Stir ingredients together.

 EACH SERVING: 232 cal., 12 g total fat (4 g sat. fat), 69 mg chol., 238 mg sodium, 9 g carbo., 3 g fiber, 23 g pro. Daily Values: 70% vit. A, 115% vit. C, 7% calcium, 11% iron.

Chicken with Grilled Summer Relish

PREP: 20 MINUTES **GRILL:** 12 MINUTES

- 2 Tbsp. olive oil
- 2 tsp. Mexican seasoning
- 2 medium zucchini and/or yellow summer squash, halved lengthwise
- 1 red onion, cut into 1-inch slices
- 4 skinless, boneless chicken breast halves
- 1 6-oz. jar marinated artichoke hearts
- 3 plum tomatoes, coarsely chopped
- 2 Tbsp. snipped fresh cilantro (optional)
  Salt (optional)

1. In a small bowl combine olive oil and Mexican seasoning Brush zucchini and onion with half of the oil mixture. Brush chicken breasts on both sides with remaining oil mixture.
2. For a charcoal grill, place chicken and brushed vegetables on the rack of an uncovered grill directly over medium coals. Grill squash for 8 minutes and onion and chicken for 12 to 15 minutes or until chicken is no longer pink (170°F), turning chicken once halfway through grilling and turning vegetables occasionally to brown evenly. (For a gas grill, preheat grill. Reduce heat to medium. Place chicken and vegetables on grill rack over heat. Cover and grill as above.)
3. Transfer chicken to a serving platter; cover and keep warm. Coarsely chop zucchini and onion. Drain artichokes, reserving marinade. Coarsely chop artichokes. In a large mixing bowl combine chopped artichokes, reserved marinade, zucchini, onion, tomatoes, and, if desired, cilantro. Serve with chicken. If desired, season to taste with salt. Makes 4 servings.

 EACH SERVING: 292 cal., 12 g total fat (2 g sat. fat), 82 mg chol., 312 mg sodium, 12 g carbo., 2 g fiber, 36 g pro. Daily Values: 14% vit. A, 48% vit. C, 6% calcium, 11% iron.

Orange-Coriander Chicken Lo Mein

START TO FINISH: 40 MINUTES

- 1 tsp. finely shredded orange peel
- ³/₄ cup orange juice
- ¼ cup reduced-sodium soy sauce
- 2 Tbsp. light-colored corn syrup
- 4 tsp. cornstarch
- 1 Tbsp. rice vinegar
- 12 oz. skinless, boneless chicken breast halves, cut into thin strips
- 2 tsp. ground coriander
- ⅛ to ¼ tsp. crushed red pepper
- 6 oz. linguine, broken
- 1 Tbsp. cooking oil
- 1 tsp. toasted sesame oil
- 3 Tbsp. sliced green onions
- 1 tsp. grated fresh ginger
- 2 cups shredded bok choy or napa cabbage
- 1 cup snow pea pods, cut into thin strips
  Snipped fresh cilantro (optional)

1. For sauce, in a medium bowl combine orange peel, orange juice, soy sauce, corn syrup, cornstarch. and vinegar. Set aside. Sprinkle chicken with coriander and crushed red pepper; set aside
2. Cook linguine according to package directions. Drain and keep warm.
3. Meanwhile, in a very large skillet heat oils over medium-high heat. Add green onions and ginger to skillet. Cook and stir about 30 seconds. Add chicken; cook and stir for 2 to 3 minutes or until no longer pink. Push from center of skillet.

4. Stir sauce; add to center of skillet. Cook and stir until thickened and bubbly. Stir in bok choy, pea pods, and cooked linguine. Cook and stir 2 minutes more. Transfer to serving plate. If desired, sprinkle with cilantro. Makes 4 servings.

 EACH SERVING: 388 cal., 7 g total fat (1 g sat. fat), 49 mg chol., 655 mg sodium, 52 g carbo., 2 g fiber, 28 g pro. Daily Values: 39% vit. A, 82% vit. C, 9% calcium, 16% iron.

Southwest Chicken Salad with Mango Salsa

PREP: 30 MINUTES **MARINATE:** 30 MINUTES
GRILL: 12 MINUTES

- 2 Tbsp. chili powder
- 1 tsp. salt
- 1 tsp. garlic powder
- 1 tsp. ground cumin
- ½ tsp. ground black pepper
- ¼ tsp. cayenne pepper
- 3 Tbsp. olive oil or cooking oil
- 6 skinless, boneless chicken breast halves
- 3 medium mangoes, seeded, peeled, and cubed
- 1 cup blueberries
- ⅓ cup finely chopped red onion
- 3 Tbsp. lime juice
- 2 Tbsp. snipped fresh mint
- 2 Tbsp. honey
- ¼ tsp. crushed red pepper
- 8 cups torn mixed greens

1. In a small bowl stir together chili powder, salt, garlic powder, cumin, black pepper, and cayenne pepper. Stir in oil. Brush mixture on both sides of chicken breasts. Place in a shallow dish; cover and chill in the refrigerator for 30 minutes.
2. Meanwhile, for mango salsa, in a medium bowl combine mango, blueberries, red onion, lime juice, mint, honey, and crushed red pepper.
3. For a charcoal grill, place chicken on the rack of an uncovered grill directly over medium coals. Grill for 12 to 15 minutes or until chicken is longer pink (170°F), turning once halfway through grilling. (For a gas grill, preheat grill. Reduce heat to medium. Place chicken on grill rack over heat. Grill as above.)
4. Slice chicken into bite-size strips; toss with greens and salsa. Makes 6 servings.

 EACH SERVING: 335 cal., 10 g total fat (2 g sat. fat), 77 mg chol., 497 mg sodium, 31 g carbo., 5 g fiber, 33 g pro. Daily Values: 38% vit. A, 66% vit. C, 6% calcium, 13% iron.

PICNIC IDEAS

Minted Iced Tea

PREP: 20 MINUTES **COOK:** 5 MINUTES **STAND:** 5 MINUTES
CHILL: 4 HOURS

- 7 cups water
- 2 cups sugar
- 8 bags orange pekoe tea
- 8 sprigs fresh mint
- 8 cups cold water
- 2 cups orange juice
- ³⁄4 cup lemon juice
  Ice cubes (optional)
  Fresh mint sprigs (optional)

1. In a large saucepan combine 7 cups water and the sugar. Bring to boiling, stirring to dissolve sugar; reduce heat. Simmer, uncovered, for 5 minutes. Remove from heat. Add tea bags and 8 mint sprigs; cover and let stand for 5 minutes. Using a slotted spoon, remove tea bags and mint sprigs; discard.
2. Transfer tea to a heatproof 1½- to 2-gallon bowl or container. Add 8 cups cold water, orange juice, and lemon juice. Cover and chill at least 4 hours or up to 2 days. If desired, serve tea over ice and garnish with additional mint sprigs. Makes 16 to 18 (8-ounce) servings.

TIP: Halve recipe, if desired.

EACH SERVING: 110 cal., 0 g total fat (0 g sat. fat), 0 mg chol., 3 mg sodium, 28 g carbo., 0 g fiber, 0 g pro. Daily Values: 1% vit. A, 37% vit. C, 1% calcium, 3% iron.

Sicilian Escarole Salad

Fast! **PREP:** 20 MINUTES

- 1 recipe White Wine Vinaigrette
- 6 cups torn escarole
- 6 cups torn leaf lettuce
- 1 large English cucumber, quartered lengthwise and cut into ½-inch pieces
- 1 cup pitted ripe olives or oil-cured black olives, chopped
- 1 cup thinly sliced red or Vidalia onion
- 3 cups assorted stir-ins: chopped roasted red sweet peppers, drained and rinsed cannellini beans, drained and flaked Italian tuna (packed in oil), Parmesan croutons, tomato slices, snipped fresh basil, snipped fresh oregano, chopped salami, chopped mortadella, cubed Asiago cheese, shredded provolone cheese

1. Prepare White Wine Vinaigrette. In a very large salad bowl combine escarole, lettuce, cucumber, olives, and onion. Add desired stir-ins. Just before serving, pour White Wine Vinaigrette over salad and toss well. Makes 12 to 16 servings.
WHITE WINE VINAIGRETTE: In a screw-top jar combine ⅓ cup olive oil; 2 tablespoons white wine vinegar; one 2-ounce can anchovy fillets, drained and chopped; 3 cloves garlic, minced; ½ teaspoon dried basil, crushed; ½ teaspoon dried oregano, crushed; ¼ teaspoon sea salt or salt; ¼ teaspoon crushed red pepper; and ⅛ teaspoon ground black pepper. Cover and shake well. Set aside.

EACH SERVING (WITHOUT STIR-INS): 93 cal., 8 g total fat (1 g sat. fat), 4 mg chol., 319 mg sodium, 4 g carbo., 2 g fiber, 2 g pro. Daily Values: 54% vit. A, 14% vit. C, 5% calcium, 7% iron.

Apple-Walnut Bread Salad with Cranberry Vinaigrette

 START TO FINISH: 25 MINUTES

    4   cups cubed Italian or French bread
        (4 ounces)
 1/2   cup coarsely chopped walnuts
 1/3   cup cranberry juice
 1/3   cup snipped dried cranberries
 1/4   cup olive oil
    1   Tbsp. finely chopped shallots
    2   tsp. sugar
 1/2   tsp. snipped fresh rosemary
 1/4   tsp. salt
 1/8   tsp. ground black pepper
    2   large apples, cored and chopped
    5   cups torn romaine lettuce
    1   small cucumber, halved lengthwise,
        seeded, and sliced

1. Preheat oven to 350°F. Spread bread cubes and walnuts in a 15×10×1-inch baking pan. Bake for 8 to 10 minutes or until nuts are toasted, stirring once.
2. Meanwhile, in a 3-cup nonmetal covered container combine cranberry juice, dried cranberries, oil, shallots, sugar, rosemary, salt, and pepper. Stir in apples. Pack in an insulated container or cover and chill for up to 4 hours.
3. In a large covered container combine romaine, cucumber, bread cubes, and walnuts. Pack in an insulated container or cover and chill for up to 4 hours.
4. To serve, gently shake dressing in covered container to combine; pour over romaine mixture and toss to combine. Makes 8 to 10 side-dish servings.
EACH SERVING: 211 cal., 12 g total fat (2 g sat. fat), 0 mg chol., 166 mg sodium, 25 g carbo., 3 g fiber, 3 g pro. Daily Values: 42% vit. A, 24% vit. C, 4% calcium, 7% iron.

Barley Corn Salad

PREP: 15 MINUTES **COOK:** 45 MINUTES
STAND: 30 MINUTES

    1   cup regular barley
    2   14-oz. cans chicken broth
 1 1/2   cups fresh corn kernels (3 ears)* or one
        15 1/4-oz. can whole kernel corn, drained
    1   large red sweet pepper, chopped (1 cup)
 1/2   cup chopped red onion
    1   small bunch parsley, finely snipped
        (1/2 cup)
 1/2   cup drained pimiento-stuffed green
        olives, sliced
 1/4   cup rice vinegar
    3   Tbsp. olive oil
    1   tsp. salt
 1/2   tsp. lemon-pepper seasoning

1. In a large saucepan combine barley and chicken broth. Bring to boiling; reduce heat. Cover and simmer for 45 minutes or until barley is tender and most of the liquid is absorbed. Drain; rinse with cold water. Drain again.

2. In a large bowl stir together barley, corn, sweet pepper, onion, parsley, and olives. For dressing, in a small bowl whisk together rice vinegar, olive oil, salt, and lemon-pepper seasoning. Pour dressing over vegetable mixture and toss to coat. Cover and let stand for 30 minutes before serving. (Or cover and chill up to 24 hours. Let stand at room temperature for 30 minutes before serving.) Makes 10 to 12 servings.
***NOTE:** If using fresh corn, cook corn, covered, in boiling water for 4 minutes or until corn is just tender. Drain. Set aside to cool. When cool enough to handle, use a sharp knife to cut kernels from cobs.
EACH SERVING: 145 cal., 6 g total fat (1 g sat. fat), 1 mg chol., 771 mg sodium, 21 g carbo., 4 g fiber, 4 g pro. Daily Values: 16% vit. A, 59% vit. C, 2% calcium, 7% iron.

Cheese and Salmon Lasagna Bites

PREP: 25 MINUTES **CHILL:** 2 HOURS

    3   lasagna noodles
    1   4-oz. container semisoft cheese with
        garden vegetables or garlic and herb
    2   Tbsp. crème fraîche or dairy sour cream
    1   tsp. finely shredded lemon peel
    1   Tbsp. lemon juice
    1   3-oz. piece smoked salmon (skin and
        bones removed), flaked
    1   Tbsp. finely snipped fresh chives

1. Cook lasagna noodles according to package directions. Drain, rinse with cold water, and drain again. Pat dry with paper towels. Halve noodles crosswise. Set aside.
2. In a small bowl stir together cheese, crème fraîche, lemon peel, and lemon juice. Gently stir in salmon and chives. Spread mixture evenly on lasagna noodles. Roll up and wrap each in plastic wrap. Cover and chill at least 2 hours. Cut each roll in half crosswise. Cover and chill for up to 24 hours.
3. Pack in an insulated container with an ice pack. Makes 12 appetizer rolls.
EACH ROLL: 70 cal., 4 g total fat (3 g sat. fat), 14 mg chol., 57 mg sodium, 4 g carbo., 0 g fiber, 3 g pro. Daily Values: 2% vit. A, 2% vit. C, 1% calcium, 1% iron.

Hazelnut Picnic Cake

PREP: 15 MINUTES **BAKE:** 30 MINUTES

    1   16-oz. pkg. pound cake mix
    2   Tbsp. chocolate-hazelnut spread
 1/3   cup hazelnuts (filberts), toasted, skinned,*
        and chopped
 1/3   cup toffee pieces
 1/3   cup chocolate-hazelnut spread (such as
        Nutella)
 3/4   cup miniature semisweet chocolate
        pieces

1. Preheat oven to 350°F. Grease a 13×9×2-inch baking pan; set aside.
2. In a large mixing bowl prepare cake mix according to package directions, except add 2 tablespoons chocolate-hazelnut spread to bowl before beating the batter. Spread batter in the prepared pan. In a small bowl combine hazelnuts, toffee pieces, and 1/3 cup chocolate-hazelnut spread (mixture will be thick). Spoon mixture on top of cake in 25 to 30 small mounds (about 1 rounded teaspoon each).
3. Bake for 30 to 35 minutes or until a wooden toothpick inserted near the center comes out clean. Sprinkle chocolate pieces on top of hot cake. Cool cake completely on a wire rack. If chocolate pieces are too soft after cooling cake, chill the cake for 15 minutes before serving. Makes 16 to 18 servings.
***TIP:** To toast and skin hazelnuts, preheat oven to 350°F. Spread hazelnuts in a shallow baking pan. Bake for 5 to 8 minutes or until skins flake off easily. Using a clean cloth kitchen towel, gently rub nuts together to remove most of the skins.
EACH SERVING: 222 cal., 10 g total fat (3 g sat. fat), 31 mg chol., 132 mg sodium, 32 g carbo., 1 g fiber, 3 g pro. Daily Values: 2% calcium, 4% iron.

Honey Lime Potato Salad

PREP: 30 MINUTES **CHILL:** 4 HOURS

    3   lb. small red potatoes
    1   small red onion, finely chopped (about
        1 cup)
 1/2   cup chopped pecans, toasted
 1/4   cup coarsely chopped fresh celery leaves
    1   8-oz. carton dairy sour cream
    3   Tbsp. bottled Key lime juice or lime juice
    2   Tbsp. honey
    2   Tbsp. sweet-hot mustard
 1/2   tsp. salt
 1/2   tsp. freshly ground black pepper
        Salt and freshly ground black pepper
    2   Tbsp. snipped fresh chives

1. Scrub potatoes. In a large pot cook potatoes, covered, in enough lightly salted boiling water to cover for 20 to 25 minutes or until tender; drain. Set aside to cool. When cool enough to handle, cut potatoes into bite-size pieces. In a very large bowl combine potato, red onion, pecans, and celery leaves.
2. In a small bowl stir together sour cream, Key lime juice, honey, mustard, 1/2 teaspoon salt, and 1/2 teaspoon pepper until smooth. Add to potato mixture; toss gently to coat. Season to taste with additional salt and pepper. Cover and chill at least 4 hours or up to 24 hours. Garnish with chives before serving. Makes 12 to 14 servings.
EACH SERVING: 156 cal., 7 g total fat (3 g sat. fat), 8 mg chol., 154 mg sodium, 21 g carbo., 2 g fiber, 3 g pro. Daily Values: 3% vit. A, 25% vit. C, 4% calcium, 7% iron.

BIRTHDAY PARTY RECIPES

CAROLYN OLESEN, TECUMSEH, NEBR.

PAMELA HASKIN, CENTRAL, ALASKA

Breakfast Birthday Cake
PREP: 25 MINUTES **COOK:** 10 MINUTES

   1 16-oz. round loaf sourdough or whole grain bread
   3 eggs
$^2/_3$ cup milk
   1 Tbsp. sugar
   1 Tbsp. vanilla
   2 Tbsp. butter
   3 cups fresh strawberries, sliced
$^1/_2$ cup strawberry preserves
   1 recipe Double Whipped Topping

1. Preheat oven to 300°F. Remove crust from bottom of loaf. Slice bread loaf horizontally into three equal layers. Save the top layer for another use (such as bread pudding or croutons). Set remaining bread portions aside. In a 2-quart square baking dish beat together eggs, milk, 1 tablespoon sugar, and 1 tablespoon vanilla; set aside. In a large nonstick skillet or on a griddle melt 1 tablespoon of the butter over medium-high heat. Dip the larger bread portion into egg mixture, letting bread soak about 1 minute on each side. Add soaked bread portion to skillet. Decrease heat to medium. Cook about 5 minutes or until golden brown, carefully turning bread slice once. Place on baking sheet and keep warm in oven. Repeat with remaining butter, bread portion, and egg mixture.

2. Meanwhile, place strawberries in a large bowl. Melt preserves in a small saucepan; pour over berries and toss to coat. Set mixture aside.

3. Place larger bread portion on a serving platter. Top with 2 cups of the strawberry mixture. Top with second bread portion. Top with some of the Double Whipped Topping and remaining strawberry mixture. Serve immediately. Cut carefully into wedges to serve. Pass remaining Double Whipped Topping. Makes 10 servings.

DOUBLE WHIPPED TOPPING: In a medium chilled bowl combine 1 cup whipping cream; $^1/_2$ of an 8-ounce container whipped cream cheese ($^1/_2$ cup); 1 tablespoon sugar; and $^1/_2$ teaspoon vanilla. Beat with an electric mixer or wire whisk until soft peaks form. Set aside.

EACH SERVING: 363 cal., 18 g total fat (10 g sat. fat), 115 mg chol., 386 mg sodium, 43 g carbo., 2 g fiber, 8 g pro. Daily Values: 13% vit. A, 45% vit. C, 9% calcium, 9% iron.

Peach Macaroon Cobbler
PREP: 15 MINUTES **BAKE:** 55 MINUTES **COOL:** 30 MINUTES

   2 29-oz. cans peach slices, drained
   1 Tbsp. cornstarch
   2 Tbsp. lemon juice
   2 Tbsp. butter, cut into small pieces
$^1/_2$ cup all-purpose flour
$^1/_2$ cup granulated sugar
$^1/_2$ tsp. baking powder
$^1/_4$ tsp. salt
   1 egg, slightly beaten
   2 Tbsp. butter, melted
$^1/_2$ tsp. vanilla
$^3/_4$ cup flaked coconut
   1 recipe Birthday Whipped Cream

1. Preheat oven to 375°F. In a large bowl combine drained peaches, cornstarch, and lemon juice; toss well. Transfer to a 2-quart square baking dish. Dot with 2 tablespoons butter. Bake for 20 minutes or until bubbly.

2. Meanwhile, for topping, in a medium bowl combine flour, granulated sugar, baking powder, and salt. Add egg, melted butter, and vanilla; stir well. Fold in $^1/_4$ cup of the coconut. Drop spoonfuls of topping over peach filling. Sprinkle with remaining coconut. Bake for 35 minutes, covering with foil after 20 minutes to prevent overbrowning. Cool about 30 minutes.

3. Serve cobbler warm with Birthday Whipped Cream. Makes 8 servings.

BIRTHDAY WHIPPED CREAM: In a medium bowl combine 1 cup whipping cream and 2 tablespoons powdered sugar; beat on medium-high speed until soft peaks form (tips curl).

EACH SERVING: 414 cal., 22 g total fat (14 g sat. fat), 84 mg chol., 195 mg sodium, 56 g carbo., 4 g fiber, 4 g pro. Daily Values: 28% vit. A, 11% vit. C, 4% calcium, 7% iron.

Fruit-Flavored Birthday Cake

Kid Friendly

PREP: 40 MINUTES **BAKE:** SEE PACKAGE **CHILL:** 1 HOUR

- 1 pkg. 2-layer-size white cake mix
- 2/3 cup frozen juice concentrate blend, thawed (any orange, peach, pineapple, or cranberry juice blend)
  Food coloring (optional)
- 1 cup tiny marshmallows
- 1 2.6-oz. pkg. whipped dessert topping mix (2 envelopes)

1. Preheat oven to 350°F. Grease and flour two 8- or 9-inch round cake pans; set aside. Prepare cake mix according to "egg white" package directions, except substitute 1/3 cup of the thawed juice concentrate for 1/3 cup of the water* called for in the directions. If desired, tint batter with food coloring. Divide batter evenly between prepared pans. Bake according to package directions. Let cool in pans on for 10 minutes. Remove from pans. Cool completely.

2. In a small saucepan combine remaining 1/3 cup juice concentrate blend and the marshmallows. Cook and stir over medium-low heat until melted. Cool for 15 minutes.

3. For frosting, in a large deep bowl prepare both packages of dessert topping mix according to package directions. When thick, gradually beat in cooled marshmallow mixture. If desired, tint with food coloring.

4. Fill and frost cake with frosting. Chill at least 1 hour before serving. Store, lightly covered, in refrigerator. Makes 12 servings.

***TIP:** Place the 1/3 cup concentrate in a 2-cup glass measure and add water to equal the amount of water called for on the package.

ONE-LAYER RECTANGULAR CAKE: Prepare cake as above but bake in a greased and floured 13×9×2-inch pan according to package directions. For frosting, prepare 1 envelope whipped topping and melt 2/3 cup tiny marshmallows in 1/4 cup juice concentrate.

EACH SERVING: 263 cal., 6 g total fat (1 g sat. fat), 0 mg chol., 308 mg sodium, 50 g carbo., 0 g fiber, 3 g pro. Daily Values: 45% vit. C, 6% calcium, 10% iron.

German-Style Pasta Salad

PREP: 40 MINUTES **CHILL:** 4 HOURS

- 12 oz. dried medium shell macaroni
- 2 hard-cooked eggs, chopped
- 1 4-oz. pkg. thinly sliced smoked salmon (lox-style), chopped
- 1/3 cup chopped red onion
- 2 Tbsp. capers, drained
- 1 8-oz. carton dairy sour cream
- 1/3 cup milk
- 1/4 cup chopped fresh dill
- 2 Tbsp. mayonnaise
- 1/2 tsp. salt
- 1/4 tsp. freshly ground black pepper
  Milk

1. Cook pasta according to package directions; drain. Rinse with cold water; drain again. In a large bowl combine drained pasta, eggs, salmon, onion, and capers.

2. For dressing, in a small bowl combine sour cream, 1/3 cup milk, fresh dill, mayonnaise, salt, and pepper.

3. Pour dressing over pasta mixture. Toss lightly to coat. Cover and chill for 4 to 24 hours. If necessary, before serving stir in additional milk to moisten. Makes 10 to 12 side-dish servings.

EACH SERVING: 230 cal., 9 g total fat (4 g sat. fat), 58 mg chol., 441 mg sodium, 27 g carbo., 1 g fiber, 9 g pro. Daily Values: 5% vit. A, 1% vit. C, 5% calcium, 7% iron.

Lemon Layer Cake with Buttercream Frosting

PREP: 30 MINUTES **BAKE:** 30 MINUTES

- 2 1/4 cups all-purpose flour
- 2 tsp. baking powder
- 1/4 tsp. baking soda
- 1/2 tsp. salt
- 2/3 cup butter, softened
- 1 1/2 cups granulated sugar
- 3/4 cup cold water
- 1 Tbsp. finely shredded lemon peel
- 2 tablespoons lemon juice
- 4 egg whites
- 1 recipe Lemon Syrup
- 1/2 cup butter, softened
- 6 cups powdered sugar (about 1 1/3 pounds)
- 2 tsp. finely shredded lemon peel
- 4 tsp. lemon juice
- 1 to 3 Tbsp. milk
  Fresh raspberries

1. Preheat oven to 375°F. Grease and flour two 8-inch round cake pans; set aside. In a medium bowl combine flour, baking powder, baking soda, and salt; set aside.

2. For cake, in a large bowl beat 2/3 cup butter with an electric mixer on medium to high speed for 30 seconds. Add 1 1/2 cups granulated sugar; beat until well combined. Combine water, the 1 tablespoon lemon peel, and the 2 tablespoons lemon juice. Alternately add flour mixture and lemon mixture, beating well after each addition. Thoroughly wash beaters. In another medium bowl beat egg whites until stiff peaks form (tips stand straight). Fold about one-fourth of the egg whites into the butter mixture; fold in remaining whites. Spread batter into prepared pans.

3. Bake for 30 minutes or until toothpicks inserted near centers come out clean. Cool cake layers in pans on wire racks for 10 minutes. Remove cake layers from pans. Gently prick layers with a long-tined fork. Spoon warm Lemon Syrup over cake layers.

4. For frosting, in a large bowl beat 1/2 cup butter on medium to high speed for 30 seconds. Beat in 3 cups of the powdered sugar; beat in 2 teaspoons lemon peel and 4 teaspoons lemon juice. Beat in remaining powdered sugar and enough milk to make spreading consistency.

5. Frost tops and sides of cake with lemon frosting. Garnish with fresh raspberries. Makes 10 to 12 servings.

LEMON SYRUP: In a small saucepan combine 1/4 cup sugar, 1/4 cup water, and 2 tablespoons lemon juice; heat and stir just until warm and sugar dissolves. Set aside.

EACH SERVING: 672 cal., 23 g total fat (12 g sat. fat), 60 mg chol., 382 mg sodium, 115 g carbo., 1 g fiber, 4 g pro. Daily Values: 14% vit. A, 11% vit. C, 3% calcium, 7% iron.

Warm Banana Bread Cobbler

PREP: 20 MINUTES **BAKE:** 25 MINUTES

- 1 cup self-rising flour
- 1 cup granulated sugar
- 3/4 cup milk
- 1/2 cup butter, melted
- 1 tsp. vanilla
- 4 medium bananas, peeled and sliced (about 4 cups)
- 1 cup rolled oats
- 3/4 cup packed brown sugar
- 1/2 cup self-rising flour
- 1/2 cup butter
- 1/2 cup chopped walnuts
  Vanilla ice cream

1. Preheat oven to 375°F. Butter a 3-quart rectangular baking dish; set aside.

2. In a medium bowl stir together 1 cup self-rising flour and granulated sugar; add milk, 1/2 cup melted butter, and vanilla. Stir until smooth. Spread evenly in prepared baking dish. Top with sliced bananas.

3. In a large bowl combine oats, brown sugar, and 1/2 cup self-rising flour. Using a pastry blender, cut in 1/2 cup butter until crumbly. Stir in walnuts. Sprinkle mixture over bananas. Bake for 25 to 30 minutes or until browned and set. Serve warm with vanilla ice cream. Makes 12 to 16 servings.

EACH SERVING: 420 cal., 21 g total fat (9 g sat. fat), 44 mg chol., 327 mg sodium, 57 g carbo., 3 g fiber, 5 g pro. Daily Values: 11% vit. A, 6% vit. C, 10% calcium, 9% iron.

CHEESE IDEAS

Manchego-Mushroom Quesadillas

Fast! **PREP:** 25 MINUTES **COOK:** 2 MINUTES PER BATCH

- 4 slices bacon, chopped
- ¼ cup chopped onion
- 1 clove garlic, minced
- 8 oz. portobello or button mushrooms, cut into bite-size pieces
- ¼ tsp. crushed red pepper
- ¼ tsp. Worcestershire sauce
- 2 Tbsp. snipped fresh cilantro
- 1 Tbsp. butter, cut into 4 pieces
- 4 oz. Manchego or Monterey Jack cheese, shredded (1 cup)
- 4 7- or 8-inch flour tortillas
- ½ cup dairy sour cream
- ⅓ cup chopped tomato
- ⅓ cup chopped green sweet pepper and/or 2 Tbsp. chopped, seeded jalapeño pepper*
- 2 Tbsp. sliced green onion

1. Preheat oven to 300°F. In a large skillet cook bacon over medium heat until bacon starts to crisp, stirring often. Add onion and garlic; cook and stir for 5 minutes or until onion is tender. Add mushrooms; cook and stir until tender. Remove from heat. Stir in crushed red pepper, Worcestershire sauce, and cilantro.
2. In another large skillet melt 1 piece of the butter over medium heat. For quesadilla, sprinkle ¼ cup of the cheese over half of each tortilla. Top cheese with ⅓ cup mushroom mixture. Fold tortillas in half, pressing gently. In prepared skillet cook one quesadilla for 2 to 3 minutes or until lightly browned, turning once. Remove from skillet; place on baking sheet. Keep warm in a 300°F oven. Repeat with remaining butter and quesadillas. Spoon sour cream into a bowl; sprinkle with tomato, sweet pepper, and green onion. Cut quesadillas into wedges; serve with sour cream sauce. Makes 4 appetizer servings.
***NOTE:** Because hot chile peppers, such as jalapeños, contain volatile oils that can burn your skin and eyes, avoid direct contact with chile peppers as much as possible. When working with chile peppers, wear plastic or rubber gloves. If your bare hands do touch the chile peppers, wash your hands with soap and water.
EACH SERVING: 392 cal., 28 g total fat (14 g sat. fat), 52 mg chol., 683 mg sodium, 23 g carbo., 2 g fiber, 13 g pro. Daily Values: 15% vit. A, 24% vit. C, 21% calcium, 9% iron.

Cheese Rolls

PREP: 40 MINUTES **RISE:** 1 HOUR 40 MINUTES **BAKE:** 25 MINUTES **COOL:** 30 MINUTES

- 1 cup warm water (105°F to 115°F)
- 1 pkg. active dry yeast
- ¼ cup sugar
- 1 egg
- ¼ cup shortening
- 3¼ to 3½ cups all-purpose flour
- 1 tsp. salt
- 2 cups shredded cheddar cheese (8 oz.)
- ¼ cup finely chopped onion
- ¼ cup snipped fresh chives
- 1 tsp. garlic salt

1. In a large mixing bowl combine water and yeast; stir until yeast is dissolved. Stir in sugar. Add egg, shortening, 1 cup of the flour, and salt. Beat with an electric mixer on low speed until combined. Beat on medium speed for 3 minutes. Using a wooden spoon, stir in as much of the remaining flour as you can. Turn dough out onto a lightly floured surface. Knead in enough of the remaining flour to made a moderately soft dough that is smooth and elastic (3 to 5 minutes total). Shape dough into a ball. Place in a greased bowl; turn once. Cover; let rise in a warm place until double in size (about 1 hour).
2. Punch dough down; turn out onto a lightly floured surface. Cover; let rest for 10 minutes. Meanwhile, lightly grease a 9×9×2-inch baking pan. In a medium bowl combine cheese, onion, chives, and garlic salt. Roll dough into a 15×12-inch rectangle. Sprinkle cheese mixture over dough. Roll up starting from a long side. Seal seam. Cut into 9 slices. Place, slices cut sides, down in prepared pan. Cover and let rise 40 minutes or until almost double in size.
3. Preheat oven to 375°F. Bake for 25 to 30 minutes or until tops are golden. Cool in pan on wire rack for 10 minutes. Remove from pan. Cool about 20 minutes more before serving. Makes 9 rolls.
EACH ROLL: 336 cal., 15 g total fat (7 g sat. fat), 50 mg chol., 531 mg sodium, 38 g carbo., 1 g fiber, 12 g pro. Daily Values: 7% vit. A, 2% vit. C, 19% calcium, 13% iron.
FROZEN BREAD DOUGH OPTION: If desired, in place of the yeast dough mixture, thaw a 1-pound loaf frozen bread dough and let rise according to package directions. Roll out, fill, slice, let rise, and bake as directed above.

Apricot-Lime Almond Spread

PREP: 20 MINUTES **CHILL:** 1 HOUR
STAND: 30 MINUTES

- ½ cup dried apricots
- 1½ tsp. finely shredded lime peel
- 2 Tbsp. lime juice
- 4 oz. Havarti cheese, cubed
- 1 8-oz. tub cream cheese spread
- ¼ tsp. salt
- ¼ cup almonds, toasted
    Pear slices, apple slices, and/or assorted crackers (optional)

1. Place apricots, lime peel, and lime juice in a food processor bowl.* Cover and process with on/off turns until chopped, stopping and scraping down sides occasionally (do not puree). Transfer mixture to a small bowl; set aside.
2. Add Havarti, cream cheese, and salt to food processor. Cover and process until creamy. Add almonds; cover and process until nuts are finely chopped. Transfer mixture to bowl with apricot mixture; stir until combined. Cover and chill for at least 1 hour and up to 24 hours. Let stand at room temperature for 30 minutes before serving. If desired, serve with fruit slices and crackers. Makes 2 cups.
***NOTE:** If you don't have a food processor, snip apricots with kitchen scissors and stir together with lime peel and lime juice; set aside. Shred Havarti cheese and let cheeses stand at room temperature for 30 minutes to soften. In a medium bowl beat cheeses with salt until creamy. Finely chop almonds and stir into cheese mixture. Stir in apricot mixture. Chill and serve as above.
EACH SERVING (2 TABLESPOONS): 93 cal., 8 g total fat (3 g sat. fat), 22 mg chol., 133 mg sodium, 4 g carbo., 1 g fiber, 3 g pro. Daily Values: 6% vit. A, 1% vit. C, 5% calcium, 1% iron.

Chipotle Scalloped Sweet Potatoes

PREP: 35 MINUTES **BAKE:** 40 MINUTES
STAND: 10 MINUTES

- 2½ lb. sweet potatoes (about 3 large), peeled and thinly sliced
- ½ cup chopped onion
- 2 Tbsp. butter
- 2 Tbsp. all-purpose flour
- ½ tsp. salt
- 1½ cups milk
- 1½ tsp. finely chopped canned chipotle peppers in adobo sauce
- 6 oz. queso quesadilla, queso blanco, or Monterey Jack cheese, shredded (1½ cups)

1. Preheat oven to 350°F. In a 4-quart Dutch oven or pot cook sweet potato slices in lightly salted boiling water for 5 minutes. Drain. Set aside. Grease a 2-quart rectangular baking dish; set aside.
2. In a small saucepan cook onion in butter for 5 minutes or until tender. Stir in flour and salt. Add milk all at once; stir in chipotle peppers. Cook and stir over medium heat until thickened and bubbly. Remove from heat. Stir in cheese.
3. Place half of the sliced potatoes in prepared baking dish. Cover with half of the sauce. Repeat potato and sauce layers.
4. Bake, covered, for 25 minutes. Uncover and bake for 15 minutes more or until bubbly. Let stand for 10 minutes before serving. Makes 8 to 10 servings.
EACH SERVING: 169 cal., 6 g total fat (3 g sat. fat), 19 mg chol., 234 mg sodium, 24 g carbo., 3 g fiber, 6 g pro. Daily Values: 273% vit. A, 32% vit. C, 15% calcium, 5% iron.

Dried Fig, Pistachio, and Cheese Bruschetta

PREP: 25 MINUTES **BROIL:** 4 MINUTES
STAND: 30 MINUTES

- 1 8-oz. baguette
- 3 Tbsp. olive oil
    Dash cayenne pepper
- 1 3-oz. pkg. cream cheese
- 2 oz. fontina or provolone cheese, shredded (½ cup)
- 3 oz. goat cheese (chèvre)
- ¼ cup snipped dried figs
- 1 Tbsp. balsamic vinegar
- ½ cup chopped pistachio nuts

1. Cut baguette into ¼-inch slices. Combine olive oil and cayenne pepper; brush on both sides of bread slices. Broil slices 3 to 4 inches from heat about 2 minutes per side or until toasted.
2. In a medium bowl let cream cheese, fontina, and goat cheese stand at room temperature for 30 minutes. In a small bowl combine figs and vinegar; let stand at room temperature for 30 minutes. With an electric mixer beat cheese until well combined; stir in figs.
3. To serve, place toasts in a basket, place cheese mixture in a serving crock, and place pistachios in a small bowl. Let guests assemble their own bruschetta. Makes 16 servings.
MAKE AHEAD: Baguette slices may be prepared 1 day ahead. Store at room temperature in an airtight container. Prepare cheese mixture up to 2 days ahead. Store, covered, in refrigerator. Let stand at room temperature for 30 minutes before serving.
EACH SERVING: 139 cal., 9 g total fat (3 g sat. fat), 12 mg chol., 166 mg sodium, 11 g carbo., 1 g fiber, 4 g pro. Daily Values: 2% vit. A, 5% calcium, 4% iron.

Individual Swiss and Spinach Dips

PREP: 10 MINUTES **BAKE:** 8 MINUTES
COOK: 5 MINUTES

- 8 hard rolls
- 1 Tbsp. butter
- ¼ cup chopped onion
- 1 10-oz. pkg. frozen chopped spinach, thawed and well drained
- 1 8-oz. container Swiss cold-pack cheese food
- 2 Tbsp. milk
- 3 Tbsp. grated Parmesan cheese
- ¼ cup sliced almonds, toasted
    Vegetable dippers

1. Preheat oven to 400°F. Cut a slice from the top of each hard roll. Hollow out rolls, leaving a ¼- to ½-inch shell (save tops and hollowed-out portion to use for soft bread crumbs). Arrange rolls, hollowed sides up, on a baking sheet. Bake for 8 to 10 minutes or until lightly toasted.
2. Meanwhile, in a medium saucepan melt butter; add onion. Cook until onion is tender. Stir in spinach, cheese, and milk; cook and stir until cheese melts and mixture is heated through. Remove from heat. Stir in 2 tablespoons Parmesan cheese. Divide mixture among prepared rolls. Sprinkle with almonds and remaining Parmesan.
3. Serve with vegetable dippers. Makes 8 servings.
EACH SERVING: 317 cal., 14 g total fat (6 g sat. fat), 29 mg chol., 840 mg sodium, 34 g carbo., 3 g fiber, 15 g pro. Daily Values: 109% vit. A, 5% vit. C, 32% calcium, 13% iron.

Couscous Salad with Garlic-Buttered Shrimp

PREP: 30 MINUTES **MARINATE:** 1 HOUR **COOK:** 3 MINUTES

- 24 large fresh or frozen shrimp in shells
- 1 Tbsp. olive oil
- 4 cloves garlic, minced
- 1 tsp. dried tarragon, crushed
- 1/2 tsp. dried thyme, crushed
- 1/4 tsp. Old Bay seasoning
- 1 5.6-oz. pkg. toasted pine nut-flavored couscous mix
- 1 1/4 cups chicken broth
- 1 8-oz. jar oil-packed dried tomatoes, drained and chopped
- 2/3 cup sliced green onions
- 1/3 cup lemon juice
- 1/4 cup butter, melted
- 1 6-oz. pkg. fresh baby spinach
- 12 pitted kalamata or ripe olives, halved
- 1 Tbsp. snipped fresh parsley (optional)
  Shredded Parmesan cheese

1. Thaw shrimp, if frozen. Peel and devein shrimp, removing tails. Rinse shrimp; pat dry with paper towels. Place shrimp in a large resealable plastic bag. Add olive oil, garlic, tarragon, thyme, and Old Bay seasoning. Seal and turn to coat shrimp evenly. Marinate in the refrigerator for 1 hour.
2. Meanwhile, prepare couscous according to package directions using the 1 1/4 cups chicken broth and stirring tomatoes and onions in with couscous. Set aside.
3. In a small bowl combine lemon juice and butter; set aside. In a large skillet cook and stir shrimp with marinade over medium heat for 3 to 5 minutes or until shrimp turn opaque. Pour half of the butter mixture over shrimp.
4. To serve, arrange spinach on a serving platter or divide among 4 bowls. Spoon couscous mixture over spinach. Arrange shrimp over couscous and spoon remaining butter mixture over all. Top with olives and, if desired, parsley. Sprinkle with Parmesan cheese. Makes 4 to 6 servings.
EACH SERVING: 605 cal., 31 g total fat (10 g sat. fat), 211 mg chol., 1,362 mg sodium, 51 g carbo., 9 g fiber, 36 g pro. Daily Values: 112% vit. A, 142% vit. C, 25% calcium, 36% iron.

Mushroom-Artichoke Soup

PREP: 40 MINUTES **COOK:** 35 MINUTES

- 1 lb. fresh cremini mushrooms, sliced
- 1 lb. fresh shiitake mushrooms, stemmed and sliced
- 1 cup thinly sliced shallots
- 2 large carrots, sliced
- 1/4 cup butter
- 3 Tbsp. all-purpose flour
- 1/2 tsp. dried thyme, crushed
- 1/2 tsp. garlic powder
- 1/2 tsp. salt
- 1/2 tsp. ground black pepper
- 1/4 tsp. crushed red pepper (optional)
- 2 14-oz. cans chicken broth
- 2 13 3/4- to 14 3/4-oz. cans artichoke hearts, drained and quartered
- 1/4 cup oil-packed dried tomatoes, drained and chopped
- 1 bay leaf
- 1 cup half-and-half or light cream
  Green onions, sliced or cut in thin strips (optional)

1. In a 5 1/2- or 6-quart Dutch oven cook mushrooms, shallots, and carrots in hot butter about 15 minutes or until mushrooms are tender, stirring occasionally. Stir in flour, thyme, garlic powder, salt, black pepper, and, if desired, crushed red pepper. Add broth all at once. Cook and stir until soup is slightly thickened and bubbly.
2. Stir in artichokes, tomatoes, and bay leaf. Cover and simmer for 15 minutes. Stir in half-and-half; heat through. Discard bay leaf. If desired, garnish with green onions. Makes 10 appetizer servings.
EACH SERVING: 172 cal., 9 g total fat (4 g sat. fat), 23 mg chol., 762 mg sodium, 20 g carbo., 4 g fiber, 6 g pro. Daily Values: 51% vit. A, 11% vit. C, 7% calcium, 14% iron.

Asian Salmon with Oven-Roasted Sweet Potatoes

PREP: 30 MINUTES **ROAST:** 35 MINUTES
COOK: 5 MINUTES

2 lb. sweet potatoes (4 medium)
1 Tbsp. cooking oil
2 Tbsp. toasted sesame oil
    Salt and ground black pepper
1/3 cup reduced-sodium teriyaki sauce
2 cloves garlic, minced
2 Tbsp. apricot preserves
2 Tbsp. dry sherry or orange juice
1 Tbsp. finely chopped pickled ginger or
    2 teaspoons grated fresh ginger
1 tsp. Dijon-style mustard
1/4 tsp. freshly ground black pepper
1 1 3/4-lb. salmon fillet, skinned
1/4 cup sliced green onions
1 Tbsp. sesame seeds, toasted

1. Preheat oven to 425°F. Peel sweet potatoes. Cut into 1 1/2-inch chunks. In a large bowl combine potatoes, cooking oil, and 1 tablespoon of the sesame oil. Sprinkle lightly with salt and pepper. Toss to coat. Place sweet potatoes in a large roasting pan. Roast, uncovered, for 15 minutes.

2. Meanwhile, in a small saucepan stir together teriyaki sauce, garlic, apricot preserves, dry sherry, ginger, remaining 1 tablespoon sesame oil, mustard, and pepper. Bring to boiling; reduce heat. Simmer, uncovered, for 5 minutes or until slightly thickened, stirring occasionally. Reserve 1/4 cup sauce.

3. Push sweet potatoes to the outside of the roasting pan; place salmon in center. Spoon remaining sauce over salmon and potatoes.

4. Roast, uncovered, for 20 to 25 minutes or until fish flakes easily. Carefully transfer fish and potatoes to a serving platter. Drizzle with reserved sauce. Sprinkle with green onions and sesame seeds. Makes 6 servings.

EACH SERVING: 470 cal., 22 g total fat (4 g sat. fat), 77 mg chol., 500 mg sodium, 35 g carbo., 5 g fiber, 30 g pro. Daily Values: 398% vit. A, 56% vit. C, 7% calcium, 10% iron.

Gorgonzola-Sauced Tortellini with Artichokes

Fast! **START TO FINISH:** 30 MINUTES

2 9-oz. pkg. refrigerated cheese-filled spinach tortellini
1 lb. bulk sweet or hot Italian sausage
12 oz. cremini, stemmed shiitake, or button mushrooms, sliced
1 large onion, cut into thin wedges
8 oz. Gorgonzola cheese, crumbled
2 14 1/2-oz. cans diced tomatoes with basil, garlic, and oregano, drained
1 13 3/4- to 14 3/4-oz. can artichoke hearts, drained and quartered
2 Tbsp. finely shredded Parmesan cheese
2 Tbsp. thinly sliced fresh basil

1. Cook tortellini according to package instructions; drain. Meanwhile, in a 6-quart Dutch oven cook sausage, mushrooms, and onion until sausage is no longer pink and onion is tender, breaking up sausage with a wooden spoon. Drain off fat.

2. Add Gorgonzola cheese; cook and stir over low heat until cheese melts. Gently stir in tortellini, tomatoes, and artichokes. Heat through. Top with Parmesan cheese and basil. Makes 8 servings.

EACH SERVING: 483 cal., 25 g total fat (12 g sat. fat), 83 mg chol., 1,575 mg sodium, 36 g carbo., 4 g fiber, 25 g pro. Daily Values: 23% vit. A, 18% vit. C, 38% calcium, 24% iron.

Green Bean Salad with Salmon and Walnuts

START TO FINISH: 45 MINUTES

1 1/2 lb. fresh green beans or three 9-ounce pkg. frozen whole green beans
1 large red sweet pepper, seeded and cut into thin strips
1 4-oz. pkg. cracked pepper smoked salmon, skinned and broken into chunks
1/2 cup chopped red onion
1/4 cup olive oil
1/4 cup balsamic vinegar
1 Tbsp. honey
1 Tbsp. Dijon-style mustard
1 clove garlic, minced
1/4 tsp. salt
1 recipe Sugared Walnuts

1. Remove ends and strings from fresh beans. In a 4-quart Dutch oven cook fresh green beans, covered, in lightly salted boiling water for 5 to 7 minutes or until crisp-tender. Or cook frozen beans according to package directions. Drain. Submerge beans in a very large bowl of ice water to cool quickly; drain well. Combine beans, sweet pepper, salmon, and red onion. Divide bean mixture among 8 salad plates or transfer to a serving dish.

2. In a small bowl whisk together olive oil, vinegar, honey, mustard, garlic, and salt. Drizzle over bean mixture. Top with Sugared Walnuts. Makes 8 servings.

SUGARED WALNUTS: Preheat oven to 325°F. Lightly coat an 8×8×2-inch baking pan with nonstick cooking spray. In a small bowl combine 1/2 cup broken walnuts, 1 tablespoon light-colored corn syrup, 4 teaspoons sugar, and 1/8 teaspoon cayenne pepper. Spread mixture evenly in bottom of prepared pan. Bake, uncovered, for 15 minutes, stirring once. Spread on foil, separating nuts. Cool at least 15 minutes. Makes about 3/4 cup.

EACH SERVING: 202 cal., 13 g total fat (2 g sat. fat), 10 mg chol., 308 mg sodium, 18 g carbo., 4 g fiber, 6 g pro. Daily Values: 22% vit. A, 81% vit. C, 4% calcium, 7% iron.

Southwest Chicken Salad with Cilantro-Lime Dressing

PREP: 45 MINUTES **GRILL:** 12 MINUTES

1 recipe Cilantro-Lime Dressing
3 8- to 10-inch flour tortillas (plain, tomato, and/or spinach)
4 skinless, boneless chicken breast halves
1 Tbsp. cooking oil
    Salt and ground black pepper
1/4 teaspoon chili powder
6 cups torn red tip leaf lettuce
1 large tomato, chopped
1 cup fresh or frozen whole kernel corn, thawed*
1 avocado, halved, seeded, peeled, and sliced
1/2 cup sliced green onions

1. Prepare Cilantro-Lime Dressing. Preheat oven to 350°F. Cut tortillas into thin strips; arrange in a 15×10×1-inch baking pan. Bake for 8 to 10 minutes or until crisp. Set aside.

2. Brush both sides of chicken breast halves with oil. Sprinkle with salt, pepper, and chili powder. Grill chicken on the rack of an uncovered grill directly over medium heat for 12 to 15 minutes or until chicken is no longer pink, turning once halfway through grilling. Cool chicken slightly; cut into bite-size strips.

3. Divide lettuce among 4 dinner plates. Top with tomato, corn, avocado, and green onions. Top with chicken and some of the tortilla strips. Spoon Cilantro-Lime Dressing over salads. Pass remaining tortilla strips. Makes 4 servings.

CILANTRO-LIME DRESSING: In a blender container or food processor bowl combine 1/2 cup dairy sour cream; 1/2 cup mayonnaise; 1/4 cup lime juice; 1/3 cup snipped fresh cilantro; 2 teaspoons sugar; 2 cloves garlic, minced; 1/4 teaspoon chili powder; 1/4 teaspoon ground cumin; and a dash of cayenne pepper. Cover and blend or process until smooth. Cover and chill until serving time.

*TIP: If desired, cook the fresh corn in lightly boiling salted water for 4 minutes; drain. Chill before serving.

EACH SERVING: 687 cal., 43 g total fat (9 g sat. fat), 113 mg chol., 511 mg sodium, 39 g carbo., 7 g fiber, 40 g pro. Daily Values: 150% vit. A, 61% vit. C, 14% calcium, 21% iron.

OUR FAVORITE TOPPINGS

Pumpkin Pistachio Cream Cannoli

Fast! **START TO FINISH:** 25 MINUTES

- ¹/₂ of an 8-oz. carton mascarpone cheese
- ³/₄ cup powdered sugar
- ³/₄ cup canned pumpkin
- ¹/₂ cup ricotta cheese
- 1 tsp. pumpkin pie spice
- ¹/₂ cup chopped roasted pistachio nuts or toasted pecans
- ¹/₂ cup whipping cream
- 12 purchased cannoli shells*
  Powdered sugar or granulated sugar

1. In a large bowl stir together mascarpone cheese, powdered sugar, pumpkin, ricotta cheese, and pumpkin pie spice until smooth. Stir in ¹/₄ cup of the nuts. Set aside.

2. In a chilled medium mixing bowl beat whipping cream until stiff peaks form. Fold into pumpkin mixture. If desired, cover and chill up to 4 hours.

3. To serve, spoon pumpkin mixture into a resealable plastic bag. Snip a ³/₄-inch hole in one corner. Pipe filling into cannoli shells, filling shells so pumpkin mixture is exposed on ends. Sprinkle ends of each cannoli with remaining nuts. Arrange on serving platter; sprinkle with powdered sugar. Makes 12 servings.

EACH SERVING: 276 cal., 20 g total fat (7 g sat. fat), 31 mg chol., 29 mg sodium, 22 g carbo., 2 g fiber, 7 g pro. Daily Values: 52% vit. A, 2% vit. C, 4% calcium, 7% iron.

*NOTE: If purchased cannoli are not available, brush sixteen 4-inch flour tortillas (trim larger tortillas if necessary) with cooking oil. Roll up, forming a cannoli shape, and secure with a wooden toothpick. Place a rolled piece of foil in the center for support. Place on a baking sheet; brush outside with oil and bake in a 375°F oven about 15 minutes or until golden brown. Place on a wire rack to cool. Remove foil and toothpicks; fill with pumpkin mixture. Makes 16 servings.

Silky Fruit Parfaits

PREP: 35 MINUTES **CHILL:** 25 HOURS

- 2 cups plain yogurt* or one 8-oz. carton mascarpone cheese
- 1¹/₂ cups pomegranate juice
- ¹/₃ cup granulated sugar
- ¹/₃ cup whipping cream
- 2 Tbsp. powdered sugar
- 1 tsp. vanilla
- 6 oranges, peeled and sectioned
  Pomegranate seeds or finely shredded orange peel (optional)

1. If using yogurt, line a yogurt strainer, sieve, or small colander with 3 layers of 100%-cotton cheesecloth or a clean paper coffee filter. Suspend lined strainer over a bowl. Spoon yogurt into strainer. Cover with plastic wrap. Chill for 24 hours to 48 hours. (If using mascarpone cheese, omit this step.)

2. Meanwhile, for pomegranate syrup, in a medium saucepan combine pomegranate juice and granulated sugar. Bring to boiling; reduce heat. Boil gently, uncovered, for 20 to 25 minutes or until reduced by half (about ³/₄ cup). Transfer to a small bowl; cover and chill for 1 to 24 hours.

3. Remove yogurt cheese from refrigerator, if using. Discard liquid in bowl; set yogurt aside. In a chilled medium bowl beat whipping cream, powdered sugar, and vanilla with an electric mixer on medium speed or a wire whisk until soft peaks form. Fold in yogurt or, if using, mascarpone cheese. Cover and chill for 1 hour to 4 hours.

4. Divide oranges among 6 dessert dishes. Spoon yogurt mixture on top; drizzle with desired amount of pomegranate syrup. If desired, sprinkle with pomegranate seeds or orange peel. Makes 6 servings.

*NOTE: Use yogurt that contains no gums, gelatin, or fillers. These ingredients may prevent the curd and whey from separating to make the yogurt cheese.

EACH SERVING: 247 cal., 6 g total fat (4 g sat. fat), 23 mg chol., 65 mg sodium, 44 g carbo., 3 g fiber, 6 g pro. Daily Values: 11% vit. A, 129% vit. C, 21% calcium, 3% iron.

Cinnamon Plum Cobbler with Candied Ginger Topping

PREP: 25 MINUTES **BAKE:** 30 MINUTES
COOL: 45 MINUTES

  8 cups sliced, pitted plums (about 8 plums)
1/3 cup granulated sugar
  1 Tbsp. cornstarch
1/4 cup orange or apple juice
  2 tsp. ground cinnamon
1 1/2 cups all-purpose flour
1/2 cup granulated sugar
  2 tsp. baking powder
1/4 tsp. salt
  6 Tbsp. butter, cut up
  1 egg, slightly beaten
3/4 cup milk
  1 cup whipping cream
1/2 cup dairy sour cream
  2 Tbsp. packed brown sugar
  3 Tbsp. finely chopped crystallized ginger

1. Preheat oven to 350°F. Lightly grease a 13×9×2-inch baking pan; set aside. In a large saucepan toss together plums, 1/3 cup granulated sugar, cornstarch, and orange juice. Cook and stir until mixture comes to boiling; stir in cinnamon. Pour into prepared pan. Set aside.

2. In a food processor bowl place flour, 1/2 cup granulated sugar, baking powder, and salt. Cover and process with on/off turns to combine. Add butter; cover and process until mixture resembles coarse crumbs. (Or combine flour mixture in a medium bowl. Use a pastry blender to cut in butter.) Transfer mixture to a medium bowl. Combine egg and milk; stir into flour mixture. Drop dough in 10 to 12 mounds on top of hot plum mixture.

3. Bake about 30 to 35 minutes or until a wooden toothpick inserted in topper comes out clean. Cool about 45 minutes.

4. Meanwhile, in a chilled medium bowl combine whipping cream, sour cream, and brown sugar. Beat with an electric mixer until soft peaks form. Fold in ginger. Serve immediately with warm cobbler. Makes 10 to 12 servings.

EACH SERVING: 396 cal., 20 g total fat (11 g sat. fat), 79 mg chol., 190 mg sodium, 53 g carbo., 3 g fiber, 5 g pro. Daily Values: 23% vit. A, 27% vit. C, 9% calcium, 8% iron.

Fluffy Fruit Topper

PREP: 15 MINUTES **CHILL:** 1 HOUR

  1 6- to 8-oz. carton berry-flavored yogurt
1/2 jar (7-oz.) marshmallow creme (about 1 cup)
  2 Tbsp. dairy sour cream
  1 8-oz. container frozen whipped dessert topping, thawed
1/2 tsp. ground cinnamon
  1 cup blueberries and/or sliced strawberries
1/2 cup chopped pecans, toasted
    Cake squares or slices

1. In a medium bowl beat yogurt, marshmallow creme, and sour cream with an electric mixer until smooth. Fold in whipped topping, cinnamon, berries, and pecans. Cover and chill for 1 to 24 hours. Serve on squares or slices of cake. Makes 12 servings.

EACH SERVING: 135 cal., 7 g total fat (4 g sat. fat), 2 mg chol., 15 mg sodium, 16 g carbo., 1 g fiber, 1 g pro. Daily Values: 2% vit. C, 2% calcium, 1% iron.

Little Pots of Irish Cream

PREP: 20 MINUTES **CHILL:** 2 1/2 HOURS

  1 cup whipping cream
1/2 cup mascarpone cheese
  6 Tbsp. Irish cream liqueur
  1 Tbsp. sugar
1/4 tsp. vanilla
  2 oz. bittersweet or semisweet chocolate, chopped
    Chocolate Spoons (optional)

1. Chill a large mixing bowl and the beaters of an electric mixer for about 30 minutes. In chilled bowl place whipping cream, mascarpone, 4 tablespoons of the liqueur, the sugar, and vanilla. Beat with electric mixer on medium speed until soft peaks form.

2. Divide cream mixture evenly among 12 shot glasses or demitasse cups. Cover and chill for 2 to 24 hours.

3. Just before serving, in a small saucepan combine chopped chocolate and remaining 2 tablespoons liqueur. Heat and stir until chocolate is melted. Spoon on top of each cup. If desired, serve with Chocolate Spoons. Makes 12 servings.

EACH SERVING: 139 cal., 12 g total fat (8 g sat. fat), 36 mg chol., 17 mg sodium, 6 g carbo., 0 g fiber, 2 g pro. Daily Values: 6% vit. A, 1% calcium, 1% iron.

CHOCOLATE SPOONS: In a small saucepan heat 2 ounces chopped bittersweet or semisweet chocolate over low heat just until melted. Dip 12 small spoons into chocolate, tapping handle of spoon against side of pan to remove excess chocolate. Sprinkle tips of spoons with white nonpareils. Place spoons on waxed paper; chill for 30 minutes.

Raspberry Cloud Cookie Cups

PREP: 30 MINUTES **BAKE:** 15 MINUTES
COOL: 5 MINUTES

    Nonstick cooking spray
1/2 cup butter, softened
1/3 cup granulated sugar
  1 egg yolk
1/2 tsp. salt
1/4 tsp. almond extract
1 1/4 cups all-purpose flour
1/2 of an 8-oz. pkg. cream cheese, softened
2/3 cup fresh raspberries
  3 Tbsp. powdered sugar
1/4 cup frozen whipped dessert topping, thawed
    Fresh raspberries

1. Preheat oven to 325°F. For cookie cups, coat twenty-four 1 3/4-inch muffin cups with nonstick spray; set aside. In a medium mixing bowl beat butter with an electric mixer on medium speed for 30 seconds. Add granulated sugar; beat until combined, scraping sides of bowl occasionally. Beat in egg yolk, salt, and almond extract until combined. Beat in as much flour as you can. Stir in remaining flour.

2. Roll dough into 1-inch balls (about 2 teaspoons). Press dough into the bottoms and up the sides of prepared muffin cups. Bake for 15 to 18 minutes or until golden. Cool in pan on a wire rack for 5 minutes. Carefully remove and let cool completely.

3. Meanwhile, in a food processor bowl combine cream cheese, 2/3 cup fresh raspberries, and powdered sugar. Cover and process until combined. Transfer to a medium bowl. Fold in whipped dessert topping. Cover and chill until ready to serve.

4. To serve, spoon raspberry mixture into cookie cups and garnish with additional fresh raspberries. Makes 24 pastries.

EACH PASTRY: 93 cal., 6 g total fat (3 g sat. fat), 24 mg chol., 92 mg sodium, 9 g carbo., 0 g fiber, 1 g pro. Daily Values: 4% vit. A, 1% vit. C, 1% calcium, 2% iron.

Balsamic Berries with Cream

PREP: 30 MINUTES **STAND:** 30 MINUTES

  4 cups sliced fresh strawberries
  2 cups fresh blackberries
1/2 cup sugar
  2 Tbsp. balsamic vinegar
1/2 pkg. (8-oz.) reduced-fat cream cheese (Neufchâtel), softened
1/2 cup cream of coconut
1/2 container (8-oz.) frozen vanilla-flavored whipped dessert topping,* thawed
1/3 cup shredded or flaked coconut, toasted (optional)

1. In a large bowl combine strawberries, blackberries, sugar, and balsamic vinegar. Cover and let stand for 30 minutes.

2. Meanwhile, for topping, in a large bowl beat the cream cheese with an electric mixer on medium speed until smooth. Gradually add cream of coconut, beating on low speed, just until combined. Fold in whipped dessert topping.

3. To serve, spoon berries into dishes and add topping. If desired, sprinkle with toasted coconut. Makes 8 servings.

***NOTE:** If vanilla-flavored whipped dessert topping is unavailable, use regular whipped dessert topping and add 1/2 teaspoon vanilla with the cream of coconut.

EACH SERVING: 216 cal., 11 g total fat (9 g sat. fat), 11 mg chol., 59 mg sodium, 27 g carbo., 4 g fiber, 3 g pro. Daily Values: 5% vit. A, 84% vit. C, 3% calcium, 5% iron.

EIGHT FOR THE SLOW COOKER

Oriental Beef Brisket

PREP: 20 MINUTES **COOK:** 10 HOURS (LOW); 5 HOURS (HIGH)

    1   lb. baking potatoes, peeled and cut into 1-inch cubes
    1   lb. sweet potatoes, peeled and cut into 1-inch cubes
    1   3- to 3 1/2-lb. fresh beef brisket, fat trimmed
  1/2   cup bottled hoisin sauce
  1/2   cup bottled salsa
    2   Tbsp. quick-cooking tapioca
    2   cloves garlic, minced

1. In a 5- to 6-quart slow cooker place baking potatoes and sweet potatoes. Top with beef brisket. In a small bowl combine hoisin sauce, salsa, tapioca, and garlic. Pour sauce mixture over brisket and potatoes; spread evenly.

2. Cover and cook on low-heat setting for 10 hours or on high-heat setting for 5 to 5 1/2 hours. Remove meat from cooker to a cutting board. Cut across the grain into slices. Serve cooking liquid and potatoes over beef. Makes 8 servings.

Healthy **EACH SERVING:** 344 cal., 11 g total fat (3 g sat. fat), 103 mg chol., 382 mg sodium, 22 g carbo., 2 g fiber, 38 g pro. Daily Values: 104% vit. A, 24% vit. C, 4% calcium, 22% iron.

Three-Bean Vegetarian Chili

PREP: 20 MINUTES **COOK:** 6 HOURS (LOW); 3 HOURS (HIGH)

    1   15-oz. can no-salt-added red kidney beans, rinsed and drained
    1   15-oz. can small white beans, rinsed and drained
    1   15-oz. can very low sodium black beans, rinsed and drained
    1   14 1/2-oz. can diced tomatoes with green chiles, undrained
    1   cup beer or chicken broth
    3   Tbsp. chocolate-flavored syrup
    1   Tbsp. chili powder
    2   tsp. Cajun seasoning
        Dairy sour cream (optional)
        Shredded cheddar cheese (optional)

1. In a 3 1/2- or 4-quart slow cooker combine kidney beans, white beans, black beans, undrained tomatoes, beer, chocolate syrup, chili powder, and Cajun seasoning.

2. Cover and cook on low-heat setting for 6 to 8 hours or on high-heat setting for 3 to 4 hours. Ladle into soup bowls. If desired, garnish with sour cream and cheese. Makes 4 servings.

Healthy **EACH SERVING:** 308 cal., 1 g total fat (0 g sat. fat), 0 mg chol., 569 mg sodium, 60 g carbo., 21 g fiber, 21 g pro. Daily Values: 18% vit. A, 10% vit. C, 17% calcium, 31% iron.

NOTE TO READER: The "eight" in the title of this category refers to the number of ingredients (eight or less) in each of these slow-cooker recipes. The number does not include optional ingredients, salt, pepper, water, nonstick cooking spray, or slow-cooker liners.

Chicken, Barley, and Leek Stew

PREP: 20 MINUTES **COOK:** 4 HOURS (LOW);
2 HOURS (HIGH)

- 1 lb. skinless, boneless chicken thighs, cut into 1-inch pieces
- 1 Tbsp. olive oil
- 1 49-oz. can chicken broth
- 1 cup regular barley (not quick-cooking)
- 3 medium leeks, halved lengthwise and sliced
- 2 medium carrots, thinly sliced
- 1 1/2 tsp. dried basil or Italian seasoning, crushed
- 1/4 tsp. cracked black pepper
  Slivered fresh basil or snipped fresh parsley (optional)

1. In a large skillet cook chicken in hot oil until browned on all sides. In a 4- to 5-quart slow cooker combine chicken, chicken broth, barley, leeks, carrots, basil, and pepper.
2. Cover and cook on low-heat setting for 4 to 5 hours or on high-heat setting for 2 to 2 1/2 hours or until barley is tender. Season to taste with *salt* and *ground black pepper*. If desired, sprinkle with fresh basil or parsley before serving. Makes 6 servings.
EACH SERVING: 254 cal., 7 g total fat (1 g sat. fat), 63 mg chol., 1,027 mg sodium, 28 g carbo., 6 g fiber, 22 g pro. Daily Values: 55% vit. A, 8% vit. C, 4% calcium, 13% iron.

Spicy Sunday Dinner Greens

PREP: 30 MINUTES **COOK:** 7 HOURS (LOW)

- 2 lb. collard greens, trimmed and coarsely torn
- 1 large onion, chopped
- 4 cloves garlic, minced
- 3 slices bacon or turkey bacon, coarsely chopped
- 1/4 cup light-colored molasses
- 2 Tbsp. balsamic vinegar
- 1 tsp. bottled hot pepper sauce
- 1 tsp. celery salt

1. In a 5- to 6-quart slow cooker combine all ingredients and 3 1/2 cups *water* (cooker will be full). Add 1/2 teaspoon *salt* and 1/4 teaspoon *ground black pepper*. Cover and cook on low-heat setting for 7 to 8 hours, stirring once after 4 hours of cooking.
2. Using a slotted spoon, transfer greens to a serving dish, reserving cooking liquid. If desired, pass cooking liquid and spoon over each serving to moisten. Makes 8 to 10 servings.
EACH SERVING: 83 cal., 2 g total fat (1 g sat. fat), 3 mg chol., 413 mg sodium, 15 g carbo., 3 g fiber, 3 g pro. Daily Values: 82% vit. A, 26% vit. C, 12% calcium, 5% iron.

Nutty Pumpkin Pie Pudding

PREP: 20 MINUTES
COOK: 2 1/2 HOURS (HIGH)

- Nonstick cooking spray or slow-cooker liner
- 1 15-oz. can pumpkin
- 1 5-oz. can evaporated milk
- 1/3 cup sugar
- 2 Tbsp. pumpkin pie spice
- 1 1-layer-size yellow cake mix
- 1 cup pecans or walnuts, toasted and chopped
- 1/4 cup butter, melted
  Frozen whipped dessert topping, thawed (optional)

1. Coat a 3 1/2- or 4-quart slow cooker with nonstick cooking spray or line with a slow-cooker liner. In the slow cooker combine pumpkin, evaporated milk, sugar, and 1 tablespoon of the pumpkin pie spice. Spread evenly to cover the bottom of the cooker. In a medium bowl combine cake mix, pecans, and remaining 1 tablespoon pumpkin pie spice. Sprinkle mixture evenly on top of pumpkin mixture. Drizzle butter over cake mix mixture.
2. Cover and cook on high-heat setting for 2 1/2 hours.
3. Uncover and let stand 30 to 45 minutes before serving. Spoon into bowls. If desired, top with whipped dessert topping. Makes 8 servings.
EACH SERVING: 349 cal., 20 g total fat (5 g sat. fat), 21 mg chol., 278 mg sodium, 42 g carbo., 3 g fiber, 4 g pro. Daily Values: 170% vit. A, 5% vit. C, 8% calcium, 12% iron.

Scotch Broth

PREP: 25 MINUTES **COOK:** 6 HOURS (LOW);
3 HOURS (HIGH)

- 1 lb. lean boneless lamb, cut into 1/2-inch pieces
- 1 Tbsp. cooking oil (optional)
- 1 cup dry yellow split peas
- 2 stalks celery, chopped (1 cup)
- 2 medium carrots, chopped (1 cup)
- 1 large onion, chopped (1 cup)
- 1/2 cup regular barley (not quick-cooking)
- 2 32-oz. cartons chicken broth (8 cups)
- 1 tsp. dried leaf sage, crushed

1. If desired, in a large skillet brown lamb in hot oil; drain. In a 4- to 5-quart slow cooker combine lamb, split peas, celery, carrots, onion, and barley. Stir in chicken broth and sage.
2. Cover and cook on low-heat setting for 6 to 8 hours or on high-heat setting for 3 to 4 hours. Ladle soup into bowls. Makes 6 servings.
EACH SERVING: 245 cal., 5 g total fat (1 g sat. fat), 46 mg chol., 1,017 mg sodium, 28 g carbo., 6 g fiber, 24 g pro. Daily Values: 55% vit. A, 5% vit. C, 4% calcium, 12% iron.

Savory Roast with Peppers and Onions

PREP: 10 MINUTES **COOK:** 8 HOURS (LOW)
PLUS 30 MINUTES (HIGH); 4 1/2 HOURS (HIGH)

- Nonstick cooking spray or slow-cooker liner
- 1 2 1/2- to 3-lb. beef chuck pot roast
- 1 tsp. dried thyme, crushed
- 1/4 tsp. cayenne pepper
- 1 14 1/2-oz. can diced tomatoes with basil, garlic, and oregano, undrained
- 1 10 1/2-oz. can condensed French onion soup
- 1 Tbsp. Worcestershire sauce
- 1 16-oz. pkg. frozen (yellow, green, and red) peppers and onion stir-fry vegetables
- 1 1/2 cups instant white rice

1. Lightly coat a 4- to 5-quart slow cooker with nonstick cooking spray or line with a slow-cooker liner. Trim fat from roast. If necessary, cut roast to fit slow cooker. Place roast in cooker. Sprinkle roast with thyme and cayenne pepper. Add undrained tomatoes, soup, and Worcestershire sauce to cooker.
2. Cover and cook on low-heat setting for 8 to 9 hours or on high-heat setting for 4 to 4 1/2 hours. If using low-heat setting, turn to high-heat setting. Add stir-fry vegetables and rice to slow cooker; stir into mixture. Cover and cook on high-heat setting for 30 minutes. Makes 6 servings.
EACH SERVING: 534 cal., 14 g total fat (4 g sat. fat), 121 mg chol., 3,677 mg sodium, 52 g carbo., 6 g fiber, 51 g pro. Daily Values: 10% vit. A, 8% vit. C, 13% calcium, 39% iron.

Cheddar-Jelly Thumbprints

PREP: 30 MINUTES **BAKE:** 15 MINUTES PER BATCH

- 6 oz. white cheddar cheese or extra-sharp cheddar cheese, shredded (1¹/₂ cups)
- ¹/₂ cup finely shredded Parmesan cheese
- ¹/₂ cup butter, softened
- 1 egg yolk
- ¹/₄ tsp. ground black pepper
- 1 cup all-purpose flour
- 1 egg white
- 1 Tbsp. water
- 1¹/₄ cups finely chopped pecans
- ¹/₃ to ¹/₂ cup green and/or red jalapeño jelly

1. Preheat oven to 350°F. Line 2 large baking sheets with parchment paper or lightly grease baking sheets; set aside. In food processor bowl combine cheddar cheese, Parmesan cheese, and butter. Cover and process until well combined. Add egg yolk and pepper; process until combined. Add flour. Process with on/off turns until a soft dough forms; set aside. (Or in mixing bowl beat butter with electric mixer for 30 seconds; beat in cheeses until well combined. Beat in yolk and pepper until combined. Add flour; beat until soft dough forms.)

2. In a small bowl combine egg white and water. Place pecans in a shallow dish. Shape dough into ³/₄-inch balls. Roll balls in egg white mixture, then in pecans. Place balls 1 inch apart on prepared baking sheets. Press your thumb into the center of each ball, reshaping as necessary.

3. Bake about 15 minutes or until edges are firm and cookies are light golden. Press puffed centers down using the rounded side of a measuring teaspoon. Transfer to a wire rack and let cool. Just before serving, place a small amount of jelly into the center of each thumbprint. Makes about 42 appetizers.

MAKE AHEAD: Prepare as directed. Place unfilled thumbprints in layers separated by waxed paper in an airtight container. Store in the refrigerator up to 3 days or freeze for up to 3 months. Thaw in container at room temperature; fill.

EACH APPETIZER: 81 cal., 6 g total fat (2 g sat. fat), 16 mg chol., 60 mg sodium, 4 g carbo., 0 g fiber, 2 g pro. Daily Values: 3% vit. A, 5% calcium, 1% iron.

Shrimp Pinwheels

PREP: 30 MINUTES **CHILL:** 1 HOUR

- 1 ripe avocado, halved, seeded, and peeled
- ¹/₂ pkg. (8-oz.) cream cheese, softened
- ¹/₄ cup ketchup
- 1 Tbsp. prepared horseradish
- 1 tsp. finely shredded lemon peel
- 2 Tbsp. lemon juice
- ¹/₂ tsp. chili powder
- 6 9- to 10-inch tomato, spinach, and/or plain flour tortillas
- 3 cups shredded spinach leaves
- ²/₃ cup smoked almonds, chopped
- 10 oz. peeled and deveined cooked shrimp, chopped

1. In a medium bowl mash avocado with potato masher or fork. Add cream cheese; stir until smooth. Stir in ketchup, horseradish, lemon peel, lemon juice, and chili powder.

2. Spread ¹/₄ cup avocado mixture on 1 tortilla, leaving a 1-inch border around edges. Top with a layer of spinach. Sprinkle with a scant 2 tablespoons almonds and about ¹/₄ cup shrimp. Roll up tightly. Repeat with remaining tortillas, avocado mixture, spinach, almonds, and shrimp.

3. Place rolled tortillas on a tray or platter. Cover and chill for 1 to 4 hours. To serve, cut each rolled tortilla into 1-inch slices, trimming ends. If necessary, secure with party picks. Arrange slices on a serving platter. Makes about 36 appetizers.

EACH APPETIZER: 82 cal., 4 g total fat (1 g sat. fat), 19 mg chol., 137 mg sodium, 8 g carbo., 1 g fiber, 4 g pro. Daily Values: 7% vit. A, 4% vit. C, 4% calcium, 3% iron.

Artichoke-Gruyère Melts

 PREP: 20 MINUTES **BROIL:** 3 MINUTES

- 1 8-oz. baguette
- 2 Tbsp. olive oil
- 3 cloves garlic, minced
- 1 9-oz. pkg. frozen artichoke hearts, thawed
- 2 Tbsp. fresh flat-leaf parsley leaves
- 2 Tbsp. fresh oregano or 1/2 teaspoon dried oregano, crushed
- 1/4 tsp. salt
- 1/8 tsp. ground black pepper
- 6 ounces Gruyère cheese, shredded (1 1/2 cups)
- 1/4 to 1/2 tsp. crushed red pepper (optional)

1. Preheat broiler. Slice baguette into 16 slices about 1/2 inch thick. Arrange slices on a large baking sheet; set aside.
2. In a small skillet heat olive oil over medium-high heat for 1 minute. Add 2 cloves of the garlic; cook and stir for 30 seconds. Remove skillet from heat. Brush both sides of bread slices with oil mixture. Broil bread slices 3 to 4 inches from the heat for 2 to 3 minutes or until light golden, turning once. Remove and set aside.
3. In a food processor bowl combine artichokes, remaining garlic, parsley, oregano, salt, and black pepper. Cover and process until finely chopped. (Or finely chop garlic, parsley, and oregano; stir in salt and black pepper.) Stir in 1/3 cup of the cheese. Spread about 1 tablespoon artichoke mixture on each bread slice. Sprinkle with remaining cheese.
4. Broil 3 to 4 inches from the heat for 1 to 2 minutes or until cheese melts and just starts to brown. If desired, sprinkle with crushed red pepper. Serve warm. Makes 16 appetizers.
MAKE AHEAD: Prepare bread slices as directed. Cover and store at room temperature for 24 hours. Prepare artichoke mixture as directed. Cover and chill for up to 24 hours. Assemble and broil as directed.
EACH APPETIZER: 106 cal., 6 g total fat (2 g sat. fat), 12 mg chol., 169 mg sodium, 9 g carbo., 1 g fiber, 5 g pro. Daily Values: 3% vit. A, 4% vit. C, 13% calcium, 3% iron.

Berry-Cheese Baguette Bites

PREP: 45 MINUTES
BROIL: 2 MINUTES PER BATCH **CHILL:** 1 HOUR

- 1 12-oz. baguette, cut diagonally into 1/4-inch slices
- 1/2 pkg. (8-oz.) cream cheese, softened
- 1 cup mayonnaise
- 1 cup shredded mozzarella cheese (4 oz.)
- 1 cup shredded cheddar cheese (4 oz.)
- 3 green onions, finely chopped
- 1/3 cup seedless raspberry preserves
- 1/3 cup dried cranberries or dried blueberries
- 1 recipe Basil-Pecan Gremolata

1. Preheat broiler. Place baguette slices in a single layer on 2 large baking sheets. Broil one sheet at a time 3 to 4 inches from heat for 2 to 4 minutes or until lightly toasted, turning once. Cool on a wire rack.
2. In a large mixing bowl beat cream cheese and mayonnaise with an electric mixer until combined. Beat in mozzarella cheese, cheddar cheese, and onions. Cover and chill for 1 to 24 hours. Meanwhile, in a small bowl combine preserves and dried cranberries; cover and chill for 1 to 24 hours.
3. Just before serving, spread baguette slices with cheese mixture. Top with a small amount of berry mixture. Lightly sprinkle with Basil-Pecan Gremolata. Makes 26 appetizers.
BASIL-PECAN GREMOLATA: In a small bowl combine 1/3 cup finely chopped toasted pecans, 2 tablespoons finely snipped fresh basil, and 1 1/2 teaspoons finely shredded lemon peel.
EACH APPETIZER: 181 cal., 12 g total fat (4 g sat. fat), 19 mg chol., 227 mg sodium, 14 g carbo., 1 g fiber, 4 g pro. Daily Values: 3% vit. A, 1% vit. C, 7% calcium, 4% iron.

Mini Cajun Mushroom Tarts

PREP: 25 MINUTES **BAKE:** 12 MINUTES

- 1 1/2 cups chopped fresh mushrooms
- 2 Tbsp. butter
- 1 tsp. Cajun seasoning
- 1/2 tsp. lemon juice
- 1/4 tsp. ground black pepper
- 1 5.2-oz. pkg. semisoft cheese with garlic and herb
- 1 egg, beaten
- 2 Tbsp. milk
- 4 oz. fresh or frozen peeled crawfish tails, thawed, or 4 oz. cooked shrimp, coarsely chopped
- 2 Tbsp. snipped fresh parsley
- 2 2.1-oz. pkg. baked miniature phyllo dough shells (30 shells)

1. Preheat oven to 350°F. In a large skillet cook mushrooms in hot butter until tender and liquid is evaporated. Add Cajun seasoning, lemon juice, and pepper. Cook 1 minute more. Cool slightly.
2. In a medium bowl combine cheese, egg, and milk. Stir in mushroom mixture, crawfish, and parsley.
3. Place miniature phyllo dough shells on a baking sheet. Spoon cheese mixture into phyllo shells. Bake for 12 to 15 minutes or until set. Serve hot. Makes 30 appetizers.
EACH APPETIZER: 56 cal., 4 g total fat (2 g sat. fat), 16 mg chol., 29 mg sodium, 3 g carbo., 0 g fiber, 2 g pro. Daily Values: 1% vit. A, 1% vit. C, 1% calcium, 2% iron.

Italian Eggplant Slices

PREP: 45 MINUTES **BAKE:** 3 MINUTES

- 1 1-lb. eggplant
- 1 Tbsp. kosher salt or salt
- 2 eggs, beaten
- 1 Tbsp. water
- 3/4 cup seasoned fine dry bread crumbs
- 2 Tbsp. grated Parmesan cheese
- 2 to 3 Tbsp. cooking oil
- 3/4 cup purchased pasta sauce
- 3 oz. provolone cheese, shredded
- 2 oz. thinly sliced prosciutto, cut into short, thin strips
- 1/4 cup walnuts, toasted and finely chopped

1. With a vegetable peeler, remove 1-inch-wide strips lengthwise down the eggplant at equal intervals. Cut eggplant crosswise into 1/2-inch slices. Place slices on a double layer of paper towels. Sprinkle eggplant with the salt, turning to lightly coat both sides. Let stand for 15 to 30 minutes or until liquid is visible on the surfaces. Rinse salt and liquid off eggplant rounds; pat dry with paper towels. Halve or quarter large eggplant slices.
2. Preheat oven to 425°F. In a shallow dish combine eggs and water. In another shallow dish place bread crumbs and Parmesan cheese. Dip eggplant slices in egg mixture and then in bread crumb mixture to coat both sides.
3. In a large skillet heat 2 tablespoons of the oil over medium-high heat. Add half of the eggplant slices; cook about 2 minutes per side or until golden. Transfer to baking sheet(s). Add remaining oil to skillet; repeat with remaining eggplant slices.
4. Place about 1 teaspoon pasta sauce on top of each eggplant slice. Combine cheese, prosciutto, and walnuts; place a small mound on top of each slice. Bake, uncovered, for 3 to 4 minutes or until cheese melts. Makes about 36 appetizers.
EACH APPETIZER: 43 cal., 3 g total fat (1 g sat. fat), 15 mg chol., 220 mg sodium, 3 g carbo., 1 g fiber, 2 g pro. Daily Values: 1% vit. A, 1% vit. C, 3% calcium, 1% iron.

MICHAEL ROSENTHAL, WOODLAND HILLS, CA

LISA VOLPE HACHEY, HOPKINTON, MA

Cherry and Tangerine Oatmeal

PREP: 15 MINUTES **CHILL:** 8 HOURS **COOK:** 5 MINUTES

- 1 cup steel-cut oats
- 1/2 cup dried tart cherries
- 2 tsp. finely shredded tangerine or orange peel
- 1/4 tsp. ground cinnamon
- 1/8 tsp. salt
  Dash ground nutmeg
- 2 cups milk
- 2 Tbsp. butter
  Milk, warmed (optional)
- 4 tsp. raw (turbinado) or granulated sugar
- 1/4 cup hazelnuts,* pecans, almonds, or walnuts, toasted and chopped

1. In a nonmetal bowl combine oats, cherries, tangerine peel, cinnamon, salt, and nutmeg. Stir in milk; cover and chill for 8 to 24 hours.

2. To serve, transfer oatmeal mixture to a medium saucepan. Heat just to boiling; reduce heat and simmer, uncovered, for 5 minutes or until oatmeal is thickened, stirring occasionally. Remove from heat. Stir in butter until melted. If desired, add warm milk to make desired consistency. Spoon into 4 individual serving bowls; sprinkle with sugar and nuts. If desired, serve with additional warm milk. Makes 4 servings.

*TO TOAST HAZELNUTS: Spread hazelnuts in a single layer in a shallow baking pan. Bake in a 350°F oven about 10 minutes or until light golden brown, watching carefully and stirring once or twice. Cool slightly. Place the nuts on a clean kitchen towel, fold towel over top, and rub vigorously to remove the skins.

EACH SERVING: 398 cal., 17 g total fat (5 g sat. fat), 26 mg chol., 177 mg sodium, 51 g carbo., 6 g fiber, 13 g pro. Daily Values: 18% vit. A, 4% vit. C, 16% calcium, 5% iron.

Baked French Toast with Caramelized Pears and Brie

PREP: 35 MINUTES **CHILL:** 1 HOUR **BAKE:** 40 MINUTES
STAND: 10 MINUTES

- 3 medium pears, peeled, cored, and thinly sliced
- 2 Tbsp. packed brown sugar
- 1/2 tsp. snipped fresh rosemary
- 2 Tbsp. butter
- 14 to 16 1/2-inch-thick slices French bread
- 8 oz. Brie cheese, rind removed and thinly sliced
- 2 Tbsp. butter, melted
- 3 Tbsp. granulated sugar
- 1 tsp. ground cinnamon
- 2 1/2 cups milk
- 3 eggs
- 1 Tbsp. vanilla
- 1/4 tsp. salt
  Warm maple syrup, fresh berries and honey, or purchased cranberry conserve

1. Grease a 3-quart rectangular baking dish; set aside. In a large skillet cook pear slices, brown sugar, and rosemary in 2 tablespoons butter over medium heat for 4 to 5 minutes or until pears are just tender.

2. Arrange 7 to 8 of the bread slices in a single layer in the prepared baking dish. Spoon pear mixture over bread slices; arrange Brie over pear mixture. Top with remaining bread slices in a single layer. Brush bread slices with melted butter. In a small bowl combine granulated sugar and cinnamon. Sprinkle evenly over bread slices.

3. In a medium bowl whisk together milk, eggs, vanilla, and salt. Slowly pour over bread slices. Cover and chill for 1 to 24 hours.

4. Preheat oven to 375°F. Bake, uncovered, for 40 to 45 minutes or until edges are puffed and golden. Let stand for 10 minutes. Serve warm with maple syrup, fresh berries and honey, or cranberry conserve. Makes 8 servings.

EACH SERVING: 405 cal., 19 g total fat (10 g sat. fat), 130 mg chol., 623 mg sodium, 44 g carbo., 3 g fiber, 15 g pro. Daily Values: 12% vit. A, 5% vit. C, 19% calcium, 11% iron.

Broccoli Soy Strata

PREP: 20 MINUTES **CHILL:** OVERNIGHT
BAKE: 50 MINUTES **STAND:** 10 MINUTES

- 2 cups cut-up fresh broccoli or 2 cups frozen broccoli cuts, thawed
- 4 cups 1-inch cubes country or crusty Italian bread cubes
- 4 oz. process Gruyère cheese, cut up
- 6 eggs, lightly beaten
- 1 1/2 cups soymilk or milk
- 1 Tbsp. honey mustard
- 1/2 tsp. salt
- 1/4 tsp. ground black pepper
- 1/4 tsp. ground nutmeg
- 4 green onions, thinly sliced

1. In a medium saucepan cook broccoli, covered, in a small amount of boiling salted water for 3 minutes; drain. Rinse with cold running water until cool; drain again.

2. In a greased 2-quart square baking dish spread half of the bread cubes. Top with broccoli and cheese. Add remaining bread cubes.

3. In a medium bowl combine eggs, soymilk, honey mustard, salt, pepper, and nutmeg. Pour egg mixture over bread cubes in baking dish. Sprinkle with green onions. Cover and chill overnight.

4. Preheat oven to 325°F. Bake, uncovered, for 50 to 55 minutes or until an instant-read thermometer inserted in center registers 170°F. Let stand for 10 minutes before serving. Makes 6 servings.

EACH SERVING: 278 cal., 13 g total fat (6 g sat. fat), 232 mg chol., 535 mg sodium, 22 g carbo., 3 g fiber, 18 g pro. Daily Values: 14% vit. A, 36% vit. C, 26% calcium, 14% iron.

Brunch Omelet Cannelloni

PREP: 50 MINUTES **CHILL:** OVERNIGHT
BAKE: 25 MINUTES

- 2 lb. fresh spinach, washed and chopped
- 1 8-oz. tub cream cheese spread with chive and onion
- 3/4 cup finely shredded Parmesan cheese
- 1/4 cup finely shredded carrot
- 1/4 cup oil-packed dried tomatoes, drained and chopped
- 6 eggs, separated
  Cooking oil
- 1 26- to 28-oz. jar pasta sauce or two 16-oz. jars light Parmesan Alfredo pasta sauce

1. For filling, steam spinach in a small amount of water for 6 to 7 minutes. Drain well. Stir in cream cheese, 1/2 cup of the Parmesan, the carrot, and dried tomatoes. Set aside.

2. For omelets, in a small mixing bowl beat egg yolks with an electric mixer on high speed for 4 minutes or until thick and lemon colored; set aside. Thoroughly wash beaters. In a large mixing bowl beat egg whites until soft peaks form (tips fold over). Pour egg yolks over whites; fold together.

3. Brush a medium nonstick skillet lightly with cooking oil; preheat over medium heat. Add about 2/3 cup of the egg mixture, spreading evenly. Cook for 2 minutes or until browned on bottom and nearly set through but top is moist. Use a wide spatula to turn omelet over or slide onto a plate and flip over back into pan. Cook second side about 30 seconds or just until set. Remove from pan. Repeat with remaining egg mixture to make 8 omelets, brushing skillet with additional oil as necessary.

4. Spoon about 1/3 cup of the spinach mixture down center of each omelet; roll up and place in a 3-quart rectangular baking dish or au gratin dish. Spoon pasta sauce over filled omelets. Cover and chill overnight.

5. Preheat oven to 375°F. Bake omelets, uncovered, for 25 minutes or until heated through. Sprinkle with remaining Parmesan cheese. Makes 8 servings.

EACH SERVING: 312 cal., 19 g total fat (10 g sat. fat), 191 mg chol., 822 mg sodium, 23 g carbo., 4 g fiber, 13 g pro. Daily Values: 179% vit. A, 32% vit. C, 25% calcium, 21% iron.

Chiles and Cheese Individual Casseroles

PREP: 30 MINUTES **CHILL:** OVERNIGHT
BAKE: 40 MINUTES **STAND:** 10 MINUTES

- 2 4-oz. cans whole green chile peppers, drained and patted dry with paper towels
- 1 cup 1-inch pieces fresh asparagus or frozen cut asparagus, thawed
- 1 small red onion, quartered and thinly sliced
- 1 Tbsp. butter
- 4 oz. Monterey Jack cheese with jalapeño peppers or Monterey Jack cheese, shredded (1 cup)
- 1 Tbsp. all-purpose flour
- 4 eggs, beaten
- 1 1/4 cups half-and-half, light cream, or milk
- 1/4 tsp. salt
- 1/4 tsp. ground black pepper
- 1 medium tomato, chopped

1. Lightly grease four 12- to 16-ounce individual au gratin dishes. Make a slit along one side of each chile pepper and lay flat. Remove and discard any seeds. Pat dry with paper towels. Arrange chile peppers in the bottom of prepared dishes in a single layer, cutting as necessary to fit.

2. In a medium skillet cook asparagus and onion in hot butter about 5 minutes or just until tender; divide among prepared dishes. Toss cheese with flour; sprinkle evenly among dishes.

3. In a medium bowl beat together eggs, half-and-half, salt, and black pepper. Divide evenly among dishes. Cover and chill overnight.

4. Preheat oven to 350°F. Place casseroles in a 15×10×1-inch pan. Bake, uncovered, for 40 to 45 minutes or until set. Let stand 10 minutes before serving. Top each with chopped tomato. Makes 4 servings.

EACH SERVING: 342 cal., 26 g total fat (14 g sat. fat), 272 mg chol., 578 mg sodium, 11 g carbo., 1 g fiber, 18 g pro. Daily Values: 27% vit. A, 43% vit. C, 40% calcium, 13% iron.

French Toast with Cranberry Filling

PREP: 20 MINUTES **CHILL:** OVERNIGHT
BAKE: 45 MINUTES

- 12 slices whole wheat bread, halved diagonally
- 6 eggs
- 1 32-oz. carton vanilla low-fat yogurt
- 1 Tbsp. finely shredded orange peel
- 1/2 cup orange juice
- 1/4 cup sugar
- 1/4 tsp. ground nutmeg
- 1 cup canned whole cranberry sauce
- 1/2 cup ricotta cheese
- 1/3 cup chopped pecans

1. Preheat oven to 300°F. Place bread on a large baking sheet in a single layer. Bake, uncovered, for 10 minutes, turning pieces once.

2. In a large bowl whisk eggs until blended. Whisk in yogurt, orange peel, orange juice, sugar, and nutmeg. Pour half of the egg mixture into a greased 3-quart rectangular baking dish.

3. Combine cranberry sauce and ricotta cheese. Spread evenly on half of the bread triangles; top with remaining triangles forming sandwiches. Arrange sandwiches in the dish. Pour remaining egg mixture over sandwiches. Cover and chill overnight.

4. Preheat oven to 350°F. Uncover and sprinkle with pecans. Bake, uncovered, for 45 minutes or until set. If necessary, cover with foil during the last 10 minutes of baking time to prevent overbrowning. Makes 6 servings.

EACH SERVING: 520 cal., 6 g total fat (5 g sat. fat), 230 mg chol., 466 mg sodium, 75 g carbo., 4 g fiber, 21 g pro. Daily Values: 9% vit. A, 23% vit. C, 39% calcium, 17% iron.

FOOD GIFTS

Honey-Wine Jelly

START TO FINISH: 1 HOUR

> 2 cups dry red wine, such as Cabernet Sauvignon, Shiraz, or red Zinfandel
> 1 1³/₄-oz. pkg. regular powdered fruit pectin
> 3¹/₂ cups honey
> ¹/₄ tsp. butter, margarine, or oil

1. In a 4- or 5-quart Dutch oven or kettle combine wine and pectin. Cook and stir over high heat until mixture comes to a full rolling boil. Add honey all at once. Return to boiling; add butter and boil for 2 minutes, stirring constantly. Remove from heat. Quickly skim off foam with a metal spoon.
2. Ladle at once into hot, sterilized half-pint canning jars, leaving a ¹/₄-inch space at the top. Wipe jar rims. Adjust lids. Process canning jars in a boiling-water canner for 5 minutes (start timing when water returns to boil). Remove jars; cool on wire racks. Makes about 5¹/₂ cups jelly (about 6 half-pint jars).
WINE TUMBLERS: If desired, prepare jelly as above, except do not place in canning jars or process. Pour mixture into short wine tumblers or decorative jars. Cover with plastic wrap; set aside to cool completely. Chill for up to 3 weeks.
EACH SERVING (1 TABLESPOON): 47 cal., 0 g total fat, 0 mg chol., 2 mg sodium, 12 g carbo., 0 g fiber, 0 g pro. Daily Values: 1% iron.

Hazelnut Sundae Sauce

Fast! **PREP:** 15 MINUTES **COOK:** 8 MINUTES

> 1 12-oz. pkg. semisweet chocolate pieces
> 1 13-oz. jar chocolate-hazelnut spread
> 1 12-oz. can evaporated milk
> ¹/₂ cup sugar
> ³/₄ cup coffee liqueur or strong coffee
> 2 cups hazelnuts, toasted and coarsely chopped (optional)

1. In a large heavy saucepan melt chocolate pieces and chocolate-hazelnut spread over low heat, stirring occasionally. Add evaporated milk and sugar, stirring until smooth. Bring to boiling over medium-high heat, stirring constantly. Reduce heat. Cook, uncovered, for 8 minutes, stirring frequently. Remove from heat and stir in coffee liqueur.
2. Spoon mixture into 6 clean decorative half-pint jars, leaving a ³/₄-inch space at the top; cover and chill. If desired, divide hazelnuts among 6 small plastic bags. Decorate jars and plastic bags as desired. Chill for up to 2 weeks. Reheat sauce before serving. Serve sauce over ice cream. If desired, sprinkle with nuts. Makes 6 half-pint jars.
EACH SERVING (2 TABLESPOONS): 128 cal., 6 g total fat (2 g sat. fat), 3 mg chol., 20 mg sodium, 17 g carbo., 1 g fiber, 2 g pro. Daily Values: 2% calcium, 1% iron.

Asian Pineapple Cream Cheese Spread

PREP: 20 MINUTES **CHILL:** 2 HOURS

- 3 8-oz. pkg. cream cheese, softened
- 2 Tbsp. packed brown sugar
- 2 Tbsp. lime juice
- 2 Tbsp. chili garlic sauce
- 1 20-oz. can crushed pineapple, drained
- 1/4 cup sliced green onions
- 1/4 cup snipped fresh cilantro
- 1 tsp. grated fresh ginger
  Assorted crackers

1. In a large mixing bowl beat cream cheese with an electric mixer on medium speed until smooth. Beat in brown sugar, lime juice, and chili garlic sauce until combined. Stir in pineapple, onions, cilantro, and ginger. Divide evenly among six 10-ounce containers. Chill for 2 hours to 3 days.

2. Wrap containers, tie with ribbon, and give with crackers as gifts. Makes 6 containers.

EACH SERVING (1 TABLESPOON): 40 cal., 3 g total fat (2 g sat. fat), 10 mg chol., 34 mg sodium, 2 g carbo., 0 g fiber, 1 g pro. Daily Values: 3% vit. A, 2% vit. C, 1% calcium, 1% iron.

Cocoa Spiced Pecans

PREP: 15 MINUTES **BAKE:** 20 MINUTES

- 1 egg white
- 1 tsp. water
- 5 cups pecan halves
- 1 cup sugar
- 1 Tbsp. unsweetened cocoa powder
- 1 tsp. salt
- 1/2 tsp. cayenne pepper

1. Preheat oven to 325°F. Grease a 15×10×1-inch baking pan; set aside. In a large bowl beat together egg white and water. Add nuts; toss to coat. In a small bowl combine sugar, cocoa powder, salt, and cayenne pepper. Sprinkle sugar mixture over nuts; toss to coat.

2. Spread nuts in prepared baking pan. Bake for 20 minutes. Spread on waxed paper; cool. Break into pieces. Divide among 6 small airtight containers. Store for 2 weeks at room temperature or freeze for longer storage. Makes 6 (1-cup) gifts.

EACH SERVING (1/4 CUP): 188 cal., 16 g total fat (1 g sat. fat), 0 mg chol., 99 mg sodium, 11 g carbo., 2 g fiber, 2 g pro. Daily Values: 1% vit. A, 2% calcium, 3% iron.

Fiery Cheese Spread

PREP: 20 MINUTES **STAND:** 30 MINUTES
CHILL: UP TO 1 WEEK

- 2 8-oz. pkg. cream cheese, softened
- 4 oz. Monterey Jack cheese, shredded (1 cup)
- 4 oz. smoked cheddar cheese, shredded (1 cup)
- 1/4 cup butter
- 2 Tbsp. red or green jalapeño jelly
- 1/3 cup pickled jalapeño slices, drained and finely chopped
- 1/4 cup almonds, toasted and finely chopped
- 1 Tbsp. paprika
- 1/2 tsp. cayenne pepper
  Assorted crackers

1. In a large mixing bowl combine cheeses and butter; let stand at room temperature for 30 minutes. Beat with an electric mixer on low to medium speed until combined. Add jalapeño jelly and chopped jalapeños. Beat on low speed just until combined.

2. Spoon a scant 1/2 cup of mixture into each of seven 4-ounce individual crocks or containers with lids.

3. In a small bowl combine almonds, paprika, and cayenne pepper. Sprinkle mixture evenly over cheese mixture in each container.

4. Cover each container with plastic wrap or the lid. Chill for up to 1 week. Give crocks with assorted crackers as gifts. Makes 7 (4-ounce) containers.

EACH SERVING (1 OUNCE): 116 cal., 11 g total fat (6 g sat. fat), 30 mg chol., 145 mg sodium, 2 g carbo., 0 g fiber, 4 g pro. Daily Values: 9% vit. A, 1% vit. C, 8% calcium, 2% iron.

Pumpkin Fudge

PREP: 10 MINUTES **COOK:** 20 MINUTES
COOL: 2 HOURS **CHILL:** UP TO 1 WEEK

- 3 cups sugar
- 3/4 cup butter
- 1 5-oz. can evaporated milk
- 1/2 cup canned pumpkin
- 1 10-oz. pkg. cinnamon-flavored pieces
- 1 7-oz. jar marshmallow creme
- 3/4 cup chopped walnuts, toasted

1. Line a 13×9×2-inch baking pan with foil, extending foil over the edges of the pan. Butter foil; set pan aside.

2. In a heavy 3-quart saucepan combine sugar, butter, evaporated milk, and pumpkin. Cook and stir over medium-high heat until mixture boils. Clip a candy thermometer to side of pan. Reduce heat to medium-low. Continue boiling at a moderate, steady rate, stirring frequently, until the thermometer registers 234°F, soft-ball stage (20 to 25 minutes). Adjust heat as necessary to maintain a steady boil.

3. Remove saucepan from heat. Stir in cinnamon-flavored pieces until melted. Stir in marshmallow creme and walnuts.

4. Pour mixture into prepared pan, spreading evenly. Allow fudge to cool 2 hours or until firm. Use foil to lift it out of pan. Cut fudge into 1-inch squares.

5. To store, place fudge in layers separated by waxed paper in an airtight container; cover. Chill for up to 1 week. Do not freeze. Makes 96 pieces.

EACH PIECE: 68 cal., 3 g total fat (2 g sat. fat), 4 mg chol., 14 mg sodium, 10 g carbo., 0 g fiber, 0 g pro. Daily Values: 5% vit. A, 1% calcium.

Pumpkin Pudding Bread

PREP: 30 MINUTES **BAKE:** 40 MINUTES
COOL: 10 MINUTES

- 1 15-oz. can pumpkin
- 6 eggs, lightly beaten
- 2/3 cup cinnamon applesauce
- 1/2 cup cooking oil
- 2 cups all-purpose flour
- 1 1/2 cups sugar
- 1 4-serving-size pkg. cook-and-serve vanilla pudding and pie filling mix
- 1 4-serving-size pkg. cook-and-serve butterscotch pudding and pie filling mix
- 1 Tbsp. pumpkin pie spice
- 2 tsp. baking powder
- 1/2 tsp. baking soda
- 1/2 tsp. salt

1. Preheat oven to 350°F. Grease the bottoms and 1/2 inch up sides of five 5 3/4×3×2-inch loaf pans or ten 4 1/2×2 1/2×1 1/2-inch loaf pans; set aside.

2. In a large mixing bowl whisk together pumpkin, eggs, applesauce, and oil; set aside. In a very large bowl stir together flour, sugar, vanilla pudding, butterscotch pudding, pumpkin pie spice, baking powder, baking soda, and salt. Stir pumpkin mixture into flour mixture just until combined. Spoon batter into prepared pans, using 1 1/3 cups for each large pan or 2/3 cup for each small pan.

3. Bake for 55 to 60 minutes for large pans or 40 to 45 minutes for small pans or until a wooden toothpick inserted near the centers comes out clean. Cool in pans on wire racks for 10 minutes. Remove from pans. Cool completely on wire racks. Wrap and store overnight before slicing. Makes 5 large (8 slices each) or 10 small (4 slices each) loaves.

EACH SLICE: 108 cal., 4 g total fat (1 g sat. fat), 32 mg chol., 95 mg sodium, 18 g carbo., 1 g fiber, 2 g pro. Daily Values: 34% vit. A, 1% vit. C, 1% calcium, 3% iron.

MENUS

SERVE DINNER IN STYLE WITH THESE IRRESISTIBLE MENU IDEAS. BUT DON'T STOP THERE! MIX AND MATCH THE RECIPES THROUGHOUT THIS BOOK TO COME UP WITH MENUS OF YOUR OWN.

Chocolate-Berry Meringue
page 276

Menus for Family and Friends

Our Prize Tested Recipes® are simply delicious when served alone or as part of a menu. But it's easy to feel overwhelmed when you have so many choices! To help you make the best possible selections, we've put together 24 menus to get you started on mouthwatering dinner parties, celebrations, and weeknight suppers.

Nutty Biscotti
page 268

Shortbread Brownies
page 264

Grilled Thai Leg of Lamb
page 266

Hoisin Beef and Broccoli Kabobs
page 274

company's coming

IT'S YOUR TURN TO HOST A SPECIAL-OCCASION DINNER FOR FRIENDS AND FAMILY, AND THIS IS THE PERFECT TIME TO IMPRESS YOUR GUESTS. FOR ANY EVENT DURING THE YEAR, THERE'S A MENU THAT MATCHES THE SITUATION PERFECTLY.

BIRTHDAY CELEBRATION

Asian Salmon with Oven-Roasted Sweet Potatoes
(page 291)

Blue and Green Salad (page 273)

French bread served with butter

Balsamic Berries with Cream
(page 293)

Sparkling water

RINGING IN THE NEW YEAR

Citrus-Chile Glazed Pork Chops with Rice and Posole Pilaf
(page 263)

Roasted zucchini and red sweet pepper chunks

Purchased dinner rolls

Four-Nut Caramel-Chocolate Tart (page 269)

Dry red wine

GRADUATION GATHERING

Garlic-Chili-Rubbed Lamb (page 278)

Grilled Avocados (page 278)

Hot cooked basmati rice

Chocolate-Berry Meringue (page 276)

Iced tea or hot tea

ANNIVERSARY FAVORITES

Middle Eastern Chicken Kabobs (page 275)
(with Tomato Relish)

Warm pita bread

Sliced cucumber and red onion with purchased creamy garlic dressing

Herb and butter rice pilaf (from mix)

Quick Walnut Mousse (page 269)

Fruit-flavored iced tea

Chocolate-Berry Meringue
page 276

Garlic-Chili-Rubbed Lamb
page 278

Grilled Avocados
page 278

for a crowd
(serves 8 or more)

THERE'S A HUNGRY CLAN ON THE MOVE TOWARD YOUR HOUSE, AND YOU'RE SUPPOSED TO FEED THEM ALL! WHEN THE GROUP GETS LARGE AND RAVENOUS, CHECK OUT THESE MENUS TO SATISFY THEIR CRAVINGS.

FAMILY FARE
Oriental Beef Brisket (page 294)
Mixed greens salad with purchased vinaigrette dressing
Buttered egg noodles
Purchased dinner rolls
Apple-Cranberry Dessert (page 256)
Hot tea or iced tea

FOOD FOR FRIENDS
Dried Fig, Pistachio, and Cheese Bruschetta (page 289)
Greek-Style Lasagna (page 258)
Sauteed zucchini and yellow summer squash
Marzipan Cheese Tart with Warm Berry Sauce (page 277)
Sparkling water or dry red wine

HOLIDAY SPREAD
Roast Pork Tenderloin with Apple Cider Pecan Salsa (page 263)
Steamed green beans
Boiled new potatoes with herbed butter
Buttermilk biscuits
Nutty Apricot Bars (page 269)
Apple cider or flavored coffee

DINNER PARTY EXTRAVANGZA
Grilled Thai Leg of Lamb (page 266)
Honey Lime Potato Salad (page 285)
Grilled pita bread
Honeydew melon slices
Very-Almond Cheesecake (page 269)
Ice water with lemon or lime slices

Grilled Thai Leg of Lamb
page 266

Apple-Cranberry Dessert
page 256

Greek-Style Lasagna
page 258

dining by the season

EACH SEASON HAS ITS OWN FLAVORS: LIGHT AND AIRY FOR SPRING, RICH AND HEARTY FOR WINTER. WITH THESE MENUS, THERE'S NO NEED TO GUESS—YOU'LL GET THE FOOD RIGHT EVERY TIME OF YEAR.

WINTER MORNING BREAKFAST

Baked French Toast with Caramelized Pears and Brie
(page 298)

Easy Florentine Soufflé Rolls (page 272)

Sausage links and bacon strips

Grapefruit with pomegranate seeds

Nutty Biscotti (page 268)

Fruit juice, milk, hot coffee, and/or hot tea

EARLY LUNCH IN SPRING

Salmon-Asparagus Lasagna Rolls (page 259)

Baby greens salad with purchased raspberry vinaigrette

Purchased focaccia bread

Fresh mozzarella, cherry tomato, and black olive kabobs

Raspberry-Rhubarb Pie (page 260)

Flavored iced tea with lemon slice

SUMMER AFTERNOON SUPPER

Chicken with Grilled Summer Relish (page 283)

Deli potato salad

Corn on the cob

Mixed Berry Cream Pie (page 277)

Minted Iced Tea (page 284)

AUTUMN DINNER

Pork with Hot Pear Relish (page 263)

Cheese Rolls (page 288)

Wild rice pilaf (from mix)

Roasted acorn squash wedges with butter

Crunchy Caramel Apple Cake (page 257)

Hot apple cider or flavored coffee

Raspberry-Rhubarb Pie
page 260

Nutty Biscotti
page 268

Easy Florentine Soufflé Rolls
page 272

pack a picnic

WHO SAYS SUMMER IS THE ONLY TIME FOR A PICNIC? ALL FOUR SEASONS ARE PERFECT FOR SPREADING A BLANKET, LAYING OUT THE FOOD, AND DIGGING IN WITH FAMILY AND FRIENDS.

SPRING FLING IN THE PARK
Shrimp Pinwheels (page 296)
Honey Lime Potato Salad (page 285)
Watermelon and cantaloupe slices
Deep Chocolate Brownies (page 264)
Lemonade or flavored water

SUMMER HIKE IN THE HILLS
Cold fried chicken
Barley Corn Salad (page 285)
Corn bread sticks
Baked beans
Shortbread Brownies (page 264)
Sweetened iced tea or iced coffee

AUTUMN STROLL IN THE COUNTRYSIDE
Barbecue and Blue Dip with Peppery Pita Crisps
(page 255)
Ham slices wrapped around pepperoncini chiles or sweet pickles
Chilled Spinach Couscous Salad (page 272)
Oaty Doodle Hearts (page 260)
Strawberry lemonade

WINTER ESCAPE INDOORS
Roast beef sandwiches with horseradish on kaiser rolls
Dill pickle spears
German-Style Pasta Salad (page 287)
Potato chips
Hazelnut Picnic Cake (page 285)
Cold beer or root beer

Shortbread Brownies
page 264

Oaty Doodle Hearts
page 260

Chilled Spinach Couscous Salad
page 272

family dinners

WHETHER IT'S A MEAL FIT FOR KIDS OR DINNER JUST FOR MOM AND DAD, THESE MENUS WILL CATER TO EACH FAMILY MEMBER. FOR DAYS WHEN THE WHOLE GROUP DINES TOGETHER, TRY THE MENU DESIGNED FOR EVERYONE.

PERFECT FOR MOM AND DAD

Shrimp with Vermicelli (page 271)

French bread

Assorted olives and relish tray

Mixed greens salad with purchased Italian salad dressing

Decadently Delicious Dark Chocolate Cookies (page 261)

Sparkling water or white wine

FAVORITES FOR KIDS

Make-Ahead Chili-Cheese Hoagies (page 267)

Dill and sweet pickles

Deli coleslaw

Corn chips

Chocolate Brownies with Peanut Butter Swirl (page 265)

Milk or iced tea

FOR VISITING GRANDPARENTS

Hoisin Beef and Broccoli Kabobs (page 274)

Hot cooked rice

Spinach salad with mandarin oranges and purchased vinaigrette dressing

Purchased soft breadsticks

Fluffy Fruit Topper (page 293) over purchased pound cake

Hot tea or hot coffee

SUPPER FOR EVERYONE

Chicken, Vegetables, and Tortellini (page 271)

Purchased garlic bread

Mixed greens salad with purchased creamy Italian dressing

Silky Fruit Parfaits (page 292)

Coffee or milk

Hoisin Beef and Broccoli Kabobs
page 274

weeknight favorites

EACH MENU HAS ITS DESIGNATED DAY OF THE WEEK, BUT DON'T BE AFRAID TO TRY TEX-MEX ON SATURDAY OR TURKEY ON MONDAY.

TURKEY TUESDAY
Stuffed Turkey Burgers (page 279)
Deli potato salad
Fresh fruit kabobs or fresh fruit salad
Baked beans
Warm Banana Bread Cobbler (page 287)
Assorted soft drinks

TEX-MEX THURSDAY
Fiesta Manaña (page 267)
Sweet and Hot Black Bean Dip (page 255) with tortilla chips and vegetable sticks
Mexican rice (from mix)
Sliced tomatoes
Raspberry Cloud Cookie Cups (page 293)
Margaritas or limeade

FRIDAY FUN
Bacon Cheeseburger Lasagna (page 259)
Carrot sticks and celery sticks served with bottled ranch dressing or vegetable dip
Malted Fudge Brownies (page 265)
Flavored water and milk

SUNDAY SUPPER
Pork with Raisin Sauce (page 262)
Mashed sweet potatoes with butter
Steamed green beans
Corn bread squares
Chocolate Brownies with Peanut Butter Swirl (page 265)
Apple cider or sparkling water

Pork with Raisin Sauce
page 262

ANNUAL Recipes INDEX

D

Nutrition information.

With each recipe, we give important nutrition information you easily can apply to your own needs. You'll find the calorie count of each serving and the amount, in grams, of total fat, saturated fat, cholesterol, sodium, carbohydrates, fiber, and protein to help you keep tabs on what you eat. You can check the levels of each recipe serving for vitamin A, vitamin C, calcium, and iron, if they are present. These are noted in percentages of the Daily Values. The Daily Values are dietary standards determined by the Food and Drug Administration (FDA). To stay in line with the nutrition breakdown of each recipe, follow the suggested number of servings.

How we analyze.

The Better Homes and Gardens® Test Kitchen computer analyzes each recipe for the nutritional value of a single serving.

- The analysis does not include optional ingredients.
- We use the first serving size listed when a range is given. For example: If we say a recipe "Makes 4 to 6 servings," the nutrition information is based on 4 servings.
- When ingredient choices (such as butter or margarine) appear in a recipe, we use the first one mentioned for analysis. The ingredient order does not mean we prefer one ingredient over another.
- When milk and eggs are recipe ingredients, the analysis is calculated using 2 percent (reduced-fat) milk and large eggs.

What you need.

The dietary guidelines below suggest nutrient levels that moderately active adults should strive to eat each day. There is no real harm in going over or under these guidelines in any single day, but it is a good idea to aim for a balanced diet over time.

Calories: About 2,000
Total fat: Less than 65 grams
Saturated fat: Less than 20 grams
Cholesterol: Less than 300 milligrams
Carbohydrates: About 300 grams
Sodium: Less than 2,400 milligrams
Dietary fiber: 20 to 30 grams

Healthy Icons.

Certain recipes throughout the book have icons next to the nutrition information that indicates the recipe is healthy. For a recipe to earn this icon, it must meet certain nutritional requirements. For a main dish, one serving should contain about 400 calories, have no more than 12 grams of fat, 5 grams of saturated fat, 700 milligrams of sodium, and 100 milligrams of cholesterol. One serving of a side dish should have less than 150 calories, 8 grams of fat, and 300 milligrams of sodium. Occasionally, an element will slightly exceed one of these numbers in a selected recipe, but typically they remain below the listed amounts.

Emergency substitutions.

If you don't have:	Substitute:
Bacon, 1 slice, crisp-cooked, crumbled	1 tablespoon cooked bacon pieces
Baking powder, 1 teaspoon	$^{1}/_{2}$ teaspoon cream of tartar plus $^{1}/_{4}$ teaspoon baking soda
Balsamic vinegar, 1 tablespoon	1 tablespoon cider vinegar or red wine vinegar plus $^{1}/_{2}$ teaspoon sugar
Bread crumbs, fine dry, $^{1}/_{4}$ cup	$^{3}/_{4}$ cup soft bread crumbs, or $^{1}/_{4}$ cup cracker crumbs, or $^{1}/_{4}$ cup cornflake crumbs
Broth, beef or chicken, 1 cup	1 teaspoon or 1 cube instant beef or chicken bouillon plus 1 cup hot water
Butter, 1 cup	1 cup shortening plus $^{1}/_{4}$ teaspoon salt, if desired
Buttermilk, 1 cup	1 tablespoon lemon juice or vinegar plus enough milk to make 1 cup (let stand 5 minutes before using), or 1 cup plain yogurt
Chocolate, semisweet, 1 ounce	3 tablespoons semisweet chocolate pieces, or 1 ounce unsweetened chocolate plus 1 tablespoon granulated sugar, or 1 tablespoon unsweetened cocoa powder plus 2 teaspoons sugar and 2 teaspoons shortening
Chocolate, sweet baking, 4 ounces	$^{1}/_{4}$ cup unsweetened cocoa powder plus $^{1}/_{3}$ cup granulated sugar and 3 tablespoons shortening
Chocolate, unsweetened, 1 ounce	3 tablespoons unsweetened cocoa powder plus 1 tablespoon cooking oil or shortening, melted
Cornstarch, 1 tablespoon (for thickening)	2 tablespoons all-purpose flour
Corn syrup (light), 1 cup	1 cup granulated sugar plus $^{1}/_{4}$ cup water
Egg, 1 whole	2 egg whites, or 2 egg yolks, or $^{1}/_{4}$ cup refrigerated or frozen egg product, thawed
Flour, cake, 1 cup	1 cup minus 2 tablespoons all-purpose flour
Flour, self-rising, 1 cup	1 cup all-purpose flour plus 1 teaspoon baking powder, $^{1}/_{2}$ teaspoon salt, and $^{1}/_{4}$ teaspoon baking soda
Garlic, 1 clove	$^{1}/_{2}$ teaspoon bottled minced garlic or $^{1}/_{8}$ teaspoon garlic powder
Ginger, grated fresh, 1 teaspoon	$^{1}/_{4}$ teaspoon ground ginger
Half-and-half or light cream, 1 cup	1 tablespoon melted butter or margarine plus enough whole milk to make 1 cup
Molasses, 1 cup	1 cup honey
Mustard, dry, 1 teaspoon	1 tablespoon prepared mustard (in cooked mixtures)
Mustard, prepared, 1 tablespoon	$^{1}/_{2}$ teaspoon dry mustard plus 2 teaspoons vinegar
Onion, chopped, $^{1}/_{2}$ cup	2 tablespoons dried minced onion or $^{1}/_{2}$ teaspoon onion powder
Sour cream, dairy, 1 cup	1 cup plain yogurt
Sugar, brown, 1 cup packed	1 cup granulated sugar plus 2 tablespoons molasses
Sugar, granulated, 1 cup	1 cup packed brown sugar or 2 cups sifted powdered sugar
Tomato juice, 1 cup	$^{1}/_{2}$ cup tomato sauce plus $^{1}/_{2}$ cup water
Tomato sauce, 2 cups	$^{3}/_{4}$ cup tomato paste plus 1 cup water
Vanilla bean, 1 whole	2 teaspoons vanilla
Wine, red, 1 cup	1 cup beef or chicken broth in savory recipes; cranberry juice in desserts
Wine, white, 1 cup	1 cup chicken broth in savory recipes; apple juice or white grape juice in desserts
Yeast, active dry, 1 package	about $2^{1}/_{4}$ teaspoons active dry yeast

Seasonings

Apple pie spice, 1 teaspoon	$^{1}/_{2}$ teaspoon ground cinnamon plus $^{1}/_{4}$ teaspoon ground nutmeg, $^{1}/_{8}$ teaspoon ground allspice, and dash ground cloves or ginger
Cajun seasoning, 1 tablespoon	$^{1}/_{2}$ teaspoon white pepper, $^{1}/_{2}$ teaspoon garlic powder, $^{1}/_{2}$ teaspoon onion powder, $^{1}/_{2}$ teaspoon cayenne pepper, $^{1}/_{2}$ teaspoon paprika, and $^{1}/_{2}$ teaspoon black pepper
Herbs, snipped fresh, 1 tablespoon	$^{1}/_{2}$ to 1 teaspoon dried herb, crushed, or $^{1}/_{2}$ teaspoon ground herb
Poultry seasoning, 1 teaspoon	$^{3}/_{4}$ teaspoon dried sage, crushed, plus $^{1}/_{4}$ teaspoon dried thyme or marjoram, crushed
Pumpkin pie spice, 1 teaspoon	$^{1}/_{2}$ teaspoon ground cinnamon plus $^{1}/_{4}$ teaspoon ground ginger, $^{1}/_{4}$ teaspoon ground allspice, and $^{1}/_{8}$ teaspoon ground nutmeg

Metric Information

The charts on this page provide a guide for converting measurements from the U.S. customary system, which is used throughout this book, to the metric system.

Product Differences

Most of the ingredients called for in the recipes in this book are available in most countries. However, some are known by different names. Here are some common American ingredients and their possible counterparts:

- Sugar (white) is granulated, fine granulated, or castor sugar.
- Powdered sugar is icing sugar.
- All-purpose flour is enriched, bleached or unbleached white household flour. When self-rising flour is used in place of all-purpose flour in a recipe that calls for leavening, omit the leavening agent (baking soda or baking powder) and salt.
- Light-colored corn syrup is golden syrup.
- Cornstarch is cornflour.
- Baking soda is bicarbonate of soda.
- Vanilla or vanilla extract is vanilla essence.
- Green, red, or yellow sweet peppers are capsicums or bell peppers.
- Golden raisins are sultanas.

Volume and Weight

The United States traditionally uses cup measures for liquid and solid ingredients. The chart below shows the approximate imperial and metric equivalents. If you are accustomed to weighing solid ingredients, the following approximate equivalents will be helpful.

- 1 cup butter, castor sugar, or rice = 8 ounces = $\frac{1}{2}$ pound = 250 grams
- 1 cup flour = 4 ounces = $\frac{1}{4}$ pound = 125 grams
- 1 cup icing sugar = 5 ounces = 150 grams

Canadian and U.S. volume for a 1 cup measure is 8 fluid ounces (237 ml), but the standard metric equivalent is 250 ml.

1 British imperial cup is 10 fluid ounces.

In Australia, 1 tablespoon equals 20 ml, and there are 4 teaspoons in the Australian tablespoon.

Spoon measures are used for smaller amounts of ingredients. Although the size of the tablespoon varies slightly in different countries, for practical purposes and for recipes in this book, a straight substitution is all that's necessary. Measurements made using cups or spoons always should be level unless stated otherwise.

Common Weight Range Replacements

Imperial / U.S.	Metric
$\frac{1}{2}$ ounce	15 g
1 ounce	25 g or 30 g
4 ounces ($\frac{1}{4}$ pound)	115 g or 125 g
8 ounces ($\frac{1}{2}$ pound)	225 g or 250 g
16 ounces (1 pound)	450 g or 500 g
$1\frac{1}{4}$ pounds	625 g
$1\frac{1}{2}$ pounds	750 g
2 pounds or $2\frac{1}{4}$ pounds	1,000 g or 1 Kg

Oven Temperature Equivalents

Fahrenheit Setting	Celsius Setting*	Gas Setting
300°F	150°C	Gas Mark 2 (very low)
325°F	160°C	Gas Mark 3 (low)
350°F	180°C	Gas Mark 4 (moderate)
375°F	190°C	Gas Mark 5 (moderate)
400°F	200°C	Gas Mark 6 (hot)
425°F	220°C	Gas Mark 7 (hot)
450°F	230°C	Gas Mark 8 (very hot)
475°F	240°C	Gas Mark 9 (very hot)
500°F	260°C	Gas Mark 10 (extremely hot)
Broil	Broil	Grill

*Electric and gas ovens may be calibrated using Celsius. However, for an electric oven, increase Celsius setting 10 to 20 degrees when cooking above 160°C. For convection or forced air ovens (gas or electric) lower the temperature setting 25 degrees for Fahrenheit and 10 degrees for Celsius when cooking at all heat levels.

Baking Pan Sizes

Imperial / U.S.	Metric
9×1$\frac{1}{2}$-inch round cake pan	22- or 23×4-cm (1.5 L)
9×1$\frac{1}{2}$-inch pie plate	22- or 23×4-cm (1 L)
8×8×2-inch square cake pan	20×5-cm (2 L)
9×9×2-inch square cake pan	22- or 23×4.5-cm (2.5 L)
11×7×1$\frac{1}{2}$-inch baking pan	28×17×4-cm (2 L)
2-quart rectangular baking pan	30×19×4.5-cm (3 L)
13×9×2-inch baking pan	34×22×4.5-cm (3.5 L)
15×10×1-inch jelly roll pan	40×25×2-cm
9×5×3-inch loaf pan	23×13×8-cm (2 L)
2-quart casserole	2 L

U.S. / Standard Metric Equivalents

$\frac{1}{8}$ teaspoon = 0.5 ml	
$\frac{1}{4}$ teaspoon = 1 ml	
$\frac{1}{2}$ teaspoon = 2 ml	
1 teaspoon = 5 ml	
1 tablespoon = 15 ml	
2 tablespoons = 25 ml	
$\frac{1}{4}$ cup = 2 fluid ounces = 50 ml	
$\frac{1}{3}$ cup = 3 fluid ounces = 75 ml	
$\frac{1}{2}$ cup = 4 fluid ounces = 125 ml	
$\frac{2}{3}$ cup = 5 fluid ounces = 150 ml	
$\frac{3}{4}$ cup = 6 fluid ounces = 175 ml	
1 cup = 8 fluid ounces = 250 ml	
2 cups = 1 pint = 500 ml	
1 quart = 1 litre